THE FINE ART OF MIXING DRINKS

THE FINE ART
OF MIXING DRINKS

DAVID A. EMBURY

A Dolphin Handbook
Doubleday & Company, Inc.
Garden City, New York

TO my daughter and her husband, who, with their tongues in their cheeks, persuaded me that I owed it to posterity to commit to paper the wisdom and learning herein contained, this book is affectionately dedicated.

The Fine Art of Mixing Drinks was originally published by Doubleday & Company, Inc. in 1948. The Dolphin Books edition is published by arrangement with Doubleday & Company, Inc.

Dolphin Books edition: 1961

Copyright, © 1948, 1952, 1958, by David A. Embury
All Rights Reserved
Printed in the United States of America

PREFACE TO THIRD AMERICAN EDITION

In the preface to the second American edition of this book in 1952 and to the British edition in 1953, I said that, despite the time that had elapsed since the first American edition went to press in 1948, there was surprisingly little that I felt should be altered.

That is still true today. The basic principles of drink mixing which I have tried to analyze and explain—an undertaking which, so far as I know, no one previously ever had the temerity to attempt—are fixed and changeless. As a pioneer in this field making no claim to omniscience, I should normally have expected a certain percentage of errors, including (what I most feared) a few colossal boners. They may be there—I freely admit it—but, thus far, very few have shown up. There was, however, one caustic comment by a West Coast bartender on the "strength" of my drinks. On this point, see "When Is a Martini Strong?" (page 119).

However, when it comes to details as opposed to basic principles, there are almost daily changes. Some of the liquors that I strongly recommended ten years ago have entirely disappeared from the market; others still exist but no longer, in my opinion, are entitled to highest rank. Here today; gone tomorrow! Also there are various new drink mixtures, some, in my opinion, decidedly inferior, which have hit the headlines and created at least a temporary furor, and about which my readers might like to know.

What is the Moscow Mule, the Waltzing Matilda, the Bloody Mary, the Screwdriver, the Grasshopper?

Perhaps the outstanding example of what I mean is vodka—a wholly characterless, dilute grain alcohol that has streaked across the firmament of mixed drinks like Halley's Comet. As I said in the first edition, "It makes an excellent cocktail base and, having no pronounced flavor of its own, it will blend with anything." On the other hand—and just because it is wholly characterless in itself—it has definite limitations. It is hard to conceive of any worse cocktail monstrosity than the Vodka Martini, the Vodka Old-Fashioned, or Vodka on Rocks. Why? Well, that is one of the things I have tried to point out in this edition.

And, finally, once again, as I said in the preface to the first edition, "Here's How!"

PREFACE

In the preface or foreword to a book of this kind it is customary to explain how the author got that way, and to elaborate on his many years of experience in the liquor business, the hotels and restaurants he has managed, the bars over which he has presided, and the celebrities he has served and for whom he has graciously named some of his extra-special drinks.

In order that there may be no misunderstanding, therefore, I want to make it clear at the outset that I have never been engaged in any of the manifold branches of the liquor business. I am not a distiller, an importer, a bottler, or a merchant of liquors. I am not even a retired bartender. My practical experience with liquors has been entirely as a consumer and as a shaker-upper of drinks for the delectation of my guests. This book is, therefore, purely and distinctly a book written by an amateur for amateurs.

On the other hand, I have always possessed an insatiable curiosity about the whys and wherefores of many things and particularly of food and drinks. For years it has been my practice, when served with some especially delicious dish at a hotel or restaurant, to worm my way into the confidence of the chef and discuss with him every minute detail of its preparation. Furthermore, I chance to have a mind that is both analytical and faintly skeptical. I always want to know not only the "how" but also the "why."

Because of these personal traits, whenever I have been served with some drink that was either extra fine or extra poor, I have always tried to ascertain what it was that made it good or that made it bad. These bits of information, gleaned piecemeal over a period of some forty years, I have collated, classified, and filed away in mental cabinets for future reference. And now I have emptied out the contents of these mental files and have compiled what I regard as the more important of them for your information and guidance.

In doing this I have assumed that, like myself, you, too, would like to know the "why" as well as the "how"; that you would not particularly care about a mere conglomeration of recipes, some good, some indifferent, and some definitely bad; but that you would like to know what principles to follow and what pitfalls to avoid in mixing palatable—and not merely potable—drinks from whatever liquors might chance to be available for use. If any pastry cook were to see a cake recipe calling for 2 pounds of butter, 1 teaspoon of flour, 5 pounds of sugar, 1 cup of baking powder, and 2 cups of vanilla, he would know that either it was written by a lunatic or it was printed by a drunken typesetter. He would know that the quantity given for every ingredient was completely ridiculous. But that is because he would know the respective functions of the shortening, the sweetening, the leavening, and the flavoring agents and the approximate quantities of each, in relation to the quantity of flour, necessary to perform those functions.

Yet many cocktail recipes are just as ridiculous as my theoretical cake recipe. The relative proportions of basic liquors, modifying agents, special flavoring agents, etc., are just as important in the mixing of a cocktail as are the relative proportions of flour, shortening, and other ingredients in the mixing of a cake. Your chef may use one egg in making one cake and a dozen eggs in making another, but he knows exactly the difference in the type and texture of the cake that will result from this variation. You, too, should know the difference in the type of drink that will result from varying proportions of the several classes of cocktail ingredients. Yet, so far as I have been able to ascertain, no book has ever heretofore attempted to teach the art of mixing cocktails in this simple and logical manner.

The contents of this book are based primarily on personal experience but also on information gleaned over many years from the reading of scores of books, pamphlets, and articles of all kinds having to do with the production, distribution, and consumption of alcoholic beverages. That part of the book dealing with the manufacture of liquors is, in the language of the old-time securities prospectus, "not guaranteed, but has been obtained from sources that are believed to be reliable." Comments on various medical aspects of the subject are based on personal discussion with leading physicians and surgeons and on articles found in publications of the American Medical Association and similar authoritative works.

All remarks concerning the superior flavor of one liquor as against another are, of course, based on personal preference and taste. The same is true regarding brands I have recommended. Those that I have named are the ones I like. Moreover, drinks that I have mixed with them have won the enthusiastic approval of my friends. I make no pretense, however, of having tried all brands of all liquors on the market. It may well be that there are other brands of one liquor or another that are just as good as any I have named or even better. Few writers on the subject of liquors have the temerity to mention brands at all. But, as already stated, I have written this book for the benefit of amateurs, some of whom may not know one brand from another. Of what avail, then, to be told that good cocktails can be made only with good liquors unless you also know at least one or two brands that are good?

In short, then, I have tried to include in this book at least the substance of everything that I should want to know if I were starting in, a complete greenhorn, to learn how to mix and serve in my own home various drinks, particularly that crowning glory of all mixed drinks—the American Cocktail.

Is that what you want to know? Then, gentlemen, "Here's How!"

CONTENTS

Preface to Third American Edition   5
Preface   7

BASIC PRINCIPLES   19

    What, Then, Is a Cocktail?   21
    Cocktail Ingredients   22
    The Base   22
    The Modifying Agent   23
    Special Flavoring and Coloring Agents   25

GLASSWARE, GIMMICKS, AND GADGETS   27

    Glasses   28
    Shakers   34
    Miscellaneous Equipment   36
    Table of Measurements   38

LIMES, LEMONS, AND LIQUORS   39

    Gin   39
    Whisky   46
    Rum   58
    Cognac and Other Grape Brandies   63
    Other Fruit Brandies   71
    Miscellaneous Spirits   72
    Southern Comfort   73
    Aquavit   74

Vodka	75
Tequila	78
Absinthe	79
Ojen	80
Arrack and Okolehao	80
Mead or Metheglin	81
Aguardiente	81
Borovicka	81
Apéritif Wines	82
Fortified Wines	87
Liqueurs	92
Bitters	94
Fruit Juices and Syrups	97
Eggs and Cream	101
Ice	102
Soda and Ginger Ale	103

PERTINENT POINTERS — 105

Measuring	105
To Stir or to Shake	108
Crushed Ice or Cubes	109
"And a Twist of Lemon"	111
Chilling and Frosting the Glasses	112
Proper Glassware	113
"Reaction Time"	113

SIX BASIC COCKTAILS — 115

The Martini	115
When Is a Martini Strong?	119
The Ideal Martini	120
The Manhattan	121
The Old-Fashioned	124
The Daiquiri	127
The Cocktail King and His Daiquiris	129
The Side Car	132
The Jack Rose	133

CONTENTS

ROLL YOUR OWN — 135

- Restatement of Basic Principles — 136
- Sours — 138
- *Cocktails Based on the Gin Sour* — 142
- *Cocktails Based on the Rum Sour* — 149
- *Cocktails Based on the Whisky Sour* — 156
- *Cocktails Based on the Brandy Sour* — 162
- *Cocktails Based on the Applejack Sour* — 166
- Aromatic Cocktails — 170
- *Gin Cocktails of the Aromatic Type* — 171
- *Rum Cocktails of the Aromatic Type* — 177
- *Whisky Cocktails of the Aromatic Type* — 180
- *Scotch Cocktails of the Aromatic Type* — 186
- *Brandy Cocktails of the Aromatic Type* — 189
- *Applejack Cocktails of the Aromatic Type* — 194
- Aromatic Wine Cocktails — 195

LIQUEURS — 199

THE USE AND ABUSE OF LIQUOR — 209

- Overindulgence — 209
- Popular Misbeliefs — 211
- Does Alcohol Warm the Body? — 211
- Alcohol, the Inevitable Concomitant of Progress — 212
- Social Effects of Overindulgence — 213
- How to Keep Sober — 215
- Alcohol and Arteriosclerosis — 217
- Alcohol and Ulcers — 217
- Alcohol and Feeble-mindedness — 217
- Does Regular Drinking Increase Capacity? — 218
- Is Alcohol Essential to Life? — 218
- Is Alcohol a Stimulant? — 219
- Is Liquor Fattening? — 219
- Is Mixing Drinks Fatal? — 220

JUDGING LIQUOR — 225

CONTENTS

BUREAUCRATIC AND OTHER IDIOSYNCRASIES	229
Internal Revenue Taxes	229
Jiffy Quick Junk	231
VODKA DRINKS	233
SHORT DRINKS, INCLUDING MORE COCKTAILS	239
Absinthe Drinks	240
After-Dinner Cordials	242
Champerelles	253
Crustas	257
Flips	263
Frappés	264
Frozen Cocktails	265
Holland Gin Cocktails	268
Knickebeins	272
Pousse-Cafés	281
Pousse l'Amour	283
Shakes	287
Sherry (or other Wine) and Egg	288
Smashes	290
Zombies	298
Zooms	300
TALL DRINKS	301
Highballs	302
Concerning Carbonated Beverages	307
Bucks	308
Rickeys	309
Collinses	312
Fizzes	314
Daisies and Fixes	320
Juleps	322
Cobblers	326
Coolers	328
Sangarees	330

CONTENTS

Slings and Toddies	332
Lemonades, Limeades, and Orangeades	333
Individual Punches	335
Puffs	337
Miscellaneous	340
Squirts	342

PARTY DRINKS — 344

Punches and Cups	344
Prohibition Punches	355
Swizzles	356
Shrubs	357
Wassail Bowl	359
Nogs	360

HOT DRINKS — 365

Possets	365
Mulls	366
Negus	367
Bishops	368
Grogs	369
Coffee Drinks	371
Blue Blazer	372
Scandinavian Hot Drinks	373

PICKER-UPPERS — 374

FOOD AND DRINK — 377

CONCLUSION — 379

INDEX — 381

THE FINE ART OF MIXING DRINKS

BASIC PRINCIPLES

Anyone *can* make good cocktails. The art of mixing drinks is no deep and jealously guarded secret. Nor is it a skill to be acquired only as the result of years of painstaking effort. It can be learned practically overnight.

Yet actually few people *do* make good cocktails. Nor is this disability limited to the amateur serving drinks in his own home. Far too many professional bartenders likewise seem wholly incapable of turning out drinks that are uniformly pleasing both to the eye and to the palate. Why is this? I am convinced that there are two principal reasons.

First, people fail to realize the absolute necessity of using *only* liquors of the highest quality. They are unwilling to pay $5.00 for a bottle of high-proof, well-aged liquor when perhaps they can get by with a low-proof, immature substitute at $2.89. But, as has been well said, a chain is no stronger than its weakest link. By the same token, a cocktail is no better than its poorest ingredient. A good Martini, for example, requires *both* top-quality gin and top-quality vermouth. Just a few drops of inferior vermouth can ruin the flavor of the finest gin and vice versa.

Second, people fail to understand the basic principle of the cocktail. Either they regard a cocktail as any haphazard conglomeration of spirituous liquors, wines (aromatic or plain), bitters, fruit juices, sugar or sugary syrups, milk, eggs, cream, and anything else that happens to be left over from last week's picnic supper, or they woodenly follow with drop-by-drop accuracy the formulas to be found in some one of the myriad recipe books now available at every bookstore. Unfortunately a large proportion of these recipes would seem to have been devised by persons with no more experience and understanding of the principles of blending liquors than the tyro who so innocently purchases and so slavishly follows them.

Most of the present generation learned to drink and most of the present-day bartenders learned their profession during the past thirty-seven years. The first fourteen years of that period were devoted to the famous "experiment, noble in purpose," and the remaining years have not yet been sufficient to erase wholly the ignoble effects of that era. During prohibition the overwhelming majority of available liquor consisted of bathtub gin and Scotch "just off the boat" (ferryboat from either Hoboken or Brooklyn). So unutterably vile were these synthetic concoctions that the primary object in mixing a cocktail became the addition of a sufficient amount of sweetened, highly flavored, and otherwise emollient and anti-emetic ingredients (cream, honey, Karo, canned fruit juices, etc.) to make it reasonably possible to swallow the resultant concoction and at the same time to retain a sufficient content of renatured alcohol to insure ultimate inebriety. Just how much dilution of the "gin"-bottle contents might be necessary to accomplish this supposedly salutary result depended largely on the intestinal fortitude and esophageal callosity of the particular individual involved. However, only the most rugged Spartan with at least ten years of vigorous prohibition training could be expected to survive—or, indeed, to get down—a drink containing as much as 50 per cent of the gin, whisky, brandy, or what have you of those days.

Small wonder, then, that this period gave birth to such pernicious recipes as the Alexander—equal parts of gin, crème de cacao, and sweet cream; the Orange Blossom —equal parts of gin and orange juice, with or without the white of an egg; the Bee's Knees—equal parts of gin, lemon juice, and honey; and so on *ad nauseam*. And it is only by regarding them as a more or less logical, albeit regrettable, aftermath of prohibition influence that one can account for the many ridiculous formulas still found in the average book of cocktail recipes of today.

WHAT, THEN, IS A COCKTAIL?

And by a "cocktail" I mean an apéritif cocktail—i.e., one to be taken before a meal as a stimulant to the appetite and an aid to digestion. Probably as good a definition as is to be found in any dictionary is that contained in Macmillan's Modern Dictionary: "iced drink made of spirits, bitters, flavoring, and sugar." Even this, however, is not strictly accurate, for by no means do all cocktails contain all four of these ingredients. However, before attempting to evolve a definition of a cocktail, let us first make sure that we understand its function. We cannot satisfactorily determine what ingredients it should contain and in what proportions until we are sure we know what purpose it is to serve. While there may be other desirable attributes of the cocktail, these are the most important:

1. It must whet the appetite, not dull it. This first basic requirement of a good cocktail automatically eliminates a host of over-sweetened, over-fruit-juiced, over-egged, and over-creamed concoctions customarily found in books of cocktail recipes. For example, while an Alexander, like a glass of good port wine, may be a delightful midafternoon drink accompanying cake or chocolate cookies, nevertheless, in the sense of a pre-prandial apéritif, it is definitely not a cocktail.

2. It should stimulate the mind as well as the appetite. The well-made cocktail is one of the most gracious of drinks. It pleases the senses. The shared delight of those who partake in common of this refreshing nectar breaks the ice of formal reserve. Taut nerves relax; taut muscles relax; tired eyes brighten; tongues loosen; friendships deepen; the whole world becomes a better place in which to live. But don't expect these results if you serve bitter drinks, syrupy drinks, watery drinks, or drinks that taste like reconditioned tin.

3. *It must be pleasing to the palate.* In order that a cocktail may satisfy both requirements 1 and 3, it must be dry (i.e., not sweet), yet smooth. Indeed, in compounding a cocktail, the first thought should be the production of a drink sufficiently dry to wake up and energize the taste buds, yet not so sour or so bitter or so aromatic as to be unpalatable.

4. *It must also be pleasing to the eye.* This requires no conscious effort, yet I have seen Martinis that looked like dishwater just recovering from a bad case of jaundice and Manhattans that resembled nothing else quite so much as rusty sludge from the radiator of a Model-T Ford.

5. *It must have sufficient alcoholic flavor* to be readily distinguishable from papaya juice, yet must not assault the palate with the force of an atomic bomb.

6. Finally (and remember I am speaking now of cocktails only and not of apéritif wines) *it must be well iced.* Of this, more later.

COCKTAIL INGREDIENTS

And now back to our consideration of the proper ingredients of the cocktail, their respective functions, and the proportions in which they should be used. Every cocktail, properly so called, must contain two distinct types of ingredients. It also may, but need not necessarily, contain a third type. They are:

1. A base;
2. A modifying, smoothing, or aromatizing agent;
3. Additional special flavoring and coloring ingredients.

Let us consider them in order.

1. *The Base* This is the fundamental and distinguish-

ing ingredient of the cocktail and *must always* comprise more than 50 per cent of the entire volume. Indeed, with a few rare exceptions it should constitute from 75 per cent of total volume upward. Strictly speaking, the base must always consist of spirituous liquors—whisky, gin, rum, brandy, etc. By common acceptance, however, combinations of vinous liquors or aromatic wines, or mixtures in which such wines predominate, have also come to be called cocktails; for example, the Vermouth Cocktail, consisting of Italian vermouth with a dash of Angostura or a mixture of Italian and French vermouth with both Angostura and orange bitters. Another example is the Bamboo Cocktail, consisting of dry sherry and French vermouth with a dash of orange bitters.

Normally, the cocktail base will consist of a single spirituous liquor, and this one liquor, being the distinguishing and predominant ingredient, determines the type of the cocktail. Thus we have gin cocktails, such as the Martini, whisky cocktails, such as the Manhattan, rum cocktails, such as the Daiquiri, and so on. Within certain limits, however, it is possible to combine two (perhaps even more, but this is dangerous) liquors as a base. For example, rye and bourbon whiskies, while differing decidedly in flavor, have the same essential characteristics and may be used pretty much either interchangeably or in combination as a base. Gin and white Cuban rum also blend very satisfactorily and may be used in combination. On the other hand, the indiscriminate mixture of three or four or five different liquors is practically certain to destroy the distinguishing flavor and aroma of all and produce a result about as palatable as a blend of castor oil and gasoline.

2. *The Modifying Agent* It is difficult to find a word that exactly describes this ingredient (or group of ingredients) and, for want of a better term, I have called it the modifying agent or modifier. It is this ingredient, in combination with the base of spirituous liquor, which characterizes the cocktail. Without this ingredient the base, no

matter how violently shaken and how thoroughly chilled, would still not be a cocktail but would remain merely chilled liquor. Its function is to smooth down the biting sharpness of the raw liquor and, at the same time, to point up and add character to its natural flavor. The flavor of the modifier itself should never predominate but should always remain submerged. The gin cocktail should still remain definitely and recognizably a gin cocktail, the whisky cocktail a whisky cocktail, but the modifier should add that elusive *je ne sais quoi* which makes the cocktail a smooth, fragrant, inspirational delight and not a mere drink of gin or whisky.

In general, modifying agents may be divided into three classes:

Aromatics, including the aromatic wines, such as French and Italian vermouth, Dubonnet, Byrrh, etc.; bitters of various types—orange, Angostura, Peychaud, Unicum, etc.; and miscellaneous aromatics such as Amer Picon and Fernet-Branca;

Fruit juices—orange, lemon, lime, etc.—with or without sugar;

Miscellaneous "smoothing" agents—sugar, cream, eggs, etc.

All of these modifiers—particularly the aromatics and, above all, the bitters—must be used with discretion. The old French maxim for salad dressing runs, "A miser for vinegar; a spendthrift for oil." This might well be paraphrased for cocktail mixing to read, "A miser for modifying agents; a spendthrift for the base." Remember always that you are making a brandy cocktail, a rum cocktail, an applejack cocktail, and not a bitters cocktail, a lemon cocktail, or an egg cocktail. Just how far you should go with each agent you will have to learn by experience, relying both on your own palate and on the comments of your friends. With bitters, a safe rule, particularly if the bitters are used in conjunction with an aromatic wine, is never more than two or three dashes to each drink.

With the aromatic wines, much depends both on the type of wine and on the base. Rye and bourbon, particularly the latter, have a natural affinity for Italian vermouth. One part of Italian vermouth and two parts of bourbon, with a small dash of Angostura, make a reasonably palatable Manhattan if you like that drink a bit on the sweet, mild side. When making Martinis, however, assuming that you are using a really high-grade matured gin, your minimum ratio should be three or four to one and, with a twist of lemon peel or a dash of orange bitters, a ratio of from five to one up to about seven to one is even better.

It is somewhat more difficult to lay down any general rule as to the use of citrus juices. This will be discussed more at length in the chapter, "Roll Your Own." In using cream or eggs, remember, first, that you are preparing a drink and not a meal. The object of the cream or eggs is merely to produce a drink that is pleasing to the eye because of its creamy, foamy texture and, at the same time, smooth and innocent-tasting. And, oh, boy, these drinks can be insidious! Also, too much of either can make you deathly sick—not because of the alcoholic content (which is, to some extent, neutralized by the eggs or cream), but because of the rich, heavy nature of the drink and the terrifically high calorie value of the combination. A reasonably safe rule for these miscellaneous smoothing agents is an absolute maximum of ½ an egg white, ¼ a whole egg, 1 tablespoonful heavy cream, or 1 teaspoonful of sugar to each drink.

3. *Special Flavoring and Coloring Agents* These include all the various cordials or liqueurs, which will be discussed later, as well as non-alcoholic fruit syrups. Moreover, the ingredient that is used as a modifier in one cocktail may be used solely for incidental flavoring or coloring in another. For example, in the Orange Blossom (one of the horrors of prohibition) the orange juice is used to modify and smooth out the gin. On the other hand, in the Bronx the modifier is the vermouth (sometimes a

combination of both French and Italian), and the orange juice is added solely for incidental flavor and color.

Of all the factors involved in the mixing of cocktails, flavoring agents are undoubtedly the most abused. As has already been pointed out, the gin cocktail should always be identifiable as a gin cocktail, the rum cocktail as a rum cocktail, and so on. Liqueurs, such as maraschino, apricot, crème de menthe, framboisette, etc., and syrups, such as orgeat (pronounced or-zhah'), grenadine, falernum, etc., are added either as a modifier or solely for color and for creating a faint, elusive, tantalizing flavor that makes the cocktail something different from the ordinary. They should *never* (with the possible exception of a very few drinks such as the Stinger, which is not really a cocktail) dominate and overpower the flavor of the base. These special flavoring agents should be measured by drops or dashes, *not* by ponies or jiggers.

Whenever you see a recipe calling for equal parts of rum, brandy, Cointreau, curaçao, and Benedictine, with a dash of absinthe, shun it as you would the very devil. Entirely apart from the fact that such a nightmare combination lacks the essential elements of a cocktail and, therefore, is not a true cocktail, there are two excellent reasons for avoiding it. First, the liqueurs themselves all have heavy, overpowering flavors which, according to how they are selected, may either blend or clash, but, in any event, taken before a meal, they will thoroughly anesthetize the nerves of smell and taste and produce the same general effect on your palate and appetite as a dose of sulphuric ether. Second, in addition to an alcoholic content averaging from 60 to 100 proof or even more, these liqueurs all possess a high sugar content. You probably would not try to eat a five-pound box of chocolates before dinner as an appetizer, and if you did try it you would probably get thoroughly sick. For precisely the same reason (only more so) you should not try to consume several cocktails whose principal ingredient is a conglomeration of heavy-bodied, high-proof, syrupy liqueurs.

GLASSWARE, GIMMICKS, AND GADGETS

Now that our cocktail-mixing objectives have been carefully defined, let us assemble our equipment. Then we will go out and buy a few bottles of liquor and, after two or three further warnings against common pitfalls and errors, we shall at last be ready to step behind the prescription counter and sing out, "Gentlemen, name your poison!"

There is practically no limit to the variety and quantity of equipment which the really serious-minded master of mixology can assemble for the purpose of simplifying (or complicating, according to the point of view) his task of compounding and dispensing cocktails, Sours, Swizzles, Collinses, Highballs, Juleps, and other drinks. On the other hand, the bare essentials which can be made to answer in an emergency are (1) something in which to mix and (2) something in which to serve. In a pinch, cups—even paper cups (but *never* tin or any other metal)—will take the place of glasses, and I have drunk cocktails shaken up in a milk bottle which, since we were in camp where all food and liquor taste their best, were hailed by all as potations handed down by the gods direct from Olympus. Measuring *can* be done with the eye (and well done if the eye is sufficiently experienced); limes and lemons *can* be squeezed with the hands and strained through a piece of old but clean cloth; two penknives, properly manipulated, make an excellent impromptu corkscrew, and so on. All these, however, are emergency measures. For simple, easy, satisfying, and gracious service in your own home you will need proper glassware and certain bar equipment.

GLASSES

First of all, your glassware, and, since our primary consideration is cocktails, let us start with cocktail glasses. You will find them in sizes ranging from about 2 to 3½ ounces. Get the large ones—not less than 3 ounces. The average bar cocktail measures about 2 to 2½ ounces, but the glass should never be filled to the brim. Not only does overfilling place too great a strain on the aplomb of the guest—especially with the second or third drink—but even the few drops of liquor which someone will inevitably spill will not improve either the guest's clothing or the top of your grand piano on which the glass may be placed.

And let your cocktail glasses be made of glass. They may be either expensive crystal from Plummer's or Steuben's or they may be the five- or ten-cent variety from Woolworth's, but be sure they are *glass*. I have friends whose pride and joy are their gold-lined, sterling cocktail "glasses." They are beautiful to look at, but any cocktail drunk from them tastes like arsenic and rusty tin. Furthermore, be sure that the glasses are long-stemmed. A stemless cocktail glass is a monstrosity. Cocktails should be sipped, not gulped, and should remain stinging cold to the last drop. This, in addition to having the cocktail itself thoroughly chilled, requires that the glass also be chilled before pouring the drink, and that the glass be handled by its stem so that the warm hand will not come in contact with the cold glass that encloses the cocktail itself. Furthermore, any glass with iced contents will "sweat" in a warm room. This is a condensation on the cold glass of moisture contained in the warm air of the room. With a long-stemmed glass this "sweating" is seldom sufficiently copious to wet the foot of the glass, thereby requiring the use of coasters, but with stemless glasses—even the footed variety—the base will invariably become damp and leave a ring on any furniture upon which it may be placed.

For your Old-Fashioneds you will, of course, need Old-Fashioned glasses. See that these are heavy. You can get them in sizes from 4 or 5 ounces upward. The usual bar size is about 4 ounces, but this allows for only one lump of ice and one jigger of whisky with but little space left over for fruit, if you wish to decorate the drink. For home use a 7- or 8-ounce size is vastly to be preferred. This will permit making a "double," using sufficient ice to keep the cocktail cold to the last drop, and will obviate the necessity of mixing a second round for any but the most hardened drinker. Even he, however, should not have a second round of this size as a prelude to a meal. I, personally, have two sets of Old-Fashioned glasses—7-ounce for ordinary occasions and a slightly larger size (15-ounce, to be specific) for extra-special occasions when serious drinking is the order of the day and the libation is not poured merely as a prelude to a heavy meal. These glasses, of course, are stemless. The ice in the glass itself keeps the cocktails cold, but, unless you are intent on making work for the furniture polishers, a coaster with each glass is an absolute "must."

Perhaps, while on the subject of glasses, it might be well to mention others that you will find useful in serving various drinks other than cocktails. Since this book does not treat of wines and beers I shall not discuss the glasses associated with those drinks except the sherry glass (for serving sherry as an apéritif) and the champagne glass, which is used for serving various cocktails—especially frozen cocktails.

The liqueur or cordial glass is the smallest and usually holds from ¾ to 1 ounce. Preferably it should be footed, but since cordials are not iced, the length of the stem is immaterial. The Pousse-Café glass is a straight-sided glass, shaped like a cordial glass but about twice as high, holding from 1½ to 2 ounces.

The whisky glass is shaped like an Old-Fashioned glass and varies in size from 1 ounce to about 2½ ounces. In the 1-ounce size it is called a pony; in the 2-ounce size a jigger, or a drink. The pony is useful only for measuring, since a

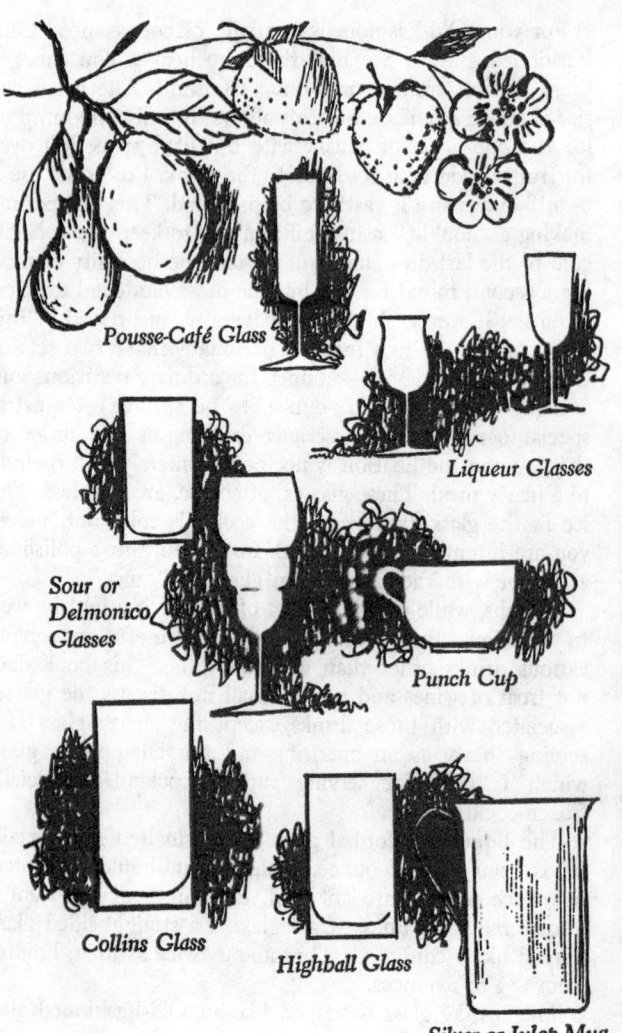

straight drink of even as little as one pony is best served in a 1½- to 2-ounce glass.

In discussing measuring glasses, it might be well to note that the word "wineglass" as frequently used in recipe books refers to quantity rather than any particular style of glass and is equivalent to 4 ounces.

The sherry glass is a footed glass holding about 2 to 3 ounces, the body of which is shaped like an inverted cone. While sherry presumably might taste equally good (or bad, depending on the sherry) from some other glass, you will find this shape important in case you ever want to serve a Sherry and Egg, a Brandy and Egg, or (God forbid!) a Pousse l'Amour.

The brandy inhaler or snifter is an egg-shaped, footed glass with a small top opening. It nestles in the palm, thereby warming the contents of the glass and holding the aroma within the glass, so that the drinker may sniff appreciatively before and during the drop-by-drop imbibing. The proper ritual is as follows: (1) Hold the glass toward the light, note the exquisite, amber translucence, and exclaim, "*Quelle beauté!*" (2) Warm the glass in the palm, sniff, and then, "*Quel bouquet, quel arome!*" (3) Warm again, sip gently, let the liquid gold roll slowly across the tongue and over the epiglottis (it should be completely evaporated and absorbed before reaching the esophagus), close the eyes, exhale gently, and reverently and rapturously whisper, "*Quel goût!*"

The champagne glass, like the cocktail glass, is long-stemmed. It is somewhat larger than the cocktail glass —usually about 5 to 6 ounces. It comes in two styles, hollow-stemmed and saucer. The hollow-stemmed glass is shaped much like the standard cocktail glass; the saucer glass is also much the same general shape but is broader and shallower. The hollow-stemmed glass is now seldom used because of the extreme difficulty in washing and drying it.

Finally we come to a group of tall, narrow (in proportion to height) glasses with fairly straight or slightly flaring sides, commonly loosely referred to as Highball glasses. These glasses vary in size from about 4 or 5 to as much as 16 ounces. Strictly speaking, the small size (about 3 to 5 ounces) is a Sour or Delmonico glass; the next size (6 to 9 ounces) a Highball glass; and the largest size (10 ounces and upward) a Collins glass. Don't expect, however, to have the Highball which you order at a bar served in anything larger than a Sour glass unless you order a double. It is a decidedly generous bar that gives you a full 2-ounce drink in a Highball (the measuring glass may *look* like 2 ounces, but note the way the bottom of the glass is constructed). Two ounces of liquor in a 14- or 16-ounce glass filled with ice and carbonated beverage would more nearly resemble the traditional Sunday-school lemonade than a Highball.

For home use I recommend three sizes of these glasses— a Sour glass of about 4- to 5-ounce size for Sours (tomato or orange juice glasses will do), a medium-sized glass (about 7 to 9 ounces) for the chap who wants just a short Highball, and the Collins glass of about 14-ounce size for use at the bridge table when you do not want to interrupt the making of a redoubled grand slam through the execution of a triple grand coup to mix a second round of drinks.

One other glass of this type that I might also mention in passing is the Zombie glass. Since the Zombie will taste just as good or just as atrocious in one glass as another and, since I trust you will serve this drink, if at all, only on rare occasions and as a curiosity, I suggest that you fall back on the good old Collins glass rather than invest in a special glass for this much-overadvertised liquid hash.

Three other containers, not strictly necessary but useful on special occasions, are the Punch cup, the Tom and Jerry mug, and the silver mug. The Punch cup, of course, goes with the Punch bowl and may be either glass or china to match the bowl. China cups and bowls have the advantage that they can be used for hot drinks—even flaming drinks—that would shatter any but the toughest laboratory glass. The Tom and Jerry mug resembles, both in shape and size, Grandfather's shaving mug or his mustache cup minus the mustache fender. Like the china Punch cup, it can be used for any hot drink. The silver mug is useful for any frosted drink that is to be sipped through straws, such as Mint Juleps. It has two advantages for this purpose over glass. First, since metal is a better conductor of heat than glass, it will frost quicker and better than even the thinnest of glass. Second, since it has a handle (and particularly if the handle is insulated from the body of the mug), the hand does not come in direct contact with the frosted surface and thus destroy the frost. The metallic taste heretofore referred to in connection with silver cocktail "glasses" is the result of direct contact of the lips with the metal and is avoided by the use of straws. This is strictly *de rigueur* with Juleps and similar tall iced drinks, but, except for frozen Daiquiris and the like, who the devil wants to drink a cocktail through a straw?

SHAKERS

Good cocktail shakers can be obtained in all manner of sizes, shapes, and materials. Since metal is a better conductor of heat than glass and, therefore, the ice in a metal shaker will melt and dilute the drinks quicker than in a glass shaker, I recommend glass shakers,[1] but with tight-fitting metal tops. The opening of the glass shaker should be large enough to take large ice cubes with ease; the opening of the metal top from which the drink is poured should be small and the construction should be such that there will be no leakage between the shaker and the top and no drip from the top after pouring. Be sure the top is

[1] There has recently appeared on the market a double-walled, insulated metal shaker which has received considerable publicity because of the length of time it will keep the contents cold without appreciable dilution. While it is undoubtedly vastly superior in this respect to the older type single-walled metal shaker, I have not been able to detect in actual use any marked advantage over a heavy, thick-walled glass shaker.

tight enough not to fly off either in shaking or in pouring, but as an extra precaution always hold one hand on the shaker and one on the top during both operations.

Chill the shaker well before using, either by leaving it in the refrigerator for a half-hour or by partially filling with cracked ice. This ice should be discarded before mixing the cocktail. The heavier the glass in your shaker, the longer it will take to chill it, but the longer the drinks in it will stay cold and undiluted. Be sure your shaker is large enough and be sure to use plenty of ice. If you are making cocktails for four and you figure two cocktails of 2½ ounces for each, this is a total of 20 ounces. A quart shaker will be none too large for this purpose. A large quantity of large cubes of ice will chill the drink quickly with less ultimate dilution and, in addition, you must have extra space to use in shaking or in stirring.

Martinis, Manhattans, and other cocktails containing wine can be stirred with a rod or long spoon in your ordinary shaker, but if you serve them with any frequency you will find a Martini pitcher with a lip designed to hold back the ice while pouring the cocktail a great convenience. With this pitcher you will need a long stirring rod, normally either of chrome-plated steel or of plastic.

The bar glass is a great convenience. I use two, both having the same size top but one large (a full quart) and the other smaller (about 20 ounces). With these I have both the regular bar-glass metal cap, also holding a full quart, and a cocktail-shaker top of the right size to fit both glasses. These make excellent shakers for making from two to eight or (with the large bar cap) even ten cocktails. When using a bar glass without a shaker top, it is easier to empty the contents into the metal cap and pour from that. It is difficult to pour directly from the bar glass without dribbling. Without the shaker top you will also need a strainer to hold back the ice while pouring. These come in two styles: a sort of oversized, perforated spoon with short handle, and a somewhat larger, flat disk with a light coiled-spring edge insuring a snug fit in the top of the bar cap. The strainer is inserted in the top of the bar cap, the handle is held between the first and second fingers, and the strainer is held in place by the tip of the forefinger while pouring.

MISCELLANEOUS EQUIPMENT

A corkscrew, a bottle opener, and a steel paring knife are absolute essentials. One of the best types of corkscrew is not a screw at all but consists of two rather thin, narrow, parallel steel blades attached at right angles to a heavy handle. These two blades are inserted with a gentle rocking motion along opposite sides of the cork, care being taken not to push down on both blades at once, thereby pushing the cork into the bottle, and when they have been thrust halfway down the cork or better, the cork is removed with a steady, twisting pull. Two excellent corkscrews are the "Korkmaster" and the "Connoisseur's Corkscrew."

There are numerous good bottle openers available on the market. Get one that is heavy and well built, not dainty and fragile. And don't rely on the bottle-opening hook of a combination can opener, corkscrew, etc., etc. I have never yet seen one that was any good, and some of them are actually dangerous.

Some type of squeezer for your citrus fruit is also needed. When only small limes were available it was necessary to have a small hand squeezer for them, but with the large Florida seedless limes now on the market, an ordinary lemon squeezer will adequately handle both lemons and limes.

Both an ice pick and an ice shaver were at one time regarded as essentials. Much better than an ice pick for breaking ice cubes is the Tap Icer. This gadget is simple, inexpensive, and unbelievably efficient. It should be included in the equipment of every home bar. The ice shaver is a relic of the days of hundred-pound ice cakes. It cannot be used with cubes from your electric refrigerator. In place of the shaver you can either wrap the cubes in a piece of heavy duck or canvas and pound them with a mallet, or you can pulverize them in an ice crusher. There are many types of the latter. Personally, I like my Dazey with its adjustable jaws for three degrees of fineness, and the same wall bracket that holds the crusher also holds my Dazey juice extractor which "squeezes" my oranges, lemons, and limes.

Unless your juice extractor embodies a coarse strainer (the Dazey does) you will need one for your fruit juices. The type that fits over the top of a glass or cup and has a flat, perforated bottom is highly satisfactory. You should also have a fine mesh wire strainer (such as a tea strainer) for straining your citrus juices to be used in fancy cocktails where you wish to retain a translucent appearance rather than the cloudy effect of such mixtures as the Daiquiri.

Just where the fetish of using loaf sugar for Old-Fashioneds originated, I do not know. However, if you wish to make yours that way, you will need a muddler—an implement that resembles a miniature wooden potato masher. The muddler is also useful in crushing mint if you decide to join the school that adheres to crushed mint in Juleps.

An ice bucket (either of the so-called vacuum variety or of heavy glass with a tight-fitting metal cover), together with a pair of small silver ice tongs, is useful in serving Highballs.

A long-handled bar spoon is also highly convenient both for measuring and for stirring. Most of the old recipe books state that the bar spoon holds one half a teaspoonful. However, I have several and I find that each one holds approximately one teaspoonful.

Finally, for use with your Old-Fashioneds and your tall drinks, have plenty of coasters. Or you may prefer to encase your tall glasses in the slips or "panties" that can be had both in woven straw and in knit twine. Maybe you can persuade some nimble-fingered friend of the fair sex to knit or crochet a set for you that will fit exactly your own glassware.

TABLE OF MEASUREMENTS

As a conclusion to our consideration of equipment, perhaps a table of measurements might be useful. How much is a dash? Well, a dash is a squirt—delivered through the squirter top of your bitters bottle or what have you. And, by the way, it will be quite helpful if you acquire a few of these tops of assorted sizes to use not only with your bitters but also in bottles of absinthe and other liqueurs that you most frequently use to flavor your cocktails. A "dash" varies in quantity according to the size of the opening in the bottle top through which it is squirted. Also like a drop, it varies according to the density and surface viscosity of the particular liquid. In theory, however, a drop equals one minim, a dash equals ten drops, and six dashes (or sixty drops) equal one teaspoonful (one dram). Accordingly we arrive at the following table:

1 drop	=	1 minim
10 drops (10 minims)	=	1 dash
6 dashes (60 drops or minims)	=	1 teaspoonful (1 dram)
8 teaspoonfuls (8 drams)	=	1 ounce
1 ounce	=	1 pony
1½ to 2 ounces [2]	=	1 jigger
4 ounces	=	1 wineglass
8 ounces	=	1 cup
16 ounces (2 cups)	=	1 pint
25⅗ ounces	=	1 fifth
32 ounces (2 pints)	=	1 quart
40 ounces	=	1 imperial quart (British and Canadian)

[2] The generally accepted size of the jigger is 1½ ounces. However, some writers have tried to standardize the size at 2 ounces instead of 1½ ounces. If you use a jigger, test it and find out how much it really holds.

LIMES, LEMONS, AND LIQUORS

At the very outset we should consider at least such of the basic principles respecting types, distinguishing characteristics, and manufacturing methods of the different kinds of liquors as may be necessary to enable us to select intelligently and with discrimination those that are to be used to start our supply shelf—gin, whisky, rum, brandy, vermouth, bitters, etc.

GIN

I mention gin first among the liquors used as a cocktail base because, in my opinion, it is the most important. If I were to be limited to just one base liquor I should unhestitatingly choose gin. That is primarily because, while gin has its own characteristic aroma and flavor and, if it is good, matured gin, needs no doctoring up with other flavors to make a palatable drink, its flavor is so subtle and delicate that it will blend satisfactorily with all manner of other flavors in a mixed drink. The second best of the more common liquors in this respect is white Cuban rum, but rum has a more pungent flavor than gin. It blends well with many other flavors, both fruity and aromatic, but, unlike gin, it clashes with some flavors and obstinately refuses to be subdued.

The second reason for regarding gin as the most important of cocktail bases is that, of all the common liquors, it gives the quickest "lift." Here, again, rum—especially the light-bodied Cuban rum—probably ranks second. Russian vodka and Danish akvavit are in the same category with gin, but they are not exactly what I have called "common liquors."

Of all the liquors in the world, gin is probably the most misunderstood, the most maligned, the most abused. So unspeakably vile were most of the synthetic concoctions, both peddled and homemade, under the name of gin during the prohibition era that it is not surprising that even today the word conjures up distasteful feelings in the minds of many who fail to realize that those horribles messes had about the same relation to real gin that iron pyrites or fool's gold has to real gold. How many people do you hear say that they simply cannot drink gin, either because they can't bear the taste of it or because it upsets them? Yet there are careful and experienced physicians who regard gin as the safest and most reliable of all liquors as a medicinal agent. And, of course, it is the *only* liquor that is a specific for the treatment of certain genito-urinary disturbances. It is quite possible that some few isolated individuals may be allergic to gin. A particular individual may be allergic to anything. Some are allergic to milk; others are allergic to bread; many are allergic to eggs. I even once heard the story of a man who was allergic to himself. On the other hand, for every genuine allergy that exists there are probably at least three or four that are merely fancied. And to say that this ratio applies to gin is undoubtedly ultra-conservative.

There are two distinct types of gin—Geneva (or Genever) and London. In mentioning two types I omit from consideration both sloe gin and bathtub gin. Sloe gin is really not a gin at all but a sloeberry liqueur; bathtub gin is less than nothing at all—made by adding essences and oils to raw alcohol and water. I have known many people who drank it during the prohibition era, but I never yet found anyone who really liked it.

Geneva gin, also called Schiedam gin and Dutch or

Hollands gin,[1] was originally made in Holland but is also now made to some extent in the Western Hemisphere. Juniper berries and other aromatics are mixed with a mash of barley malt and other grains, and the whole mash is fermented and distilled together—very much the same as whisky is distilled. This process produces a highly aromatic and somewhat bitter, acrid liquor which is unquestionably the finest of all gins for medicinal purposes. It is an excellent remedy for lumbago. It is even possible to acquire a taste for it as a drink, either straight or with a dash of bitters. As a cocktail base, however, it is practically worthless because it will not blend with other flavors—even vermouths. There are a few cocktail recipes based on Geneva gin which will be included in a later chapter of this book, but they are offered primarily as curiosities and are not recommended.

We are now fairly well recovered from the world-wide war shortage of all kinds of liquors, including gin. Not only was a good gin hard to obtain in the United States, but London gin was scarce in London, and Hollands gin was scarce in Holland. Some of the Geneva gins normally available before the war—all excellent—were Hulstkamp, Fockink,[2] and Bols. These are now again available here. Another splendid old Hollands gin, seldom seen in this country, is made by Levert & Co., Amsterdam, under the trade name of "Oorlam—zeer oude Genever."

When the Germans occupied Holland, Bols moved to Argentina where they made, among other liquors, a Geneva-type gin. It was not too bad, but it did not possess the same excellence that always characterized all the Bols

---

[1] Geneva Gin is also called schnapps (shnahps), although the word "schnapps" is also sometimes applied to whiskies and other distilled spirits.

[2] On the old building—the oldest tavern in Amsterdam—at the corner of Oude Zijds Voorburgwal and Pijlsteeg streets, there is a tablet dedicated "to the old Wynand Fockink Tavern erected in the year 1619" or, as it reads in Dutch, "Naar het Oude van Wijnand Fockink Opgericht Anno 1619."

products of the old days in Holland. Fortunately, Bols is now back in Holland and we are again getting its products.

The uninitiated would scarcely recognize Geneva and London gins as belonging to the same family or as being manufactured from the same substances. Yet the pronounced difference in taste results almost entirely from the difference in the two processes of manufacture. In the manufacture of London gin the juniper berries (together with such other seeds, roots, barks, etc., as may be used for flavoring) are placed in the still with raw alcohol, the whole mass is redistilled, and the alcohol picks up the flavor of these various substances in the process of redistillation. All real London-type gins, therefore, are double-distilled. Some are triple-distilled. Bathtub gin is not redistilled, which is one of the reasons for its gross inferiority.

There are two types of London gin, dry and sweet, although all London gin is commonly and somewhat loosely referred to as London dry. The sweet type, seldom seen on the American market, is known as Old Tom. It is simply London dry gin to which has been added sugar or some similar sweetening agent. Not only is it the ideal gin for a Tom Collins but, strictly speaking, a Tom Collins is not a Tom Collins unless it is made with Old Tom gin. The substitution of dry gin for Old Tom gin in this drink has become a common practice merely because, since prohibition, Old Tom is seldom seen in this country.

Not only is Old Tom gin the proper gin for a Tom Collins; in a pinch it can also be used for cocktails. It must be remembered, however, that this gin is already sweetened. Consequently it will not make a really dry cocktail, but this sweetness can be offset, at least in part, by an extra twist of lemon peel or an extra dash of bitters. In making gin cocktails that call for sugar, such as a Clover Club or a Gimlet, merely cut down on the sugar or omit it altogether.

Of the truly dry London gins there are still two kinds—white and yellow—although it is only lately that any substantial number of people in this country have become acquainted with yellow gin and its outstanding excellence.

Now, as the old woman said when she kissed the cow, *"Chacun à son goût."* To me, the king of liqueurs is Grand Marnier, with a few others such as Benedictine, Vieille Cure, and green Chartreuse running neck and neck for second place. Your favorite may be Parfait Amour or Forbidden Fruit—two that vie for bottom place in my list. However, this book is intended primarily for the novice who wants to know how to choose and what is good and what is bad. Therefore, at the risk of putting myself out at the extreme end of a limb and handing you a saw with which to work behind me, I intend to express frankly my own personal preferences as to types of various liquors and even as to brands.

Prior to World War II there was a plentiful supply in the market of imported London gins, including those made by Booth, Gordon, Coates, Holloway, Nicholson, Gilbey, and Burnett, to mention some of the truly good brands. Some of those named were better than others, but all were at least reasonably good. Of all of them, however, the one of predominating excellence, according to my taste, is Booth's House of Lords—a yellow gin—and I have yet to find any discriminating gin drinker who disagrees with this. Other good imported gins now available are Burrough's Beefeater (truly excellent), Berry Brothers, and Old Gentry. If you are interested in high-proof gins, you might try Deptford or Young's (both 100 proof) or Tanqueray's (94.6 proof). House of Lords (still my favorite for Martinis) is only 86 proof.

The firm of Joseph E. Seagram & Sons, Inc., has come out with a domestic yellow gin, Seagram's Golden, also known as Ancient Bottle, the first yellow gin to be produced in this country and, just as I regard House of Lords as truly representing the peerage of English gins, so do I consider Seagram's Golden as so far superior to all other American gins that it and the others should not be mentioned in the same breath. In fact, to my taste, it ranks as a close second to House of Lords and ahead of many of the English white gins.

Even before prohibition days, because of the high customs duties on imported liquors, a number of British distilleries had established branch plants for the manufacture of gin in the United States. After repeal, with the still higher taxes involved, it was only natural that these and other distilleries should again open here. Unfortunately —and I say this without fear of successful contradiction— there is no American (including the Latin Americas) gin, with the possible exception of Seagram's Golden, that can compare in flavor with that distilled in England. Just why this is true, it is rather difficult to say. It is quite understandable that Grand Marnier, a liqueur with a *Fine Champagne* (pronounced feen shaN-pahN'ya) base, could not be successfully made here where we have no brandies comparable even to an ordinary cognac or armagnac, or that the Cinzano organization could not make a truly fine Italian vermouth in the Argentine where the full-bodied wines of Italy are not available. But why experienced distillers such as Gordon, presumably using the same formulas and methods, cannot make in the United States a gin that compares with their English product is another question.

One possible explanation may be the difference in water. Strange as it may seem to the uninitiated, the water that is used in the manufacture of liquor has a profound effect on its flavor. In the manufacture of one liquor only soft water is used, with another only water from a limestone area, and with still another only water from an area abounding in red granite. Each different water results in liquor having a different taste and character.

Another reason that has been assigned is the lower proof at which gin is distilled out in England. With very few exceptions, all liquors are distilled out at proof much higher than that at which they are bottled. Scotch whisky, for example, which is usually bottled and sold at between 80 and 90 proof, is distilled out and barreled for aging at proofs running as high as 150 or even higher. In general, it may be said that the *lower* the proof at which liquor is distilled out and the *higher* the proof at which it is bottled and sold, the better the liquor.

This statement may, at first, sound paradoxical. However, the explanation is simple and entirely logical. One of the objects in distilling liquor is to retain a sufficient quantity of those flavoring elements which give the particular liquor in question its distinguishing characteristics. If liquor were distilled out at 200 proof (a purely theoretical 100-per-cent alcohol and, in practice, incapable of realization) it would be plain alcohol with no flavor whatsoever (other than the flavor, if you can call it such, of alcohol itself) and it would not make the slightest difference in flavor, body, or character whether it was made from sugar, potatoes, barley, rye, corn, or any other starchy substance. It would be pure and simple unadulterated C_2H_5OH—the most absolute of alcohol absolutes.

Now, the lower the proof (within reason) at which liquor can be distilled out, the more of these distinguishing flavoring characteristics will be retained. American gin is distilled out at about 190 proof, English gin at about 180. The English gin, therefore, has more body and character and less of the "metallic," raw-alcohol taste. Strangely enough, the exact reverse is true of the practices of the two countries in manufacturing whiskies. Scotch whisky is distilled out at 180 proof or higher, Canadian at about 160 proof, and American at 140 proof or lower. Hence the better body and superior character of American whiskies as well as the fact that the best American whiskies are bottled in bond and sold at 100 proof, whereas most Scotch whiskies, to obscure their sharp, raw alcohol taste, are watered down to about 86 proof before being bottled and sold.

In saying that the higher the proof at which liquor is sold the better the liquor, I mean simply that there is no necessity of going to a liquor store to buy water. The term "proof" with respect to liquors means ½ per cent. Thus, 100-proof (or 100°) liquor means that it has an alcoholic content of 50 per cent; 80° has an alcoholic content of 40 per cent—and so on. If you buy 100° liquor and add 25 per cent pure distilled water to it, you will have 80° liquor. One will be as pure, as wholesome, as free from deleterious substances as the other. But the 100-proof liquor will have 25 per cent more body, 25 per cent more character, and 25 per cent more alcoholic strength than will the 80-proof. And—as I said before—why go to a liquor store to buy water? You can get it much cheaper from the kitchen faucet or—if you live in the country—from the well in the back yard.

WHISKY

If gin is the most misunderstood of all spirituous liquors, whisky is probably the most controversial. What are the relative merits of Scotch, rye, and bourbon? If all the best Scotch whiskies are blends, why are straight ryes and bourbons superior to blends? Why is an eight- or ten- or twelve-year-old whisky better than one that is only three or four years old? If Irish whisky is made, not from potatoes, but from barley, the same as Scotch, why does it lack the smoky taste of Scotch? Why are rye and bourbon whiskies frequently prescribed by doctors and Scotch practically never? Is bonded whisky necessarily purer and more wholesome than other whiskies? Is Canadian rye better or worse than American rye?

These and countless other questions are wrangled back and forth by the protagonists of the various types and specific brands of whiskies, usually primarily on the basis of their own taste preferences, sometimes on the basis of superstitious notions and pseudo-scientific information picked up from genial but not too learned bartenders, but seldom on the basis of intimate knowledge of actual facts. Before buying whisky for our supply shelf let us see if we can answer some of these questions. And, first of all, let us answer the question, "What is whisky?"

There are many different definitions of whisky, but for

the present let us define it as any spirituous liquor made from grain. We have already seen how gin is made. Brandies are made from fruits, rum is made from sugar, but whiskies—all whiskies—are made from grain. Scotch and Irish whiskies are made primarily from barley, rye whisky (both American and Canadian) from rye, and bourbon whisky from corn. All the various types normally are made with a certain amount of barley malt—that is, barley that has been moistened, allowed to sprout, and then kiln-dried. Scotch and Irish whiskies use from 40 per cent to 100 per cent malt; American and Canadian whiskies, usually about 10 per cent.

Until a little more than one hundred years ago both Scotch and Irish whiskies were made entirely from barley malt and were distilled in pot stills. In 1826 the continuous still was invented which greatly reduced the cost of distillation. This still, however, produces a much lighter-bodied liquor than the pot still, one of higher alcoholic content, and one lacking the body and character of pot-still liquor.

All malt whiskies are still made in the pot still; unmalted grain whiskies come from the continuous still. Up to about a hundred years ago all Scotch whiskies were straight whiskies. Along in the eighteen-fifties, however, the practice of blending malted and unmalted whiskies originated, and this resulted in a much cheaper whisky and one of a sufficiently general appeal so that today an unblended Scotch whisky is practically unknown. Let it be understood, however, that they are all blends of *whiskies* and not blends of whisky and "neutral grain spirits"—which is simply raw alcohol distilled from grain. The blend may be one of all pot-still malt whiskies gathered from various distilleries of the four principal geographical areas of Scotland —each with its own peculiar and distinctive body, flavor, and character—or it may be a blend of these malt whiskies with grain whisky manufactured in a patent or continuous still. Furthermore, when malt and grain whiskies are blended, the whiskies are first aged separately for several years; they are then "married" in huge mixing vats and are then again stored in oak casks for still further aging. The important points with respect to Scotch "blends" are, first, that only *whiskies* are blended, no raw alcohol, no caramel, no prune juice, no sherry, and no other artificial coloring or flavoring ingredients, and, second, that the blends are aged both before and after blending. No whisky under three years of age can be sold in Great Britain and, because of our Internal Revenue provisions, no whisky under four years of age is exported to the United States. The better brands will run from seven or eight years up to twelve or more.

The principal difference between Scotch and Irish whiskies is that Irish whisky is entirely lacking in the smoky taste of Scotch. The reason for this is extremely simple. In Scotland the barley malt is dried in kilns with a porous floor directly above peat fires. The heavy, aromatic peat smoke swirls around the moist grain which drinks up the smoky flavor and retains it through subsequent processing just as hickory-smoked ham or bacon retains its smoky taste from the smokehouse, through later frying, baking, broiling, or even boiling, right to the table. In Ireland, on the other hand, the malt is dried in kilns having solid, non-porous floors, and the smoke from the fires, therefore, has no chance to reach and permeate the grain.

There are really two types of Irish whisky, that made in Northern Ireland and that made in the Irish Free State. The former is a pot-still whisky made entirely from malted barley; the latter is a blend of malt whisky with grain whisky—usually barley but also sometimes wheat, oats, or rye. Now, if you really like the peat-smoke taste of Scotch, you may prefer it to Irish, just as you may prefer smoked ham to fresh ham. From every other point of view, however, I believe that Irish is infinitely superior to Scotch. One of the tragedies of our disgraceful prohibition era is the fact that, while our country was deluged with Scotch, both genuine and synthetic, and with Canadian, there was practically no Irish. Our citizens, therefore, learned to like (or think they liked) Scotch and Canadian but I venture to guess that not one out of a thousand even knows what Irish tastes like.

Just a brief word about Canadian whisky (which, in my opinion, is all it deserves) and then we shall get down to American whiskies, which, to my taste and for my money, are the real royalty of the whisky clan. Most Canadian whisky is a rye type, although in recent years some bourbon type has also been made there. To me, Canadian whisky has always tasted like a blend of Scotch and rye and I don't like it. I admit that this is an individual idiosyncrasy. I like both Scotch and rye—but I don't like them mixed. I like both raw onions and chocolate ice cream, but I don't like them mixed.

Actually, Canadian whiskies are manufactured very much like American whiskies but with certain differences that give them an entirely different character. I have already said that the lower the proof at which whisky is distilled out and the higher the proof at which it is bottled and sold, the better the whisky. American whiskies are distilled out at 130 to 140 proof; Canadian at 150 to 160. American whiskies are bottled in bond at 100 proof and at a minimum age of four years; Canadian whiskies are bottled in bond at 90 proof and at a minimum age of two years. In taking American whisky out of bond for bottling, *nothing* can be added to the whisky other than pure distilled water for the purpose of bringing the proof down from perhaps 108 or 110 to 100; in Canada it is permissible to restore evaporation losses through the addition of either neutral grain spirits or green whisky. If you like light-bodied whiskies you may well prefer Canadian to American. But if you like a whisky that is full-bodied, mature, rich in character, and entirely free from what I call an "alcoholy" taste, you will prefer American bonded whisky, as do I.

Just a word, now, as to brands of the several foreign whiskies before we take up the American ryes and bourbons. Of all the Scotch whiskies I have ever tasted, no other can compare with Fulstrength, made by the Drambuie firm of Edinburgh. It is a well-matured, pure pot-still whisky of 114.2 proof. It is smooth as velvet—a true liqueur Scotch. Its price is higher than other Scotch whisky —and well worth it. In a highball it will go nearly half as far again as ordinary Scotch. At present it is not available on the American market. As a matter of fact, good Scotch whisky has become extremely rare in the United States today. Most of the brands mentioned in the first edition of this book, if now available at all, are comparatively green and bear no age label whatsoever. Those that are well aged are, quite understandably, priced out of all proportion to a comparable American rye or bourbon. Of the better Scotches, available at the moment, I can recommend (if you are willing to pay the price) Ambassador (25-year-old), Grant's (20-year-old), Bell's Royal Reserve (20-year-old), and Martin's (20-year-old). Not so well aged (and therefore not so excellent), are J. & B. Liqueur Scotch, Hankey Bannister, Chivas Regal, and those two that are probably still the best known of all Scotches in the United States, Johnny Walker Black Label and Haig & Haig Pinch Bottle (all twelve years old).

Of the Irish whiskies with which I am familiar, I can recommend Erin's Antique (30-year-old), John Jameson Liqueur (12-year-old), Paddy's Old Irish (10-year-old), Old Bushmill's (9-year-old), and Power's Three Swallows (7-year-old).

The most common Canadian whisky on the market is Canadian Club. It is excellent (if you like Canadian whiskies), as are also Seagram's V.O. and Seagram's Pedigree.

As has already been stated, rye whisky is made primarily from rye, and bourbon whisky primarily from corn. Under F.A.A. regulations the amount of primary grain in each case must be at least 51 per cent. In actual practice about 10 per cent barley malt is used in making whiskies, the balance being both rye and corn. The amount of corn used in making rye varies from 10 per cent to 40 per cent. The proportion of the two grains used in bourbon depends upon the process. With the "sweet-mash" process about 75 per cent corn is usually used; with the "sour-mash" process about 60 per cent. The "sour-mash" process produces a finer whisky with a magnificent bouquet and flavor. The "sweet-mash" process, however, results in a greater quantity of whisky from the same amount of grain, thereby lowering the production cost.

In the earlier editions of this book, I named my favorite American whiskies. Many of those have now disappeared from the market and, both because of idiotic governmental regulations and because the manufacture of cheap blended whiskies is much more profitable than the manufacture of superior bonded products, others are disappearing almost daily. All I can now say is that you should insist on *bonded* whiskies, preferably at least eight years old. Also examine the labels carefully and make sure that you are getting *Pennsylvania* ryes and *Kentucky* bourbons and not the vastly inferior products made (perhaps by the same distillers) somewhere in the Middle West. Some distillers are even putting out blended whiskies under the same brand name as their old bonded whiskies. I have never found any blended American whisky that, to my taste, was even reasonably satisfactory. However, there has been so much misunderstanding on the subject of bonded versus blended whiskies that before going any farther it may be well to see what the real facts on this question are.

First of all, there is no more guarantee of either purity or quality as to whisky bottled in bond than there is as to whisky withdrawn from bond for bottling elsewhere. A well-made, well-aged whisky would be just as good if it never entered a bonded warehouse, and a poorly made whisky would still be poor if it reposed twenty years in a bonded warehouse and was finally bottled there. The bottled-in-bond label does guarantee four things:

1. *That it is straight liquor, all of the same distillation and the same age, and not a blend of different liquors of different ages and different distillations;*

2. *That that age is not less than four years;*

3. *That it was bottled at not less than 100 proof;*

4. *That nothing has been added to the straight liquor other than such quantity of pure distilled water as may be necessary to bring it down to 100 proof—no neutral grain spirits or other alcohols, no sweetening agent, no coloring matter, etc.*

Blends of American whiskies are of two kinds: blends of straight whiskies (rye or bourbon as the case may be), and blends of straight whisky with neutral grain spirits. The label will always disclose which type the blend is. In straight whisky blends the label may state either the age of the youngest whisky or the age and percentage of each whisky comprising the blend. Obviously the latter method will be followed if the amount of whisky older than the youngest is at all substantial. In spirit blends the label must show both the percentage of neutral grain spirits and the age and percentage of each whisky used.

If you absolutely must buy a spirit blend because you can't get anything else (the only reasonable excuse I can think of), note particularly whether the label says "Blended Whisky" (or, perhaps, "Whisky, a Blend") without specifying the type of whisky, or whether it mentions the type, as "Blended Rye Whisky," "Blended Bourbon Whisky," "Rye Whisky, a Blend," etc. This is important. Under F.A.A. regulations "Blended Whisky" may contain as little as 20 per cent of 100-proof straight whisky, whereas if the type is named, such as "Blended Rye Whisky," the blend must contain a minimum of 50 per cent of straight whisky of that type.

Since both the neutral grain spirits and the green whiskies used in the various blends are practically sure to have a raw, pungent, disagreeable taste, the blender is permitted to add "blending agents" up to some 2 per cent of the total volume. Caramel or burnt sugar (which both sweetens and colors), prune or other fruit juices, and heavy-bodied sherries are some of the more common substances used for this purpose.

And now that you understand the difference between the term "blend" as applied to Scotch and to American whiskies, let us get back to the question of which is the better American whisky, bonded or blended. By now the answer should be obvious. Of course there is no accounting for tastes. I have known people who preferred grain alcohol or vodka, which is the same thing, and ginger ale to a Rye or Bourbon Highball. I know people who can see no particular difference in the taste of different whiskies —rye, Scotch, bourbon, Canadian, straight or blended— all are just whiskies. These people drink primarily for the "kick," not for the taste. In my opinion, such people should not drink at all. Unfortunately, however, they are usually the ones who drink the most. If they must drink, then they might as well stick to the cheapest, strongest form of liquid dynamite they can find. After all, why waste their money even on a carefully made blend to which the blender has added a heavy imported sherry in an effort to smooth out the very raw taste they crave?

Such people, however, will not be readers of this book and I therefore return to the question of the choice of the discriminating drinker. People who buy blends rather than bonded straight whiskies usually do so for one of two reasons: Either they prefer (or think they prefer) a light-bodied whisky, or they think the blend is cheaper. Let us examine the latter point first. In judging price, let us do so, not on the basis of dollars per bottle, but on the basis of dollars per pint or quart of straight whisky. I have already pointed out that blended whisky may contain as little as 20 per cent of straight whisky by volume; the rest is neutral grain spirits; i.e., alcohol and water. These ingredients are pretty cheap. In fact, if it were not for the Internal Revenue tax, the cost of the alcohol would normally be only a few cents per gallon. For practical purposes, therefore, we can pretty much forget these ingredients and figure cost on the basis of the amount of straight whisky only. There are probably very few blends on the market that contain as little as 20 per cent straight whisky, but I do know several widely advertised brands that contain 30 per cent or less. Well, figure it out. If a bottle of straight whisky costs $5.00, then, at any price in excess of $1.50 for the same size bottle, a 30-per-cent blend is the more expensive. Even on the basis of proof alone it must be remembered that, whereas all bonded whisky is 100 proof, the blends range between 80 and 90 proof. Therefore, solely on the basis of alcoholic content (not a sound basis), the blends should sell at from 10 to 20 per cent less.

All this, of course, is pretty much beside the point. I mention it merely to point out that the man who really enjoys the flavor of good whisky is simply kidding himself when he buys a blend on the theory that he is getting more whisky for less money. He is getting whisky-flavored spirits, not straight whisky. Legally, both are whisky (that has been determined under our Food and Drugs Act), but they bear the same relation to one another that a pure beef hamburger or a pure pork sausage does to a hamburger or a sausage that has been "stretched" with cereal. And the same general considerations apply, only to a lesser degree, to a blend of straight whiskies in which matured whiskies are blended with young, green whiskies.

The real test, of course, is your personal taste. Blended whiskies are lighter-bodied than straight whiskies. The closer the distillation of grain mash comes to pure alcohol, the lighter the body. The substances (known as congenerics) which give whisky its character are distilled out and left behind when the higher proofs are reached. Also, the body is increased by aging so that well-matured whiskies are not only smoother but also heavier-bodied than green whiskies. Kentucky "White Mule"—green whisky fresh from the still—is anything but heavy-bodied. I know people who like that too. I don't. If you really prefer light-bodied whiskies, then by all means buy blends. But, in that case, you should realize that you simply don't like real whisky flavor, because the acme of whisky flavor is to be found in a well-made straight whisky which has been aged in the wood for at least ten or twelve years—preferably sixteen to twenty.

There is a great difference of opinion as to the length of time during which whisky will continue to improve in the wood. Federal regulations do not permit whisky to be bottled in bond under four years. It may therefore be said with reasonable assurance that under four years a whisky cannot be regarded as sufficiently mature to be really palatable. From there on, up to some ten or twelve years, there is general agreement that whisky steadily continues to improve, but there are those who claim that after some ten or twelve years there not only is no substantial improvement but there may even be some deterioration. On the other hand, I know that immediately after the repeal of prohibition I was fortunate enough to procure Mount Vernon rye and Old Granddad bourbon eighteen to twenty years of age, and they were by far the best whiskies I have ever tasted. Later I was able to get sixteen-year-old only and, while the difference was not great, there still was a difference. From there the age dropped to ten and twelve years and the difference was pronounced. In these days when one is extremely fortunate to get a bonded bourbon or rye more than four years old, the ten-year-old that I barely tolerated before the war would be manna from heaven! Oh yes, I still have a bottle or two of these rare old jewels of perfection, but I don't drink them. I occasionally get out a medicine dropper and gently anoint my tongue with a few drops—just so I won't forget what *real* whisky should taste like.

During the war, distillers turned to the manufacture of spirit blends in order to maintain at least a reasonably high production level. Even the Mount Vernon Distillery Co., whose rye I used to consider the absolute tops, made only a blend. To make matters worse, they advertised "The mildest Mount Vernon you ever tasted." As if mere mildness were desirable! Of course all that is necessary to make it still milder is to add more water. This, surely, is a classic example of making a virtue out of necessity! Along much the same lines, one manufacturer of Scotch advertises its blend as "The Light-Bodied Scotch." These and similar ads are reminiscent of the canner of tuna fish who did much to overcome prejudice against this "white salmon" in the early days by advertising: "Guaranteed not to turn red in the can." For my part, rather than turn to whisky-flavored alcohol I preferred to wait until genuine, straight whiskies could be manufactured, aged, and again put on the market.

On account of their pronounced smoky taste most Scotches are not as adaptable to cocktail making as rye or bourbon. They should be taken straight or in a Highball. Strangely enough, while "Scotch and soda" is today the almost universal formula for a Scotch Highball, Scotch was originally drunk in the British Isles with ginger ale or, as it is there known, "ginger beer." The use of seltzer or soda developed much later. Just how the fetish or superstition started that "Scotch and soda" is the gentleman's drink and that American whiskies are plebian and inferior, it would be hard to determine. I strongly suspect that importers of Scotch, seeking some plausible reason to justify the additional cost resulting from customs duties, may have had something to do with it.

Actually, there are just three differences between Scotch and American whiskies: (1) the only grain, or at least the predominating grain, used in Scotch is barley; in American whiskies the predominating grain is either rye or corn. (2) Scotch has a smoky taste resulting from kiln-drying the barley malt over open peat fires. (3) Scotch (with few exceptions, such as Fulstrength) is a lighter-bodied, lower-proof whisky than our straight whiskies, although comparable in this respect to our blends.

One other difference respecting age should be noted. In the British Isles it is customary to age whisky in re-used casks. This is regarded as anathema by the best United States distillers. In fact, F.A.A. regulations do not permit an age label unless the aging has been in new, charred casks. Aging—i.e., the mellowing, maturing, and development of character while in the wood—is the result, in part, of slow evaporation through the pores of the wood. Naturally this evaporation results in a certain amount of clogging of the pores as well as the retention in the wood of minute quantities of vegetable matter which, in time, may impart an undesirable flavor to the contents of the cask. Unfortunately, there is no fixed ratio of this retarding of normal evaporation and maturing. It is impossible to say that four years in a new cask is equivalent to five years or six years or seven years in a re-used cask. The ratio varies as between different barrels and different whiskies. Hence the F.A.A. rule. On the other hand, the regulations do permit the green stamp pasted over the cork to state the year of distillation and the year of bottling. If the label says "Four years old," that is your guarantee that the whisky was aged four years in a new cask. If this statement is lacking but the green I.R. stamp says "Distilled in 1940. Bottled in 1944," the aging was probably in a re-used cask. But remember that a twelve-year-old Scotch whisky, because of the common practice of re-using the cooperage, will probably not be equivalent in maturity to an American whisky aged twelve years in new casks.

Another peculiarity of the three kinds of whisky is that bourbon matures and mellows much faster than rye and rye much faster than Scotch. Accordingly, a four-year-old bourbon will be smoother than a four-year-old rye, and the four-year-old rye much smoother than a four-year-old Scotch.

In the last analysis, the only test as to which is best, Scotch, Irish, Canadian, or American whiskies and, of the American, rye or bourbon, is your own individual taste. All of them—assuming equal degrees of skill and care on the part of the respective distillers—are equally pure, equally wholesome, equally safe to drink. The same is true as between straight whiskies and blends. The one final test of superiority *for you* is your own palate. To me, well-matured straight bourbon is the king of whiskies, rye a close second, and the others merely make up the field. Also, to me, any blend of straight whisky, either with neutral grain spirits or with green whiskies, is repugnant. Your taste may be different. Some people like coffee, others like chicory, still others like cereal beverages such as Postum. All these beverages are potable; all, if properly brewed, are wholesome. For you, that one is best which best suits your individual taste.

Then why do doctors never prescribe Scotch? Well, some doctors do—albeit they are few. There may be several reasons for this, but perhaps the United States Pharmacopoeia definition of whisky as "an alcoholic liquor obtained from the distillation of . . . cereal grains and containing not less than 47% nor more than 53% by volume of alcohol" may have something to do with it. If the doctor wishes to limit his prescription in accordance with the U.S.P., there are but few Scotches and, so far as I know, no American blends that could fulfill this requirement of a proof between 94 and 106. Furthermore, the U.S.P. calls for aging at least four years in the wood. This, of course, eliminates all spirit blends.

RUM

Rum might, in effect, be called a by-product of the manufacture of sugar. It can, of course, be made from the fermented juice of the entire sugar cane, but for the most part it is made from molasses, the heavy, dark syrup remaining after the greater part of the solid sugar has been crystallized out of the juice of the cane. To this molasses is added the residue from previous distillations and the mixture is fermented and distilled. In the case of Cuban and similar light-bodied rums, fermentation is induced by the addition of an artificial yeast culture; in the case of Jamaica rum, no cultured yeast is used and fermentation is the result of exposure of the mash to the air, from which it absorbs wild yeasts. This process is somewhat slower than the Cuban process but yields a rum of an entirely different body and character. After fermentation is complete the resultant mash is distilled and aged. Cuban rum is also filtered through sand and charcoal and, after filtering, caramel is added (and sometimes fruit juices or wines) to give color and flavor. The light body of Cuban rums and the absence of the pungent aroma and flavor characterizing Jamaica rums are due in part to this filtering process and in part to the higher proof at which Cuban rum is distilled out.

The various rums may be divided into three classes:

1. *The light-bodied Cuban rums;*

2. *The heavy-bodied Jamaica and Demerara rums;*

3. *The "in-betweeners," which run all the way from Barbados and New England rums—almost, but not quite as heavy-bodied as the Jamaicas—through the Virgin Islands, Martinique, Santo Domingan, Haitian, and Mexican rums, down to those Puerto Rican rums that are supposed to be (but are not) the same—or "just as good"—as the Cuban rums.*

There is still a fourth type of rum, seldom seen in this country but used a great deal in the Netherlands and the Scandinavian countries, and that is Batavia arak, a highly aromatic rum that comes from Batavia on the island of Java in the Dutch East Indies. It is extremely dry—almost like a brandy—and pungent. It is made from Javanese molasses mixed with a small quantity of Javanese red rice. Like Jamaica rum, fermentation is due entirely to wild yeasts. It is the basic ingredient of Arrack Punsch—commonly known here as Swedish Punch.

Beef liver and porterhouse steaks both come from steer beef, but there the similarity ends. Cuban and Jamaica rum are both made from sugar, but they are as dissimilar in taste and use as porterhouse and liver or as gin and whisky. The two simply cannot be substituted for one another in the mixing of drinks.

Cuban rum—especially the white label rum—has only

a faint, elusive flavor and, since this flavor is delicate and subdued, the rum will blend with almost any other liquor, fruit juice, fruit syrup, liqueur, or what have you. Like gin, therefore, it is the cocktail base par excellence. Jamaica rum, on the other hand, has a pungent, all-pervasive bouquet that definitely refuses to be subdued, tamed, or overcome by any other flavor whatsoever. It should therefore be used not as a cocktail base but as a flavoring agent. In cocktails, Cuban rum should be used by the jigger; Jamaica rum by the dash. Jamaica rum blends beautifully with all fruit flavors and with nearly all liqueurs—even those that are highly aromatic. You can readily understand the characteristics of the two rums if you will mix each of them separately with equal parts of apricot brandy. In the case of the Cuban rum mixture, you will have an apricot drink with a faint rum flavor; in the case of the Jamaica rum, you will have a rum drink with a faint apricot flavor.

But, whereas Cuban rum is the superior rum for a cocktail base, Jamaica is the better type for long drinks, such as the Planters' Punch. It is also the rum for use in cooking and in flavoring candies, sauces, ice creams, etc. It is a magnificent addition to coffee, either hot or cold, and even to tea. Both in flavoring foods and in flavoring drinks, it must be used with discretion and finesse, for it is an outstanding example of *multum in parvo*.

All liquors sold in the United States must pay the United States Internal Revenue tax. In addition, imported liquors are also subject to import duties. Because of this latter fact and because Puerto Rico is a possession of the United States and its products are not subject to import duties, there has been a tremendous growth in the manufacture of rum in Puerto Rico since prohibition repeal. At least two of the fine old distillers of Cuban rum have acquired distilleries in Puerto Rico and now make rum there as well as in Cuba. Whether it is because of the difference in water or because of differences in soil and climate, I do not know, but, in any event, the Puerto Rican rums are definitely inferior to the Cuban. Even the Puerto

Rican rum made by the fine old firm of Bacardi y Cia. can in no way compare with their rum made in Santiago de Cuba. There has been a notable improvement in the Puerto Rican rums during the last few years and some are not too bad. Of those I have tried I have found Bacardi, Ronrico, and Carioca the best. As already stated, however, none is quite as good as the better brands of Cuban rum and, of the Cuban brands, I particularly recommend Bacardi and Havana Club. The Cuban rum costs more but is well worth the difference.

Cuban rums are made in two types, white label or *carta blanca* and gold label or *carta de oro*. Traditionally, the gold label rum is sweeter, heavier, and has been aged longer, hence the price is usually somewhat higher. Today in actual practice, however, both rums obtain their color primarily from the addition of caramel rather than from aging (which is done in *uncharred* oak casks) and, since caramel is cheap, it is rather difficult to justify the higher price charged for the gold label type. The gold label type is more like a Barbados or Haitian rum and is used primarily in long drinks. The white label is definitely the type for cocktails, whether used only with fruit juices and sugar, as in the Daiquiri, or combined with other flavors, such as the various fruit liqueurs. Bacardi y Cia. also make Ron Añejo (on-yáy-ho) or very old rum, a magnificent after-dinner drink in place of cognac or armagnac.

Before the war the finest Jamaica rums were those shipped to England for aging in the bonded warehouses in London and were known as London Dock rums. The foggy, damp air of London is supposed to be responsible for their peculiar excellence. The exigencies of war interrupted the shipment and storage of these rums and when they may again be available, I have no idea. Of the various top-quality Jamaica liqueur rums, the finest I have ever found are Myers's Mona (aged for some thirty years), Wray & Nephews' Special Reserve (eighteen years), Bellows' Liqueur (seventeen years), and Lemon Hart Liqueur. These are all true liqueur rums with a mellow smoothness, bouquet, and flavor comparable to fine old brandies. It is really a sacrilege to use any of them in a cocktail or any other mixed drink. They should be taken straight, the same as a Fine Champagne, an armagnac, or any fine old cordial. Of the rank and file of Jamaica rums suitable for use in cocktails, in long rum drinks, and in cooking, there are many excellent brands. I particularly recommend Portal, Dingwall & Norris's Bellows; Wray & Nephews' Three Dagger; Charley's Royal Reserve; Lemon Hart; and Myers & Son's Planters' Punch.

Demerara rums are made from sugar produced in the Demerara River section of British Guiana. While they are both darker and heavier-bodied than Jamaica rums, they lack the pungent bouquet of the Jamaica rum. They are sold in high proofs—up to 151°—and are most useful in making high-powered drinks that still do not taste strongly alcoholic. They are therefore useful in making hot toddies and grog and heavy-bodied punches, not to mention (and perhaps it might be just as well if I did not mention it) the Zombie, which contains an almost microscopic amount of 151-proof Demerara floated on top. Demerara rum does not have sufficient aroma and character to make good tall drinks, and it is practically useless for cocktails. Bellows and Lemon Hart are both acceptable.

You can get along very nicely with two rums only for your supply shelf, Cuban white label for a cocktail base and Jamaica for tall drinks and for adding a spicy flavor to some of your ultra-ultra cocktails. However, for the sake of variety, you may also want to add to your collection one or two bottles of the "in-betweeners." These are all sufficiently heavy-bodied to use in tall drinks and they will work reasonably well—at least as well as a Cuban gold label—as a base for certain cocktails. For example, the Barbados rum cocktail and the Haitian rum cocktail are made exactly like a Daiquiri except for the rum used. They are similar to a Daiquiri, yet different. Because of their heavier body, many like them better than a true Daiquiri.

In making cocktails in which liqueurs or fruit syrups are

used for flavoring, however, you must exercise discretion and do a certain amount of experimenting. These rums all blend well with fruit flavors, but the fruit flavor does not stand out the same as it does in combination with Cuban white rum. Accordingly, in order to get the peach, cherry, apricot, or other flavor you are seeking it may be necessary to use so much of the liqueur that the cocktail is entirely ruined by oversweetness. In general, it may be said that, while Cuban white rum blends well with fruit *liqueurs*, it will be best with the heavier rums to use fruit *brandies*. For example, use Cherry Heering to flavor Cuban rum, but use kirschwasser (a cherry brandy) with Barbados, Haitian, or New England rum.

Of the various Barbados rums, I suggest Lightbourn's, Goddard's, or Cockade; of the Martinique rums, Bardinet's Negrita, Marie Brizard's Charleston, or Ernest Lambert's St. James; and of the Haitian rums, Sarthe. Most of these, unfortunately, are hard to find here in the States.

I have never yet tasted a good Virgin Islands rum, but Old St. Croix is probably the best I have tried and Government House the worst.

Mexican rums vary all the way from the unbelievably vile up to one of the smoothest, most palatable, medium-bodied rums I have ever known. This particular rum, Berreteaga, unfortunately, is not exported to the United States, but if you chance to live near the border you might be able to find it. It is made in the state of Tabasco, Mexico, and is said to acquire its delightful, mellow flavor from aging in prune-soaked oak casks.

Good, well-aged New England rums are hard to find, but Old Medford and Austin, Nichols & Co.'s Old New England are the two best I have found. The latter is well aged and is excellent.

COGNAC AND OTHER GRAPE BRANDIES

Brandy is not only the oldest of all liquors but is universally recognized as the finest. In our pharmacopoeia it used to be known as Sp. Vini Gall.—*Spiritus Vini Gallici*—or French spirit of the grape. This has now been changed to *Sp. Vini Vitis*, or spirit of the grape vine. It is the Latin *aqua vitae*, the French *eau de vie*, or water of life. For centuries its use was confined almost exclusively to medicinal purposes and it was prescribed for almost every conceivable ailment.

Although the term "brandy" is usually accepted as connoting grape brandy, in its broader sense the term applies to liquor distilled from any fruit as distinguished from those distilled from grain (whiskies) and from sugar (rums). Thus, in addition to grape brandies, we have cherry brandy (kirsch), prune or plum brandy (slivovitz, quetsch, and mirabelle), apple, peach, and apricot brandies, and—although but little known—even an orange brandy. The firm of Zwack of Budapest, Hungary, also makes a delicious raspberry brandy called Himbeergeist —the spirit of the raspberry—and in France and Switzerland, essentially the same type of raspberry brandy is called framboise (pronounced frahn-bwahze).

Of all the grape brandies of the world, practically every connoisseur will agree that cognac is the finest and that the best of the cognacs is a Fine Champagne. All cognac comes from the Cognac district lying along the Charente River in South France, not far from Bordeaux. This area is divided into eight zones, and at the very heart of the district lies the Grande Champagne from which come the Fine Champagnes, the aristocracy of the cognacs. The grapes that go into all cognacs are grown, picked, pressed, fermented, distilled, aged, and bottled in this same Cognac region. Not a single drop of any other wine or brandy is ever allowed to enter a bottle of cognac.

The peculiar excellence of this liquor is due, first, to the soil and climate of the region where the grapes are produced and, second, to the loving care and fierce pride with which every operation, beginning with the cultivation of the grapes and culminating in the aging and bottling of the brandy itself, is performed. The soil is rich in limestone and is fine and light as an ash heap. Throughout the entire summer the grapes luxuriate in a superabundance of golden sunlight. Throughout the entire growing season, therefore, the fruit drinks in both from the soil and from the air those elements that are transmuted by the alchemy of nature into the juice which later is to become the liquid gold called cognac.

It should be mentioned in passing that the Champagne subdivision of the Cognac district is an entirely different district from that of North France from which we get our sparkling champagne wine. In fact, strangely enough, the wines themselves from which cognac is made are sour, brackish, and distinctly unpalatable. It is only after they have been distilled and aged that they acquire the smoothness, the bouquet, and the character that make them the toast not only of France but of the entire world.

The wines are distilled only in pot stills and every step is under strict governmental supervision. Each still is locked and sealed, and during the entire distilling season, which may run to six months or more, the stills are in continuous operation day and night and every day including Sundays. Each and every step of the operation is performed with meticulous care and with painstaking perfection of detail. This, as has already been suggested, is a labor of love for the greater glory of the district and its product.

Since American connoisseurs are definitely age-conscious respecting most liquors and especially brandies, it seems strange, at first blush, that the French Government, which is so extremely painstaking in protecting cognacs against adulteration by so much as a single drop of wine from a different district even of France itself, should give practically no consideration to the question of age. No attempt whatsoever is made to register casks in bond as to age, to certify the age, or even to prevent bottlers from mislabeling as to age. On second thought, however, the reason becomes apparent. We in this country buy our liquors by the label; the Frenchman buys by the taste. It is altogether possible that one twenty-year-old brandy may be infinitely superior to another of twice that age. The Frenchman tastes first, then buys. We in this country, under the customary strict laws differentiating between sales for "on premises" and "off premises" consumption—between the package store and the saloon—must buy first and taste afterward. We dare not even draw the cork from the bottle until we have left the premises where the purchase was made. We must therefore rely first of all on the integrity of the bottler and, since the same bottler may put out a half dozen or more grades of varying ages, on his statement as to the age.

Reliable exporters (and their American distributors) are loath to allege a definite age which they cannot accurately determine. Under existing circumstances it is in many cases practically impossible to state the exact age of a cognac, particularly since the constant loss from evaporation during the aging process is made up from time to time and not always with brandy of exactly the same age. Partly for that reason it has become customary to use on brandy labels letters indicating quality rather than age. These letters and their meanings are as follows:

E   *extra* or *especial*
F   *fine*
M *mellow*
O *old*
P *pale*
S *superior*
V *very*
X *extra*

These letters, unfortunately, mean little as to true age. Even the common three-star label has no particular significance. One three-star brandy may be five or six years, another eight or ten years, and still another twelve or fifteen years old. In general, however, it may be said that three-star is the youngest of the brandies labeled as to quality (except those of bottlers—if there still be any—who use one- or two-star labels), V.O. the next older,

V.S.O. the next, V.S.O.P. the next, and V.V.S.O.P. the oldest, with the various E, M, and X labels falling in between according to the fancy of the individual producer.

There is a great difference of opinion among connoisseurs and experts as to the effect of aging beyond a period of perhaps forty or fifty years. Beyond that age many claim that the liquor has a tendency to break down and actually deteriorate. Of course this refers—as does the aging of all spirituous liquors—to aging in the wood and, in the case of cognacs, to aging in casks of uncharred oak from the forests of Limoges. Once bottled and tightly sealed, the liquor will be the same a hundred years later as it was the day it was bottled. All I can say on the subject of age is that I still have cognacs (some Fine Champagnes and some not) of ten, twenty, forty, and sixty years, respectively, one bottle of Monnet 1858 (supposedly eighty years old), and one bottle labeled "Napoleon 1811." Up to the forty-year-old the difference in quality is approximately in proportion to the respective ages; the sixty-year-old (a Marie Brizard Fine Champagne) is slightly better than the forty-year-old but not proportionately better; and the Monnet 1858 is the best of the lot but by no means twice as good as the forty-year-old. The alleged Napoleon 1811 is perhaps somewhat better than the ten-year-old but does not compare with the twenty-year-olds.

For cocktails, such as the Side Car, a three-star cognac is entirely adequate, although a ten-year-old cognac will produce a better drink. I cannot deny that a still smoother and more delightful drink would result from using a cognac of twenty years or more, but I do say that to mix this nectar of the gods with any other substance whatsoever—even a single drop of water—would be sacrilege, pure and simple.

One other point should be mentioned before leaving the subject of cognacs and that is that practically all brands today are blends and that it is this skillful blending that produces the finest brandies. This, of course, is a blending of certified cognac brandies only, the only other additions permitted being distilled water to bring the liquor down to the required proof of some 80° to 90° and, in some cases, a small amount of caramel to deepen the color. The various cognacs are selected—one for its strength, another for its mellowness, another for its color, and so on—and mixed in huge vats where they remain for several months until thoroughly blended, after which they are bottled.

The next time you sip a Fine Champagne with your after-dinner coffee, just pause and reflect on the painstaking labor that goes into the cultivation, harvesting, and pressing of sufficient grapes to produce a single quart of wine; on the further labor of fermenting, settling, and decanting that wine; on the still further labor of distilling it and laying it away in casks, in tending the casks, refilling them, and in finally blending and bottling their contents; reflect on the 90-per-cent loss in quantity resulting from distillation and on the still further losses due to evaporation during the many years of aging; and, finally, reflect on the twenty, forty, or sixty years that this liquor lay aging in heavy oak casks buried in cellars deep down in the ground. Just make yourself realize that it took an entire quart of wine—the product of I know not how many grapes—plus all that work and all those years to produce the one small glass of brandy you hold in your hand. Then, and then only, can you fully appreciate the true value of real cognac.

With the end of the war, an abundance of good cognacs has again appeared on the market. Among my favorite brands are Monnet (moh-nay'), Marie Brizard (bree-zahr'), Otard Dupuy (oh-tar' dee-pwee'), Rémy Martin (ray'-mee mar-ten'), Gautier (goat-yay'), and Courvoisier (koor-vwahs-yay'). I also find Cusenier (kee-sen-yay'), Bisquit Dubouché (bis'-kwee deë-boo-shay'), and Jules Robin (zhul ro-ben') highly satisfactory. Two other well-known old brands are: Get (zhay), made by Get Frères, and Rouyer (roo-yay') made by Rouyer, Guillet & Cie.

Armagnac (pronounced ar'-men-yahk) is another French brandy which, at least, is a close second to cognac in quality and (in France) in popularity. In fact, there are many who prefer armagnac. This brandy comes from an area still farther south than the Charente where cognac is made. There are slight differences in the two processes of distillation, and the casks in which the liquor is aged are made of a different type of oak. As the city of Cognac is the center of the Cognac trade, so Condom (pronounced cawn'-dawn) is the heart of the armagnac trade.

From shortly after the repeal of prohibition until the outbreak of the war, the firm of Marquis de Caussade of Condom, France, had done much to popularize armagnac in this country. Unfortunately the war cut off the supply from France. An attempt was made to manufacture a similar brandy in the United States but without success, and for several years the armagnacs were practically nonexistent here. They have now reappeared. I can testify to the outstanding excellence of the product of Marquis de Caussade. Two or three other brands, also from Condom, also enjoy an excellent reputation. Because these brandies are less highly commercialized than the cognacs, it is normally possible to buy an armagnac at a much lower price than a cognac of equal age and quality. Also, misrepresentation of age and other characteristics of quality, so common with cognacs, are almost completely absent with the armagnacs. The armagnacs, generally speaking, are somewhat better-bodied and drier than the cognacs.

Another brandy that is a great favorite with a number of my good French friends is made from the last press of the grapes and has a strong woody taste. It is known as *eau de vie de marc* (pronounced oh-de-vee-de-mar) customarily shortened to marc (mar). It is extremely dry, is anything but mellow, and, to the average American taste, is rather unpalatable. The same type of brandy (but don't tell my French friends I said it was the same) is produced in Italy under the name of grappa. The brand of Italian grappa most commonly found here is the product of Martini & Rossi. A similar brandy is also produced in small quantity in California. If you like a cocktail that is very dry and you do not mind a flavor that is more like the stem of the grape than the grape itself, you might try marc or grappa. Otherwise, I do not recommend them for cocktail making.

Another grape brandy that I definitely do not recommend comes from Peru and is known as Pisco. Such aging as it receives (and, to judge by its flavor, that is very little) is done in unglazed crocks or jars and not in wood. I am told that it is quite popular in Peru—which is one reason I am satisfied to remain in the United States.

Since it was not possible to manufacture beverage brandy in this country after the Eighteenth Amendment went into effect and until 1933, there are few if any really good American brandies as yet. Fairly substantial stocks are being put aside each year for maturing in addition to the very large quantities (running into millions of gallons) that are used annually in manufacturing cordials and in fortifying sherries and similar heavy wines. While some American brandies come from other states, such as New York, by far the greatest quantity is produced in California. These brandies are highly satisfactory for cooking, flavoring sauces, etc. None that I have yet found can in any sense replace a cognac or an armagnac as a beverage—even in a cocktail such as a Side Car. Of course they are very much cheaper than French brandies. Many of them are carefully made and are pleasant to the taste if you judge them on their own merits and not as a substitute for French brandies. Their flavor—even many that are called cognac type—is muscat. They are, for the most part, distinctly heavier-bodied than French brandies and they lack the mellow smoothness and finesse of a cognac or armagnac.

Two other grape brandies should be mentioned in passing, those from Spain and those from Greece. Both are dark and extremely heavy. Neither can compete in any way with good French brandies, but each, in its own way, is quite good—especially the Spanish. This is a brandy distilled from sherry wine and it retains a distinct sherry flavor. It is much sweeter than cognac and fuller-bodied.

It has many devotees and, as an after-dinner drink, is excellent. It can be used in cocktails but *not* as a substitute for cognac. I use it extensively in cooking, my favorite brand being the twenty- or twenty-five-year-old Fundador made by Pedro Domecq. Another excellent brand is that made by Gonzales, Byass & Co. If you like to broil steaks over charcoal, try anointing them gently with Fundador (the ten-year-old will do for this) while cooking. This is truly food for the gods. The Greek brandy, on the other hand (Metaxa being the brand best known in this country), has a rather sharp taste and has failed to gain the popularity here that has been achieved by the Spanish brandies. Nevertheless, it is a more satisfactory cocktail substitute for cognac because it lacks the sweet sherry flavor of Spanish brandy.

OTHER FRUIT BRANDIES

The first in importance among the brandies made from fruit other than grapes is apple brandy—or, as it is commonly called, applejack. This liquor, if properly made and sufficiently aged, is a splendid drink either straight or in a cocktail. Unfortunately, it is next to impossible to find any well-aged apple brandy in the market. In the Normandy peninsula of France the same brandy, known as calvados (with the accent on the last syllable), is made with meticulous care and is aged in the wood for ten years or more before being sold. This is a truly magnificent liquor, but it seems to have found but little market here, presumably because of the mistaken notion that applejack is just plain applejack, wherever made. A large percentage of the apple brandies sold here is not more than three or four years old. One is extremely fortunate if he can find any that is as much as six years old. That is not a sufficient age for apple brandy, any more than it is for cognac, to produce a smooth, mellow drink. Another reason for the superiority of calvados is that it is distilled in pot stills and is distilled out at low proofs. The American variety is made in patent stills and is distilled out at a proof of from 10° to 20° higher than the Norman product.

In making this brandy, carefully selected apples are used, part sweet and part sour, but all preferably of the winter and not of the early fall varieties. Every apple must be sound and ripe, but not overripe. Slight imperfections in the fruit or any lack of care in pressing, fermenting, and storing the product will result in an off-flavor brandy. The fruit is crushed in a press and the juice is drained from the pulp through canvas cloths, strained, and stored in a cool cellar where it slowly ferments. The fresh juice is known as sweet cider; after fermentation it is known as hard cider. The hard cider is double-distilled and then stored in oak casks to age. Like other liquors, it acquires its color from aging in the wood. Sad to relate, the best apple brandy in this country is to be found in the cellars of farmers who, in total defiance of Internal Revenue laws, distill "Jersey Lightning" for their own personal use. Since these amiable lawbreakers (many of them rigid Puritans in all other respects) usually put down a quantity every year, it is not unusual for them to have small stocks from ten to twenty years old. This, however, is strictly for personal use and the entertainment of friends and is not commercially available.

At the very bottom of the palatability scale of brandies (at least as measured by my palate) stands a plum brandy known as slivovitz. Traditionally it is supposed to be a favorite Jewish drink, but among my many Jewish friends I have yet to find one who likes it. It is sharp, harsh, and unpleasant to swallow and leaves an aftertaste on a par with quinine or bitter aloes. How such a distasteful liquor can be distilled from so pleasant a fruit as the plum is, to me, a complete mystery. This brandy is known in France as quetsch or mirabelle.

Next to apple brandy in importance comes the cherry brandy known as kirschwasser (pronounced keersh'-vahsser) or kirsch. I still have a small quantity of Schwarzwälder Kirsch made by the famous Zwack firm of Budapest.

To me at least, that is the kirsch par excellence of the entire world. Even before the war, however, this was seldom found in this country and, when it could be found, the price was almost prohibitive. Fortunately, there are also reasonably good kirschwassers made both in Switzerland and in France and an excellent kirsch made in Denmark under the name of Kirsebaer. Of the Swiss brands I recommend Rigi and Brunnen; of the French brands, Marie Brizard. Both types are sweeter than the Schwarzwälder (made from cherries grown in the famous Black Forest region of Germany), and neither leaves the same lingering, delightful aftertaste. Nevertheless, either the Swiss or the French kirsch is an excellent drink, either can be used with good results in cocktails, and either will make a splendid flaming dessert. Kirsch is a true brandy and is not to be confused with cherry cordials or liqueurs. Zug (pronounced tsook) and Basel, Switzerland, are noted for their kirsch and many excellent brands are made there.

I cannot leave the subject of fruit brandies without mentioning the excellent blackberry, pear, apricot (Barack Pálinka), and raspberry (Himbeergeist) brandies made by the firm of Zwack & Co. These are all true brandies, not liqueurs or cordials (although Zwack also makes excellent liqueurs). They are splendid after-dinner drinks, dry, fiery, and with an aftertaste not to be found in any of the syrupy cordials. They are pretty expensive for use in cocktails, but if for some extra-special occasion you want a cocktail that is ultra-ultra, try one with a gin or white Cuban rum base, a lime-juice modifier, sugar to taste, and a few dashes of one of these fruit brandies!

MISCELLANEOUS SPIRITS

Southern Comfort While this 100-proof liquor is made from a supposedly secret formula, it is, at least in taste, a peach-flavored bourbon. It has been made for many years but has only recently come into common use north of the Mason and Dixon Line. It is a grand drink straight or as a liqueur, and it can be substituted for bourbon in practically any whisky drink, but because of the peach content the resulting drink will not be as dry as it would with straight bourbon. Proof of the popularity of this liquor is to be found in the fact that it has been quite extensively imitated.

Aquavit This is the great drink of the Scandinavian countries. It is made in the same manner as gin is made —that is to say, neutral grain [3] spirits are redistilled in the presence of flavoring materials. Several flavoring substances are used, but, whereas the principal flavoring ingredient of gin is juniper, in the case of aquavit it is caraway. The liquors of the several Scandinavian countries differ somewhat from one another, the Danish being the driest and the Swedish the sweetest. The natives of each country, as might be expected, usually prefer the type of their homeland. Outside of Norway and Sweden, however, it is quite generally recognized that Aalborg Taffel Akvavit from Denmark is the driest and the best. In all three countries,

---

[3] Perhaps "neutral potato spirits" would be more accurate. Irish whisky is commonly but erroneously referred to as "potato whisky." There is also prevalent an erroneous belief that vodka is always made from potatoes. Actually, ethyl alcohol can be made from any starch; and potatoes, like the cereal grains, are rich in starches. Therefore, any liquor that uses ethyl alcohol in the process of its manufacture—like aquavit, gin, and the blended American whiskies—can use an alcohol made from either grain or potatoes. As a practical matter, distillers will use whichever is more abundant and is cheaper. Scandinavia produces many potatoes but little grain, hence aquavit is commonly made with potato alcohol. Russia is a great grain-producing country, hence vodka is commonly made from grain rather than potatoes. Furthermore, true vodka is an unaged, high-proof, straight whisky and, while whisky can be made from a potato mash, it is grossly inferior to grain whiskies in body, in flavor, and in character. During the recent post-war scarcity of cereal grains in the United States a large proportion of the so-called "neutral grain spirits" used in the manufacture of American whisky blends was made from potatoes. Czechoslovakia is a potato-producing country and there vodka is frequently made from potatoes.

Denmark, Sweden, and Norway, the manufacture of aquavit is now strictly controlled by government monopoly. There is therefore little use of discussing brands. Outside of Aalborg from Denmark, what is usually to be found here is 1ma Aquavit, made by Aktiebolaget Vin & Spritcentralen, Gothenburg, Sweden, and Løitens, made by A/S Vinmonopolet, Oslo, Norway.

Aquavit should be served stinging cold, but it is best when ice is not allowed to come in contact with the liquor and thus dilute it. The better Scandinavian restaurants which make a specialty of aquavit freeze the bottle in a small cube of ice to chill the liquor. The glasses, of course, should also be pre-chilled. Aquavit may also be used as a cocktail base either straight or blended with gin, but in so using it one must remember its strong caraway flavor and not attempt to blend it with incompatible flavors such as peach, apricot, etc. It is best, however, straight. Like vodka, the normal-sized drink of about an ounce to an ounce and a half should be downed at one swallow—not sipped. Like vodka, also, it is a grand apéritif. The Scandinavians like a beer chaser, but I do not recommend this as a pre-prandial potion. The accompanying Scandinavian toast is *"Skaal"* (pronounced skoal), which is equivalent to the German *"Gesundheit."*

Vodka What aquavit is to Scandinavia, vodka is to Russia and Poland. However, where aquavit is made like gin, vodka is made like whisky. In fact, it actually is a straight grain whisky, usually wheat or corn or rye, with (as in the case of other whiskies) a small amount of malt. Neither aquavit nor vodka is aged. Both are bottled at once or stored in glass until bottled. Vodka should be taken straight and very, very cold, like aquavit. It also makes an excellent cocktail base and, having no pronounced flavor of its own, it will blend with anything. In this respect it is superior to aquavit for use in cocktails. Unfortunately, there is no Russian vodka available in the United States at the present time. Of the domestic vodkas that I have tried, the Smirnoff brand is by far the best. Vodka is also made in green, yellow, and pink colors. You can make a yellow variety for yourself by grating a small quantity of lemon peel, drying it for two or three days, and then adding it to the vodka—about a 2-ounce measure of the dry grated peel to a 25-ounce bottle of vodka. Allow it to stand for a week or ten days, shaking occasionally, and then decant off the liquid. The green (really a yellowish-green) variety is made by infusing the vodka with a small quantity of zubrowka grass. It is sold under the name of Zubrowka (pronounced zu-brof'-ka). It is really an aromatized vodka. The pink or whisky-colored variety is made in a similar manner except that red-colored berries from the mountain ash are used instead of zubrowka grass. It is called Jarzebiak (pronounced yar-zhen'-bee-ak).

My hat is off to the American vodka manufacturers and their advertising departments, particularly Heublein, manufacturers of the Smirnoff brand, for what I regard as the most outstanding job of advertising and sales promotion that this country has ever witnessed. I am not so keen about the claim that vodka "does not have an unpleasant liquor taste." If you don't like the taste of liquor, why drink it? But the blurb that it "leaves you breathless," with its *double-entendre*, is one of the cleverest advertising slogans I have seen.

Due, I believe, in large part to the magnificent advertising and sales promotion tactics, the sale of vodka in this country has attained an almost unbelievable record. First of all, when this campaign started, vodka was almost unknown in the United States. It was a mysterious liquor from behind the Iron Curtain and, for quite understandable reasons, we are rather allergic to anything emanating from behind the Iron Curtain. The people (principally Heublein) who set out to popularize vodka had everything against them and practically nothing in their favor.

Second, from the point of view of a liquor with an outstanding taste appeal, such as cognac, bourbon, rye, etc., they started with an absolute blank. Vodka, as will be shown below, is a liquor with absolutely no taste appeal

THE FINE ART OF MIXING DRINKS

whatsoever. Except for the alcoholic content, one might as well try to promote the appeal of distilled water! And look what has happened.

In the last half of 1950, the first period for which figures were published by the federal government, there were less than 387,000 gallons of vodka bottled in the United States. For the year 1955, that figure had jumped to almost seven million gallons. Of this amount, well over one third was sold on the Pacific coast and Heublein alone sold over 40 per cent of the total.

And just what is this liquor which, against all the normal and understandable resistance to its use, has achieved such a miraculous sales record? Well, that is the most extraordinary part of the whole story. It is nothing but pure, high-proof grain alcohol and water. It is nothing but the "Mountain Dew," "White Mule," or "Cawn Likker" (and a substantial part of it is made from corn) so well known in our own Southland, only distilled out at an even higher proof and, therefore, having even less character and flavor. (See pages 44–46.)

Our federal regulations on the "Production of Distilled Spirits," 1950 edition, provide (Section 183.531) that "All spirits distilled at or above 190 degrees of proof shall be branded 'Neutral Spirits' followed by a word or phrase descriptive of the material from which distilled." They then proceed to define vodka (Section 183.533) as "Neutral spirits which are reduced to not more than 110 degrees of proof and not less than 80 degrees of proof and, after such reduction, are so treated by one of the following methods as to be without distinctive character, aroma, or taste . . ." The methods of treatment for neutralizing or removing the congenerics are threefold; two are continuous flow over charcoal or constant agitation in contact with charcoal for at least eight hours, and the third is any other method approved by the Commissioner for rendering the product "equally without distinctive character, aroma, or taste."

Now, as I have already said (page 45), in general, the *lower* the proof at which liquor is distilled out and the *higher* the proof at which it is bottled, the better the liquor; a 200-proof liquor (actually impossible to attain) would be pure, unadulterated alcohol absolute. Well, ordinary commercial grain alcohol averages only 190 to 196 proof—much of it even less. If, therefore, you need grain alcohol to dilute your tincture of iodine or to rub on your back and the corner drug store is closed, just use vodka. Of course the vodka is half distilled water but that won't harm your back at all.

I have had no Russian or Polish vodka for quite a number of years and I have no completely authoritative information as to just how it is (or used to be) made. To the best of my recollection, however, it was even better than our Smirnoff. Also, it is my understanding that it was distilled out at about 150° to 160° which, if correct, would account for its superior character and flavor even though it might not leave you quite so "breathless."

Tequila From the plant known as maguey, a species of aloe, grown extensively in Mexico, come the two Mexican drinks, pulque and tequila. The sap of the maguey ferments very rapidly and this fermented juice is called pulque. The pulque, when distilled, is known as tequila (pronounced te-kee'-la). My first introduction to this drink was from a bottle brought up from Mexico by a Mexican friend during prohibition days. When the cork was drawn there emanated from the bottle an odor faintly resembling a combination of overripe eggs and limburger cheese. Out of deference to my friend, I managed to perform the ceremony of the MEXICAN ITCH. This consists of shaking a dash of salt on the back of the left hand. The fingers of that hand grasp a wedge of lemon and the right hand holds a pony of tequila. The salt is licked from the back of the hand, the lemon is squeezed onto the tongue with the salt, and then the whole is washed down with the tequila.

Of course lemon (citric acid) in combination with salt (sodium chloride) produces a dilute hydrochloric acid, and it seems that this is essential to overcome the hydrogen sulphide (ripe egg) odor of the tequila prior to swallowing it. Once the liquor reaches the stomach, however, I must admit that it gives rise to a warm, mellow glow that gradually spreads from the stomach to the fingers, toes, and even to the hairs of the head.

During the period of the gin famine, circa 1944, a considerable amount of tequila was exported from Mexico to the United States for use as a cocktail base in place of gin. With me it could never replace even an unaged gin, although it might, perhaps, be called comparable to bathtub gin. However, I did find one brand—Cuervo (pronounced kwair'-voh)—from which the unpleasant odor above mentioned seemed almost completely absent. In a pinch it might be used in a cocktail. In general, however, the only liquor I have ever tasted that I regard as worse than tequila is slivovitz.

Absinthe This liquor, in its original form, is not only illegal in the United States; it is and for many years has been illegal even in Switzerland, its birthplace, and in France. Its manufacture and sale were forbidden because it was supposed to be habit-forming and to result in insanity and sterility. The ingredient blamed for all this evil was wormwood—the *absinthium* variety of Artemisia or sagebrush. There is, however, at least a respectable difference of opinion on this question. From my own personal experience I can say that as a child I was constantly dosed—as were the other children of that neighborhood and time—with copious draughts of wormwood tea, along with catnip tea, thoroughwort tea, and various other medicinal "teas." Let one of the good old ladies of the town hear of a child—or even a barnyard animal—with worms, and every child in the community was loaded, steeped, drenched, and force-fed with wormwood tea until the scare was over. I can find no evidence that this resulted either in any increase in insanity or in any decrease in the birth rate of that community as against other communities not similarly addicted to the use of this good old vermifuge.

The old pre-war absinthe, made by Pernod Fils of France, was labeled "Extrait d'Absinthe." The modern and legal substitute—without the wormwood—exported from France by Pernod Fils is labeled "Liqueur d'Anis." A still better substitute is made by Pernod S.A. in Tarragona, Spain, under the name of "Liqueur Veritas." There is also one made in Louisiana called "Herbsaint," pronounced, not herb-saint, but airb-saN, which is close enough to the correct French pronunciation of absinthe to sound almost identical. None of these substitutes quite takes the place of genuine absinthe with its somewhat bitter, aromatic flavor. They are, however, reasonably acceptable, both in an Absinthe Drip or Absinthe Frappé and as a flavoring ingredient in cocktails.

Ojen (pronounced o-hen) This Spanish liquor, properly considered, is not an absinthe substitute but is an absinthe-*flavored* liquor. It is practically a ready-mixed cocktail, requiring only a dash of bitters and icing to make a delicious drink. It can also be used to give an absinthe flavor to other cocktails, but when so used it should be combined in approximately equal parts with the gin or other cocktail base, whereas with Pernod, Veritas, or similar absinthe substitutes, only a few dashes should be used.

Arrack and *Okolehao* (pronounced oh"-koh'-le-hah"-oh) These two liquors are indigenous to Hawaii and are seldom seen in the continental United States. In fact, one composer, joking about the lack of familiarity with this liquor whose name sounds like that of a musical instrument, has written a song around the key phrase: "While playing on my little okolehao." Both liquors are made by distilling the fermented mash of rice and molasses. In the case of okolehao proper there is added a quantity of juice extracted from the root of the taro plant, and the distillate is aged in charred oak casks.

The white okolehao or arrack uses coconut juice in place of the taro and the distillate is aged in uncharred barrels. It lacks the smoky taste of the okolehao proper and has but very little color. Both liquors are bottled at 90 proof or less. Arrack is said to be of Chinese origin, presumably because of the use of rice in making the mash. It should be noted that this is an entirely different drink from Batavia arak or arak rum (p. 59), used principally in the manufacture of Swedish Punch (p. 207).

Mead or *Metheglin* (pronounced me-theg'-lin) This good old liquor of great-grandpappy's day was made (usually homemade) of an artificially fermented mash of malt, water, and honey. It was sweet and fairly potent but rather characterless when unflavored. For that reason it was frequently combined with one or more spices according to taste. There has been organized in England a society—Mead Makers, Ltd.—concerned with the revival of mead making and drinking, but it is doubtful whether any popularity which this drink may acquire there will spread to the United States.

And this may be as good a place as any to mention, as curiosities, a couple of liquors which I do not recommend but about which you might like to know.

Aguardiente (ah-gwar'-dee-en"-tee) This is seldom seen in the United States, which is perhaps just as well, but is quite popular in Spain and the various Latin American countries with those who want a cheap, high-powered liquor, regardless of taste. The name means "burning water," which is fairly descriptive and reminds one of "fire water," the Indians' name for whisky. There are two types: aguardiente uva, made from grapes, and aguardiente de caña, made from sugar cane or molasses. The former is, by far, the better of the two.

In either case, whether made from grapes or from sugar cane, the middle run of the still (discarding both the "heads" and the "tails") is bottled just as it comes from the still, without aging or rectification, but watered down from a proof of 160° or better to 100° or less. It is analogous to vodka and to the "White Mule" of our own Southland. It can be used as a substitute for vodka with very little difference in flavor effect.

Borovicka (bo-ro-veet's-kah) This is an unaged 90-proof juniper brandy made by Rudolf Jelenik Distilleries of Vizovice, Czechoslovakia. It is dry, and can be used as a substitute for gin in almost any gin drink but is not satisfactory as a substitute for other brandies as an after-dinner drink. I doubt that it is a true brandy made solely from juniper berries, but I do not know.

APÉRITIF WINES

Next to the citrus-fruit juices, aromatized wines constitute the principal modifying, blending, or smoothing agent used with liquor bases in making cocktails. All of these apéritif wines are also excellent as straight appetizers. Since they average only 18 or 19 per cent alcoholic strength, they are much milder than cocktails in which the liquor base runs from 43 to 50 per cent alcohol. Throughout Europe they are used either straight or with a dash of bitters or a twist of lemon.

Today you will see vermouth concerns advertising that the wine should be served "well iced, with a twist of lemon." This, however, raises a highly controversial question. If French vermouth is to be taken straight it undoubtedly should be well chilled to bring out the tang of the aromatics. In France, the home of French vermouth, however, only the sweet or Italian vermouth is used as an apéritif. French vermouth is made for export trade, principally to the United States, for use in making Martinis and other cocktails. And, almost without exception, your native Frenchman, your true lover of vermouth and similar apéritif wines, takes his apéritif just as it comes from the bottle —at room temperature. The same is true in other European countries where apéritif wines are used rather than cocktails.

On the other hand, your American insists on well-iced drinks, particularly his pre-prandial apéritif, and it is largely in an effort to popularize these apéritif wines with the American public that the practice of icing them has sprung up. As a result of this, many so-called "American bars" in Europe today, when serving vermouth, quinquina (pronounced keN-kee'-nah), or any other apéritif wine to an American customer, add an ice cube to the glass of wine.

Your individual taste must be the guide to your answer to this controversial question. Undoubtedly too much chilling destroys the bouquet and aroma of wine, particularly a red wine. The "well-iced" school answers this argument by saying that chilling brings out the tang of the aromatics and an apéritif wine is taken for the flavor of the aromatics rather than of the wine itself. Also, they say that only the thoroughly chilled pre-prandial drink will properly stimulate the taste buds and wake up the appetite. They compare the warm vermouth of the Italian and the Frenchman with the Englishman's horror of all horrible drinks—warm beer! My suggestion is that you try your vermouth and other apéritif wines, first, at room temperature; second, chilled by icing the bottle or leaving it for an hour or more in the refrigerator; and, finally, chilled by adding an ice cube to the glass or, still better, by *stirring* gently with ice in the shaker. Whatever you do, however, *never* shake the wine or any cocktail containing wine with ice. Shaking will result in a cloudy, muddy, disgusting-looking drink.

The most commonly used of the apéritif wines are the vermouths, of which there are two types, the Italian or sweet and the French or dry. The Italian vermouth "marries" perfectly with whisky, the French vermouth with gin. True, there are cocktail recipes that use these combinations in reverse, but there is always likely to be something wrong, something not quite satisfactory, about a blend either of dry vermouth and whisky or of sweet vermouth and gin.

The best Italian vermouths are made in Torino, Italy. By far the best brand is Cinzano (pronounced chin-zah'-no). This famous old vermouth is made by Francesco Cinzano & Cia., which was organized in 1835. Despite the dark color of the vermouth, the wines used are all white wines, some dry and some sweet. These wines, none of which is less than one year old, are infused with some thirty different herbs, each of which has been previously distilled or macerated with alcohol. The mixture is then aged, decanted, filtered, clarified, pasteurized, and refrigerated. The clarification process alone consumes from three to five months. The combined process of pasteurization and refrigeration (which is done at about 9° below zero) is most interesting in results. This treatment was originally undertaken for the purpose of destroying the bacteria of fermentation and insuring good keeping qualities in the tropics as well as in the arctic. Not only was this result accomplished, but it was found that the treatment resulted in maturing the wine to a degree approximately equivalent to aging it some four or five years in the wood.

My own favorite Italian vermouth is Cinzano Bianco, a vermouth as light in color as the French vermouths but a true Italian vermouth made in Torino by the same Francesco Cinzano & Cia. Manhattans made with it, for example, are still Manhattans but different and superb.

French vermouth is made primarily from the light and rather flavorless wines pressed from grapes grown in the Hérault section of France, which, however, are mixed with some Algerian grapes to reduce the extreme dryness of the wine. The wine is fortified with a brandy containing natural grape sugar and alcohol and, as in the case of Italian vermouth, infused with some thirty or more aromatizing herbs. In general it may be said that the processes of manufacturing French and Italian vermouths are quite similar, the differences in the character of the two products being due to differences in the kinds of grapes and, to a lesser extent, the herbs used. The wines used in making French vermouths require longer aging than those used in making Italian vermouths. Very roughly, it may be said that it takes at least two years to make a good Italian vermouth and from three to four years to make a good French vermouth. Before the war, the outstanding French vermouth was Noilly Prat (pronounced nwah'-ee prah, and *please* don't call it "noy-lee-pratt") from Marseille. Since the war, apparently two things have happened. First, it is believed by many people (myself included) that the present product, while gradually improving, does not quite measure up to this company's pre-war standard. Second, a number of other manufacturers have greatly improved their vermouths and now offer products which are vastly better than before the war. My own favorite French vermouth today is Lillet (pronounced lee'-lay), made by Lillet Frères of Podensac, France. Do not confuse it with the Lillet apéritif made by the same company and originally sold under the name of Kina Lillet. Except for Lillet, I still regard Noilly Prat as probably the best.

I cannot leave the subject of current brands of French vermouth without commenting on Boissière (pronounced bwah'-see-air), made by Ets. Chambéry-Comoz of Chambéry, France, "Inventors of the White Vermouth." Actually, while there are others better, it is not a bad vermouth. The trouble is that, however horrified the manufacturers may be at this result, it has been a godsend to the gyp bars. A 3-to-1 or even a 2-to-1 Martini made with Boissière will be lighter in color than a 7 to 1 made with most other vermouths. Unfortunately all too many untrained drinkers judge the dryness of their Martinis, not by the flavor, but by the color. Who, then, can blame the bar, in business primarily for profit, for copping an extra dime by taking advantage of their lack of sophistication and educated taste? Other vermouth manufacturers are now copying this trick and, to my taste, have completely ruined their products thereby.

In the first year after prohibition for which figures were available (1935) there were 4,081,440 bottles of vermouths imported to and 113,280 manufactured in the United States. By 1940 these figures had risen to 6,029,760 bottles imported and 1,689,000 manufactured here. By 1943 imports had entirely ceased (except comparatively small quantities from South America), but domestic manufacture had risen to 9,473,280 bottles. The famous old Cinzano organization, among others, moved to South America early in the war period and opened plants in several countries, notably Argentina and Chile. The same man who had operated their plant in Torino, Italy, came to South America and took over. The same secret formulas and processes were used. The same meticulous care was exercised in every minute detail of the manufacturing process. The same herbs were obtained from the same sources. The same wines, of course, could not be had, and to this I attribute primarily the difference in the products. Nevertheless, excellent wines are made in South America, particularly in Chile. Despite all the effort and all the care, however, the South American vermouth of Cinzano was no more like Cinzano from Torino, Italy, than a brisket of beef is like a porterhouse steak.

Of course when imports from France and Italy were cut off by the war, the domestic organizations did not have two to four years in which to prepare their product. This, alone, is sufficient to account for the poor quality of many of the domestic vermouths that came on the market overnight. They were, in effect, bathtub vermouths, like the bathtub gin of prohibition days. Most of the numerous brands that so quickly appeared disappeared with equal speed. A few survived and deserve credit for making a reasonably acceptable product under almost impossible conditions. Most of the American vermouths now on the market are not only pure and wholesome but are also fairly palatable.

Several other apéritif wines should also be mentioned, principally Dubonnet (dew-boh-nay'), Byrrh (beer [4]), and St. Raphael (san raff"-ay-ell'). All three of these apéritif wines are generally similar to vermouth, but each has its own individual characteristics. They can be taken as a straight apéritif or substituted for vermouth in cocktails. In fact, some interesting variations in standard cocktails can be made just by this simple change in the modifying agent. For example, try one Manhattan made with ver-

---

[4] "Byrrh" is pronounced exactly like our word "beer." This is somewhat confusing for us. There is no confusion in France, where Byrrh is made, because there the word for beer is *bière*, pronounced bee-ayr'.

mouth, another with Dubonnet, and a third with Byrrh. You will find them similar, yet each will be different from the others just as a Daiquiri made with lemon differs from one made with lime.

FORTIFIED WINES

By far the most important of the fortified wines (i.e., wines whose alcoholic strength has been increased by the addition of grape brandy or some similar spirit) is sherry. True sherry comes from Jerez (pronounced hay-reth'), a city in the southern part of Spain. The quality of the wine is the result partly of the chalky soil and favorable climate of that small section of Andalusia where the grapes are grown and partly of the special methods of aging and blending the various wines that go into the finished product. It takes many, many years to produce a high-grade sherry. The "solera" or mother wine which is the heart of the blend may have been started as much as eighty or a hundred years ago, and each solera is tended with meticulous care to make certain that, as it is replenished from time to time, there are added to it only wines of the same type and quality. Other countries, including the United States, may produce wines of a taste similar to sherry, but only in this one small section of Spain are the true sherries to be found.

Nor can the producer tell until the wine has fermented and has clarified how much of what type of sherry a given press of grapes will produce. From the selfsame grapes, pressed and barreled at the same time, the wine in some of the casks will be pale, in others dark; in some the flavor will be delicate, in others more or less harsh; some will make sherries of the finest delicacy and character, some will be fit only for distilling into brandy. Also, after the new wine has been barreled and is left to "flower" (a secondary fermentation peculiar to sherry), still further unpredictable changes take place. Some of the wines will be light and dry, some will be heavy and rich, some will be in between, and some may have turned sour and be fit only for use in vinegar.

The casks of each of the various types of wine are now placed in storage with the soleras of the same type. The solera is always the oldest wine of that particular type. As wine is drawn from the solera for bottling, the space thus emptied is filled with wine from the next oldest casks, these are refilled from the next, and so on down to the youngest. Thus there is no such thing commercially as a sherry of any given year's vintage. All sherries are continuous blends. If the label bears a statement such as "Solera 1858," that means only that the solera or mother wine was started a hundred years ago and not that the contents of the bottle are a hundred years old.

In addition to the straight wine soleras, the producer also maintains soleras of color wine which are obtained by reducing unfermented wines to some 20 to 30 per cent of their original volume and thus securing a dark, heavy, sweet syrup which is then mixed with regular sherry in varying proportions. The final sherry blend as it is bottled will consist of wines of various ages drawn from the appropriate solera together with the necessary amount of color wine to give the desired color and sweetness and (if needed) sufficient grape brandy to fortify the wine to the desired alcoholic strength.

In general, the sherries exported to the United States are of four types:

FINO (*fee'-no*) *Pale and very dry.*

AMONTILLADO (*a-mon"-te-yah'-doh*) *Also pale and dry but not so extremely dry as fino.*

OLOROSO *Golden color and medium sweet.*

CREAM *Dark-colored, sweet, and very rich.*

Manzanilla (mahn-zah-neel'-yah) is the same general type as the fino but is extremely light-bodied and even drier than the fino. Vino de pasto (vee'-no de pah'-stoh) falls between the fino and the amontillado. It is somewhat lacking in character and does not possess the nutlike flavor of the amontillado. Amoroso is similar to the oloroso but drier and somewhat lighter in color. Unless you are sure of the reliability of the producer, however, do not rely too much on the label as an indication of the type of sherry. Many a bottle labeled amontillado is merely an inferior pale dry sherry, and many a bottle labeled oloroso lacks the full-bodied richness of the true golden oloroso.

The pale dry sherries—manzanilla, fino, and vino de pasto—are useful principally as a substitute for vermouth in cocktails and as cooking sherries. The best sherry for use straight as an apéritif is the amontillado. Dry sack is also excellent. The amontillado is dry enough to act as a stimulant to the appetite and has a character and finesse that are almost wholly lacking in the other pale dry types. The oloroso and other sweet sherries are dessert wines. They are too sweet and heavy for use, either straight or in cocktails, as an apéritif. They are excellent for use in sauces and make a delightful midafternoon drink. The outstanding sherry brands are those of Duff Gordon, Gonzales Byass, Pedro Domecq, Sandeman, John Harvey & Sons, and Williams & Humbert, all of Jerez. John W. Burdon, of Port St. Mary, Spain, also makes a very excellent sherry. All of these firms produce excellent sherries, both apéritif and dessert. As a dessert wine, however, Harvey's Bristol Cream is the king of them all.

Another fine old wine, extremely popular in colonial days but almost never seen today, is Madeira. While the manufacturing processes differ widely from those used in producing sherry, nevertheless, like sherry, Madeira has a range varying all the way from a light, medium-dry, apéritif wine to a heavy-bodied dessert wine that rivals even a port. Like port and the sweeter sherries, it is a magnificent midafternoon drink and it is unsurpassed as a cooking wine. Its tonic qualities, like those of port, are exceptionally good and it has a sharp tang not to be found even in the finest sherries. The best of these wines come from Funchal in the island of Madeira. One of the lightest (both in body and in color) of the Madeiras is Rain Water made by Welsh Bros. The driest and most acceptable as an apéritif is Gloria Mundi made by Leacock & Co. Unfortunately it is now difficult to find either Rain Water or Gloria Mundi in the United States. Blandy also produces an excellent Madeira, as does Sandeman, whose house is famous for its ports and, to a somewhat lesser extent, for its sherries.

Port wine should probably not be mentioned at all in connection with apéritif drinks because all ports—even the tawny variety—are very sweet and therefore unfit for use as an apéritif. The one possible exception is a white port which is used to some extent as an apéritif in Europe but is seldom if ever seen in the United States. I mention port here because it is extremely useful in making some mixed drinks other than cocktails. It also is useful in the kitchen and it is a splendid midafternoon drink. At the table it is a wine to be taken after, not with, a sweet dessert or as an accompaniment to cheese. Like a sherry, it should be sipped slowly in order to enjoy to the utmost its rich bouquet and undertone. It is also extensively used for medicinal purposes.

Port wine derives its name from the city of Oporto, Portugal, where it is made. It is made not from one but a number of different types of grapes, all of which, however, are grown along the Douro River valley. Fermentation begins at once after the grapes are pressed, but, unlike sherry, which goes through two processes of fermentation, port is allowed to progress only half to two thirds through the fermentation process when the fermentation is stopped by the addition of Portuguese brandy. It is the unfermented sugar still remaining in the wine that gives it its sweetness.

Port wine, perhaps, illustrates better than any other the difference between aging processes as applied to wines and spirits. It has already been pointed out that spirituous liquors, such as brandy and whisky, age only in the wood. Once they are bottled, they remain unchanged. They will be no smoother nor more mature a hundred years after bottling than the day they were put in the bottle. Wine, on the other hand, because of the grape sugar which still remains unfermented and undistilled, will continue to age in the bottle for many, many years. This is particularly true of port, the fermentation of which was arrested when it was little, if any, more than half complete. Experts claim that any of the heavy-bodied ports (that is, the vintage or crusted varieties) must rest in the glass for at least eight to ten years before they are ready to use, and the truly fine ports are aged from twenty-five to forty years after bottling.

There are two types of the better ports: vintage and crusted. Vintage port, of course, is the finest of the ports. However, only little of it is seen in America because it does not keep well in transit. Crusted port, like the vintage variety, forms a solid crust on the sides of the bottle requiring the decanting of the wine before use. It is really the same type of wine as vintage port but of a slightly inferior character. Tawny and ruby ports, the types most commonly found in this country, are aged in the wood. Their crusting is done while in the wood. The tawny port is "fired" from time to time to remove the crusty sediment, and each firing leaves it paler in color—hence the name "tawny." Ruby port is simply a blend of young port with the older and lighter-colored tawny. A real tawny is composed of good wine, well matured in the wood, and is really delightful and delicate in taste although it cannot compare in body and bouquet with a vintage or even a crusted port. A ruby port will have a more fruity flavor but will lack the delicacy and finesse of a tawny.

Perhaps one other fortified wine, marsala, should be mentioned in passing. It is a dark, sweet, heavy wine, with a sharp taste somewhat resembling Madeira. It is of little use in the making of mixed drinks and of no use as an apéritif. Its chief use is in cooking, where it serves somewhat the same purpose as sherry but with a different and distinctive flavor.

LIQUEURS

A later chapter will be devoted to an enumeration of the various liqueurs and cordials in common use. For the present, however, let it suffice to mention a few basic principles respecting the use of liqueurs in preparing cocktails and other mixed drinks without going into details as to the distinguishing characteristics of the numerous varieties available.

To begin with, the distinction between a liqueur or cordial and a brandy should be kept clearly in mind. This is especially important because, unfortunately, the two terms are sometimes used somewhat indiscriminately on labels. A true brandy is distilled from the fermented mash of the fruit and is dry, not sweet. Under F.A.A. regulations, its sugar content must be less than 2½ per cent. Liqueurs, on the other hand, are made by macerating or infusing the fruits or other flavoring materials in a spirituous liquor such as brandy, filtering or, perhaps, redistilling the flavored liquor, and then adding sugar syrup to obtain the required sweetness. In the better-made liqueurs this product (irrespective of the age of the spirits used in preparing it) is still further aged in the wood. The infused liqueurs may absorb sufficient color from the fruits that are combined with the brandies. The distilled liqueurs, however, are colorless as they come from the still and acquire their color either by aging in the wood or by the addition of artificial (preferably vegetable) coloring agents. Liqueurs are used for two purposes: straight, as an after-dinner cordial in place of a cognac or other brandy, and as a flavoring agent for cocktails and other mixed drinks.

The use to which the liqueur is to be put should determine the brand you purchase. Of course some of the better liqueurs, such as Benedictine, Grand Marnier (pronounced grahN marn-yay'), Drambuie, etc., are not only trademarked but are made by secret processes and formulas and have never been successfully imitated. The Grand Marnier people, during the war, tried making their product in the

United States but, owing to their total inability to obtain a brandy even approximating the Fine Champagne which forms the base of this exquisite cordial, gave up the attempt. Many other liqueurs, however, especially the fruit liqueurs, are made both here and abroad. I have never yet found any liqueur made in the Western Hemisphere which I regarded as in any way comparable to the better brands made in Europe, particularly France, Hungary, and the Netherlands. They may have the full flavor of the fruit or aromatic herbs, they may be equally high in proof, they may have the proper sugar content. They may even taste pretty much the same on the way down. Somehow or other, though, they lack the finesse of the European products and, in particular, the aftertaste and effect are of cloying sweetness without the delightful bouquet and lingering delicacy that distinguish the high-grade cordial from the ordinary.

On the other hand, if the liqueur is to be used by merely adding a dash or two to a cocktail as a flavoring agent, it would be the height of extravagance and an almost criminal waste of heaven-sent nectar to use the delicate, expensive imported brands. The domestic liqueurs—or even a plain fruit syrup from your corner-drugstore soda fountain—will give you the desired peach, raspberry, apricot, pineapple, or similar flavor. Keep your liqueurs made by Zwack in Hungary, by Fockink or Bols in Holland, or by Garnier or Marie Brizard in France as an after-dinner treat for your gourmet friends and use the cheaper domestic varieties to spice your cocktails. A real Cointreau (pronounced kwen'-troh) will give you a somewhat better Side Car than will a domestic Triple Sec; a real Chartreuse (pronounced shahr-trerz') will give you a better cocktail than a domestic liqueur verte, granted. The difference, however, will be barely discernible and will be out of all proportion to the relative costs of the two liquors. Spend your good money for the best in a cocktail base and for the best in your vermouths, which are of prime importance. To use an expensive, imported liqueur in a cocktail where only a few dashes are wanted for a faint, elusive flavor would be like adding beef tenderloin to your stew in making a *boeuf en daube*.

Of the imported liqueurs I recommend Benedictine Society, Fécamp, France, for Benedictine; Pères Chartreux, Tarragona, Spain, for Chartreuse; Peter Heering, Copenhagen, Denmark, for Cherry Heering; Cointreau S.A.R.L., Angers, France, for Cointreau; Rocher Frères, France, for curaçao (kew'-ra-soh); H. Severy, Hasselt, Belgium, for kümmel (kim'-mel) (Allasch Doppelt Kümmel); G. A. Jourde, Bordeaux, France, for Cordial Médoc; Ditta Giuseppe Alberti, Benevento, Italy, for Liqueur Strega (stray'-ga); Drambuie Liqueur Co., Edinburgh, Scotland, for Drambuie; Union of South Africa, Cape of Good Hope, South Africa, for Van der Hum; Ets. Marnier Lapostolle, France, for Grand Marnier; A. B. Vin & Spritcentralen, Gothenburg, Sweden, for Carlshamm's Punsch (Swedish Punch); l'Abbaye de Çenon, Bordeaux, France, for Vieille Cure (vee'-ya kewr); and, for the miscellaneous fruit and other cordials, any of the following houses: Zwack (tsvahk) of Hungary, Fockink and Bols of Holland, and Bardinet (bar-di-nay'), Cusenier (kee-zen-yay'), Garnier (garn-yay'), Get Frères (zhay frayr), Marie Brizard (bree-zahr'), and Rocher Frères (ro-shay' frayr), all of France.

Of the domestic brands (strictly for use in cocktails) I have found several satisfactory, including the firms of Bardinet, De Kuyper, and Nuyens, all of whom now have American distilleries. The products of Jacquin (zha-ken) and Leroux (lee-roo'), both of Philadelphia, are also good.

BITTERS

Bitters are an essential ingredient of a large number of cocktails. Strangely enough, while they are distinctly bitter when tasted straight, their effect on a cocktail is almost the exact reverse. A raw, sharp, acrid, bitter whisky can be smoothed out tremendously by the addition of a sufficient quantity of bitters. Some bitters have an alcoholic content nearly as high as that of gin, rum, and many whisky blends, yet they are not subject to the Internal Revenue tax on alcoholic liquors because they have pronounced medicinal value and are used, even by strict prohibitionists, as aids to the digestion. This freedom from tax applies to all the aromatic bitters. On the other hand, the non-medicinal bitters that are used solely for flavoring purposes in mixing drinks are subject to the tax. This applies to the citric-flavored bitters such as orange bitters and the less common lemon and lime bitters. One of the anomalies of the New York State liquor laws is that only alcoholic beverages—all subject to Internal Revenue taxes—can be sold in a liquor store. Consequently, medicinal bitters, the same as ginger ale, soda, citrus fruits, and other "mixings," cannot be bought there. You can, however, obtain them at your favorite grocery or drugstore. Most aromatic bitters are made according to secret formulas. They are more or less interchangeable, but, though all are bitter, each will give to a drink a slightly different tone than any of the others. In the oldest recipe book that I possess (printed in 1880) more than half of the recipes that call for bitters add the admonition "Bokers genuine only." If this particular brand is still made it has at least been many years since I have seen it on the market. The same is true of Hostetters, another famous old medicinal bitters which, however, was not used in mixing drinks.

By far the most commonly used bitters today is Angostura. This is a *sine qua non* both for a real Old-Fashioned and for a real Manhattan. One trouble with many Manhattans today, both homemade and served at bars, is that the bitters are omitted. This is largely a result of prohibition drinking, when it was too much trouble to mix a real drink and, even though a liberal dash of Angostura would have smoothed out, to some extent, the vile whisky of those days, people just didn't bother. Consequently, today many have become used to drinking their cocktails without bitters and really prefer them that way—or at least think they do. For that reason bartenders hesitate to use bitters in a drink such as a Manhattan unless specifically requested.

Next to Angostura, the best-known American bitters is Abbot's, made by C. W. Abbot & Co., Baltimore, Maryland. Another excellent and well-known old bitters which has recently reappeared on the market is Boonekamp, made by Bols of Holland. Peychaud, from France, is an absolute "must" in the Sazerac cocktail. At present, however, it is almost impossible to find. Two very fine bitters come from Italy, Campari and Fernet. The latter is now manufactured also by a branch of the old Italian firm of Fernet-Branca in New York. Campari is more than a mere bitters; it is really a highly aromatic liqueur. Zwack of Budapest also makes an excellent bitters called Unicum. It blends particularly well with brandies.

Two excellent brands of orange bitters are made in England, one by Field, Son & Co. and the other by Holloway's Distillery. Holloway's also makes an orange bitters in this country, using the same formula as in England. Another good domestic brand of orange bitters is De Kuyper's. Recently there have appeared on the market a number of orange bitters which are laxative. Being of a medicinal nature, they, like the aromatic bitters, escape the Internal Revenue tax. Probably the amount of rhubarb and cascara sagrada in these brands is not sufficient for the few dashes used in a cocktail to produce any pronounced laxative effect. Nevertheless, it is preferable to use an orange bitters that is made strictly and solely for beverage purposes if it can be obtained.

No discussion of bitters would be complete without mentioning Amer Picon, a bitter liquor made by G. Picon, Levallois-Perret, France. This is not ordinarily used as a true bitters to smooth out and blend a cocktail but is diluted with water and sometimes sweetened with grenadine or some other fruit syrup or liqueur and taken as an apéritif. It also blends most satisfactorily with vermouth, particularly Italian vermouth. Fernet-Branca and Campari are also sometimes used in a somewhat similar manner, and I still have nostalgic memories of the Little Hungary restaurant of pre-prohibition days with its gypsy violinist and the wine decanters with poppet valves in the bottom for refilling your glasses. Three wines were served with every dinner, the final, dessert wine being a Hungarian tokay. The apéritif (which, like the wines, was included as part of the table d'hôte dinner) was always a Unicum cocktail in which the outstanding ingredient was Zwack's Unicum bitters.

FRUIT JUICES AND SYRUPS

I entitled this somewhat lengthy chapter "Limes, Lemons, and Liquors." If you have read all up to this point you should be reasonably familiar with the basic facts respecting liquors. Now let us consider the limes and lemons.

The first commandment with respect to fruit juices is to use nothing but fresh fruit, freshly squeezed. By fresh fruit I mean fruit that is ripe but not overripe, and is firm and sound. The citrus fruits other than lemons turn soft and show rotten spots as they age, but lemons frequently shrivel up and turn hard instead of rotting. Do not use them unless the skin is still a bright yellow or greenish-yellow and is tender. The inside of a brown, hard lemon may look all right, but you can be sure that a drink made with it will not taste right. The chemical changes that have withered the fruit and hardened the skin have also seriously affected the flavor of the juice.

It should scarcely be necessary to caution you never, *never*, NEVER to use unsweetened canned juices. Among the exceptionally vile concoctions of the prohibition era (and their names were legion) was a combination of bathtub gin and canned orange or grapefruit juice, with or without sweetening. At least they did blend because one was about as unpalatable as the other, both having a similar sharp, harsh, acrid, tinny taste. Neither was wasted on the other; each succeeded in bringing out all the obnoxious qualities of the other. From that point of view it was an ideal drink—ideally odious. But, for the love of all that is holy, don't spoil good liquor by mixing it with canned fruit juices.

I know that some people claim they like canned orange and grapefruit juice; my own wife is one of them. If you are another, then *please* drink it straight, not mixed with liquor. And, by the same token, don't use any of the synthetic jiffy-quick lemon juice substitutes. I know at least one of these that is wholesome and stimulating. In fact, our Red Cross blood banks, during the war, used it extensively and with excellent results. That, however, does not make it a good substitute for fresh lemon juice in a cocktail. Tomato juice is also wholesome and, to me at least, delicious, but I trust you would not use it with rum and sugar in making a Daiquiri.

And when I say to use only freshly squeezed fruit juices, I mean squeezed when you make the cocktail—not the day before, not an hour before, not even a half-hour before. All fruit juices commence to ferment as soon as the skins are removed and the juice is exposed to the air. I am not particularly concerned about the loss of vitamin content, because for a period of several hours that is negligible, especially if the juice is kept refrigerated. The enzymes or digestive ferments in the fruit, however, start working *immediately* upon exposure of the juice to the air. If you want to see a visible demonstration of this, squeeze a glass of lemon or lime juice and set it aside. Look at it every ten minutes for an hour and note the separation with a clear, watery liquid at the bottom and a constantly thickening, curdled-looking mess floating on top. No, that is not just the pulp separating from the juice; that is fermentation going on. The chemical changes that bring about this separation also affect the taste and tend to give the juice an off-flavor, brackish taste. So buy 'em fresh; squeeze 'em fresh; use 'em fresh!

Occasionally you will find a recipe that calls for pineapple juice. How does one squeeze a pineapple? Obviously it cannot be done in a Dazey juice extractor or with one of the old-fashioned conical glass extractors. If you are the fortunate possessor of a Waring Blendor or similar high-speed mixer your problem is solved. This machine will extract the juice from any kind of fruit or vegetable. While I never tried it, it would not surprise me to see it get juice from a stone! Just beat up your fruit in the Blendor and strain. Failing one of these marvels of multiple uses, your next best bet is a small fruit press, and in that category I include those juice extractors that consist of two flat plates mounted on a tripod and operated by a long handle which exerts a tremendous pressure on the fruit that is placed between the plates. Once again, just squeeze, then strain. Oh yes, in the case of pineapple, you first peel it, remove the eyes and core, and slice it.

Believe it or not, there are a few recipes that call for unusual juices such as coconut juice and the juice of papaya or other melons. I even have one recipe (the Red Snapper) that calls for tomato juice and Worcestershire sauce! If you must make one of these exotic misfits and you want coconut juice or melon juice, a Waring Blendor is practically indispensable.

Now, thus far I have been talking about unsweetened fruit *juices*, as distinguished from fruit *syrups*. Many recipes call for fruit syrups, especially raspberry syrup. Raspberry syrup was one of the stock articles of the preprohibition bar. Even the old-type Pousse-Café called for a layer of raspberry syrup. You may also want (particularly after you once start to "roll your own") other fruit syrups —apricot, cherry, peach, and what not. For the most part, liqueurs of these flavors will be better than non-alcoholic syrups, but if you do want a non-alcoholic syrup just take a small bottle down to the corner drugstore and ask your favorite soda jerker to fill it with whatever syrup you are seeking. You can also, in a pinch, use the juice from canned fruits—especially those put up in glass. I do not particularly recommend this, but on occasion I have used them myself with pretty fair results. The sweetened juices from canned fruits somehow do not acquire that horrible brackish flavor, suggestive of a combination of stale dishwater and quinine, that is to be found in the canned unsweetened fruit juices. Remember, though, that the juice from your canned fruits is neither as heavy nor as sweet as either soda-fountain syrups or liqueurs.

Probably the most important of all syrups is sugar syrup or simple syrup or gum syrup or, as ye olde-tyme bartenders' manuals called it, gomme syrup. I long since abandoned the agony of softening and muddling loaf sugar in making Old-Fashioneds and of wasting time trying to effect a complete dissolution of either granulated or powdered sugar in a Daiquiri or similar drink to the end that there might be no undissolved sugar left in the bottom of the cocktail glass. The solution is simple—dissolve the sugar in advance; i.e., use gum syrup. Essentially, this is merely granulated sugar and water heated to the boiling point and then cooled. Some of the old-time recipes call for the addition of a small quantity of either glycerin or gum arabic for the purpose of arresting the tendency of the sugar to crystallize out of the solution, but in my opinion this is neither necessary nor desirable. The object in determining the ratio of sugar and water is to make the syrup as heavy as possible without getting later crystallization. I have found that a mixture of about 3 cups of sugar to each cup of water yields a very satisfactory syrup. Add the sugar to cold water in a saucepan, heat it, and allow it to boil vigorously for a few minutes. Cool and then bottle. I use old pint liquor bottles with screw tops. This solution will keep indefinitely and will save you weary hours of time in making all manner of drinks calling for the use of sugar—and, what is more important, it will make better drinks with no sediment in the bottom of the glass.

At this point I suggest that you turn to the chapter on liqueurs and look up grenadine and orgeat, two non-alcoholic syrups that are most useful in cocktail mixing. These and other fruit syrups—unlike simple syrup—have a tendency to ferment and mold after exposure to air and must be carefully watched. If you live in a state where it is possible to purchase grain alcohol, I suggest that after opening a bottle of one of these syrups you add about 6 to 8 per cent alcohol for the purpose of preserving it. If, however, you live in some place like New York where you can buy every kind of alcohol except alcohol, add about 10 to 15 per cent of vodka, which, after all, is nothing but dilute grain alcohol.

One final caution regarding the use of sugar, sugar syrups, and all non-alcoholic heavy syrups such as grenadine, orgeat, honey, etc. All forms of sugar, dry or in syrup, blend with liquor and other liquids best when warm. Contact with ice, even if it does not crystallize out the sugar content of a syrup, will at least harden it enough to prevent ready mixing with the other ingredients. It is better, therefore, to stir or shake the ingredients so as to blend them thoroughly before adding ice to the shaker. Furthermore, when syrups, alcoholic or non-alcoholic, are added for color effect—such as grenadine, green crème de menthe, Parfait Amour, etc.—a clearer, more colorful cocktail will be produced if the ingredients are mixed before icing. Pouring the colored syrup on the ice will give a muddy effect. It should also be noted that sugar does not dissolve well in alcohol. If you use dry sugar for Daiquiris and similar cocktails, the sugar should be thoroughly dissolved in the lemon or lime juice before adding the liquor.

EGGS AND CREAM

It should not be necessary to point out that when eggs, cream, or even milk are used in a mixed drink they must be strictly fresh. In using milk or cream with citrus juices, remember that the citrus juice is full of citric acid and that any acid will curdle milk. It is therefore best to blend the other ingredients in the shaker first and add the milk or cream last.

The exact reverse is true of eggs. In this case, the alcohol will tend to "cook" the egg. It is therefore best to blend the egg thoroughly with the lemon or other citrus juice and sugar first and then add the liquor, a small portion at a time, shaking well after each addition. Another method sometimes used is to shake up everything but the egg first in order to thin out the liquor as much as possible and then add the egg last. This works reasonably well with egg whites but is not so satisfactory when yolks are used. If you are able to get dried egg powder you can avoid all worry about curdling. Just dump the powder in with the other ingredients and shake. The flavor, however, particularly of the powdered yolks, is far from satisfactory.

ICE

It is strange, indeed, that most amateur bartenders fail to recognize the fact that ice is one of the essential ingredients of a cocktail and that absolute purity is just as important in the case of ice as of any other ingredient. You can feel reasonably well assured that the ice delivered to you by any metropolitan ice company is pure. But what about the ice from your own kitchen refrigerator? If your city water tastes of chlorine, your ice will taste of chlorine and so will your cocktails.

Furthermore, ice drinks up the odors of a refrigerator as a sponge drinks up water. If your cocktail has a faint aroma of Camembert cheese or of leftover broccoli, interview the major-domo of your kitchen and ascertain whether leftover foods are kept in tightly covered dishes or are left open in the refrigerator. Point out to her that keeping foods in closed dishes is not only essential to the purity of the ice but that it prevents the drying out of the foods and is, therefore, good economy.

At the same time ascertain how often the box is defrosted. I have seen refrigerators so caked up with ice that it was necessary to use a jimmy to get an ice tray out. This, again, is poor economy. A refrigerator, if not the self-defrosting type, should be defrosted as soon as a substantial film of ice (say, 1/16" to 1/8") has formed in the freezing compartment. Frequent defrosting results in better refrigeration, lower operating costs, and longer life of the refrigerating machinery. Ice is a highly efficient insulating material. When your refrigerating compartment is surrounded by a solid mass of ice a quarter of an inch thick or more, that compartment is completely insulated from the part where the food is stored. The cold does not reach the food. Since the temperature of the food compartment is thermostatically controlled, the refrigerating unit works overtime in a violent effort to offset the negligence of the operator. Electric or gas bills (according to the type of box) go up and the machinery wears out.

The ice that forms on the refrigerating unit is the condensed moisture from the foods stored in the box. This moisture is laden with odors from the food whence it escaped. The quarter-inch coating on the outside of the compartment that holds your ice trays, therefore, is not just ice—it is frozen parsnips, potatoes, chicken, and what have you. And all these delicate but inappropriate flavors will be communicated to the ice in your trays and thence to your drinks.

SODA AND GINGER ALE

Waters of any kind, carbonated or plain, sweetened or unsweetened, have no place in a cocktail. An Old-Fashioned, for example, with *any* water—even a few squirts—in it is no longer a cocktail but a short Highball. With all the care you can possibly exercise, any cocktail that stands five minutes or more in contact with ice will be diluted to an appreciable extent and the use of still more water in mixing the cocktail is anathema.

However, ginger ale and the various carbonated waters, usually called club sodas, are essential ingredients of Highballs and other long drinks. The two essentials of any carbonated beverage are high carbonation and good retention. Unfortunately, this is a combination difficult to achieve. Frequently, especially with ginger ales, the beverage that is not highly carbonated retains its life longest, whereas the one that boils out like a volcano in eruption when the cap is removed goes flat in a few minutes. It is also generally true that the beverages in which the gas rises in minute quantities retain their life longer than those that give off their gas in larger bubbles.

Ginger ales should also be really dry and pale. The old-time heavy, brown, syrupy ginger ale has no place in drink mixing. The sugar content should be medium and there should be a fairly sharp acid taste.

There are innumerable brands both of club soda and of ginger ale on the market. Unfortunately, for one reason or another, most of them fall below any reasonably high standard for carbonated beverages. One brand is off taste, another is off color, another has insufficient carbonation, etc. Some houses make either good soda but a poor ginger ale or vice versa. I particularly recommend Canada Dry brand both of water and of ginger ale. And, whatever you do, don't fall for the "calory-free" hooey in mixing your tall drinks. The liquor you use is loaded with calories; the few extras to be found in the dry ginger ale (if you are using ginger ale) you could put in your eye and never notice them. Don't ruin a good drink for the sake of a silly fetish. One concern even puts out a calory-free club soda! The best sodas made are simply charged water, and if there is any calory count in carbon dioxide, medical science has not yet discovered it. The chemicals used in the other type of soda are definitely not of a fattening type and any appreciable amount of sugar in it would ruin it.

PERTINENT POINTERS

We have now learned the basic principles of cocktail mixing, we have acquired our cocktail shaker, glasses, and other necessary implements, and we have learned how to select our ingredients and, let us assume, have collected at least a few bottles of liquor and a supply of limes, lemons, and so on. Before actually measuring out our first cocktail and shaking it up, however, let us give heed to a few final hints and warnings.

MEASURING

There are two ways of measuring your ingredients: with a measuring glass and by the eye. Immediately after repeal, the average bartender treated his jigger as if it were an indispensable part of his left hand—a sort of sixth digit. There were two reasons for this. First, many bartenders lacked the experience and "know-how" to measure with reasonable accuracy by eye alone. Second, the proprietor fixes his prices on the basis of just so many drinks from each bottle. If he pays five dollars for a full quart of bonded whisky and he allows two ounces to a drink, he knows that he should get sixteen drinks from the bottle and that the liquor in each drink will cost him slightly over thirty cents. If the bartender pours three-ounce drinks, however, the cost to the house will average nearly fifty cents per drink. Accuracy is essential for profit.

In the good old days before prohibition the bartender set

out the whisky bottle, the Highball glass, the ginger ale or soda, and a measuring glass and let the customer pour his own drink for a Highball. He noted whether the customer poured one, two, or three "fingers" of liquor and charged accordingly. That same bartender would toss into the shaker the ingredients for anywhere from one to six cocktails, shake, line up the glasses, and pour the cocktails. Each glass would be full to the brim with not a single drop left over. Today's bartenders are again acquiring this knack.

The home entertainer is not mixing and selling drinks for profit and therefore need not use a medicine dropper or pipette to portion out his liquor. He is not dispensing hundreds of bottles of liquor per day, and a ha'penny's difference in the cost per drink need not seriously worry him. Nevertheless, he is likely to gather the idea from many of the modern recipe books that laboratory accuracy in measurement is a vital essential, and that unless he follows that particular author's proportions with meticulous accuracy the drink will be utterly ruined. This is largely the bunk! If you will read a dozen recipe books you will find few, if any, drinks as to which all the authors agree on the proportions of the several ingredients. Who is right? The answer is to learn the proportions that best please your own taste and that of your discriminating guests and then stick to these proportions with *reasonable* accuracy. A few grains of sugar, a few drops of bitters, or a few spoonfuls of liquor more or less will make no noticeable difference.

Now, at first, you may have little idea just how much of this and that to put in the shaker to make two drinks, four drinks, or ten drinks. It is easy to learn. Start with the bitters, since it is well in practically all cases to pour this ingredient first. Remember that 6 dashes equal 1 teaspoonful. With the shaker held diagonally so that the liquid will collect in one spot, measure into it successively ½ teaspoonful, 1 teaspoonful, 2 teaspoonfuls, etc., of water and note how much of the bottom is covered. Suppose your recipe calls for 3 dashes to a drink. You will now be able to visualize how much to put in for 2, 4, 8 drinks, etc.

Now for your total quantity of ingredients. It is written in the book of the law of good fellows that wherever two or three are gathered together each will want a couple of drinks. Accordingly, you will seldom mix less than four drinks. Take your cocktail glass and fill it with water to within about ¼" to ⅜" of the top. Empty it into the shaker and repeat. Note the height to which 2 glasses, 4 glasses, and so on, fill the shaker. Until you feel that you can trust both your eye and your memory you may, if you have a glass shaker, make a series of narrow scratch marks with a sharp file on one side of the shaker to indicate the height to which it should be filled for any successive number of drinks. After a little practice you will find you do not need these guides.

But those guide lines are only for the total quantity of all ingredients. If your Manhattan is to be made 3 to 1 and your Martini 5 to 1, how do you gauge the proportions? Well, brother, with the line before your eye showing the total amount of liquid needed, if you cannot pour with reasonable accuracy one sixth or one fourth of that amount, then you better buy a micrometer caliper with a vernier scale and forget all I have said about using your eye.

In nearly all cases the liquors are poured into the shaker first and the ice is added last. In the few cases where that is not done, measure out in a separate glass the liquors that are to be added last. Never try to measure by eye after the ice has been put in.

Experiment from time to time with different proportions in your drinks, but do this alone or with a trusted friend who is somewhat of a connoisseur. Try a Manhattan that is 2 to 1, 3 to 1, 4 to 1. If the 3 to 1 seems too strong and the 2 to 1 too mild, try 2½ to 1. But once you have decided on your proportions, *stick to them*. Two things will result in encomiums from your guests. The first is that your Manhattans, Martinis, Side Cars, or what-have-you always taste *exactly* the same—not good today and poor tomorrow. The second is that every so often you bring forth some new delight to stimulate their palates and warm both their stomachs and their hearts.

TO STIR OR TO SHAKE

Here, again, the instructions in most recipe books are far from enlightening. The reader is told to stir or to shake, as the recipe calls for, under penalty of spoiling the drink. Why he should do the one or the other, however, is seldom explained. And even professional bartenders do not always know. I once heard a bartender—and a fairly good one at that—assure a customer that he could not shake a Martini because "shaking bruises the gin"!

The real distinction between the two methods is simple. Shaking produces a colder cocktail quicker than stirring. Therefore, since frigidity is highly desirable in all cocktails, shaking is normally the preferable method. However, with some cocktails another consideration enters into the picture, and that is "eye appeal." A substantial part of the charm of certain cocktails such as the Martini and the Manhattan is their clear, almost scintillating translucence. A stirred cocktail will remain clear; a shaken cocktail will be cloudy or even muddy in appearance. This result is particularly noticeable where vermouth or any other wine is an ingredient. Therefore, you should never shake a cocktail containing any wine unless you want a muddy-looking drink. This cloudiness will clear somewhat as the drink stands, but it will never have quite the limpid appeal of the drink that is stirred. Some people care more for the stinging cold of the shaken cocktail than they do for its appearance. So if you do not mind a muddy-looking drink, shake to your heart's content.

Incidentally, there are very few cocktails that can be made with the beautiful translucence of the Martini and the Manhattan. This is because more cocktails are made with citrus juices than with vermouths, and the citrus juices themselves are not translucent. It is, however, possible to make a fairly clear cocktail with lemon or lime juice if only a small quantity is used and if it is strained through a very fine wire mesh (such as a tea strainer) or through cloth.

And when you stir, stir; do not churn. It is possible to stir so fast, and with an up-and-down as well as a circular motion, that the stirring practically amounts to shaking. On the other hand, when you shake, shake like the very devil! Do not rock or swish or revolve or merely agitate. Throw your biceps into high gear and push the accelerator down to the floor board.

One word of caution should be given respecting Highballs and other tall drinks using carbonated beverages. These must be stirred with a long spoon or stirring rod (an iced-tea spoon will do) to blend the liquor with the ginger ale or soda. Stir quickly and briefly. Too long stirring will cause the gas to escape and result in a flat drink. And, whatever else you do, be sure to use plenty of ice —two large cubes in a short Highball (Sour-glass size) and four or five in a large Highball or Collins glass. I believe it was Charles H. Baker, Jr., in one of his excellent articles who said, "A lukewarm drink means a lukewarm guest." True, Cholly, my boy, absolutely true!

CRUSHED ICE OR CUBES

As a usual thing ice cubes are used for stirred drinks and cracked or crushed ice for those that are shaken. Many cocktail books state that a drink that is stirred will be stronger than one that is shaken, and that one in which ice cubes are used will be stronger than one in which crushed ice is used. As a practical matter this is usually true; in theory it is absolutely untrue. The reason that it is usually true in practice is that, regardless of the kind of ice used and regardless of whether the drink is stirred or shaken, the mixologist devotes approximately the same length of time to the chilling operation.

When ice melts it absorbs heat from whatever substance

it chances to be in contact with—in this case the cocktail liquor. The heat absorption by the ice—and the resultant melting of the ice and dilution of the drink—are in direct proportion to the surface area of ice exposed to the liquor. The finer the particles of ice, the greater the exposed area and the quicker the drink can be chilled to any given temperature. You can chill your cocktail quicker with crushed ice than with cubes and you can chill it quicker by shaking than by stirring. But chilling to the same temperature will result in exactly the same amount of dilution, whether you shake or stir. Except for one thing, the same should be true whether you use crushed ice or cubes. That one thing depends on the temperature of your ice. Your ice should come from the freezing compartment (if you don't leave the trays out to warm up) at about 10 degrees below freezing. It should, therefore, be *theoretically* possible to reduce the temperature of your cocktail (depending on the specific heat of your particular mixture and assuming an equal quantity of cocktail and ice) approximately 10 degrees *before melting a single drop* of the ice. Furthermore, because of the principle of latent heat of fusion, you will still further reduce the temperature of your cocktail by the mere melting of the ice and the changing of it from ice at a temperature of 32 degrees to water at the same temperature.

As I have said, these considerations are largely theoretical. Just one practical consideration remains and that is that, stirred or shaken, whole cubes or cracked, *the more ice, the less dilution*. One author—I regret that I can't remember who it was—used to delight in concocting new drinks for his friends and concluded every recipe with— "and two tons of ice." He was absolutely right!

For absolutely perfect cocktails only one round should be shaken at a time, because after the drink is shaken and poured and while it is being consumed the ice will continue to melt in the shaker and will further dilute any liquor that is held back for a second round. Furthermore, in shaking a second round, any leftover ice should be discarded and only fresh ice direct from the refrigerator used. This is because the leftover ice will be partly melted and "honey-combed." There may easily be ten or twelve degrees' difference in the temperature of ice fresh from the electric refrigerator and ice that has been used in the shaker and is at or near the melting point of 32° Fahrenheit. For the same reason, ice trays should *never* be taken from the refrigerator and allowed to stand and warm up before using the ice. Always use the ice the minute it is taken from the box.

As a practical matter, however, it may not always be convenient to shake and drink one round and then shake and drink a second, particularly with guests who like (as do I) to put away their first cocktail with reasonable speed and then linger a bit longer over the second. Some writers condemn the "dividend" cocktail as one of the iniquitous survivals of prohibition days. They are correct in saying that the holdover drink will be weaker than the one that is freshly shaken and immediately consumed and that it will not have quite the same sparkle and life. The dilution, however, can be greatly reduced by using all cubes instead of crushed ice or by using cubes in combination with a small amount of crushed ice. If not more than five to ten minutes elapse between pouring the first and second drinks, the dilution from further melting of large cubes will not be too great.

In making Old-Fashioneds it is customary to use cubes only—just why I do not know. I find that the drink can be chilled much quicker and more satisfactorily and that it is easier to drink if the cubes (or, with an extra-large glass where several cubes are used, one or two of them) are cracked.

"AND A TWIST OF LEMON"

Many cocktail recipes call for a twist of lemon or, more specifically, of lemon peel. Use only fresh, soft lemons with a clear, unblemished skin. With a razor-sharp paring knife slice off thin strips of the peel about ⅜" wide, lengthwise the lemon. Be careful that the knife does not go deep enough to cut off any of the white, pulp-like layer under the yellow skin. After your drink is poured, take the peel between the thumb and middle finger and give it a sharp pinch over the glass. Orange peel can be used in place of lemon peel but with a quite different taste effect. Lime peel, however, has a sharp, acrid taste that most people find repugnant.

Remember that the peel of citrus fruits contains a sharp, rather bitter oil. Used with restraint, it points up a drink with a delicious fragrance. Too much of it, however, can ruin a drink. Therefore, unless the recipe specifically calls for it, or unless you know that you (or your guest, as the case may be) really like the heavy bitter flavor, do *not* put the peel in the drink. Merely twist it over the top.

CHILLING AND FROSTING THE GLASSES

There are two methods of pre-chilling cocktail glasses before pouring your drinks. Where crushed ice is at hand the simplest and most effective method is to fill the glass with the crushed ice, allow it to stand while the drink is being shaken, and then discard the ice. Another reasonably satisfactory method is to place an ice cube in the glass, grip the stem at the base between the thumb and fingers, and, with a rotary motion of the entire glass, spin the cube around the inside.

"Frosting" a glass has nothing to do with its temperature but refers to giving it a frosted appearance. This is done by moistening the rim of the glass and dipping it in powdered sugar. Sometimes the rim of the glass is immersed to a depth of ⅛" or more in a colored liqueur or syrup, such as grenadine. Probably the best method, however, is to run a wedge of lemon or lime (cut so the juice will flow freely) around the rim of the glass. The glass is then inverted, any excess moisture is shaken off, and the wet rim of the glass is dipped in a saucer of powdered sugar. If powdered sugar is not available, fine granulated sugar can be substituted. Never use XXXX or confectioner's sugar. Frosting adds greatly both to the appearance of the drink and, in the case of certain cocktails such as the Daiquiri, to their flavor.

PROPER GLASSWARE

Use the right glass for the particular drink you are serving. The reason is undoubtedly purely psychological, but the fact remains that champagne in a Sour glass, a cocktail in a whisky glass, or sherry in a coffee cup simply does not taste as it should. Drinking, as distinguished from guzzling, is a fine art. The perfect drink must appeal to the sense of sight as well as to the sense of smell and the sense of taste. If you would win the acclaim of your guests, observe those nuances that may sound trifling but actually make all the difference in the world.

"REACTION TIME"

I once had a guest say to me, "Dave, that is the most delicious cocktail I ever tasted, but I wish you had put a little liquor in it." Twenty or thirty minutes later and after two of them, he said, "Great heavens, what kind of dynamite did you conceal in that drink?" The answer, of course, was that the cocktail contained a fairly substantial amount of a heavy liqueur and was smoothed out with egg white.

Different types of drinks have different reaction times. Liquors that are unaged or only slightly aged, such as gin, vodka, or akvavit, give a quicker lift than those that are old and mellow, such as well-aged whiskies. Dry drinks give a much quicker reaction than sweet drinks. Even the use of Italian vermouth will slow down the reaction time. The use of eggs, milk, or cream not only smooths out and covers up the sharp, biting tang of the drink but also greatly lengthens the reaction time. Eggs, cream, and sugar do *not* make a drink milder—they only make it taste milder and postpone its effect. The alcoholic content of the drink will, sooner or later, reach the blood stream and, according to the capacity of the individual, will produce the same effect whether it be thirty seconds or thirty minutes after the drink is consumed. That is why sweet drinks and creamy drinks are dangerous. They taste harmless, so the drinker has another and another and, maybe, still another. Later on he experiences the cumulative effect of the entire lot. Furthermore, such drinks do not stimulate the appetite; they smother it. One of the deadliest of this type of drink is the Alexander. It is not a prelude to a meal; it is a meal in itself. And, by the same token, probably the most perfect apéritif cocktail ever invented is the Martini. It sharpens the taste; it makes the stomach fairly cry out for food; and, since its reaction time is practically instantaneous, it gives fair warning to the drinker not to take too many.

SIX BASIC COCKTAILS

The average host, who makes no pretense of being an expert on liquors, can get along very nicely with a knowledge of how to mix a half dozen good cocktails. In fact, if he can make only two or three and always makes them well he will stand much higher in the regard of his guests than will the indiscriminate chop-suey dispenser who throws together a little of everything that chances to be lying around loose with no regard whatsoever for the basic function to be performed by each ingredient. Let us therefore start off with just six cocktails and learn to make them well. They are the *MARTINI*, using gin; the *MANHATTAN* and the *OLD-FASHIONED*, using whisky; the *DAIQUIRI*, using rum; the *SIDE CAR*, using cognac; and the *JACK ROSE*, using applejack.

THE MARTINI

I have already referred to the Martini as the most perfect of apéritif cocktails. Unfortunately, however, the average Martini served either at home or over a bar is anything but perfect. This is due in part to poor-quality liquors and in part to the proportions used. The usual recipe book specifies one-third vermouth and two-thirds gin. In violent protest against this wishy-washy type of cocktail there have sprung up the *VERMOUTH RINSE* and *VERMOUTH SPRAY*. The first consists of rinsing the inside of the cocktail glass with vermouth, pouring it back in the bottle, and then filling the glass with iced gin. The second uses a special vermouth atomizer, although a perfume atomizer will do. The iced gin is poured into the cocktail glass and then given a light spray of vermouth. With good, imported gin, both are acceptable, but are they Martinis?

Today when one mentions a Martini he invariably refers to the so-called *DRY MARTINI*; i.e., one made with French vermouth. Yet, strangely enough, the Martini was originally made with Italian vermouth, like a Manhattan. Italian vermouth and gin, however, do not make a wholly pleasing combination, and this cocktail is pretty much forgotten. Nevertheless, you will find many books of cocktail recipes that list three types of Martinis as follows (and I do *not* recommend any of them):

1. DRY MARTINI
- 1 part French Vermouth
- 2 parts Gin
- 2 dashes Orange Bitters to each drink

Some recipes even call for equal parts of gin and vermouth.

2. MEDIUM MARTINI
- 1 part French Vermouth
- 1 part Italian Vermouth
- 2 to 4 parts Gin
- 1 dash Orange Bitters & 1 dash Angostura to each drink

Some recipes call for orange bitters only and some omit the bitters altogether.

This cocktail also goes under the name of the *PERFECT*. Someone once said that whoever named near-beer was a darned poor judge of distance. I say that whoever named the "Perfect" cocktail was a mighty poor judge of perfection.

It is also sometimes called the *SOMERSET* and, if

made with equal parts of French vermouth, Italian vermouth, and gin, the *QUEEN*.

3. SWEET MARTINI
    1 part Italian Vermouth
    2 parts Gin

Some recipes call for orange bitters, some for Angostura, and some for no bitters whatsoever. Also, as in the case of the so-called Dry Martinis, some recipes call for equal parts of vermouth and gin.

An olive, either plain or stuffed, is ordinarily added to the Dry Martini, a maraschino cherry to the Medium and Sweet Martinis.

The above recipes are given merely in order that you may know the difference between these various types of Martinis as set forth in most recipe books and as served at most bars. My advice is to forget them all and, in your own home, serve one of the following:

MARTINI DE LUXE or *GIBSON DE LUXE*
    1 part Lillet Vermouth
    7 parts imported English Gin [1]

Stir [2] well in a bar glass or Martini pitcher with large cubes of ice and pour into chilled cocktail glasses. Twist lemon peel over the top.

The distinction between the Martini and the Gibson is simple. The Martini is served with an olive, the Gibson with a small pickled cocktail onion.

If you can get olives stuffed with any kind of nuts, they make the perfect accompaniment to a Martini. In choosing cocktail onions, get the hard, light-colored, sour onions, not the dark, sweet ones.

---

[1] The Martini made with yellow gin is sometimes known as the *GOLDEN MARTINI*.
[2] If you shake the Martini, it becomes a *BRADFORD*.

After extensive experimentation I have arrived at the ratio of 7 to 1 as the proportion most pleasing to the average palate. I know some who prefer a ratio as high as 10 to 1. Try out different mixtures and ascertain which you like best. I have found, however, that everyone who likes mixed drinks at all likes a 7-to-1 ratio with the right vermouth and with the right gin—even those who never before would drink a Martini at all.

Please note that this cocktail absolutely requires a gin of the highest quality. With ordinary run-of-the-mill (or should I say run-of-the-still?) gin you will simply have to use a higher proportion of vermouth to overcome the harsh, raw-alcohol taste of the gin. That is the real reason for the common 2-to-1 formula. With a larger proportion of vermouth (even the best vermouth), however, and with an inferior gin, regardless of proportions, you will have a decidedly inferior cocktail. Unless you have a good French vermouth, such as Lillet, I suggest that you use a good dry sherry, preferably an imported amontillado. Martinis made with dry sherry are excellent. Many people prefer them to those made with vermouth. I have also found that sherry conceals the harsh, tinny taste of an inferior gin much better than vermouth. Here is an excellent variation of the Martini, using sherry in place of vermouth:

GORDON

1 part Duff Gordon Amontillado Sherry
5 parts *imported* Gordon Gin

Prepare and serve like the Martini de Luxe.

If you are in a hurry or if you do not have lemon peel available, a few dashes of orange or lemon bitters (not more than two or three dashes to each drink) make a reasonably satisfactory substitute.[8] Also, some people like *both* the bitters and the twist of lemon.

---

[8] Few people realize the importance of the "twist of lemon" in the preparation of cocktails, particularly the Martini. Some regard it as a fancy, rather frivolous, and wholly meaningless gesture.

As occasional interesting variations in your Martinis try the addition of any one of the following:

A few dashes of curaçao (sometimes called the FLYING DUTCHMAN).

A few dashes of Chartreuse (either green or yellow)—see the NOME.

A few dashes of absinthe. This is sometimes called the INTERNATIONAL. This name is also sometimes applied to a Medium Martini flavored with a few dashes of crème de cassis or Benedictine.

Martinis are also sometimes made with some other liquor substituted for gin as a base—particularly a liquor of neutral flavor such as vodka or tequila. When so made, they are known as the *VODKA MARTINI, TEQUILA MARTINI, RUM MARTINI,* and so on.

WHEN IS A MARTINI STRONG?

In California, one of the reviewers of the first edition of this book asked the opinion of his favorite bartender, a chap of the type that I have elsewhere referred to as "genial but not too learned." The reviewer, however, apparently had great confidence in him because he was a real old-timer whose experience dated back to the days of the swinging front doors, the crystal chandeliers, and the mahogany bar and brass rail. His answer was, "If I mixed 'em the way this guy says to do it, I'd have our customers reeling down the street, stumbling over match sticks like they was logs."

Nothing could be farther from the truth. The lemon must be fully ripe but the skin must be soft and flexible. A hard, dried-out skin will not exude its oil when twisted. When the bit of lemon peel is twisted over the glass, the surface of the cocktail should be sprayed as if by an atomizer with the oil of the lemon. This simple operation transforms a mediocre cocktail into a good one and raises a good cocktail to the level of frankincense and myrrh!

I have asked dozens of my friends how much difference they thought there was between the alcoholic strength of a 3-to-1 and a 7-to-1 Martini. Two classes of people—chemists and accountants (who have any familiarity with liquors)—give the correct answer: "practically none." All others, of course, reply that 7 to 1 is approximately twice as strong. Well, let's see. For the purpose of our test, I am going to use House of Lords gin (my favorite for Martinis) and Noilly Prat vermouth. House of Lords gin is 86 proof or 43 per cent alcohol; Noilly Prat vermouth is 38 proof or 19 per cent alcohol. All French vermouths run 18 to 19 per cent alcohol, there is a much wider range in the alcoholic content of the various brands of gin. Using these two brands, then, we arrive at the following figures:

For our 3-to-1 Martini (3 times 43 for the gin) plus (1 times 19 for the vermouth), or 129 plus 19 equals 148. One hundred forty-eight divided by 4 (the total number of parts) equals 37, the alcoholic percentage of our 3-to-1 Martini.

For our 7-to-1 Martini (7 times 43 for the gin) plus (1 times 19 for the vermouth), or 301 plus 19 equals 320. Three hundred twenty divided by 8 (total number of parts) equals 40, the alcoholic percentage of our 7-to-1 Martini. Forty minus 37 equals 3, the exact difference in alcoholic percentage between our 3-to-1 and our 7-to-1 Martinis *before icing* and using House of Lords gin. Icing dilutes the alcoholic content by about ¼ to ⅓. There is, therefore, approximately 2 to 2½ per cent difference in the alcoholic content of a 3-to-1 and a 7-to-1 Martini, as iced and served, using House of Lords gin in both.

THE IDEAL MARTINI

So much has been written on the subject of Martinis that it may seem like carrying coals to Newcastle to indulge in further comment on this King of Cocktails. However, so much of what has been written is pure hooey and balderdash that I cannot refrain from popping off about some of it.

To begin with, the original Martini (or Martinez, as it apparently was first named) was made with equal parts of Old Tom gin, a sweetened gin, and Italian vermouth, the only vermouth then in existence, with a bit of sugar syrup, a few dashes of bitters, and a dash, perhaps, of curaçao or of absinthe. The Dry Martini, as we now know it, using French vermouth and no sugar syrup or cordials, has been a matter of slow and rather painful evolution.

Now, as I have pointed out elsewhere, the ideal proportions of *any* drink (and this, of course, includes the Martini) are those that best suit *your* particular taste. What raises my hackle feathers is the insistence of some writers that a given drink *must* be made with exactly their specified proportions. I have particularly in mind one chap who shall be nameless because he is only one of many. This gentleman is a facile and highly interesting writer and, except as to gin, rum, and whisky, I have found many of his comments on drinks and drink mixing thoroughly sound. But, when it comes to the Martini, phooey! He insists that the ideal ratio "may be generalized at about 3.7 to one," although he admits that it may not be too bad up to about four to one. I suppose that his absolutely perfect ratio would be something like 3.690412 to 1! And then, to make matters worse, he insists that the gin must be American gin and that "whatever imported gin may be for, it isn't for Martinis." Well, if he won't use real imported English gins, perhaps he should be excused for using an excess of vermouth (if it is a good vermouth) to help conceal the tinny, raw alcohol taste of most American gins.

Waiter, another 7-to-1 House of Lords Martini, please!

THE MANHATTAN

I list the Manhattan second among our six basic cocktails because, of all the hundreds of so-called cocktails listed in recipe books and the dozens listed on the liquor cards of hotels and restaurants, more Martinis and Manhattans are sold than any other kind. In fact, if we leave out Daiquiris and Old-Fashioneds, there are more Martinis and Manhattans sold than all other kinds put together.

Just as in the case of Martinis, you will find Manhattan recipes varying all over the lot in their proportions. In fact, there are recipes that even suggest two parts of vermouth to one part of whisky. The usual recipe, however, is one part vermouth and two parts whisky.

A further complication enters the Manhattan field that is not found with Martinis. With Martinis it is recognized that, irrespective of the proportions of vermouth and gin, a Sweet Martini is made with Italian vermouth, a Dry Martini with French vermouth, and a Medium Martini with a combination of the two types of vermouth. The same distinction is usually made in the case of Manhattans. However, the combination of French vermouth and whisky is not pleasing to most palates and, accordingly, on the assumption that a Manhattan is always made with Italian vermouth only, some people now use the terms Dry, Sweet, and Medium to designate the proportions of vermouth and whisky, a Sweet Manhattan being one made with 50 per cent or more of vermouth, a Medium Manhattan with about two parts of whisky to one of vermouth, and a Dry Manhattan with three or four parts of whisky to one of vermouth.

Both the Manhattan and the Old-Fashioned are usually made with rye whisky. I have already pointed out the fact that rye and bourbon can be used more or less interchangeably in most drinks and that they can be used in combination in most drinks. Many people—and I am one of them—prefer the flavor of bourbon to that of rye. If you are ordering one of these drinks at a bar and want it made with bourbon, you should specify "Bourbon Manhattan" or "Bourbon Old-Fashioned." Also, you should specify a bonded whisky. Otherwise the bartender will probably use a blended whisky—and whatever blend gives the proprietor the greatest margin of profit.

In all recipes in this book where either rye or bourbon can be used according to individual taste, I shall simply use the word "whisky." Scotch, however, is not interchangeable with American whiskies. Therefore, in recipes calling for the use of Scotch, the word "Scotch" will be used instead of "whisky."

Let us now return to our three types of Manhattans as set forth in most recipe books. They are as follows:

1. *MANHATTAN (SWEET)*
    1 part Italian Vermouth
    2 parts Whisky
    1 dash Angostura to each drink [4]

As above noted, some recipes call for equal parts of whisky and vermouth and some for other proportions.

2. *MANHATTAN (MEDIUM)*
    1 part Italian Vermouth
    1 part French Vermouth
    4 parts Whisky
    1 dash Angostura to each drink

Here again the relative proportions of whisky and the vermouths vary with different authors. Also, some recipes call for orange bitters as well as Angostura.

3. *MANHATTAN (DRY)*
    1 part French Vermouth
    2 parts Whisky
    1 dash Angostura to each drink

---

[4] The Sweet Manhattan made without bitters but with both orange peel and lemon peel in the mixture and shaken instead of stirred is called the *ARMY*. The plain Sweet Martini, made half and half, is sometimes called the *NAVY*. See also the *VIRGIN*.

The comments respecting proportions as well as those respecting the use of orange bitters set forth above for the Medium Manhattan also apply to the Dry Manhattan. It is also quite common to add a twist of lemon and drop the peel into the Dry Manhattan.

As in the case of the usual Martini recipes, the above Manhattan recipes are given for general information only. Once again I recommend that you forget them all and that, in your own home, you serve the following:

MANHATTAN DE LUXE

1 part Cinzano Italian Vermouth
5 parts Bonded Whisky
1 dash Angostura to each drink

Stir well in a bar glass or Martini pitcher with large cubes of ice and pour into chilled cocktail glasses. Add a maraschino cherry to each glass. Unless the cherries have stems attached, spear each cherry on a toothpick or use glass fruit spears.

As in the case of Martinis, interesting variations of the Manhattan may be effected very simply by the addition of a few dashes of curaçao or Chartreuse. I do not recommend the addition of absinthe. If you like an absinthe-whisky combination, go whole hog on it and mix a Sazerac.

Also, as with Martinis, Manhattans are sometimes made with different base liquors, and are then called the *SCOTCH MANHATTAN, RUM MANHATTAN, BRANDY MANHATTAN, APPLEJACK MANHATTAN*, etc. These are made with Italian vermouth, the various Martinis with French vermouth.

THE OLD-FASHIONED

If properly made, this is a truly magnificent cocktail. The principal reason that it does not enjoy an even greater popularity than it now claims is that what is usually served as an Old-Fashioned is actually a short Highball rather than a cocktail. Water, either plain or charged, has no more place in an Old-Fashioned than it has in a Manhattan or a Martini. The water is usually added ostensibly for the purpose of dissolving the sugar. You can make perfect Old-Fashioneds *only* by using sugar syrup. However, if you do not have sugar syrup available you can make a fairly passable cocktail by using loaf sugar as follows:

Put one medium-sized lump of sugar in the Old-Fashioned glass and add enough lukewarm water to cover it completely. Watch carefully until the sugar starts to dissolve and then pour off *all* the water. Add three dashes of Angostura, crush the sugar with a muddler, and blend sugar and bitters thoroughly. Add a small quantity of whisky and stir with a small spoon until the sugar is *completely* dissolved and blended with the liquor. Then, and then only, complete the cocktail. It takes about twenty minutes to make a satisfactory Old-Fashioned starting with dry sugar; it takes about two minutes starting with sugar syrup. Also, the sugar syrup makes a smoother, better drink. Therefore, let's make our Old-Fashioneds this way, using medium-sized Old-Fashioned glasses (about 5 to 7 ounces):

OLD-FASHIONED DE LUXE Pour into each glass 1 to 2 teaspoonfuls simple syrup and add 1 to 3 dashes Angostura. Stir with a spoon to blend the bitters with the syrup. Add about 1 oz. whisky and stir again. Add 2 large cubes of ice, cracked but not crushed (see page 109). Fill glass to within about ⅜" of top with whisky and stir again. Add a twist of lemon and drop peel in the glass. Decorate with a maraschino cherry on a spear. Serve with short stir rod or Old-Fashioned spoon.

I have been intentionally somewhat indefinite about the quantity of sugar and bitters for two reasons. First, you should experiment and determine for yourself just how sweet you like the drink and just how much of the bitters flavor suits you best. Second, I have stated the recipe in terms of filling your Old-Fashioned glasses to within about ⅜" of the top and I do not know the exact size of your glasses. Tastes vary somewhat, of course, but I have found that most people like about 1 teaspoonful of sugar and 1 to 2 dashes of Angostura to each 2 ounces of whisky.

Also, please note that I have suggested only a cherry and a bit of lemon peel for decorations. You will frequently find Old-Fashioneds served with lemon, orange, cherry, and pineapple. The bartenders' manuals of the Gay Nineties were replete with illustrations of cocktails, Sours, Crustas, Smashes, Cobblers, and other drinks decorated with all the above fruits together with strawberries, grapes, raspberries, etc., according to the available supply and the fancy of the writer. At the other extreme stand those who contemptuously refer to any cocktail decoration as "the garbage." My own opinion is that fruit flavors and liquors blend exquisitely and that, for a midafternoon or an evening drink, an Old-Fashioned is greatly improved in its over-all appeal by the judicious addition of a few fruits. Fruits, however, properly belong at the end of a dinner rather than at the beginning. Accordingly, when serving Old-Fashioneds as an apéritif, I recommend using only the lemon peel with no fruit at all or, at the most, a cherry or a slice of orange.

Note that in the Old-Fashioned the only modifying agents used are the bitters and sugar. The reaction time of this cocktail is slower than that of a Martini both because of its sugar content and because whisky is slower than gin. Don't be deceived by this. It is not a lighter drink than the Martini; it is stronger. Its action is merely delayed.

As an occasional variation in your Old-Fashioned try adding a teaspoonful of the juice from your bottle of maraschino cherries or a dash of curaçao, Cointreau, Chartreuse, or Liqueur Strega.

Old-Fashioneds are also frequently made with liquors other than rye or bourbon. Southern Comfort makes an excellent OLD-FASHIONED but is a bit on the sweet side. This can be offset by using less sugar. There are also GIN OLD-FASHIONEDS,[5] SCOTCH OLD-FASHIONEDS, BRANDY OLD-FASHIONEDS, RUM OLD-FASHIONEDS, APPLEJACK OLD-FASHIONEDS, etc. All are made exactly the same as the Whisky Old-Fashioned except for the liquor used. With Gin and Rum Old-Fashioneds, orange bitters may be substituted for or used in combination with Angostura.

THE DAIQUIRI
also sometimes spelled Dykaree

At one time the generally accepted distinction between a BACARDI and a Daiquiri was that one was made with grenadine and the other with sugar. The firm of Bacardi y Cia., proprietors of the Bacardi trade-mark, however, objected to the use of the name "Bacardi" as applied to any drink not made with Bacardi rum and maintained in the courts of the United States their exclusive right to the use of that name. Accordingly, the cocktail made with sugar is now known as a DAIQUIRI and the one made with grenadine as a DAIQUIRI GRENADINE or PINK DAIQUIRI. If vermouth instead of citrus juice is used with the grenadine, the name is EL PRESIDENTE.

The original and correct recipe for the Daiquiri is stated in terms of a single cocktail as ½ teaspoonful sugar, juice of half a lime, and 1 jigger of white label rum. This is a cocktail that is difficult to improve upon. It is dry, yet smooth. The reaction time is short. The lime and rum blend perfectly. The Daiquiri, like the Old-Fashioned, deserves an even greater popularity than it now enjoys. For example, it is, in my opinion, a vastly superior cocktail to the Manhattan, yet most bars sell many more Manhat-

---

[5] The GIN OLD-FASHIONED is also sometimes called the STUBBY COLLINS, presumably because it is a Collins without the charged water. When made with yellow gin it is sometimes called the GOLDEN SPIKE.

tans than Daiquiris. So far as I can ascertain there are two reasons why more Daiquiris are not sold: the use of inferior rums and the use of improper proportions.

In the chapter on limes, lemons, and liquors, I pointed out the inferiority of Puerto Rican rums as compared with the Cuban and the gross inferiority of Virgin Island rums. Nevertheless, because of the price differential, the overwhelming proportion of rum actually used both by bars and in private homes is Puerto Rican. There are, it is true, some reasonably good Puerto Rican rums, but none as good as the Cuban. Many of the brands are not even fairly good and you can't make a good Daiquiri without good rum. Many bar cocktails are made with lemon instead of lime juice and with lemons squeezed far in advance of making the cocktails. Furthermore, since lemon juice is much cheaper than good rum, it is a common practice to use more lemon juice and less rum. Since stepping up the quantity of lemon juice alone might make the cocktail too sour, the quantity of sugar is also increased and the result is a cocktail that is anything but dry.

A reasonably good Daiquiri can be made with lemons instead of limes, but, to most tastes, it will not be as good as one made with limes. Also, other sweetening agents, particularly *falernum* and *orgeat*, can be substituted for the sugar. Both of these syrups have a slight almond flavor that blends well with the rum. Falernum, in fact, was invented in the West Indies specifically for use with rum drinks. Personally, I think that the slight ginger flavor of falernum makes it a better sweetening agent for Jamaica or the other heavier-bodied rums than for Cuban rum. Orgeat, I consider ideal for use with Cuban white label rum. *Crème d'ananas* is also excellent.

Following, then, are three varieties of the Daiquiri, all of which are excellent:

DAIQUIRI

1 part Sugar Syrup
2 parts Lime Juice

8 parts White Label Cuban Rum

Shake vigorously with plenty of finely crushed ice and strain into chilled cocktail glasses.

DAIQUIRI GRENADINE Same as above, but use slightly less sugar and add two dashes of grenadine for each drink. Stir sugar, grenadine, and lime juice together thoroughly before adding the rum. This is sometimes called the *SANTIAGO*.

DAIQUIRI DE LUXE
- 1 part Orgeat or Crème d'Ananas
- 2 parts Citrus Juice made by mixing the juice of one large Lemon with that of three or four large Limes
- 8 parts Cuban White Label Bacardi or Havana Club Rum

Shake vigorously with plenty of finely crushed ice and strain into chilled and frosted cocktail glasses.

No decoration should be used with the Daiquiri because it is a cloudy cocktail. Cherries, olives, etc., are used largely as a matter of eye appeal and therefore belong primarily with clear, translucent cocktails such as the Martini and the Manhattan.

All rum drinks (except hot toddies and the like) should be frigid when served. Rum, like vodka and aquavit, is at its best when stinging cold. For that reason it is best to use finely crushed ice, pre-chill both shaker (to minimize dilution) and glasses, and, when shaking, shake as if you were suffering a super-acute attack of ague and Saint Vitus dance combined. The *FROZEN DAIQUIRI* and other frozen drinks will be discussed in a later chapter.

THE COCKTAIL KING AND HIS DAIQUIRIS

For approximately forty years prior to his death in early December 1952, Constante Ribalagua presided over the bar at La Florida (Flo-ree'-dah), known in recent years as the Floridita to distinguish it from another restaurant of the same name. He is said to have squeezed over 80 million limes and to have made over 10 million Daiquiris. This restaurant, at the corner of Obispo and Monserrate streets in Havana, became known as "La Catedral del Daiquiri"—The Temple of the Daiquiri—and Ribalagua as the Cocktail King—"El Rey de los Coteleros." The title was, indeed, well deserved. His limes were gently squeezed with his fingers lest even a drop of the bitter oil from the peel get into the drink; the cocktails were mixed (but not overmixed) in a Waring Blendor; the stinging cold drink was strained through a fine sieve into the glass so that not one tiny piece of the ice remained in it. No smallest detail was overlooked in achieving the flawless perfection of the drink.

If you acquire a cocktail recipe book from any of the bars in Cuba, watch out for their translation of the word "limon" (lee-moan'), which means *both* lime and lemon. This is almost invariably incorrectly translated into English as "lemon." Sometimes the author specifies "limon verde" to avoid this confusion but the translator is likely to render this as "green lemon" or even "unripe lemon." Actually lemons are almost unknown in Cuba, whereas lime trees grow in everyone's own yard.

Here, then, are the recipes for the Cocktail King's five famous Daiquiris, together with several others served at the Floridita and other Havana bars. All are to be mixed in a Blendor and strained into the glass.

DAIQUIRI NO. 1

    1 teaspoonful Sugar
    Juice of ½ small Lime
    2 ounces White Label Rum

It is difficult to restate this in terms of numbers of parts but, bearing in mind the small size of Cuban limes, it should average about 1:4:16 in place of my standard

1:2:8. Note that this is *not* stronger than my 1:2:8, but merely not quite so sweet. It is the same as 1/2:2:8.

DAIQUIRI NO. 2   The same as No. 1, with the addition of a teaspoonful of orange juice and a few dashes of curaçao to each drink.

DAIQUIRI NO. 3   The same as No. 1, with the addition of 1 teaspoonful each of grapefruit juice and maraschino to each drink.

DAIQUIRI NO. 4   The same as No. 1, except that gold label rum is used together with 1 teaspoonful of maraschino to each drink.

DAIQUIRI NO. 5 or PINK DAIQUIRI   The same as No. 1, with the addition of 1 teaspoonful each of maraschino and grenadine to each drink.

GOLDEN GLOVE   The same as No. 1, with the addition of 1 teaspoonful of Cointreau to each drink. See the MORNING ROSE.

RAMONCITA LOPEZ SPECIAL   The same as No. 1, with the addition of 1 egg white to each two drinks. Compare SEPTEMBER MORN, and SNOW WHITE.

PINEAPPLE BACARDI   Use either fresh pineapple juice and sugar or pineapple cordial in place of plain sugar.

BANANA BACARDI   Use *Bandana from Havana* in place of sugar.

HAVANA BEACH   Equal parts of fresh pineapple juice and white label rum with ½ a lime and 1 teaspoonful of sugar to each drink.

NACIONAL   Equal parts white label rum and apricot brandy with ½ a lime and 1 teaspoonful of sugar to each drink. Compare the MARY PICKFORD, CUBAN, and TROPICAL.

THE SIDE CAR

This cocktail is the most perfect example I know of a magnificent drink gone wrong. It was invented by a friend of mine at a bar in Paris during World War I and was named after the motorcycle sidecar in which the good captain customarily was driven to and from the little bistro where the drink was born and christened. As originally concocted it contained some six or seven ingredients in place of the three now set forth in practically all recipe books. The simplification of the recipe by reducing the number of ingredients should not, in itself, affect the desirability of the cocktail. Unfortunately, however, the proportions are usually stated as equal parts of lemon juice, Cointreau, and brandy. This may not be a bad formula for a midafternoon drink, but for an apéritif it is simply horrible because of its sickish sweetness.

Essentially the Side Car is nothing but a Daiquiri with brandy in the place of rum and Cointreau in the place of sugar syrup or orgeat. Some Side Car recipes specify lime juice, just as some Daiquiri recipes specify lemon juice. However, to most palates, lemon combines more pleasingly with both brandy and whisky than does lime.

In making our Side Cars for service at home, therefore, let us stick to the same proportions as are used in our Daiquiris as follows:

SIDE CAR DE LUXE
- 1 part Cointreau or Triple Sec
- 2 parts Lemon Juice
- 8 parts Cognac or Armagnac

Shake vigorously with plenty of cracked or crushed ice and strain into chilled cocktail glasses. A twist of lemon may be used if desired and the peel dropped into the glass. Otherwise no decoration.

The same drink may be made with applejack in place of

cognac and, when so made, it is variously known as the *KIDDIE CAR*, the *APPLE CAR*, and the *APPLE-CART*.

THE JACK ROSE

As has previously been mentioned, the principal reason that apple brandy has not gained greater favor with the drinking public is the fact that it is sold before it is well aged. I venture to say that if some enterprising distiller would put out an apple brandy made with the same loving care as cognac and aged in the wood for ten, twenty, or even forty years, it would soon rival grape brandies in popularity, especially for use in mixed drinks.

Of the various applejack cocktails, the Jack Rose is the best known and, apparently, the best liked. Once again, if you will examine a dozen books of cocktail recipes you will find formulas varying all the way from applejack and lemon juice half and half with a few dashes of grenadine to applejack and grenadine half and half with a few drops of lemon juice. But, just as the Side Car is essentially the same type of cocktail as the Daiquiri with different base liquors and sweetening agents, so is the Jack Rose essentially the same as the Side Car with apple brandy used in place of grape brandy and grenadine (primarily for color) used in place of Cointreau. In fact, a Jack Rose is nothing but a Pink Apple Car. Let us, therefore, make it that way, and this is the way:

JACK ROSE DE LUXE
- 1 part Grenadine [6]
- 2 parts Lemon Juice
- 8 parts Apple Brandy

Shake vigorously with plenty of cracked or crushed ice and strain into chilled cocktail glasses. A twist of lemon

---

[6] If you use plain sugar syrup instead of grenadine, you will have an *APPLEJACK SOUR*, also called a *JERSEY SOUR*.

may be used and the peel dropped into the glass if desired. Otherwise no decoration.

A nice touch can be added to this drink by frosting the glasses. Here, however, the rim of the glass should be moistened with grenadine instead of lemon juice before dipping it in the powdered sugar. A good way to do this is to pour a little grenadine in a saucer, dip the rim of the glass, and, still holding the glass mouth down, spin it by the stem to remove any excess liquid. Then dip in powdered sugar.

ROLL YOUR OWN

The bartenders' manual of a half century ago might contain recipes for some two or three hundred drinks, many of which are seldom or never heard of today. In addition to Sours, Rickeys, Fizzes, Punches, Highballs, and Collinses, there were Cobblers and Crustas and Cups; there were Daisies and Fixes and Flips and Groggs; Smashes and Shrubs and Toddies and Noggs; there were Slings and Gaffs and Sangarees; Knickebeins, Shamparelles, and Pousse-Cafés. Out of these several hundred assorted drinks, however, you would find not more than ten or twenty cocktail recipes.

Then along came prohibition and the cocktail really came into its own. Everyone with a bottle of bathtub gin, a basket of fruit, and some icebox leftovers invented a new cocktail. Almost any liquid short of gasoline, added to the liquor of that era, would help conceal its raw alcohol taste and would therefore improve it. Eggs and cream, in particular, smooth out the taste and disguise the alcoholic strength of liquor. And so dawned the day of poultry and dairy cocktails. If Gerald Jones discovered that wild chokecherries steeped in bathtub gin gave it a new flavor, he thereupon invented the Jerry Jounce. If Bill Smith, when given a dose of citrate of magnesia by his doctor, chanced to note its lemon-like flavor, he immediately tried it out with his latest purchase of alleged Scotch and treated his friends to his newly invented Scotch Citrate Sour. How any of us managed to survive the horrors of those fourteen fearful years will ever remain a mystery to me.

Today almost any fair-sized book on mixed drinks contains recipes for anywhere from three hundred to six or seven hundred cocktails. Out of every hundred recipes perhaps three or four will be really good and another half dozen can be made respectable by readjusting proportions. As to the rest, the less said and the sooner they are forgotten, the better. They were conceived in ignorance and born of misunderstanding. They should be allowed to die in peace and quiet.

Yet you yourself—anyone—can invent cocktails, good cocktails, palatable cocktails, delicious cocktails by the dozen—nay, by the hundred. You need no recipe book. All you need is an understanding of a few fundamental principles and a reasonably discriminating taste. No, I don't mean that you must be an expert liquor taster or a connoisseur of vintages and brands. You can tell whether a drink is sweet or dry, can you not? And you can distinguish the flavor of peaches from that of cherries? You wouldn't dream of putting sauerkraut on your ice cream nor of spreading horseradish on your strawberry shortcake? You can tell the taste of quinine from that of mint? That is about all the taste discrimination needed, if you thoroughly understand and rigidly adhere to just a few fundamentals.

RESTATEMENT OF BASIC PRINCIPLES

And at this point, unless your memory of the contents of the first chapter on basic principles is still very clear, it might not be a bad idea to turn back and reread that chapter. In any event, I will restate a few of those principles, then amplify them by giving further details, and finally show their practical application in mixing cocktails without reference to a recipe book. In other words, I shall try to show you how simple it is to "roll your own."

1. *The essential ingredients of a cocktail are (a) the base*

and (b) the modifier. To these two basic ingredients there may also be added special flavoring and coloring ingredients if desired.

2. With few exceptions, the base consists of one or more spirituous liquors such as gin, vodka, rum, whisky, brandy, etc. The base must always comprise upward of 50 per cent of the total volume of the cocktail—usually much more. In the case of cocktails where the modifier consists solely of bitters (such as the Gin Cocktail) or consists of bitters and sugar (such as the Old-Fashioned), the base will constitute practically 100 per cent of the total volume. With Sour-type cocktails, the base will usually average from 80 to 90 per cent of total volume, depending upon whether or not special flavoring and smoothing agents are used and, with cocktails employing an aromatic wine modifier, from 65 to 85 per cent.

3. While there are numerous varieties of modifiers, such as citrus juices, aromatic wines, bitters, cordials, cream, eggs, etc., all but a very few cocktails, irrespective of the liquor employed for a base, can be divided into two types, depending on the modifier used: (a) the aromatic type and (b) the Sour type.

4. The aromatic type of cocktail employs, as a modifier, bitters or one of the various aromatic wines—French vermouth, Italian vermouth, Dubonnet, Byrrh, etc.—or both. Since a dry sherry is sometimes substituted for French vermouth in Martinis and similar cocktails, such cocktails, although not strictly aromatic, may, for the sake of convenience, be grouped with the aromatic type.

5. The Sour type is so named not because it tastes sour but because it is patterned after the various Sours; i.e., it consists of lemon or lime juice, sugar or some other sweetening, and a spirituous liquor. If you will examine practically any book of cocktail recipes you will find that a very large percentage of the recipes are of this type. That is because the citrus juices blend well with all kinds of spirituous liquors

and all kinds of cordials and fruit juices. The vermouths and other aromatic wines, on the other hand, do not blend well with most cordials or other sweetening agents. If the cordial is itself an aromatic liqueur, such as Benedictine, Chartreuse, Van der Hum, or Liqueur Strega, it may be blended with an aromatic wine, but a mixture of aromatic wine with plain fruit flavors such as apricot, peach, maraschino, grenadine, etc., results in a brackish, unpalatable taste. The combination is analogous to sprinkling sage or poultry seasoning (both of which are aromatics) on your raspberry sherbet.

SOURS

Since the overwhelming majority of our cocktails are of the Sour type, let us first learn how to make Sours. Sours are usually served at bars in a Sour or Delmonico glass and are garnished with a cherry, a slice of orange, and sometimes a pineapple stick or a slice of lemon. However, there is no reason why they should not be served (with the decorations or "garbage" omitted) in a cocktail glass.

Most recipe books state their formulas in terms of teaspoonfuls of sugar, juice of a lime, juice of half a lemon, etc.—i.e., in terms of each individual drink. However, for reasons heretofore stated, I assume that the reader will seldom mix less than four cocktails at one time. Accordingly, in giving recipes for drinks to be mixed in a shaker (as distinguished from Highballs and other drinks individually prepared) I shall do so in terms of relative proportions; i.e., so many *parts* of each ingredient, and the same proportions, of course, will apply whether mixing one drink or twenty. Moreover, I greatly prefer the recipe that specifies the quantity or the number of parts of citrus juices to the one that simply says "juice of one lime" or "juice of half a lemon." I have squeezed some lemons that yielded only a scant half ounce of juice and others that yielded nearly two ounces. The same variation will be found in the other citrus fruits. What price, then, "juice of one lemon"?

As has already been stated, a Sour is simply a combination of citrus juice (lemon or lime or both), sugar or other sweetening, and liquor. As with other drinks, the proportions vary all over the map, according to the personal whims and individual taste of the author of the recipe. The bartenders' manual of a half century ago specified for each individual drink ½ tablespoonful sugar, 3 or 4 dashes lemon juice, and 3 to 4 ounces of liquor. Other writers have tried to standardize on "1 sweet, 2 sour, 3 strong." Still others advise as much as 6 parts of lemon juice to 1 part of sugar. And with a variance among professional bartenders ranging all the way from 1 sour and 4 sweet to 1 sweet and 6 sour and all the way from 2 to 8 parts of liquor for each part of combined lemon and sugar, many of these writers still warn the gullible reader that he *must* follow proportions with meticulous accuracy lest the entire drink be ruined!

The truth of the matter is, of course, that that proportion of sweet and sour is best which best pleases the taste of the individual drinker, provided, always, that for the apéritif cocktail the final blend with the liquor base will produce a drink that is dry, not sweet. Just how dry, again, is a question of personal preference, but let it *never* be sweet. This is a matter not of ruining the drink but of ruining the appetite and the digestion.

In the true Sour, served in a tall glass and garnished with fruit, the proportion of citrus juice (particularly where lemon is used) to liquor may properly be quite a bit higher than in the Sour type of cocktail. This is both because the drinker expects, in a Sour, more of the sour taste and lemon flavor than he does in a cocktail and because the fruit with which the drink is decorated to some extent counteracts the acidity of the citrus juice. For the cocktail, and using sugar syrup instead of dry sugar, I have found that for most palates the proportion of 1 sweet, 2 sour, and 8 strong is about right. Experiment with it for yourself. If you find it a bit too sour or a bit too sweet for your individual taste, change the proportions of the citrus juice and sugar accordingly. Using this proportion, however, we arrive at the following recipes for Sours:

GIN SOUR
    1 part Sugar Syrup
    2 parts Lime or Lemon Juice
    8 parts Gin

A dash or two of lime, lemon, or orange bitters to each drink may be added if desired.

Citrus juice and sugar smooth down the raw alcohol taste of white gin much more than does vermouth. Therefore, while yellow gin is a "must" for a perfect Martini, white gin, particularly imported English gin, is satisfactory in Sours and Sour-type cocktails.

RUM SOUR
    1 part Sugar Syrup
    2 parts Lime or Lemon Juice
    8 parts Rum

Now, supposing that we specify lime juice and white Cuban rum, does this recipe sound familiar? Right! The famous Daiquiri. For a Daiquiri, *mes enfants*, is nothing more or less than a Rum Sour!

WHISKY SOUR
    1 part Sugar Syrup
    2 parts Lemon Juice
    8 parts Rye or Bourbon

Two or three dashes of Angostura to each drink constitute a pleasing addition to this drink. Lime juice may be used in place of lemon, but, to most tastes, lemon combines more pleasingly with whisky than does lime. Scotch or Irish may be used in place of rye or bourbon, but the smoky taste of Scotch does not combine pleasingly with citrus juices.

A Whisky Sour without the sugar is sometimes called a *PALMER*.

BRANDY SOUR
- 1 part Sugar Syrup
- 2 parts Lime or Lemon Juice
- 8 parts Cognac or Armagnac

As in the case of the Whisky Sour, lemon juice gives a somewhat more pleasing combination than lime juice.

Does this also sound somewhat familiar? Suppose we stick to lemon juice and substitute Cointreau or Triple Sec for the sugar syrup. What do we have? Right again—the Side Car!

APPLEJACK SOUR
- 1 part Sugar Syrup
- 2 parts Lime or Lemon Juice
- 8 parts Apple Brandy

As in the case of the Whisky and Brandy Sours, lemon is preferable to lime juice.

Now let us once again substitute Triple Sec for the sugar syrup. Result: the *KIDDIE CAR* or *APPLE CAR*.

Or, again, instead of the Triple Sec, substitute grenadine. Result: the *JACK ROSE*.

Do you begin to see how, with just a few fundamental principles and two or three basic formulas, it is simple and easy to produce new cocktails *ad infinitum*? As a matter of fact, the only difficult feat in foisting new cocktails on an unsuspecting public is naming them! That I leave to the lady who, according to tradition, is paid huge sums by the Pullman Company for naming new sleeping cars. I never (well, hardly ever) attempt it.

Any spirituous liquor (but *not* a liqueur) can, of course, be substituted for the gin, rum, whisky, etc., in the above recipes and, with such substitution of the appropriate liquor, you can have a VODKA SOUR, a TEQUILA SOUR, an AQUAVIT SOUR, an APRICOT BRANDY SOUR, a KIRSCH SOUR, and so on—as long as your varieties of spirituous liquors hold out. I suppose you could even have a Slivovitz Sour, though why, I wouldn't know. On second thought, perhaps a bit of lime juice and sugar might tame that otherwise fractious and unbridled liquor down to a point where it could be swallowed without inducing convulsions. I must make a note to try it someday. And I might also try an Eau de Vie de Marc Sour.

Now that we fully understand the general principle of making Sours, let us experiment with a few interesting variations. As we improvise we must always remember that the Sour is the underlying melody. Sometimes the bass will carry the air and sometimes the treble. We may introduce arpeggios, trills, runs, octaves, and other variations; we may play in 2/4, 4/4, 6/8, or even waltz time; we may even syncopate the time; but always one of the Sours will stand out as the theme about which we are extemporizing. And, since gin is the most versatile of all liquors for blending purposes, let us begin with

COCKTAILS BASED ON THE GIN SOUR

During prohibition days it was my good fortune to have to make frequent business trips to what was then the great oasis of the North American desert—Canada. At Montreal I was regularly entertained for luncheon at that magnificent old institution, the St. James Club, and there the standard cocktail was called simply a GIN SOUR. Actually, it was a Gin Sour embellished with egg white—that, and nothing more. It is a splendid drink, smooth, palatable, easy to take, yet dry enough not to dull the appetite. As the first of our variations, therefore, I give you the

MONTREAL GIN SOUR
    1 part Sugar Syrup
    2 parts Lemon Juice

8 parts Gin
1 Egg White to each 2 drinks

Put all ingredients except the gin in the shaker with cracked ice. Shake vigorously until thoroughly blended and creamy. Add ¼ to ½ the gin and combine, then add balance of gin and shake. Strain into chilled cocktail glasses.

You will remember that in the Side Car we substituted Cointreau or Triple Sec for sugar. The same substitution in the Montreal Gin Sour gives us the

WHITE LADY
1 part Cointreau or Triple Sec
2 parts Lemon Juice
8 parts Gin
1 Egg White to each 2 drinks

Follow directions for Montreal Gin Sour. Lime juice, in place of lemon, makes an interesting variation.

The ladies may like this a bit sweeter, in which case you can increase the Cointreau to 2 parts.

One of the best examples I have ever seen of how new cocktails are created occurred when my older daughter returned home after an appendectomy. I set out to mix a White Lady for the good doctor and myself as a fitting celebration of the child's recovery. Unfortunately, however, upon strict search I found myself entirely destitute of Cointreau. I did, nevertheless, have a full bottle of R.O.C. curaçao and this, I decided, would answer in place of the Cointreau. Since the curaçao is orange-colored, I also decided to use a whole egg instead of egg white. And thus was born the

APPENDICITIS
1 part Curaçao

  2 parts Lemon Juice
  8 parts Gin
  1 Whole Egg to each 4 drinks

Follow directions for mixing Montreal Gin Sour but add the gin to the other ingredients in 3 or 4 installments instead of 2.

Since that time I have found that the drink can be still further improved by substituting Grand Marnier for the curaçao and lime for the lemon and using only the white of the egg. I call this the

APPENDICITIS DE LUXE
  1 part Grand Marnier
  2 parts Lime Juice
  8 parts Gin
  1 Egg White to each 2 drinks

Follow directions for mixing the Appendicitis.

Early in the book I spoke in disparaging terms of the Bee's Knees. This, however, was because as it originally came out during prohibition days it consisted of equal parts of lemon juice, honey, and gin. If made as a variation of the standard Gin Sour, merely substituting honey for the sugar syrup, it is acceptable.

BEE'S KNEES
  1 part Honey
  2 parts Lemon Juice
  8 parts Gin

Shake vigorously with cracked ice. The addition of a small amount of orange juice (about 1 to 2 parts) makes an interesting variation.

  The same drink, except for the use of white Cuban rum in place of the gin, is known as the *HONEY-*

SUCKLE. The same drink with Jamaica rum is the *HONEY BEE*. The Honeysuckle is also sometimes called the *AIRMAIL*.

If we substitute maraschino liqueur for the sugar syrup or honey we shall have the

AVIATION
    1 part Maraschino
    2 parts Lemon Juice
    8 parts Gin

Shake vigorously with cracked ice.

The same drink, except for the use of rum in place of the gin, is known as the *BEACHCOMBER*.

An interesting variation of this cocktail is the substitution of maraschino and Cointreau, equal parts, in place of the plain maraschino. Some recipe books list, under the name of *Aviation*, an entirely different drink consisting of equal parts of Dubonnet and sherry.

Now note how small a change can produce a different cocktail—or, at least, a different name.

CASINO
    1 part Maraschino
    1 part Lemon Juice
    1 part Orange Juice
    8 parts Gin

Follow directions for mixing the Aviation.

Here again it should be noted that at least one recipe book lists, under the name of "Casino" a quite different cocktail made with gin, whisky, Cointreau, slivovitz, and Italian vermouth. Horror of horrors!

Another spawn of the prohibition toad that I have already

denounced is the Orange Blossom, consisting of equal parts of gin and orange juice. If, however, this drink is treated as a Sour-type cocktail and made accordingly, it is not too bad. In doing this it must be borne in mind that orange juice is sweeter and less pungent than either lime or lemon juice. Hence, the quantity of sugar must be cut down and that of the citrus juice increased.

ORANGE BLOSSOM

½ part Sugar Syrup
4 parts Orange Juice
8 parts Gin

Shake vigorously with cracked ice. The zest and flavor of this drink may be improved by adding 2 or 3 dashes of lime juice for each drink.

This drink is sometimes incorrectly called the *GIMLET*. Actually the Gimlet is a *GIN RICKEY* and is made with sugar, lime juice, gin, and carbonated water. It is served in a Delmonico or Sour glass. It is also served as a cocktail, omitting the carbonated water.

The Orange Blossom is also sometimes called the *ADIRONDACK* and the *FLORIDA*.

Now let us try one or two cocktails in which a special coloring agent is introduced.

BLUE DEVIL or BLUE MOON

1 part Crème Yvette or Parfait Amour
2 parts Lemon Juice
8 parts Gin

Strain the lemon juice through a cloth or fine mesh strainer to remove as much pulp as possible. Stir ingredients with large ice cubes. This cocktail is sometimes made with the addition of egg white, in which case it can be shaken instead of being stirred and it is not necessary to strain the lemon juice.

In Paris I heard loud praises sung of the *OISEAU BLEU* or *BLUE BIRD*, made with a teaspoonful each of lemon juice and "blue curaçao" to each glass of gin. I have never heard of any such animal as *blue curaçao* and I therefore started investigating. It is merely white curaçao or Triple Sec to which blue vegetable coloring matter has been added.

GREENBACK
   1 part Green Crème de Menthe
   2 parts Lime Juice
   8 parts Gin

Strain the lime juice, as in the case of the Blue Moon, and stir with large ice cubes. As an occasional variation, add three dashes absinthe for each drink.

Now turn back for a moment to the *APPENDICITIS DE LUXE*. If we leave out the egg white and add grenadine we shall have the

RED LION
   ½ part Grand Marnier
   ½ part Grenadine
   2 parts Lime Juice
   8 parts Gin

Shake vigorously with cracked ice.

There are two fairly common gin cocktails of the Sour family employing egg whites, one made with gin only and one with both gin and applejack.

CLOVER CLUB
   1 part Grenadine or Raspberry Syrup
   2 parts Lemon Juice [1]

---

[1] Some recipe books prescribe 1 part each of French and Italian vermouth in addition to the lemon juice. This is incorrect and results in a much inferior cocktail.

1 Egg White to each 2 drinks
8 parts Gin

Follow directions for mixing Montreal Gin Sour. This same cocktail with a small sprig of mint floated on top of the drink is called the CLOVER LEAF.

PINK LADY
1 part Grenadine
2 parts Lemon or Lime Juice
2 parts Apple Brandy
6 parts Gin
1 Egg White to each 2 drinks

Follow directions for mixing Montreal Gin Sour. Compare Opalescent.

And, finally, to conclude our cocktails of the Gin Sour type, here are two that show how easy it is to combine a half dozen or more liqueurs in a cocktail and still produce a dry, palatable, and wholly satisfactory drink, provided the basic proportions of a Sour are maintained. Both of these drinks have always been hailed with enthusiasm when I have served them.

THE SHEIK Mix in a separate shaker or glass equal parts of grenadine, peach, apricot, Cointreau, curaçao, maraschino, and Grand Marnier. Combine in the shaker:
1 part of the above Liqueur mixture
2 parts Lime Juice
1 part Jamaica Rum
7 parts Gin

Shake vigorously with cracked ice and strain into chilled and frosted cocktail glasses.

QUEEN OF SHEBA Same as The Sheik but with the addition of one egg white for each 2 drinks. Shake lime juice, liqueurs, and egg white together before adding

Jamaica rum and gin. Then add these liquors in 2 or 3 installments, shaking after each addition.

These are the recipes for fifteen cocktails all based on the theme of the Gin Sour. For the sake of simplicity and uniformity, I have written all but one on the basis of 1 sweet, 2 sour, 8 strong, but this is by no means an inflexible rule. Taste your cocktail. If you think it a bit too sour, add more sugar or other sweetening; if you think it a bit too sweet, add more lemon or lime juice; if you think the citrus flavor or the liqueur flavor stands out too much, add more gin. You probably will not find any of the above recipes stated in exactly the same proportions in any other book on mixed drinks. For example, I have one book that prescribes equal parts of lime juice and grenadine for the Pink Lady; another specifies ½ ounce lime juice and 4 dashes grenadine; and still another, equal parts of grenadine and applejack with a few dashes of lime juice. There are just three rules that you should follow in mixing your cocktails:

1. *The base of spirituous liquor should always predominate; i.e., it should be a Gin Cocktail, a Rum Cocktail, etc., and not a Sugar Cocktail, a Grenadine Cocktail, a Lemon Cocktail, or an Egg Cocktail.*

2. *It should always be dry, not sweet.*

3. *Within these limitations, it should contain such proportions of the various ingredients as best suit your personal taste or that of your guests for whom you are mixing it. The only merit I claim for the 1-2-8 formula is that I have found, with most cocktails of the Sour type, that is the ratio that seems to be most pleasing to the taste of the greatest number of people.*

COCKTAILS BASED ON THE RUM SOUR

Of course the outstanding cocktail of the Rum Sour type is the Daiquiri, which is a Rum Sour, pure and simple.

I have already described the Daiquiri Grenadine or Pink Daiquiri, using grenadine, and the Daiquiri de Luxe, using orgeat or crème d'ananas. I have also mentioned the fact that falernum may likewise be substituted for the sugar with a resulting flavor somewhat similar to that of the Daiquiri de Luxe. If we substitute equal parts of maraschino and Cointreau in place of the sugar syrup we have the

BEACHCOMBER   See AVIATION recipe.

If we substitute honey we have the

AIRMAIL or HONEY BEE or HONEYSUCKLE   See BEE'S KNEES recipe.

If we add egg white to our Pink Daiquiri we get the

SEPTEMBER MORN
    Slightly less than 1 part Sugar Syrup
    2 parts Lime Juice
    8 parts White Cuban Rum
    2 to 3 dashes Grenadine to each drink
    1 Egg White to each 2 drinks

Blend the egg whites with the sugar, grenadine, and lime juice before adding the rum. Shake vigorously with finely crushed ice and strain into chilled and frosted cocktail glasses.

If, in place of sugar in our Daiquiri, we use curaçao and grenadine and if we substitute lemon for lime juice, we have the

MORNING ROSE
    1 part Curaçao or Cointreau
    2 parts Lemon Juice
    5 parts White Cuban Rum
    2 or 3 dashes Grenadine to each drink

Shake with finely crushed ice and strain into chilled cocktail glasses.

Here is another variation closely similar to the Morning Rose—in fact, I think it is at its best if made exactly according to the Morning Rose formula, merely substituting apricot liqueur for the curaçao or Cointreau. However, the following is the original formula as given me by Herb Smith of the Spanish Room at the Deshler-Wallick Hotel in Columbus, Ohio, one of the best bartenders I have met since prohibition repeal. He takes his profession seriously, really studies his liquors, and really knows them. He takes keen pride in his work and in making your drink exactly as *you* like it. His besetting sin is that, personally, he likes them a bit on the sweet side, which accounts for the somewhat ladylike (and, therefore, insidious) quality of the

MAÑANA
- 1 part Lemon Juice
- 1 part Grenadine
- 2 parts Marie Brizard Apry
- 6 parts White Cuban Rum

Shake and serve like the *MORNING ROSE*. This drink may also be given a rather pleasing quirk by the addition of 1 dash of Boonekamp bitters to each drink. Compare the *CUBAN APRICOT*.

If we add pineapple juice and egg white to our Rum Sour, we have the

SNOW WHITE
- 1 part Sugar Syrup
- 2 parts Lime Juice
- 2 parts Pineapple Juice
- 6 parts White Cuban Rum
- 1 Egg White to each 2 drinks

Follow directions for mixing the *SEPTEMBER MORN*. If fresh pineapple juice is not available, a somewhat similar cocktail (but not so good) can be made by substituting pineapple syrup for the sugar syrup.

Mint blends well with all the spirituous liquors and, when fresh mint is not available, crème de menthe may be used with a somewhat similar effect. Cocktails with a mint flavor are especially well liked on hot summer days. The use of white crème de menthe in place of sugar in a Rum Sour gives us the

MIAMI
- 1 part White Crème de Menthe
- 2 parts Lemon or Lime Juice
- 8 parts White Cuban Rum

Shake with finely crushed ice. The chilled cocktail glasses may be frosted, using crème de menthe to moisten the rim of the glass before dipping it in sugar.

Another version of the Miami uses Cointreau instead of crème de menthe. This, of course, is simply a *RUM SIDE CAR*. Still another version consists of 1 part gin and 2 parts pineapple juice.

An even better mint-flavored summer cocktail is the

MAISON CHARLES (pronounced may-sawn' sharl)
- 1 part Sugar Syrup
- 2 parts Lime Juice
- 8 parts White Cuban Rum
- Fresh Mint

Gently crush a few sprigs of mint in a bar glass, cover with rum, and let it stand for 15 to 30 minutes. Pour this infusion into the shaker with the lime juice and sugar syrup. Shake with finely crushed ice.

Cut a few leaves of mint very fine, being careful not

to use even the fine stems. This may be done with a sharp paring knife or with a parsley cutter. Mix a small quantity of this finely chopped mint with powdered sugar and use for frosting the cocktail glasses.

Chill the glasses, strain the cocktail into them, and sprinkle a very few bits of the chopped mint on top as a final decoration.

The *MADISON AVENUE* is made in the same manner as the Maison Charles except that Cointreau is substituted for the sugar syrup.

Rum, like gin, blends well with many other liquors. Here is a cocktail using a rum and cognac combination as a base.

BOLERO
- 1 part Sugar Syrup
- 2 parts Lime Juice
- 4 parts Gold Label Cuban Rum
- 4 parts Cognac
- 1 teaspoonful Orange Juice to each drink

Shake with finely crushed ice.

Another cocktail employing orange juice illustrates how a slight modification of the Sour formula will give rise to a different drink.

CUBAINE
- 1 part Sugar Syrup
- 1 part Lemon Juice
- 1 part Orange Juice
- 8 parts White Cuban Rum

Shake with finely crushed ice.

All the rums blend perfectly with fruit flavors. Hence any fruit brandy can be used to advantage in combination with rum as a cocktail base. This is especially true of peach and apricot brandies.

CUBAN APRICOT or CUBAN PEACH
    1 part Sugar Syrup
    2 parts Lime Juice
    4 parts White Cuban Rum
    4 parts Apricot Brandy or Peach Brandy

Shake with finely crushed ice. As a pleasing decoration for this drink, dip a small sprig or a fair-sized leaf of mint in one of the liquors, then in powdered sugar, and float this frosted mint on the top of each drink.

Somewhat closely allied to the *SNOW WHITE*, but omitting the egg white, is the

KNICKERBOCKER
    1 part Pineapple & Raspberry Syrups, half & half
    2 parts Lemon & Orange Juice, half & half
    8 parts Rum

Shake with finely crushed ice.

The dozen or so recipes set forth above should give you an idea of what others have done with cocktails based on the Rum Sour. Like gin, rum can be blended with all manner of liqueurs, both aromatic and non-aromatic, and with any and all fruit flavors. The number of different rum cocktails you can turn out is limited only by your ingenuity and your supply of fruit syrups and liqueurs. As I have pointed out before, the corner-drugstore soda fountain can supply you with fruit syrups and your favorite package store with the liqueurs. And one of the minor blessings of cocktail mixing is that the domestic brands of liqueurs, which I would not recommend as after-dinner cordials, are satisfactory for use in cocktails.

As a grand finale to cocktails based on the Rum Sour, I give you one of my favorites which I have named after my favorite community:

LARCHMONT

    ½ part Sugar Syrup
    2 parts Lime Juice
    2 parts Grand Marnier
    6 parts White Cuban Rum

Shake vigorously with crushed or cracked ice and strain into chilled and frosted cocktail glasses. A twist of orange peel may be dropped into each drink for decoration if desired.

After I had invented the Larchmont I discovered that Colonel G. Selmer Fougner had devised a somewhat similar cocktail consisting of 1 part Grand Marnier, 2 parts rum, and just a dash of lime juice which, in honor of his wife, he had named *THE LITTLE ONE*.

Compare also the *APPENDICITIS DE LUXE* and the *RED LION*.

The following cocktail I am including at the insistence of some twenty friends to whom I served it one New Year's Eve. Several of them enthusiastically voted it by far the best cocktail they had ever tasted. It illustrates how easy it is to "roll your own" with whatever materials are at hand. I had originally intended to serve the Larchmont, but I decided to vary the above recipe somewhat because I had just obtained a box of Chinese preserved ginger, a delicacy practically unobtainable during the war years. Now a bit of preserved ginger on a spear is delicious in a rum cocktail, but the flavor blends particularly well with Jamaica rum. I therefore decided to add a dash of Jamaica rum to the cocktail. Falernum has a slight ginger flavor also, so I decided to use falernum in place of sugar syrup. This combination seemed to fit better with a somewhat heavier-bodied rum than straight Cuban white label, and I chanced to have on hand partly used bottles of several "intermediate" rums. These, therefore, went into the mixture. Following is the final result which, in honor of the new year then being ushered in, I named the

FORTY-SEVEN

- 1 part Falernum
- 1 part Grand Marnier
- 4 parts Lime Juice
- 1 part Jamaica Rum
- 1 part Haitian Rum
- 2 parts Barbados Rum
- 1 part White Cuban Rum
- 3 parts Gold Label Cuban Rum

Shake vigorously with cracked ice and strain into chilled cocktail glasses. Decorate with a bit of preserved ginger on a toothpick or spear.

Please note that there is no special merit in the use of five different rums in this drink. The cocktail would be just as good and would taste only slightly different if made with one part Jamaica rum and about six to seven parts Cuban gold label. The sole reason for using five different types instead of two was that several partly used bottles were at hand. Knowing that they would blend satisfactorily, I used them instead of opening fresh bottles of Cuban gold label.

COCKTAILS BASED ON THE WHISKY SOUR

When we leave gin and rum and take up whiskies and brandies we immediately reduce drastically the limit on the number of palatable blends in which we can indulge. Gin and rum (at least the white label Cuban rum) have bland flavors that "marry" with other flavors to produce an entirely new taste that is a perfect blend of the two. Whisky, on the other hand (and, to a somewhat lesser degree, brandy) is a grouchy old bachelor that stubbornly insists on maintaining its own independence and is seldom to be found in a marrying mood. Its flavor refuses to be subdued. When combined with some other liquor the result will frequently be two distinct flavors, possibly antagonistic to one another, instead of a new and pleasing fragrance that is merely subtly suggestive of the two original essences.

Whisky does combine quite well with the aromatic liqueurs such as Benedictine and Chartreuse. It also blends well with orange-flavored liqueurs—curaçao, Grand Marnier, and mandarine. That it can be pleasingly combined with at least some of the other fruit flavors is proved by the fact that Southern Comfort—a peach-flavored bourbon—is such a magnificent and deservedly popular liquor. Nevertheless, when you seek to combine whisky with fruit syrups or liqueurs, proceed with caution. You can substitute almost any kind of fruit syrup or liqueur for the sugar syrup in a gin or rum cocktail with supreme confidence that the mixture will be smooth and pleasing. You just can't do that with either whisky or brandy. If you want to produce some new mixture with one of these liquors as a base, try out a small quantity for yourself first. Don't mix up a shakerful and use your guests as guinea pigs. Bourbon blends with other flavors, particularly non-aromatic flavors, better than rye, and cognac blends better than apple brandy. Also, lemon juice is usually preferable to lime juice in making whisky cocktails. In the following cocktails, unless otherwise specified, "whisky" means either rye or bourbon, but preferably the latter.

BOURBON

- 1 part Benedictine
- 1 part Curaçao
- 2 parts Lemon Juice
- 6 parts Bourbon
- 1 dash Angostura to each drink

Shake with cracked ice.

Note that in the above recipe I have varied materially from the 1-2-8 formula. Whisky fights so strongly for supremacy of flavor in any drink that, in order to bring out the flavor of other ingredients to any appreciable degree, it may frequently be necessary to cut down on the amount of whisky and increase the amount of the other liquors. G. Selmer Fougner, in his famous *Along the Wine Trail* series, recommends a bourbon cocktail consisting of 1 part lemon juice, 1 part bourbon, and 2 parts Benedictine, with dashes only of curaçao and Angostura. This, however, results in a Benedictine, rather than a bourbon, cocktail and contains much too much of the syrupy cordial for a truly dry apéritif.

If we substitute grenadine for sugar in the Whisky Sour and add a bit of orange juice, the result is the famous

WARD EIGHT
- 1 part Grenadine
- 2 parts Lemon Juice
- 1 part Orange Juice
- 8 parts Whisky

Shake with cracked ice.

The Ward Eight is also frequently served in a tall glass with finely crushed ice and a small quantity of carbonated water. When thus served it is decorated with fruits and served with straws. Of course it is then no longer a cocktail.

If we substitute lime for the lemon juice and use a twist of orange peel in place of the orange juice, we have the

NEW YORKER
- 1 part Grenadine
- 2 parts Lime Juice
- 8 parts Whisky

Shake with cracked ice. Drop a twist of orange peel into each glass. A spoonful of claret may be floated on top if desired.

Another drink sometimes called the New Yorker consists of a Medium Manhattan with a few dashes of curaçao and a twist of orange peel.

The New Yorker also is sometimes served as a tall drink with carbonated water and crushed ice, like the Ward Eight. When thus served, it is sometimes made with sugar syrup instead of grenadine and, after it is strained into a glass of crushed ice and the charged water has been added and the drink stirred slightly, a small amount of claret wine is floated on the top.

Some recipes for drinks of the Whisky Sour type omit the lemon or lime juice altogether. Such a cocktail is the

MILLIONAIRE
- 1 part Grenadine or Raspberry Syrup
- 2 parts Curaçao
- 8 parts Whisky
- 1 Egg White to each 2 drinks

Shake the liqueurs and egg white thoroughly with cracked ice first, then add the whisky in 2 or 3 installments, shaking after each addition.

While the above recipe produces a very satisfactory drink, in my opinion it is improved by the addition of a small quantity of lemon juice.

Two or three dashes of absinthe for each drink convert this cocktail into the MILLIONAIRE ROYAL.

At some bars a drink is served under the name of MILLIONAIRE which consists of lime juice, sloe gin, and apricot brandy, with a few dashes of Jamaica rum. Since the sloe gin, which is a liqueur, predominates in this drink, I do not regard it as a true cocktail.

A cocktail which is nothing but a plain Whisky Sour with the addition of orange bitters is the

BUSTER BROWN
- 1 part Sugar Syrup
- 2 parts Lemon Juice
- 8 parts Whisky
- 2 dashes Orange Bitters to each drink

Shake or stir with cracked ice. Stirring will produce a clearer drink, but whenever clarity is sought the lemon juice should be strained through cloth.

A drink in which curaçao only is substituted for sugar syrup is the

CURAÇAO
>   2 parts Curaçao
>   1 part Lemon Juice
>   6 parts Whisky

Shake or stir with cracked ice. Drop a twist of lemon peel into each drink.

Note that in the Curaçao the proportions of sweet and sour have been reversed. This is in order to bring out the flavor of the curaçao. Some recipe books even recommend equal parts of whisky and curaçao, but here again we enter the realm of drinks heavy in sugar and, therefore, not properly apéritif cocktails. Many liqueurs such as curaçao, and more particularly crème de menthe and Grand Marnier, have such a strong, biting flavor that they do not taste sweet. They may be used in substantial quantity in a cocktail and the drink may still taste reasonably dry. The sugar is still there, however, and the effect on the appetite is the same whether the drink *tastes* sweet or not.

A pleasing cocktail in which both curaçao and crème de menthe are used is the

DIXIE
>   2 parts Curaçao
>   1 part Crème de Menthe
>   1 part Lemon Juice
>   6 parts Whisky
>   1 dash Angostura to each drink

Shake or stir with cracked ice.

A very good whisky cocktail using Benedictine in place of sugar is the

FRISCO
- 2 parts Benedictine
- 1 part Lemon Juice
- 6 parts Whisky

Shake or stir with cracked ice. In some recipes the lemon juice is omitted.

By using fresh pineapple juice our Whisky Sour becomes a

PINEAPPLE BLOSSOM
- 1 part Sugar Syrup
- 1 part Lemon Juice
- 2 parts Pineapple Juice
- 6 parts Whisky

Shake with cracked ice. If pineapple juice is not available, substitute 2 parts pineapple syrup for the sugar syrup and pineapple juice.

Compare the JACK IN THE BOX. See also the PINEAPPLE BLOSSOM made with gin.

And here is one using maraschino in place of sugar syrup:

TENNESSEE
- 2 parts Maraschino
- 1 part Lemon Juice
- 6 parts Whisky

Shake with cracked ice.

I do not, by any means, recommend all of the above cocktails of the Whisky Sour type. My own favorite whisky cocktails are the Old-Fashioned and the plain Whisky Sour. For fancy blends with liqueurs give me gin or rum cocktails. However, the ten variations of the Whisky Sour above listed should be sufficient to guide you in "rolling your own" if you want to play around with this type of drink.

COCKTAILS BASED ON THE BRANDY SOUR

By now you ought to be pretty much able to turn out your own Sour-type cocktails blindfolded, in the dark, with your eyes shut, and with your hands tied behind your back. However, since we started out with basic cocktails having five different liquors as their base—gin, rum, whisky, brandy, and applejack—we will "roll" at least a few Sour-type drinks with each of these liquors.

Brandy is a bit easier to combine with other liquors than is whisky, although not so easy as either gin or rum. In general, it may be said that if you can make a certain drink with a whisky base you can make the same drink with a brandy base. The taste, of course, will be different, but I know of no ingredients that can be combined with whisky that cannot be combined at least equally well with brandy.

In speaking of "brandy" I refer to grape brandy and, specifically, to either cognac or armagnac. Other fruit brandies—apple, apricot, peach, cherry, blackberry, raspberry, etc.—are, of course, something else. Delicious drinks of the Sour type can be made with them also, but, as a usual thing, they combine with other flavors in a manner quite different from the grape brandies. A heavy grape brandy, such as the Spanish, Portuguese, Greek, or South African, also produces a result differing widely from that of the cognac and armagnac brandies.

There are at least six or eight different cocktails put out by different bars under the name of the Brandy Cocktail. Some consist of nothing but brandy and bitters, others contain a spot of sugar, still others contain vermouth, or some liqueur, or even absinthe. Here is one that is merely the *CURAÇAO* with brandy substituted for the whisky, plus a dash of bitters:

BRANDY COCKTAIL (SOUR)
- 2 parts Curaçao
- 1 part Lemon Juice
- 8 parts Brandy
- 1 dash Angostura to each drink

Shake or stir with cracked ice. A twist of lemon over each glass. See also BRANDY COCKTAIL (AROMATIC).

A somewhat novel variation of this drink in that it is one of the very few cocktails using port wine is the

BETSY ROSS
- 1 part Curaçao
- 2 parts Port
- 6 parts Brandy (preferably Fundador)
- 1 dash Angostura to each drink

Stir with large cubes of ice. A twist of lemon over each glass.

Another well-known cocktail using port wine is the COFFEE. There are probably as many different recipes for the Coffee Cocktail as there are different brands of coffee on the market. One of these recipes actually calls for coffee. That, however, is a formula that is little known and seldom used. Following is the type of recipe usually found:

COFFEE
- 1 part Sugar Syrup
- 4 parts Port
- 4 parts Brandy
- 1 Whole Egg to each 4 drinks

Shake with cracked ice. Grate nutmeg over top if desired.

Neither the Betsy Ross nor the Coffee Cocktail is a true

Sour, of course. Also, since port—even the driest of the ports—is a rather sweet dessert wine and not of the apéritif type, neither of these drinks—and particularly the Coffee Cocktail—can be regarded as a true apéritif cocktail.

Another of the better-known brandy drinks is the *STINGER*. The usual recipe for this drink calls for brandy and white crème de menthe in equal parts. If green crème de menthe is used it is known as the *EMERALD*. The Emerald with a dash of red pepper added is called the *DEVIL*. Where the half-and-half formula is used the Stinger, like the Coffee, is not a true cocktail. It can, however, easily be transformed into a dry and very palatable cocktail similar to the *MIAMI*, except that brandy is used in place of rum.

DRY STINGER

1 part Lime Juice
2 parts White Crème de Menthe
6 parts Brandy

Shake with finely crushed ice and strain into chilled and frosted glasses.

An excellent variant of the Brandy Sour, using a splendid South African liqueur, is the

SUNDOWNER

1 part Lemon Juice
1 part Orange Juice
2 parts Van der Hum
6 parts Brandy

Shake with cracked ice. The original recipe calls for Cape of Good Hope (South African) brandy to match the Cape of Good Hope Van der Hum. A good cognac or armagnac will do, however. See the *SUNRISE* and the *SUNSHINE*.

Two cocktails that combine brandy with rum are the *BOLERO* and *BETWEEN THE SHEETS*. Gold label rum is rather better in combination with brandy than is white label.

BETWEEN THE SHEETS
   1 part Cointreau or Triple Sec
   2 parts Lime Juice
   3 parts Brandy
   3 parts Cuban Gold Label Rum

Shake with crushed ice. A twist of lemon over each glass.
   This drink is sometimes made with brandy only and sometimes with rum and gin. Also lemon is sometimes used in place of lime. The above is, in my opinion, the best of the many recipes I have seen.

Still another brandy-and-rum combination, but this time with the rum predominating, is called the

NATURAL
   1 part Grenadine
   1 part Orgeat
   2 parts Lemon
   3 parts Brandy
   5 parts Cuban Gold Label Rum

Shake with crushed ice.

A variation of the Side Car in which Chartreuse is used with the Cointreau is called the

KNIGHT
   1 part Cointreau & Chartreuse, half & half
   2 parts Lemon Juice
   8 parts Brandy

Shake with cracked ice.

Still another variation uses strawberry syrup and maraschino for the sweetening agent:

HARMONY
- 1 part Strawberry Syrup & Maraschino, half & half
- 2 parts Lemon Juice
- 8 parts Brandy

Shake with cracked ice.

Another cocktail called the Harmony consists of 1 part Forbidden Fruit, 2 parts lemon juice, 2 parts gold label rum, 4 parts gin, with a dash of grenadine to each drink.

In both the Knight and the Harmony, the lemon juice can be omitted, the liqueurs slightly increased, and a few dashes of orange bitters to each cocktail used in place of the lemon juice.

COCKTAILS BASED ON THE APPLEJACK SOUR

We have seen how honey, fruit syrups, and liqueurs can be substituted for plain sugar in Sour-type cocktails with a wholly new cocktail as a result. Here is one in which maple syrup is substituted. Don't shy away from it. It is not half bad.

APPLEJACK RABBIT
- 1 part Maple Syrup
- 1 part Lemon Juice
- 1 part Orange Juice
- 6 parts Apple Brandy

Shake with cracked ice.

Maple sugar may be used in place of maple syrup but has the same disadvantage that ordinary dry sugar has as compared with a sugar syrup.

This drink is also sometimes, for no reason at all, called the *APPLEJACK DYNAMITE*. The same cocktail made with a gin base plus a dash of Angostura is called the OLD VERMONT.

If you like the Jack Rabbit, try substituting maple syrup for plain sugar syrup in Sours made with other liquor bases.

The ROYAL SMILE is substantially the same cocktail as the PINK LADY, but without the egg white.

ROYAL SMILE
    1 part Grenadine
    2 parts Lemon Juice
    4 parts Gin
    4 parts Apple Brandy

Shake with cracked ice. The relative proportions of gin and applejack can be varied to suit the individual taste. Some recipes call for the addition of 1 egg white to each 2 drinks.

Another Applejack cocktail that, except for the liquor base, resembles the DAIQUIRI DE LUXE is the

SUPREME
    1 part Orgeat
    2 parts Lemon or Lime Juice
    8 parts Apple Brandy
    1 dash Grenadine to each drink

Shake well with cracked ice.

Here is a cocktail which, except for the liquor base, resembles the PINEAPPLE BLOSSOM.

JACK IN THE BOX
    1 part Sugar Syrup
    1 part Lemon or Lime Juice
    2 parts Pineapple Juice
    6 parts Apple Brandy
    1 dash Angostura to each drink

Shake with cracked ice. If fresh, unsweetened pineapple juice is used, either this cocktail or the Pineapple Blossom can be made milder by increasing the quantity of pineapple juice without any serious sacrifice of dryness.

The Jack in the Box is also sometimes called the *JERSEY CITY*. Instead of using lemon juice a strip of lemon peel may be twisted over each glass.

In the *MILLIONAIRE* we found a combination of grenadine and curaçao. Here is one which combines grenadine and Chartreuse:

DEAUVILLE
- 1 part Grenadine or Raspberry Syrup
- 1 part Chartreuse
- 8 parts Apple Brandy
- 1 teaspoonful Lemon Juice to each drink

Shake with cracked ice.

And here is one that combines curaçao and sugar syrup as sweetening agents:

COUNTRY GENTLEMAN
- 1 part Sugar Syrup
- 2 parts Curaçao
- 2 parts Lemon Juice
- 8 parts Apple Brandy

Shake with cracked ice.

Note that the Country Gentleman merely *adds* the curaçao to a plain *APPLEJACK SOUR* without omitting the sugar. With a base liquor as pungent as applejack and with a liqueur as sharp as curaçao (or with any aromatic liqueur such as Benedictine or Chartreuse), such addition may be possible within certain limits without rendering the cocktail too sickish-sweet. With a bland liquor, such as gin or white label rum, and with a heavy fruit liqueur such as peach or apricot, this would be wholly impossible.

The Honeymoon combines curaçao and Benedictine. Benedictine, being an aromatic liqueur, blends particularly well with whisky and apple brandy.

HONEYMOON
- 1 part Curaçao & Benedictine, half & half
- 2 parts Lime Juice
- 8 parts Applejack

Shake with crushed ice. This drink is also sometimes called the *FARMER'S DAUGHTER*.

Applejack can, of course, be combined with other spirituous liquors, as has already been seen. One such cocktail is the *DEPTH BOMB*, in which it is combined with cognac. Whoever named this drink apparently thought it was peculiarly potent, but don't let the name deceive you. It would be exactly as potent—no more and no less—if it were made with either liquor alone.

DEPTH BOMB
- 1 part Grenadine
- 2 parts Lemon Juice
- 4 parts Cognac
- 4 parts Apple Brandy

Shake with cracked ice.

I have already pointed out that the principal reason that apple brandy does not enjoy greater popularity is the fact that it is practically impossible to find any on the market that has been sufficiently aged to develop that mild, bland, delicious taste which characterizes all well-matured liquors. If you are fortunate enough to possess any well-made applejack that has been aged in the wood for even five or six years, but still better eight or ten, you will be reasonably safe in substituting it for cognac in practically any recipe calling for brandy. The flavor of the drink will be different, but it will be equally delightful. You can also use it as a substitute in most whisky drinks.

AROMATIC COCKTAILS

Where the Sour-type cocktail employs citrus juice and sugar or some other sweetening agent as a modifier of the liquor base, the aromatic type employs some aromatic agent such as one of the various bitters (Angostura, Peychaud, orange, Unicum, etc.), or one of the several aromatic wines (French or Italian vermouth, Dubonnet, Byrrh, etc.), or both. Dry sherry is sometimes substituted for an aromatic wine. The aromatics may be used either alone or in conjunction with sugar or some other sweetening agent. Also, at times the modifier may be an aromatic liqueur such as Benedictine or Chartreuse, or a citrus liqueur such as curaçao or Grand Marnier, which, while not truly aromatic, has a somewhat similar effect as a modifier.

As has already been pointed out, there are many more Sour-type cocktails than aromatic-type. This is because any fruit juice or liqueur can be blended with the citrus juices, but extreme caution must be observed in trying to blend them with aromatics. Remember that in your aromatic wines you will find some thirty to forty different roots, leaves, seeds, peels, etc., and that these may include such items as coriander, wormwood, marjoram, camomile, aloes, bitter orange, and even quinine. The aromatic wine will blend with an aromatic liqueur because both are aromatic. *Perhaps* it will blend with a plain-flavored liqueur such as apricot, maraschino, or crème de cacao, but then again perhaps it will not. Also remember that not only must the liqueur and the aromatic wine blend, but the combination must blend with the base liquor. A certain combination may blend satisfactorily with rum but not with whisky or vice versa.

In trying out such combinations the safest method is to mix a small quantity of the aromatic wine and the liqueur and taste the mixture. If this is reasonably palatable, then add a small quantity of the liquor base and taste again. If this mixture is not definitely unpalatable yet is not wholly satisfactory, try varying the quantities of the three types of ingredients. You might also try adding a small quantity of sugar syrup, or a dash of bitters. Or then, again, you might throw the whole mess in the sink and go back to a good old Martini, Daiquiri, or Old-Fashioned. Much will depend on your patience and how anxious you are to bring forth a new drink.

GIN COCKTAILS OF THE AROMATIC TYPE

The outstanding aromatic-type cocktails are made by simply adding a few dashes of bitters to each drink of base liquor and chilling in an Old-Fashioned glass. The bitters should be of the aromatic type—Angostura, Boonekamp, Peychaud, Unicum, etc.—rather than non-aromatic flavoring bitters such as orange, lemon, or lime. Sometimes a small quantity of sugar syrup is used and sometimes a few dashes of an aromatic liqueur. Without any sweetening agent whatsoever the drink is likely to have too strong a taste of the base liquor for most palates, especially those of the ladies. Your real two-fisted drinker, however, may prefer this and may even scoff at the sweetening as producing a sissified drink. *Chacun à son goût*.

Cocktails made by merely adding bitters to the base liquor are usually known by the name of the liquor itself. In the case of the Gin Cocktail, it is also sometimes called (particularly in England) Gin 'n' Bitters. Here it is:

GIN COCKTAIL or *GIN 'N' BITTERS* Put large cubes or cracked ice in an Old-Fashioned glass. Pour in enough House of Lords or Ancient Bottle gin to fill within ⅜" of the top. Add Angostura [2] or other aromatic bitters to taste (about 3 to 5 dashes). Stir and serve with short stir rod or spoon. Twist a strip of lemon peel over drink and drop peel in the glass. A few dashes of curaçao may be added if desired.

Another method of making this drink is to rinse the glass with bitters, shake out the excess, and then fill the glass with iced gin.

The Gin Cocktail is also sometimes served in an ordinary cocktail glass, in which case it is stirred in a bar glass or Martini pitcher and then strained into the glass.

Another good old British standby, especially in her Far Eastern possessions, is the Gin Pahit (pronounced pah-eet'), which is nothing but a Gin Cocktail, sometimes with the addition of absinthe and sometimes without it.

GIN PAHIT

House of Lords or Ancient Bottle Gin
3 dashes Angostura to each drink
2 dashes Absinthe to each drink

Stir with large cubes of ice. Add a twist of lemon to each drink. If desired, a spoonful of curaçao or Chartreuse may be floated on top of each drink.

GIN 'N' SIN Straight gin with 1 teaspoonful lemon juice, 1 teaspoonful orange juice, and a dash of grenadine to each drink.

This, of course, is a Sour- rather than an aromatic-type cocktail. It is shown here merely to bring together all the various "gin-and" drinks.

While on the subject of His Britannic Majesty's gin drinks, mention may be made of two others that have been cele-

---

[2] If Angostura bitters are used, this cocktail is frequently referred to as PINK GIN and, if orange bitters are used, as YELLOW GIN.

brated in song and story. One—Gin 'n' It—is nothing but a Sweet Martini, and the other—*GIN 'N' TONIC*—is not a cocktail but a long, cooling drink. It is referred to here, however, in order to keep it with its compatriots under the Union Jack.

GIN 'N' IT
   1 part Italian Vermouth
   3 parts Gin

Stir and serve in cocktail glass or mix in Old-Fashioned glass, following directions for Gin 'n' Bitters.

In Europe the proportions used are half and half and the drink is not iced.

There is another member of the "gin-and" family which has recently attained a certain amount of popularity with real gin lovers and that is

GIN 'N' ROCKS   Pour straight gin over ice cubes in an Old-Fashioned glass. Add a twist of lemon if desired, stir, and serve.

This, of course, is merely straight gin, iced, and, since the drink contains no modifying agent (particularly if the twist of lemon is omitted), it does not strictly conform to our definition of a cocktail. Nevertheless, cocktail or no cocktail, it does meet the requirements of a pre-prandial apéritif and, if made with a mellow yellow gin, it is, at least in the writer's opinion, infinitely superior to the usual wishy-washy bar Martini. It must be remembered that, unlike whisky, rum, and the various grape and other fruit brandies, gin is, itself, a highly aromatic liquor. The addition of further aromatics to produce a cocktail is therefore, to some extent, like carrying coals to Newcastle. There is substantial merit in the claim of the House of Seagram that their Ancient Bottle gin "is almost a Martini in itself."

The perfect aromatic gin cocktail, of course, is the *MARTINI*. Reference was made in discussing the Martini to the fact that the drink might be occasionally varied by the addition of absinthe or Chartreuse or curaçao. The *MEDIUM MARTINI* (or so-called "Perfect") with a dash of absinthe is called the

BALD HEAD
- 1 part French Vermouth
- 1 part Italian Vermouth
- 4 parts Gin
- 1 or 2 dashes Absinthe to each drink

Stir with large cubes of ice. Twist lemon peel over the drink. Decorate with a stuffed olive.

Note that the Bald Head is nothing but a Medium Martini with a dash of absinthe.

The same cocktail with anisette in place of absinthe and with a small amount of fruit juices is known as the

BEAUX ARTS
- 1 part French Vermouth
- 1 part Italian Vermouth
- 1 part Orange & Pineapple Juice, half & half
- 6 parts Gin
- 1 dash Anisette to each drink

Since the fruit juices will prevent a clear drink in any event, this cocktail may be shaken.

Another version of this drink calls for grapefruit juice instead of orange and pineapple and for applejack instead of gin.

Just to illustrate how simple it is to "roll your own" and how slight a variation of a standard formula will produce a "new" and different cocktail, here is the essence of a dozen or more cocktails taken at random from various recipe books and all based on the Martini. Different recipe books will set forth varying proportions of the several ingredients, but, in substance, this is what these cocktails are. You can try them and vary the proportions, as previously indicated, to suit your own taste.

ALLIES Dry Martini with 2 dashes kümmel to each drink. Stir.

DEEP SEA Dry Martini with a dash of anisette to each drink. Stir.

GLOOM CHASER or *GLOOM RAISER* Dry Martini with 2 dashes absinthe and 2 dashes grenadine to each drink. Stir. Compare the *INTERNATIONAL*. Another version of the Gloom Chaser consists of a Daiquiri with curaçao substituted for the sugar.

PARISIAN Dry Martini with 2 or 3 dashes crème de cassis to each drink. Stir.

Another version of the Parisian consists of 1 part lime juice to 3 or 4 parts Dubonnet. Stir.

HONG KONG Dry Martini with 1 spoon sugar syrup, 1 spoon lime juice, and 1 dash Angostura bitters to each drink. Stir.

YALE Gin Cocktail with 1 dash orange bitters and 1 dash absinthe to each drink. Stir.

YALE FENCE
- 1 part Italian Vermouth
- 1 part Applejack
- 1 part Gin

Stir. A twist of lemon over each drink.

COOPERSTOWN Medium Martini with a sprig of mint to each drink bruised and stirred with the cocktail. A twist of lemon over each drink.

BOOMERANG   Medium Martini with a dash of Angostura and 2 dashes maraschino to each drink. Stir. A twist of lemon over each drink.

LAMBS' CLUB   Medium Martini with 2 or 3 dashes Benedictine to each drink. Stir. A twist of lemon over each drink.

PLAZA   Medium Martini with 1 teaspoonful pineapple juice to each drink. Shake.

AMBER DREAM   Sweet Martini with 1 dash orange bitters and 3 or 4 dashes Chartreuse to each drink. Shake. Also called the *BIJOU* and the *GOLDEN GLOW*.

GREENBRIER   Sweet Martini with a sprig of mint to each drink. Prepare like the *COOPERSTOWN*, above.

BARRY   Sweet Manhattan with a dash of white crème de menthe to each drink. Stir.

LONE TREE   Sweet Martini with 1 dash lemon juice to each drink. Shake.

MAXIM   Sweet Martini with 1 to 2 dashes crème de cacao to each drink. Shake.

There is one old standby among the gin cocktails of the aromatic type that has more or less fallen into disrepute since prohibition, and that is the Bronx. There are few cocktails the recipes for which differ as widely as this one. Some books recommend dry vermouth, some sweet vermouth, and some both. Some specify equal parts of vermouth and orange juice and some provide only for a slice of orange peel shaken with the cocktail or a slice of orange dunked in each glass. You can try out various proportions and modifications for yourself. At the best, however, you will be able to produce only a fairly good cocktail—nothing to brag or write home about. Here is a fairly good formula for the drink:

BRONX
- 1 part French Vermouth
- 1 part Italian Vermouth
- 1 part Orange Juice
- 6 parts Yellow Gin

Shake with cracked ice. Drop a twist of orange peel into each glass.

This cocktail is sometimes called the *MECCA*. With 2 parts orange juice instead of 1 and with the French vermouth omitted, it is sometimes called the *ABBEY*.

Following are two variations of this drink:

SILVER BRONX
- 1 part Orange Juice
- 2 parts Italian Vermouth
- 6 parts Gin
- 1 Egg White to each 2 drinks

Shake ingredients other than gin with cracked ice and add gin in 2 or 3 installments, shaking after each addition.

This cocktail is sometimes erroneously called the *BROOKLYN*. See index for the true Brooklyn.

PINEAPPLE BRONX
- 1 part Italian Vermouth
- 1 part Pineapple Juice
- 6 parts Gin

Shake with cracked ice.

RUM COCKTAILS OF THE AROMATIC TYPE

The leading rum cocktail of the aromatic type is *EL PRESIDENTE*. Gold label rum is somewhat more pleasing than white label when combined with vermouth and is therefore used in this and many other aromatic-type cocktails. Not satisfied with one President, the rum hounds have concocted two, one Cuban and one American.

EL PRESIDENTE (*Cuban*)
    1 part French Vermouth
    3 parts Gold Label Rum
    1 dash Grenadine to each drink

Stir with large cubes of ice. Drop a twist of orange peel in each glass. Sometimes also decorated with a cherry. This recipe may be varied by adding 1 or 2 dashes of curaçao to each drink.

EL PRESIDENTE (*American*)
    1 part French Vermouth
    1 part Lemon Juice
    3 parts Gold Label Rum
    1 dash Grenadine & 1 dash Curaçao to each drink

Shake with cracked ice and decorate same as the Cuban President.

The manufacturers of Havana Club, one of the finest of Cuban rums, recommend the use of sweet vermouth instead of dry, thereby making the drink a *RUM MANHATTAN*. The recipe suggested by them, however, is much too sweet. Here is a modification:

HAVANA CLUB
    1 part Italian Vermouth
    3 parts Havana Club Gold Label Rum

Stir with large cubes of ice. Decorate with a cherry. This drink is improved by adding 1 dash Angostura to each drink.

If sherry is used in place of vermouth in the American President, the cocktail becomes the

HAVANA
> 1 part Sherry
> 3 parts Gold Label Rum
> 3 or 4 dashes Lemon Juice to each drink

Shake well with cracked ice. Decorate with a twist of orange peel.

Another cocktail, made of 1 part pineapple juice, 2 to 3 parts white label rum, with a dash each of grenadine and maraschino, is sometimes incorrectly called the Havana. The correct name for this drink is the *MARY PICKFORD*.

Of course, as with all the other base liquors, the wines, citrus juices, and liqueurs may be omitted altogether and the plain rum (preferably gold label) served with a spoonful of sugar syrup and a dash of Angostura. This drink is called by either of two names:

RUM COCKTAIL or RUM OLD-FASHIONED
Mix exactly the same as the *OLD-FASHIONED* but using gold label rum instead of whisky.

The Rum Cocktail is sometimes stirred in a bar glass or pitcher and served in cocktail glasses instead of in Old-Fashioned glasses. If made with a dash of orange bitters in addition to the dash of Angostura and served in a cocktail glass with a twist of orange peel it is sometimes called *MAMMY BOY*.

There is just one other rum cocktail of the aromatic type which may be worth mentioning. Actually it is merely a *RUM BRONX*. However, it is sometimes called the

THIRD RAIL
> 1 part French Vermouth
> 1 part Italian Vermouth
> 1 part Orange Juice
> 6 parts Gold Label Rum

Shake well with cracked ice. Decorate with a twist of orange peel. Some recipes call for gin instead of rum and, of course, the drink then becomes a *BRONX*, pure and simple.

I doubt that you will care much for any of the aromatic rum cocktails—at least I don't. Sour-type rum cocktails can be magnificent, but I'll take my Martinis with gin and my Manhattans and Old-Fashioneds with whisky. You can have the Presidentes, the Havana Clubs, and the Third Rails if you want them. The above examples, however, will show you how this type is made. And remember, for the Sour type use white label rum; for the aromatic type, use gold label.

WHISKY COCKTAILS OF THE AROMATIC TYPE

The outstanding aromatic whisky cocktails, of course, are the *MANHATTAN* and the *OLD-FASHIONED*. As noted under the recipes for these drinks, interesting variations of both may be had by the addition of a dash of curaçao or any aromatic liqueur. To go any farther in seeking to modify either of these two magnificent drinks strikes me as an attempt to gild the lily. However, boys will be boys, mixers will mix, and inventors will invent. Accordingly, I shall list a few of the many dozens of aromatic-type cocktails that various people have from time to time concocted with a whisky base. First, however, let me point out that, just as we have a Gin Cocktail and a Rum Cocktail consisting of the base liquor with bitters, so, too, we have the

WHISKY COCKTAIL [3] Made exactly like the *GIN COCKTAIL* except that whisky is used in place of gin.

---

[3] In all logic it would seem that a bourbon cocktail should be a whisky cocktail made with bourbon. This name, however, has been given to a cocktail of the Sour type. See recipe for the *BOURBON*.

With the addition of sugar, this cocktail becomes the *OLD-FASHIONED*. Some recipes prescribe both Angostura and orange bitters. Some also prescribe a dash of gin, but why, heaven only knows. When made with the two types of bitters, this cocktail is sometimes called the *COUNTRY CLUB*.

A modified Old-Fashioned is made with Fernet-Branca, a bitters particularly well-loved by Italians, and is called

TORONTO
  1 part Sugar Syrup
  2 parts Fernet-Branca
  6 parts Canadian Whisky
  1 dash Angostura to each drink (optional)

This cocktail may be made in Old-Fashioned glasses or may be stirred with large cubes of ice and strained into cocktail glasses. In either case, decorate with a twist of orange peel.

One variation of the Manhattan employs orange juice and Chartreuse and is known by two different names:

BARBARY COAST [4] or BISHOP [5]
  1 part Orange Juice
  1 part Italian Vermouth
  4 parts Whisky
  1 dash Chartreuse (Yellow) to each drink

Shake with cracked ice and decorate with a twist of orange peel.

[4] Another cocktail sometimes called the *BARBARY COAST* is made with 1 part crème de cacao, 2 parts gin, and 2 parts Scotch with a tablespoonful of sweet cream to each drink. Shake with cracked ice.
[5] Another cocktail sometimes called the *BISHOP* is, in effect, a Daiquiri but with 2 parts rum and 1 part claret in place of straight rum.

A cocktail quite similar to the Toronto except that it employs Amer Picon in place of Fernet-Branca is the

NEW DEAL
- 1 part Sugar Syrup
- 2 parts Amer Picon
- 6 parts Whisky

Follow directions for mixing the TORONTO.

The Lafayette is, in effect, a Medium Manhattan with Dubonnet substituted for the Italian vermouth.

LAFAYETTE
- 1 part French Vermouth
- 1 part Dubonnet
- 6 parts Whisky
- 1 dash Angostura to each drink

Stir with large cubes of ice. This cocktail is sometimes served à la Old-Fashioned.

If we substitute lime juice for the Dubonnet we have the Westchester Special. This is a *very* dry cocktail. I have already said that French vermouth does not blend as well with whisky as Italian vermouth, nor lime juice as well as lemon. Yet here is a cocktail that uses both French vermouth and lime juice and, at the Westchester Country Club at least, it seems to be reasonably popular. I know better cocktails, but I must admit it is not bad.

WESTCHESTER SPECIAL
- 1 part Lime Juice
- 1 part French Vermouth
- 4 parts Bourbon

Shake well with cracked ice.

THE FINE ART OF MIXING DRINKS 183

Every borough of Greater New York has to have its special cocktail. You have had the Manhattan and the Bronx. Here is the

BROOKLYN
- 1 part French Vermouth
- 3 parts Whisky
- 1 dash Maraschino to each drink
- 1 dash Amer Picon to each drink

Stir with large cubes of ice. If you do not have Amer Picon, you can substitute Angostura.

You will note that the Brooklyn is nothing but a Dry Manhattan with a dash of maraschino. It is supposed to be a specialty of that grand old Brooklyn hotel, the St. George. I would be willing to wager, however, that even in Brooklyn there are at least five to ten times as many Manhattans consumed as there are Brooklyns. Try both and you will understand why. Note that the *SILVER BRONX* is also sometimes called the Brooklyn.

Here are a few more concoctions selected at random, all constituting merely minor variations on the theme of one of the Manhattans:

SIDNEY or *ST. MORITZ* Dry Manhattan with 1 dash orange bitters and 2 or 3 dashes Chartreuse to each drink. Stir. At the St. Moritz Hotel this drink is served in Old-Fashioned glasses. Some recipes call for equal parts of Chartreuse and French vermouth.

NEW ALGONQUIN Dry Manhattan with the addition of the same quantity of pineapple juice as that of the French vermouth and 1 dash of Angostura to each drink. Shake.

BOULEVARD Dry Manhattan with 2 or 3 dashes of Grand Marnier to each drink. Use orange bitters, not Angostura.

A different version of this drink consists of a Medium Martini with a few dashes of grapefruit juice.

MARIANNE Medium Manhattan but with Byrrh substituted for the Italian vermouth. Stir.

Compare the Lafayette above, in which Dubonnet is used in place of Italian vermouth.

CHERBOURG This is a Medium Manhattan, pure and simple—1 part French vermouth, 1 part Italian vermouth, and 6 parts whisky—with a dash of Angostura and a dash of lemon juice to each drink. Shake.

CAPITOL Sweet Manhattan with a dash of Angostura and 1 or 2 dashes of Cointreau to each drink. Stir.

SHEEPSHEAD BAY Sweet Manhattan with a dash of Angostura and 2 or 3 dashes of Benedictine to each drink. Stir.

SHAMROCK Sweet Manhattan with a dash of Angostura and a teaspoonful of green crème de menthe to each drink. Shake.

Another version of this drink consists of 1 part green crème de menthe to 2 or 3 parts gin with a teaspoonful each of lemon and orange juice and 1 egg white to each 2 drinks.

HAWTHORNE Sweet Manhattan made with equal parts Italian vermouth and Dubonnet in place of the straight Italian vermouth. 1 dash curaçao to each drink. Stir.

UPTOWN MANHATTAN Sweet Manhattan with the addition of about half as much lemon juice as Italian vermouth. One dash Angostura to each drink. Shake or stir.

PICCADILLY Uptown Manhattan with a dash of Angostura and 2 or 3 dashes of kümmel to each drink.

HABITANT Sweet Martini with the addition of as

much maple syrup as Italian vermouth. Two dashes Angostura to each drink. Stir or shake.

This is a specialty of the Canadian Club of New York City. It can be improved upon by cutting down somewhat on the maple syrup and adding a few dashes of lemon juice.

Compare the *APPLEJACK RABBIT* and the *OLD VERMONT*.

To conclude our experimentation with whisky cocktails of the aromatic type, let us consider the *SAZERAC*, widely advertised as the drink that made New Orleans famous. This is one of the numerous drinks whose precise formula is supposed to be a deep dark secret. Somehow, the gullibility of human nature is such that the two things that seem to afford the greatest advertising value to a drink are (1) a secret formula shrouded in great mystery, and (2) the slogan "Only two to a customer."

There have been many recipes published purporting to be the true and original Sazerac. I cannot vouch for the authenticity of any of them, especially since the Sazerac Company of New Orleans still claims that its drink (which, incidentally, is sold bottled as a ready-mixed cocktail) is made from a formula that has been in use for more than a hundred years and never made public. Nevertheless, anyone at all familiar with liquors who has ever tasted this drink knows that essentially it is merely an Old-Fashioned made with Peychaud bitters instead of Angostura and flavored with a dash of absinthe. Traditionally, the Sazerac, like the Old-Fashioned, is made by first saturating a lump of sugar with bitters and then muddling it. In the interest of simplicity and better drinks, however, we have abandoned loaf sugar in favor of sugar syrup. We shall therefore make our Sazerac in this manner:

SAZERAC Fill small Old-Fashioned glasses with finely crushed ice and set aside to chill. Put into pre-chilled bar glass or pitcher for each drink:

1 tsp. Sugar Syrup
3 dashes Peychaud Bitters
2 to 2½ ounces Whisky

Stir with large ice cubes until thoroughly chilled. Empty the Old-Fashioned glasses. Put 1 dash absinthe in each glass and twirl glasses until inside is thoroughly rinsed with the absinthe, throwing out any excess liquid. Strain liquor into the chilled and rinsed glasses. Twist a strip of lemon peel over each drink and drop into glass for decoration. Serve with a glass of ice water on the side as a chaser.

The Sazerac is a sharp, pungent, thoroughly dry cocktail. To most people, however, the combination of absinthe and whisky is not particularly pleasing. Whisky lovers do not like the sharp, biting taste that the absinthe imparts. Absinthe lovers prefer their absinthe straight, dripped, frappéed, or mixed with gin rather than whisky. Even among my various New Orleans friends I have yet to find a Sazerac addict. Nevertheless, various hotels, clubs, and other bars have created simplified Sazerac-type cocktails— drinks with pretty much the same flavor as the Sazerac but which can be made with much less fuss and loss of time. Here is one that is typical of all of this group:

WEYLIN or *LOTUS CLUB SPECIAL* Dissolve a lump of sugar with a few dashes of Peychaud or Angostura bitters and muddle in a bar glass. Add a dash or two of absinthe and a drink of rye or bourbon. Stir and serve in an Old-Fashioned glass, adding a twist of lemon to the finished drink.

SCOTCH COCKTAILS OF THE AROMATIC TYPE

Thus far all the whisky cocktails we have discussed have been made with either bourbon or rye. Just why anyone should want to make a cocktail with Scotch I wouldn't know, any more than I can understand why anyone should want to kill the exquisite bouquet of a good champagne by blending it with sugar, Angostura, and lemon and calling it a champagne cocktail. However, there are Scotch cocktails, most of them of the aromatic type, and this is probably as good a time as any to mention a few.

The simplest of all Scotch cocktails, of course, is the

SCOTCH COCKTAIL [6] Made exactly like the GIN COCKTAIL but with Scotch in place of the gin.

This drink is greatly improved by the addition of 1 teaspoonful of sugar syrup to each drink. When so made, it was dubbed by Colonel G. Selmer Fougner, of *Wine Trail* fame, THE JOHN McCLAIN. It is also sometimes called the LOCH LOMOND.

Of all the Scotch cocktails sold, probably nine out of every ten are either Scotch Old-Fashioneds or Scotch Manhattans. The Scotch Manhattan, however, has been given a special name—the Rob Roy. Here they both are:

SCOTCH OLD-FASHIONED [6] Made exactly like the Old-Fashioned but with Scotch in place of rye or bourbon.

ROB ROY [6] Made exactly like the Manhattan but with Scotch in place of rye or bourbon.

If orange bitters are used instead of Angostura, this drink is sometimes called the HIGHLAND, or the HIGHLAND FLING, or the EXPRESS. An interesting variation of the Rob Roy is the

BOBBIE BURNS [6] Rob Roy with the addition of 1 dash of Drambuie for each drink. Benedictine is sometimes

---

[6] An interesting variation of these drinks may be obtained by substituting Peychaud bitters for the Angostura. Peychaud, somehow, seems to blend better than Angostura with the Scotch.

used in place of Drambuie. However, the Drambuie is preferable because it is made with a Scotch whisky base.

Some lost or misguided soul with nothing better to occupy his time has even devised the Scotch Sazerac but without the elaborate work involved in the original Sazerac. For whatever it may be worth (which is not much), here it is:

SCOTCH SAZERAC
    1 part Italian Vermouth
    6 to 10 parts Scotch (according to taste)
    1 dash Absinthe to each drink

Stir with large cubes of ice.

The above are all modifications of the Sweet Manhattan, using Scotch whisky. Other Scotch cocktails are based on the Dry and Medium Manhattan formulas. Here are a few:

AFFINITY This is simply a Medium Manhattan but with Scotch in place of rye or bourbon.

BEADLESTON A Dry Manhattan but with Scotch in place of rye or bourbon.
    If the vermouth is reduced to a few dashes to each drink, this drink is sometimes called the *BLUE BELL*.
    If, in place of Angostura in the Blue Bell, a dash of orange bitters and a dash of Cointreau are substituted, the drink is sometimes called GREEN BRIAR. Compare GREENBRIER.

Another variation of the Dry Scotch Manhattan is the

TRINITY A Dry Manhattan, using Scotch whisky with a dash of orange bitters, a dash of apricot, and a dash of white crème de menthe to each drink.

The Scotch Manhattans are sometimes varied by the addition of lemon or lime juice. These variations, too, have been named as follows:

HOLE IN ONE   A Dry Scotch Manhattan with a dash of orange bitters and a dash of lemon juice to each drink.

CHURCHILL   A Sweet Scotch Manhattan with a dash of lime juice and a dash of Cointreau to each drink.

If you particularly like Scotch and you want to play with Scotch cocktails, I suggest that you start by combining the liquor in varying proportions, first with French vermouth, then with Italian, and ascertain which combination you prefer. Then try varying this mixture by adding a dash of different aromatic liqueurs, but be extremely wary of using sweet fruit liqueurs such as maraschino, apricot, peach, etc. Drambuie blends perfectly with Scotch. Van der Hum, Benedictine, Chartreuse, and a few others blend reasonably well. If your blend seems to lack character and piquancy, try adding a dash of lemon juice. Sometimes, too, a mere change in the bitters used will change the entire character of the drink. If you are careful and have sufficient patience, you will probably succeed in evolving a few mixtures that are at least reasonably palatable. I doubt that you will ever find any Scotch combination that is really outstanding or is a substantial improvement upon the plain Scotch Manhattan or plain Scotch 'n' Bitters.

BRANDY COCKTAILS OF THE AROMATIC TYPE

Here again, as with gin, rum, and whisky, the standard *BRANDY COCKTAIL* consists simply of brandy and bitters. There are, however, numerous varieties. Most of the recipes for the Brandy Cocktail employ either sugar or some liqueur even where lemon is not used, and this, if the amount of the sweet is kept down to a few dashes, makes an excellent drink. It should scarcely be necessary to point out that a really delightful drink will result only from the use of a well-aged cognac or armagnac. Here is a typical recipe *without* any citrus juice:

BRANDY COCKTAIL To each drink (2 ounces) of cognac in the bar glass or pitcher add 3 dashes (½ teaspoonful) sugar syrup and 1 dash Angostura. Stir with large cubes of ice. A twist of lemon peel over each glass. It is, of course, simply a BRANDY OLD-FASHIONED.

This may be varied by adding for each drink 1 or 2 dashes of curaçao, maraschino, or Benedictine.

During World War I, Japan was an ally of the United States and not an enemy. Presumably it must have been around that time that someone named a very satisfactory cocktail the

JAPANESE
 1 part Orgeat
 8 parts Cognac
 1 dash Angostura to each drink

Stir with cracked ice.

As with the various aromatic whisky cocktails, many of the brandy cocktails are simply variations of one or another of the three types of Manhattans, but with cognac substituted for rye or bourbon.

DELMONICO This is a plain Manhattan with cognac substituted for the whisky. If orange bitters are used instead of Angostura, it becomes a HARVARD.

This is also sometimes called a SARATOGA. The real Saratoga, however, is made with apple brandy. There is also a DELMONICO SPECIAL which is merely a Medium Martini with 1 teaspoonful of brandy to each drink and a twist of orange peel.

ANNIVERSARY Also the Manhattan type but with equal parts of gin and cognac in place of the whisky and with 2 dashes of orange bitters to each drink in place of Angostura.

If French vermouth is used in place of Italian vermouth, this cocktail becomes a *BERMUDA*. There are also two other cocktails called the Bermuda. One is a plain Rum Sour with a dash of Angostura. The other is made with gin and peach or apricot brandy in place of cognac, and with a dash of grenadine. This latter is also called *BERMUDA ROSE*.

Another interesting cocktail that is one of the very few in which port wine is used is the

MONTANA
    1 part French Vermouth
    1 part Port Wine
    4 parts Cognac

Stir with large cubes of ice.

Here is a combination aromatic and Sour type:

COURTNEY RILEY COOPER
    1 part Cointreau
    1 part Lime Juice
    1 part Dubonnet
    4 parts Cognac

Shake well with cracked ice.

BOMBAY This is made like a Medium Manhattan with 2 or 3 dashes of curaçao to each drink and, of course, with cognac instead of whisky. Some recipes also call for a dash of anisette. Stir with cracked ice.

METROPOLITAN Made like a Dry Manhattan but

with cognac. Add 2 or 3 dashes of sugar syrup and the same amount of Angostura for each drink.

A cocktail something like *SLOPPY JOE'S* in that it uses pineapple juice in conjunction with cognac is the

EAST INDIA
- 1 part Curaçao
- 1 part Pineapple Juice
- 8 parts Cognac
- 1 or 2 dashes Angostura to each drink

Shake well with cracked ice. Decorate with a cherry and a twist of lemon. Maraschino may be substituted for the pineapple juice.

Thus far I have not mentioned any of the *SMASHES*, that is, drinks flavored with crushed mint. Ye olde-tyme bartenders' manuals featured Smashes as drinks served in a large glass filled with crushed ice and decorated with every conceivable kind of fruit. On the other hand, the flavor of mint "marries" satisfactorily with practically any spirituous liquor, and there is no reason why a Smash cannot be served in an Old-Fashioned or other small glass as a cocktail. A Brandy Smash makes an excellent cocktail. Compare the *MAISON CHARLES* and the *MADISON AVENUE*, both made with rum.

I have repeatedly pointed out that I by no means recommend all of the various recipes contained in this book. I am setting forth the recipes primarily to show you how simple it is to flit from cocktail to cocktail and, by observing a very few fundamental principles, to reach down into your supply closet at any time and bring up a new drink by just a simple twist of the wrist and without the use of mirrors. Only one out of many will be a real masterpiece. Once in a while, despite the greatest care, you will come out with a complete flop. But you can always be cheered by the thought that, blunder along as you may, you will find it difficult, if not impossible, to concoct anything worse than some of the unholy messes to be found in almost any recipe book.

For the most part, I have tried to tame down the recipes in this book where possible, to bring them within at least a reasonable approximation of my definition of an apéritif cocktail. For example, see the *BEE'S KNEES* and the *ORANGE BLOSSOM*. In some cases the effort to do this scarcely seemed worth while and I have simply set forth the proportions more or less commonly recommended and employed because, after all, I expect you to "roll your own," and all these recipes are merely to show you what others have done and how they have done it—be the results good, bad, or indifferent.

I have already expressed my opinion both of the *ALEXANDER* and of the *CHAMPAGNE COCKTAIL*. Despite all I have said, however, maybe you will like them and, if you do, here are prototypes of both in which brandy is used.

CHICAGO In a bar glass containing 1 or 2 large cubes of cracked ice, stir 1 jigger cognac with 1 dash Angostura and 2 or 3 dashes curaçao. Strain into a chilled and frosted cocktail or saucer champagne glass and fill the glass with champagne.

Compare the *MAHARAJAH'S BURRA PEG*.

PANAMA
- 1 part Sweet Cream
- 1 part Crème de Cacao
- 3 to 4 parts Cognac

Shake vigorously with cracked or crushed ice.

The Panama, of course, is not an aromatic-type cocktail. I have put it here alongside the Chicago because both of them seem to me to represent such a futile waste of good liquor. The Panama is merely a *BRANDY ALEXANDER* with cognac substituted for the gin. The original Alexander recipe calls for equal parts of the three ingredients. I have tried to cut down on the sugar bowl and cream pitcher sufficiently to make the drink halfway fit to introduce to the stomach as a prelude to the meal. As a dessert rather than an apéritif the original formula is excellent.

APPLEJACK COCKTAILS OF THE AROMATIC TYPE

The whole subject of applejack cocktails might be summed up by saying that if you can get a well-made, thoroughly matured apple brandy (let us say at least six to eight years old) you can safely use it in place of grape brandy in any brandy drink. The flavor, of course, will differ from that of cognac but only as the flavor of bourbon differs from that of rye. You may like one better than the other, just as you have a preference between strawberries and raspberries or between oysters and clams, but, except for taste preferences, the one should make just as fine a drink as the other. And, by the same token, if you cannot get an apple brandy that is well made and well aged, you cannot make good applejack drinks any more than you could make good drinks with bathtub gin or with "White Mule" fresh from the still.

As with the other liquors, the cocktail that bears the name of the base liquor consists of that liquor with bitters —nothing more:

APPLEJACK COCKTAIL One or 2 dashes Angostura to each jigger of apple brandy. Stir. Twist a slice of lemon peel over each drink.

This same drink plus 1 teaspoonful sugar syrup is known as the *CONNECTICUT*.

APPLEJACK OLD-FASHIONED Made exactly like the Old-Fashioned but using apple brandy in place of whisky.

B.V.D.[7] or *APPLEJACK MANHATTAN*   Made exactly like the Manhattan but with apple brandy in place of whisky.

APPLE BLOSSOM   Applejack Manhattan with 2 dashes grenadine and 2 dashes pineapple juice to each drink. Stir.

STAR   Made like a Dry Manhattan, using apple brandy in place of whisky. One dash Angostura to each drink. A twist of lemon over each glass.

The addition of ½ teaspoonful of sugar syrup to each drink changes the name to the *T. N. T. SPECIAL*.

The Star is also sometimes called the *KLONDIKE* and sometimes the *FARMER'S WIFE*.

AROMATIC WINE COCKTAILS

The great native American drink is the cocktail and, for the production of this drink, America draws its ingredients from all over the world—gin from England, vodka from Russia, vermouths from Italy and France, cognac and armagnac from France, rum from the West Indies, cordials from Denmark, Holland, France, and Austria, etc. It uses aromatic wines only as a modifier in conjunction with spirituous liquors.

Now all this is fine and I am one of those who greatly prefer a good cocktail with a base of spirituous liquor to any wine, aromatic or otherwise, as an apéritif. Nevertheless, the various aromatic wines, either straight or with a dash of bitters, do make light, dry, and wholly palatable apéritifs in themselves. Europeans generally take them in preference to cocktails. Moreover, some of the various bitters, such as Amer Picon, Fernet-Branca, Campari, and Unicum, when diluted, either with water or with an aromatic wine, make splendid tonics and appetizers. I am not going to compare a Picon cocktail with a Dry Martini or

---

[7] Another cocktail, sometimes called the B.V.D., is made with French vermouth, gin, and rum.

a Larchmont, but anyone interested in assorted drinks should try some of these aromatics without the addition of spirits just to see what they are like.

As previously stated, a genuine cocktail, strictly speaking, must have a base of spirituous liquor, and such liquor must comprise more than 50 per cent of the finished cocktail, but as a matter of convenience we also speak of vermouth cocktails, Dubonnet cocktails, etc., although the spirituous liquor constitutes less than 50 per cent of the whole drink or even if the drink contains no spirits whatsoever.

Here are a few "cocktails" in which the aromatic wine is used as a base instead of a modifier.

VERMOUTH Straight Italian vermouth with 1 or 2 dashes Angostura to each drink. A twist of lemon peel in each drink. If possible, chill the wine in the bottle and pour into chilled glasses. Otherwise, stir quickly and briefly with large cubes of ice.

DUPLEX or MIXED VERMOUTH French and Italian vermouths, half and half. Otherwise follow the recipe for the Vermouth.

This same drink with the addition of a dash of maraschino is known as the DIPLOMAT.

ADONIS
  1 part Italian Vermouth
  2 parts Dry Sherry
  1 or 2 dashes Bitters [8] to each drink

Stir quickly with large cubes of ice.

BAMBOO or AMOUR
  1 part French Vermouth
  1 part Dry Sherry
  1 or 2 dashes Bitters [8] to each drink

[8] Wherever the word "bitters" is used without specifying the brand, use your favorite bitters, whatever that may be.

Stir quickly with large cubes of ice. A twist of orange peel over each glass.

BAHIA or BRAZIL
- 1 part French Vermouth
- 1 part Dry Sherry
- 1 dash Orange Bitters & 2 or 3 dashes Absinthe to each drink

One half teaspoonful sugar syrup to each drink may be added if desired. Stir with cracked ice. A twist of lemon over each glass.

MERRY WIDOW
- 1 part French Vermouth
- 1 part Dubonnet
- 1 dash Orange Bitters to each drink

Stir quickly with large cubes of ice. A twist of lemon over each drink.

PICON, SWEET
- 1 part Amer Picon
- 1 part Italian Vermouth

Follow instructions for the *DUPLEX*, above.

PICON, DRY
- 1 part French Vermouth
- 2 parts Amer Picon
- 1 part Gin
- 1 dash Orange Bitters to each drink.

Stir with cracked ice. A twist of lemon over each drink.

PICON CREMAILLERE
- 1 part Amer Picon
- 1 part Dubonnet
- 2 parts Gin
- 1 dash Bitters to each drink

Follow instructions for the DRY PICON, above.

DUBONNET
    1 part Dubonnet
    1 part Gin

Follow instructions for the DRY PICON, above.

There are two cocktails made with Byrrh, one with gin and the other with rye, both of which, unfortunately, are commonly referred to as the Byrrh Cocktail. To be safe, therefore, it is best to specify the liquor as well as the wine.

BYRRH, GIN or BYRRH, RYE
    1 part French Vermouth
    1 part Gin or Rye
    2 to 4 parts Byrrh, according to taste

Stir with large cubes of ice. A twist of lemon over each glass.

And finally here is one from Switzerland, the home of that excellent cherry brandy, kirsch.

SWISS
    1 to 5 parts Kirsch
    1 part Dubonnet

Shake. Decorate with a twist of lemon. I have purposely been indefinite as to the proportions. As a devotee of dry cocktails, I like a ratio of about 5 to 1. The Swiss themselves use much more Dubonnet. But then the Swiss idea of a Martini (or, as they call it, Vermouth and Gin) is a glass of Italian vermouth with 1 or 2 teaspoonfuls of gin to the glass.
    Compare the ROSE.

LIQUEURS

In the chapter on limes, lemons, and liquors we bypassed the enumeration and description of the various cordials or liqueurs in more or less common use, stating that this would be taken up in a later chapter. That was in order that we might get down to the important business of mixing our "six basic cocktails" and learning to "roll our own." Let us now go back to the subject of liqueurs.

For the distinction between brandies (dry) and liqueurs (sweet) as well as for the names of manufacturers of some of the better liqueurs, see the section on liqueurs. Remember that, while both brandies and liqueurs are used as after-dinner drinks and while both may be used in cocktails, a brandy is used as a base liquor whereas a liqueur is used only in minute quantities as a special sweetening and flavoring agent in place of or in conjunction with sugar. Remember also that, whereas any liqueur can be used in a Sour-type cocktail, particularly with gin or rum, the aromatic and citrus-type liqueurs are the best for use in a cocktail containing aromatic wines.

Here is a list of the better-known liqueurs. While many liqueurs contain some aromatic herbs, I have indicated those that are most definitely aromatic and those that are strongly citrus so that you will know which ones are best to use in your aromatic-type cocktails. Note that this list also includes a few bottled syrups (not, strictly speaking, liqueurs) that are either non-alcoholic or of a very low alcoholic content.

Abricotine or *Apricot Liqueur* or *Apry* (ah-pree') A very sweet apricot-flavored liqueur with a grape-brandy base. *Abricotine* and *Apry* are the trade names of special brands. The latter is the product of Marie Brizard and is generally regarded as the best of all.

Advocaat (ahd-vo-kaht') A thick, heavy mixture of grape brandy, sugar, and eggs, resembling a brandy-flavored custard sauce. This is an excellent tonic drink. It is not particularly useful in cocktail mixing although it is specified in a few recipes.

Allasch See *Kümmel*, below.

Anis (ah-nees') or *Anisette* (ah-nee-set') A rather sweet, clear liqueur of aromatic type, the principal flavoring ingredient being anise seed. Marie Brizard's anisette is generally regarded as the best brand. See also *Liqueur d'Anis*, below.

Arrack Punsch A rather sickish-sweet liqueur with a base of Batavia arak which, in turn, is a molasses rum from the island of Java. See *Arak rum*.

Bacardi Elixir A delicious cordial with a pure Cuban rum base and flavor.

Bandana from Havana An excellent crème de bananes, manufactured by Nicolás Merino, Havana.

Benedictine One of the oldest and best of all liqueurs, highly aromatic, and having a base of the finest cognac. It is a proprietary liqueur made by the Benedictine Society at Fécamp, France. The familiar letters D.O.M. which are printed on the label do *not* stand for Dominican Order of Monks but for the Latin, *Deo Optimo Maximo*, meaning: "To God, the Best, the Greatest." It is made with consummate skill and is thoroughly aged. There are few liqueurs in the world that can compare with it.

Blackberry Liqueur A blackberry-flavored liqueur made from blackberry brandy, usually in combination with a small percentage of red wine.

Caloric Punsch or *Carlshamm's Punsch* Same as *Arrack Punsch*, above.

Certosa (chair-toh'-sah) An Italian liqueur, somewhat

similar to Chartreuse, but seldom seen in this country. It comes in different colors and flavors and, like Benedictine and Chartreuse, is made by a religious order.

Chartreuse Another grand old liqueur which, like Benedictine, originated with a religious order. It is not as old a liquor as Benedictine by some two hundred and fifty years, but it compares favorably in flavor, and the secret of its formula is as jealously and effectively guarded. Unlike Benedictine, it is still made by the religious order with which it originated. This order, however, has twice been forced out of France, and during their exile the fathers took their secret formula to Spain where they established a second plant. The Chartreuse made in Spain is labeled "Liqueur Fabriquée à Tarragona par les Pères Chartreux." It is normally found in two colors, yellow and green, the green being of higher proof (110°, as against 86°), decidedly drier and more aromatic, and in every respect the better of the two. There is also an Elixir Chartreuse of 150° to 160° which, however, is seldom, if ever, seen in this country. Recently the order returned to France, where they are now again manufacturing the liqueur.

Cherry Liqueur This is a rich, heavy liqueur made of wild black cherries with a base of grape brandy. The finest of all brands is *Cherry Heering* made by Peter F. Heering of Copenhagen, Denmark. Rocher Frères also make an excellent cherry.

C.L.O.C. A faintly caraway-flavored Danish liqueur produced by the manufacturers of Aalborg Akvavit. It is usually referred to as "Cloc" (pronounced klawck), although actually the name consists of the four initials of the phrase, *Cuminum Liquidum Optimum Castelli*.

Coffee Southern A very fine *Crème de Café* put out by the manufacturers of *Southern Comfort*.

Cointreau (kwen'-troh) A proprietary liqueur of the citrus type made by Cointreau, S.A.R.L., of Angers, France. White, orange flavor, 80 proof, cognac base. See also *Curaçao* and *Grand Marnier*, below.

Cordial Medoc (cord-yahl' may'-doc) A proprietary

liqueur made by J. A. Jourde of Bordeaux, France. While it is primarily a blend of orange curaçao, crème de cacao, and cognac, it cannot be classed as citrus type because the cocoa flavor so completely subdues the orange flavor of the curaçao.

Crème d'Ananas (krem dah-nah'-na) A sweet liqueur flavored with pineapple.

Crème de Bananes (krem de ba-nahn') A sweet liqueur flavored with bananas.

Crème de Cacao (kah-kah'-oh) A very sweet, syrupy liqueur of dark chocolate color and cocoa flavor.

Crème de Café (kah-fay') Very much like crème de cacao but with a coffee flavor.

Crème de Cassis (kah-see') A dark, moderately sweet liqueur flavored with black currants. The proof is very low —usually less than 40°.

Crème de Fraises (frayz) or *Crème de Framboise* (franbwahz') Two sweet liqueurs, the former flavored with strawberries and the latter with red raspberries. See *Framboise*, below.

Crème de Menthe (maNt) A moderately sweet, pungent, aromatic liqueur flavored with various mints, chiefly peppermint. It is sold in two colors, white and green, the latter being artificially colored. The white is usually somewhat drier and, therefore, is preferred by connoisseurs. *Freezomint*, made by Cusenier, is generally regarded as the best of all brands, although I have tasted one or two other brands that I liked fully as well, if not better.

Crème de Moka (moh'-ka) Same as crème de café, above.

Crème de Noyaux (nwa-yoh') A liqueur made from fruit pits and having a bitter, almost harsh, almond flavor.

Crème de Rose A sweet liqueur flavored with vanilla and rose-petal oil.

Crème de Thé (tay) Tea-flavored liqueur.

Crème de Vanille (vah-nee'-ya) Very sweet liqueur made from vanilla beans.

Crème de Violette (vee"-oh-let') or *Crème Yvette* (ee-vet') Very sweet violet-flavored liqueur.

Csaszar A pear-flavored liqueur (*crème de poire*) made by Zwack of Budapest.

Curaçao (kew'-ra-soh") A citrus liqueur made from the peel of the bitter orange grown on the island of Curaçao, Dutch West Indies, where this drink originated. The best of the brands commonly found in this country is R.O.C., made by Rocher Frères of France. Excellent curaçaos are also made in Holland. There are both orange and white curaçaos. See also *Cointreau* and *Triple Sec*.

Damiana (dah"-mee-ah'-nah) A rather nondescript French cordial seldom found in this country. Supposedly it possesses some slight aphrodisiac properties.

Danziger Goldwasser (dahn'-tsik-er golt'-vahs-ser) or *Eau de Vie de Danzig* (oh de vee de dahn'-tsik) or *Eau d'Or* (oh dawr) While Benedictine is doubtless the oldest proprietary liqueur still in existence—having originated early in the sixteenth century—"Golden Water," of which the modern German goldwasser is the prototype, is said to date back four centuries earlier. It is a rather dry, aromatic, and citrus liquor, colorless except for the tiny particles of pure gold leaf contained in it. These present a very attractive appearance when the drink is shaken or stirred.

Drambuie (drahm-bew'-ee) A proprietary liqueur that has been made for some two hundred years. Reasonably dry and aromatic in character. The only liqueur made with a base of the finest pot-still Scotch. The other principal ingredient is honey having a heather flavor. If you want a liqueur to blend with cocktails having a Scotch base, by all means try Drambuie.

Falernum (fa-lair'-num) This syrup has scarcely enough alcoholic content to be classed as a liqueur. The proof runs from 12° to 18°. It is a heavy white syrup with a base obtained in distilling rum. Aromatic in character, with a distinct almond flavor and just a faint suspicion of ginger. Excellent with rum drinks, particularly in combination with lime juice, but blends better with Jamaica and the other heavy-bodied rums than with white Cuban rum.

Fior d'Alpe (fee'-ohr dahl'-pay) or *Fiori Alpini* (fee-oh'-ree ahl-pee'-nee) or *Flora della Alpi* (ahl'-pee) A sweet, light-colored, aromatic Italian liqueur. A twig is placed inside the bottle on which the sugar forms into crystals of rock candy. When the twig is covered with the sugar crystals its appearance is very attractive. Unfortunately, however, unless the bottle is kept very cool, the sugar dissolves off and falls to the bottom of the bottle, leaving the twig bare. This does not damage the quality of the liqueur in the least.

Forbidden Fruit A proprietary, sweet, citrus liqueur invented by Louis Bustanoby. The principal flavoring agent is a West Indies grapefruit called the shaddock. The base is grape brandy. Despite the fact that this liqueur has enjoyed a huge popularity, especially with the ladies, I regard it as decidedly inferior to the other citrus liqueurs such as Grand Marnier, Cointreau, and curaçao.

Framboise (fraN-bwahz') or *Framboisette* (fraN-bwa-zet') Framboise is, or should be, a raspberry brandy rather than a liqueur. Framboisette is the same as *Crème de Framboise*, above.

Freezomint See *Crème de Menthe*, above.

Ginger Liqueur See *King's Ginger Liqueur*, below.

Goldwasser See *Danziger Goldwasser*, above.

Grand Marnier (grawn marn-yay') A dry, pungent, citrus liqueur—orange-flavored on a base of the finest grand champagne brandy. To me this is the absolute king of all liqueurs, excelling even Benedictine and Chartreuse. It lacks the antiquity of Goldwasser and Benedictine; it does not boast the religious parentage of Benedictine and Chartreuse; but for sheer excellence of flavor it is unsurpassed. It blends magnificently in all manner of cocktails, particularly of the Sour type. It is also superb in cooking, for all manner of dessert sauces, and, of course, it is an absolute "must" for crêpes suzette.

Grenadine A very sweet, reddish, non-alcoholic syrup,

mildly flavored with pomegranates. Used primarily for color rather than flavor.

Irish Mist A liqueur with a base of pure pot-still Irish whisky, the other principal ingredient being heather honey. This cordial is to Irish whisky what Drambuie is to Scotch.

Kahlua A *crème de café* or *licor de café* manufactured in Mexico.

King's Ginger Liqueur A ginger-flavored liqueur with a cognac base, made in Holland.

Kümmel (kim'-mel) A very dry, aromatic, white liqueur flavored principally with cumin, coriander, and caraway seed. The base is usually grain spirits. The proof is usually fairly high—from 82° to 100°. The kümmel made by Gilka in Germany is usually regarded as the best brand. However, Allasch Doppelt Kümmel, made by Severy in Belgium, and Bolskümmel, made in Holland, are also excellent. This drink also dates back to the sixteenth century.

Liqueur d'Anis (lee-ker' dah-nee') See *Anis*, above. Note that anis, pronounced ah-nees', comes from Spain or South America, but that liqueur d'anis, pronounced ah-nee', without the *s* sound, comes from France or, at least, bears the French name.

Liqueur Jaune (zhone) An imitation of Yellow Chartreuse.

Liqueur d'Or See *Danziger Goldwasser*, above.

Liqueur Strega (stray'-gah) A yellowish, citrus, and highly aromatic propietary liqueur made by Ditta Giuseppe Alberti of Benevento, Italy. Excellent for blending in aromatic cocktails.

Liqueur Verte (vairt) An imitation of green Chartreuse. The word *verte*, meaning green, is sometimes written *vert* (pronounced vair). This is incorrect. "Liqueur" is a French word of feminine gender and the adjective must agree in gender with the substantive which it modifies.

Mandarine or *Mandarinette* A citrus liqueur flavored with the peel of tangerines. Note also that there is an aromatic apéritif wine bearing the same name.

Maraschino (mare-as-kee'-no) or *Marasquin* (mare-as-ken′) A very sweet white liqueur flavored with the wild black marasca cherries grown in Dalmatia. Fruit and seeds or pits are crushed together in making this liqueur. Excellent for use in Sour-type cocktails in place of sugar where just a faint suggestion of a flavor that is "different" is desired. Blends perfectly with other fruit flavors—apricot, peach, cherry, raspberry, etc.

Mazarine (maz-a-reen′) A slightly aromatic citrus liqueur based on a special, supposedly secret, formula.

Monastique (mon-as-teek′) An imitation of *Benedictine*.

Nectar of Tokay A moderately sweet aromatic liqueur made by Zwack of Budapest and resembling *Liqueur Strega*. It even has a twig in the bottle, like Strega.

Noilly Cassis I have commented on the VERMOUTH CASSIS. The Noilly Prat people have now put it on the market, ready mixed.

Noyaux See *Créme de Noyaux*, above.

Orange Liqueur A sweet citrus liqueur made with a grape-brandy base and flavored with oranges.

Orgeat (or-zhah′) A sweet, non-alcoholic, almond-flavored syrup. Blends well in Sour-type cocktails and is the perfect companion to rum, especially white Cuban rum.

Ouzo (oo′-zo) An anise-flavored liqueur made in Greece.

Parfait Amour (par-fay′ tah-moor′) Same as *crème de violette*, above.

Passion-Fruit Nectar A non-alcoholic syrup made from the passion fruit, so called because of the supposed resemblance of the flower to the crown of thorns pressed upon the head of Christ on the cross (Mark, 15:17). It consists of passion-fruit juice, sugar, citric acid, and water with an infinitesimal amount of sulfur dioxide added as a preservative. Imported from Australia by Perry H. Chipernoi, Inc., N. Y. C. Blends with lime and lemon juices and with gin, rum, and vodka. Try it in place of sugar syrup for a super-excellent Daiquiri. Try it in Rum Rickeys, in Daisies and Fizzes, and in Lemonades, either plain or spiked. It makes an excellent *PROHIBITION COCKTAIL*, or *PROHIBITION PUNCH*.

Peach Liqueur or *Pêche* (pesh) Similar to apricot liqueur, above, but flavored with peaches instead of apricots. There is also a dry peach brandy called pêche.

Peppermint or *Pippermint* A peppermint syrup seldom used in this country but highly popular in French cocktail recipes. *Crème de menthe*, while differing somewhat from pippermint, can be substituted with reasonably satisfactory results. The best-known brand of pippermint is that made by Get Frères of France.

Pineapple Cordial, Cuban A *crème d'ananas* made by José Arechabala, S. A., Cardenas, Cuba.

Prunella or *Prunelle* A dark, sweet liqueur with a grape-brandy base flavored with fresh plums. Not to be confused with any of the plum or prune brandies, such as mirabelle, quetsche, and slivovitz.

Raspail A French aromatic liqueur, somewhat resembling Benedictine, but with no religious background.

Rock and Rye Just plain old-fashioned rye whisky (usually about 50 per cent) mixed with fruit juices and rock candy (crystallized sugar). In my boyhood days in the country this was a favorite cough and cold remedy, even with those who frowned on liquor as the devil's broth. And, oh boy, how the dear old prohibitionists did look forward to getting a cold!

Sloe Gin A heavy, aromatic liqueur flavored with sloeberries—a kind of small, wild plum.

Southern Comfort A proprietary liqueur whose excellence is attested by its numerous imitators. Supposedly a secret formula but has a base of excellent bourbon whisky, peach-flavored. One hundred proof and reasonably dry. Makes an excellent Manhattan (but go easy on the vermouth), Old-Fashioned, or Whisky Sour. If you find it too sweet, use a smaller quantity and add straight bourbon.

Strega See *Liqueur Strega*, above.

Swedish Punch See *Arrack Punsch*, above.

Tangerine Dolfi A citric liqueur somewhat resembling

Mandarine and the various curaçaos but with a spicy tang all its own.

Triple Sec An imitation Cointreau.

Van der Hum An excellent aromatic and citrus liqueur made by the Union of South Africa, Cape of Good Hope. The citrus flavor is from tangerine peel. Blends perfectly with brandy.

Vieille Cure (vee′-yå kewr) An excellent aromatic liqueur made by L'Abbaye de Çenon, Bordeaux, France. A worthy companion of the other two great liqueurs having a religious parentage—Benedictine and Chartreuse. Please note that there is *no* accent mark over the *e* in *Cure*. It is pronounced kewr, not kew-ray′. The name means the Old Vicarage, not the Old Curate. In fact, Vieille Curé is an impossible phrase because *Vieille* is feminine—as is *Cure* —whereas *Curé* is masculine. The Old Curate would be Vieux Curé.

THE USE AND ABUSE OF LIQUOR

OVERINDULGENCE

It is a striking fact that those things which, properly controlled and used, constitute the greatest of boons to mankind can be seriously injurious when allowed to get out of hand. Fire, for example, is an absolute essential to modern living. Fire heats our houses in winter; fire cooks our food; fire, in the form of rapid explosions of gas, runs our automobiles, our airplanes, our steamships, and our trains; fire furnishes the energy that turns the wheels of most of our industrial plants. Without fire we would either die or revert to the primitive savage, eating raw foods and living in caves. Yet fire annually destroys millions of dollars' worth of property and kills and injures thousands of persons.

Electricity lights our buildings and our streets, energizes our radio, telephone, and telegraph, washes and irons our clothes, operates countless household gadgets and implements, ignites the fuel that propels our vehicles, performs a thousand tasks both in industry and in private life that otherwise would consume millions of weary man-hours of labor. Yet instant death lurks in the innocent-looking cord that connects our reading lamp, our toaster, or our radio, and countless conflagrations, large and small, are traced to "defective wiring."

The very medicines that save thousands of lives when properly administered in the treatment of disease may cause prolonged agony and even death when taken in excessive doses or otherwise improperly used. This fact is by no means limited to medicines that are commonly known as poisons, such as arsenic, bromine, strychnine, etc. It is also true of many simple standard home remedies such as aspirin, castor oil, and various cough syrups. Even ordinary sodium bicarbonate or baking soda, so extensively used as a home remedy for acid indigestion, if taken habitually, will actually increase acidity and may cause extensive damage to the entire digestive tract.

The same is true of foods. A deficiency of one kind of food in an individual's diet is usually accompanied by an excess of some other kind, and the two dietetic errors combine to induce digestive disturbances and either temporary or even chronic ill health. An excess of starches, of sugars, of proteins, or of fats can cause serious bodily injury. Even the most perfect of foods, taken at the wrong time, may cause considerable discomfort. This is commonly erroneously attributed by the victim to some particular item of his meal. "It must have been something I et." Actually, most acute digestive disturbances are brought on by eating when very tired, when subject to high nervous tension, or when, for any other reason, the digestive organs are unable properly to perform their appointed task, and are not due to any one food that was eaten.

Liquor, of course, is no exception to the universal rule that extreme discomfort and even permanent injury may result from improper use of that which is otherwise entirely harmless and even wholesome and beneficial. Unbiased medical investigators agree that there is no evidence whatsoever that well-made liquor, when consumed in anything like normal and reasonable amounts, is, of itself, harmful in the slightest degree. On the contrary, it stimulates the appetite, promotes digestion, refreshes through relaxation, acts as a specific in many diseases, and will even maintain life for a time when the body is incapable of assimilating food.

POPULAR MISBELIEFS

There is probably no other comestible in the whole world that has been so misunderstood and misrepresented by both friend and foe as alcoholic liquor. On the one hand, it does *not* cure or even relieve certain conditions for which it is commonly supposed to be a remedy and, on the other hand, it does *not* cause many diseases for which it is frequently blamed. As an example of conditions under which, contrary to popular belief, alcohol should *never* be administered, there may be mentioned snakebites and heat prostration or other shock. The physiological action of alcohol is the exact opposite of what a patient suffering from either of these afflictions needs. An outstanding example of a disease long erroneously attributed to alcohol is cirrhosis of the liver. In my younger days this dread disease was popularly known as "beer liver." Medical science has now completely acquitted liquor of any demonstrable responsibility. It is true that more drinkers than non-drinkers suffer from cirrhosis, but that is merely because there are more drinkers than non-drinkers. By the same token there is more cirrhosis among right-handed people than among left-handed; more among people who eat three meals a day than among those who eat only one. On the other hand, such statistics as have been collected by medical authorities indicate that there is a somewhat higher *percentage* of cirrhosis among non-drinkers than among drinkers. This does not mean that liquor helps prevent cirrhosis. Apparently there is no relation of cause and effect whatsoever. It is purely fortuitous. The fact remains, however, that it is true.

DOES ALCOHOL WARM THE BODY?

Another popular fallacy is that alcohol warms the body. Its actual effect is the exact opposite. Alcohol partially inhibits the action of the vasoconstrictors, causing a dilation of the blood vessels and a rushing of the blood to the small vessels on the surface of the body. This, in a warm atmosphere or one that is moderately cool, gives a purely superficial feeling of warmth. In a cold atmosphere, however, this rush of blood to the surface causes heat to be given off by the body much faster than it is generated, with the result that the whole body is more quickly chilled. Despite the immediate *feeling* of warmth after one or two drinks and despite the increased perspiration which the liquor induces, alcohol actually *lowers* the temperature of the body. It is therefore frequently used as a diaphoretic and febrifuge. Alcoholic beverages are most useful in the tropics; they may be extremely dangerous in the arctic. Upon returning to a warm room *after* exposure to cold, a good, stiff drink, especially a hot drink, may be most helpful in strengthening the heartbeat and bringing a warm glow to the skin. Liquor taken *before* going out in the cold, however, will lower the body's resistance to the exposure.

ALCOHOL, THE INEVITABLE CONCOMITANT OF PROGRESS

Throughout the ages alcohol has been the handmaiden of religion, of philosophy, of science and invention, and of culture and appreciation of the finer things of life. From time immemorial poets have sung praises of the cup that cheers. Wine is deeply entrenched in ceremonials of both the Jewish and the Christian church. The Bible is replete with references to liquor, and by no means are all of them deprecatory. Wine was served at the Last Supper, and Christ himself did not deem it beneath his dignity to transmute water into wine in order that those who attended the wedding feast might be refreshed and cheered. History reveals that the contributions to human progress made by those nations and by those religious cults that feature total abstinence are infinitesimal compared with those made by drinking peoples. Search the records of this or any other country and you will find that, for the most part, the outstanding statesmen, generals, poets, philosophers, scientists

—the leaders in every field of human endeavor—have been men who drank. In the main, they have been men who drank as they ate—in moderation—but a surprisingly large number have been what might aptly be called "two-fisted drinkers." History affords a complete refutation of the prohibitionist theory that alcohol stifles initiative and inhibits progress.

Despite all this, it must be freely admitted that overindulgence in alcohol, either sporadic or chronic, produces undesirable results, both physical and social. Physically, an overdose of alcohol precipitates the pepsin content of the gastric juices, producing excessive secretion of mucus (gastric catarrh), hyperacidity, nausea, and vomiting. The "hang-over" is characterized by a "big head," bloodshot eyes, throbbing temples, a volcanic stomach, and a cotton mouth—the "dark brown taste of the morning after." It would seem that, for a normal human being, whatever pleasure—if it be a pleasure—can be derived from tanking up to the point of complete inebriety would be more than offset by the drastic punishment so quickly and relentlessly imposed by nature, and that one grisly experience of the resultant "heeby-jeebies" should be more than enough for an entire lifetime.

SOCIAL EFFECTS OF OVERINDULGENCE

The social effects of overindulgence are even worse than the physical. Alcohol acts on nerve tissue, including the brain, quicker than on any of the other organs. The immediate reaction (characteristic of moderate drinking) is a faster response to stimuli, quicker thinking, scintillating repartee, greater humor and geniality, a freer play of the emotions. With increased doses, however, the brain becomes anesthetized, fatigue sets in, co-ordination fails, and eventually there is a more or less complete inertia of both brain and muscle. Drunkenness, by removing normal inhibitions, may completely change a man's character. The bully may become a weakling; the shy recluse, a braggart.

The ugly drunk and the drooling, sniveling drunk are equally obnoxious. Here again it would seem that the vicarious experience just once of seeing another human being completely "blotto" should be sufficient to engender a firm and unbreakable resolution never to take a chance on making a similarly disgusting spectacle of oneself.

For the normal, intelligent human being, however, the evil effects of overindulgence are no better argument against normal drinking than the danger of electrocution is against the use of electrical equipment, or the danger of a conflagration against keeping a fire to cook one's meals or to heat one's house. Chronic alcoholism is a disease and, for the most part, a disease peculiar to the mentally unstable. There is no more reason for drinking to the point of drunkenness than there is for eating to the point of gluttony. Drinking, like eating, affords real pleasure only up to a certain point. The discriminating drinker, the man who fully appreciates the bouquet, the aroma, the delightful aftertaste of a rare vintage wine, of a pedigreed cognac, of a ripe, mellow bourbon, or of a superb liqueur, knows that after a certain number of drinks (the exact quantity varying with the individual) the exquisite character of the liquor can no longer be fully savored. He refuses either to waste good liquor by consuming it when unable to appreciate and enjoy it to the utmost or to insult the cause of intelligent and cultured drinking by imbibing for the degenerate purpose of getting a kick out of the alcoholic content.

There are, of course, a few (but, luckily, a very few) unfortunate individuals so extraordinarily sensitive to alcohol that, to them, a single drink is a knockout. There are others—also, fortunately, few—with whom a single drink seems to create an insatiable desire for more and more and yet more. To such persons there is but one sensible answer, and that is not to drink at all. True, they must miss a great deal of the relaxation and enjoyment that is granted to the average, healthy, normal person. This, however, is equally true of the person who, because of some digestive deficiency or some allergy, is not permitted to eat strawberry shortcake, or corn on the cob, or sea food, or a charcoal-broiled steak smothered in mushrooms.

HOW TO KEEP SOBER

But how, you may ask, is the average person to know exactly how many drinks he can stand? Should he go on just one good binge and have a record kept of how much he consumes in order that thereafter he may know when to stop? My answer is "No." It is best that you never find out the limit of your capacity. There is just one safe and simple rule which, if rigidly adhered to, will afford you a maximum of pleasure in your drinking with a minimum of danger of ever becoming drunk. When you reach a point where you feel absolutely sure that you could stand one more but have some slight doubt as to what two more might do to you, S T O P. If you resolutely refuse to take even the one extra that you are certain would be O.K., you will maintain your physical stability, your mental balance, and your moral aplomb.

There may, however, come a time in your life when you know that, at the fiftieth reunion of the Class of Naughty Naught or at a stag dinner given in honor of some old crony, you will be expected to drink a lot more than you really want to drink and more than you can normally carry with safety. Is there any advance preparation that may enable you to withstand the onslaught of those two or three (or perhaps more) drinks that, under ordinary circumstances, you would not think of taking? Cheer up. There is.

I have already pointed out the fact that alcohol has a peculiar affinity for nerve tissue and therefore affects the nervous system before any other organs. This is because it is absorbed by the tissues of the stomach and intestines and passes directly into the blood stream unchanged or in the form of an aldehyde—i.e., robbed of a part of its oxygen. Now, if we can prevent the liquor from coming into direct contact with the walls of the alimentary tract, we shall prevent the alcohol from being taken up and passed into the blood stream. There are two methods of partially accomplishing this result. One is by absorption and the other by insulation.

The absorption method consists of filling the stomach with food so that when the alcohol reaches the stomach, instead of being churned around by itself and washing the entire stomach lining with liquor, a large part of the alcohol is absorbed by the food. What then comes in direct contact with the cellular tissue that is so eager to drink up the alcohol and pass it on to the blood is not the alcoholic liquor but food with a relatively small alcoholic content. Each square inch of stomach wall is covered, not with a square inch of alcoholic liquid, but with a square inch of food containing perhaps 2 or 1 per cent or even less of alcohol. The best foods for this absorptive process are proteins—particularly lean meat and eggs—and whole milk. Go easy on the starches and, above all, shun all sweets. Sugar not only does not mitigate the effect of alcohol; it intensifies it.

Obviously, if this riotous affair is to be a dinner and a large part of the drinking is to be done before the food is served, you cannot very well fill up beforehand with sirloin steak, custard, and milk. In that case you must rely on the insulation method. This method depends, first, upon the fact that alcohol and oil will not mix and, second, upon the tendency of fats of any kind to adhere to the walls of the stomach and form a thin film which repels the alcohol and keeps it away from the mucous membrane. Taking liquor into an empty stomach is like pouring water over a sponge; taking liquor into a stomach that has first been given an oil bath is like covering the sponge with a sheet of cellophane and then pouring on the water. Olive oil is best for this purpose—two ounces or more taken perhaps fifteen or twenty minutes before the orgy begins. If you chance to be one of those perverted individuals who do not like this sweet, nutty oil from the sunny slopes of

Spain, you can substitute any other vegetable oil commonly sold as a salad oil.

Don't get the foolish notion that either the absorption method or the insulation method or even both in combination will enable you to consume two or three quarts of liquor and go home as sober as when the party began. These precautions will merely reduce to some extent the effect of the alcohol; they will not wholly eliminate it. And, of course, as the food in your stomach becomes more and more saturated with liquor and as the coating of fat over the stomach lining is gradually churned into the other stomach contents and passed on to the intestines, the preventive value of the treatment is gradually lessened.

Before leaving the subject of the sensible use of liquor, there are a few scientific facts that I should like to bring out and superstitious follies that I should like to explode.

1. *Alcohol and Arteriosclerosis* A popular belief is that heavy drinking may result in arteriosclerosis. Not only is this absolutely false but the person with arteriosclerosis or a tendency toward it, if he wants to survive, definitely should drink. Alcohol is a vasodilator. It relaxes the vasoconstrictors and permits the blood to flow freely from the heart through the arteries, capillaries, and veins back to the heart. One prominent physician of whom I know has said that every man over sixty should have at least one drink a day; over seventy, two; and, over eighty, three. I can't vouch for his ratio but it is a fact that a tendency toward arteriosclerosis is one of the conditions in which the moderate use of alcohol is indicated as a remedy.

2. *Alcohol and Ulcers* Also false is the contention that alcohol causes ulcers. It is true that, if you have ulcers, you should not drink, because alcohol will irritate them and retard their healing. However, there is no evidence whatsoever that alcohol tends to produce them.

3. *Alcohol and Feeble-mindedness* It is true that only

the person with some sort of psychological deficiency or psychosomatic abnormality is likely to become a confirmed drunkard. But the alcohol is not the cause; it is merely one possible outlet.

4. *Does Regular Drinking Increase Your Capacity?* Also untrue. I have already pointed out the factors that control the quantity which you can drink with impunity. Some medical authorities claim that your susceptibility to alcohol is the same at eighty as it is at eighteen, irrespective of how much you drink in between. Personally I do not believe that that is always true, although I by no means seek to pose as an authority on geriatrics. I do know that twenty years ago I could drink considerably more without feeling it than I can today. I fancy that, with another man, this equation may be reversed. This, however, has nothing whatsoever to do with how much and how regularly one drinks in the meantime.

5. *Is Alcohol Essential to Life?* I do not know whether any scientist has ever tried to dealcoholize the human blood in order to ascertain whether life would still continue or not. It is a fact, however, that the blood of every human being does contain alcohol, and this is just as true of a Carrie Nation or a Pussyfoot Johnson as it is of the Old Soak. The amount is not large. It is measured in thousandths of a per cent. Now it is not necessary to drink alcohol in order to keep the blood supplied with this essential ingredient. All that is necessary is to eat a reasonable quantity of carbohydrates and the body itself will convert them into alcohol. The human body is an extraordinarily efficient chemical laboratory. It manufactures a long array of pharmaceuticals. Some of these, like the saliva and pepsin, are harmless drugs. Others, such as adrenalin, pituitrin, and bile are definitely poisonous and, if taken in sufficient doses, could cause serious illness or even death.

Alcohol is one of the more innocuous secretions compounded within the human body. Whenever I hear some rabid prohibitionist ranting about the evils of alcohol and urging the smashing of every still in the world, I cannot help wondering if he realizes that within his own body he carries a miniature still which, despite his vociferous ululations and despite all the laws he would like to see passed, will keep right on distilling out its daily stint of alcohol until the day he dies!

6. *Is Alcohol a Stimulant?* This is an extremely difficult question to answer. The initial effect of alcohol, at least in small doses, is that of a stimulant. The frequency of respiration is stepped up. The strength of the systolic contraction of the heart is increased, resulting in a full, strong, regular pulse. The nerves respond more quickly to stimuli. Every symptom is typical of reaction to a stimulant. In larger doses, however, the effect is that of a sedative rather than a stimulant. In excessive doses, as has already been stated, the effect is that of an irritant, producing hyperacidity and acute fatigue. It would seem that the restful, refreshing effect of one or two good drinks is due, not to stimulation, but rather to relaxation. Tired muscles and tense nerves relax and are rested, which is really the exact opposite of being stimulated and prodded into further activity.

7. *Is Liquor Fattening?* This also is a tough one to answer. Alcohol, *in itself*, cannot possibly produce fat, yet those who drink in any substantial quantity are likely to put on fat, and they can control their weight to a considerable degree by abstaining from liquor for periods of three or four weeks at a time. This may sound paradoxical, but the explanation is entirely logical. Alcohol is an energy-producing food of high caloric value. It is the most readily assimilable of any food that can possibly be taken into the body, since it requires no digestive process or effort whatsoever. It furnishes about seven calories of energy per gram, which is approximately equal to the caloric value of butter, is twice that of heavy cream or granulated sugar, is five times that of lean meat, and is ten times that of whole milk.

You will therefore readily see that it does not take a very great number of cocktails to supply all the calories that are necessary for an individual leading a sedentary life. Unfortunately, however, man cannot live by calories alone. He must have proteins, carbohydrates, fats, vitamins, minerals, and a certain amount of bulk. In order to get these other essentials he must eat other foods. These additional foods furnish additional calories, in excess of what the system needs and can work off, and these excess calories are stored up in the form of fat—with most people, principally around the midriff.

8. Is Mixing Drinks Fatal? Of all the stupid superstitions that prevail respecting the use of liquor, this one seems to be the most persistent and the most widespread. If you start with gin, you must stick to gin; if you start with rum, you must stick to rum, and so on. That this belief has no foundation whatsoever in fact has been definitely determined by medical investigators, and their findings have been widely publicized, not only in the official journal of the American Medical Association, but also in other magazines. Apparently many people either have not read these articles or else, reading and knowing the truth, they still refuse to accept it. To authoritative medical assurance on this point I can also add my own personal experience of some forty years. When drinking at a bar where variety is available I would no more think of taking four or five—or even two—cocktails of the same kind than I would think of ordering, for an entire dinner, four or five plates of soup, or four or five servings of roast beef, or four or five cuts of chocolate pie. My many friends who have drunk with me on numerous occasions of this kind can testify that shifting from a Martini to an Old-Fashioned, then to a Daiquiri, and finishing with a Side Car has had no more effect on me than would four drinks of the same kind. Actually, the following are the points that will determine how your drinks affect you—and by "affect" I mean either by inducing partial mental or physical paralysis (actual "drunkenness") or by upsetting the digestive system with accompanying discomfort, nausea, and possible vomiting:

First of all is your own individual susceptibility to alcohol. One man may be completely befuddled by a single cocktail; another may drink eight or ten with impunity.

Second, and closely allied to the first point, is your physical condition, especially the condition of your alimentary tract. I have already explained the effect of food, particularly fats, proteins, and milk, on your susceptibility to alcohol. Your general state of health also has a profound influence on your capacity. Strangely enough, however, you may be more quickly affected by alcohol when in the pink of condition and ready to fight your weight in wildcats than when suffering from certain diseases. Any disease that slows down the activity of the digestive organs also slows down the rapidity with which alcohol will be absorbed in the stomach and intestines and passed into the blood stream. Moreover, certain types of influenza are characterized by intestinal catarrh. The mucus then adheres to the lining of the digestive tract and insulates it against alcohol very much the same as olive oil or other fats will furnish such insulation. I have already pointed out that excessive doses of alcohol may give rise to an intestinal catarrh; that is nature's method of insulating and protecting the system against such overdoses.

Third, your mental attitude, as well as your physical condition, will have a pronounced influence on your reaction to the mixed drinks. You may be familiar with the old practical joke in which, pursuant to a prearranged plan, when the innocent victim arrives at his office in the morning a perfect picture of glowing health, the pranksters, one after another, extend their sympathy, tell him how pale and worn out he looks, and so on, until finally he has to go home and to bed. This is purely psychological, the result of the power of suggestion, but it is none the less real to the victim. And autosuggestion can be just as powerful as any other kind. Drunkenness is primarily a mental affliction in any event. If you are thoroughly convinced that you can get drunk on milk, you probably can get drunk on milk. And if you can get drunk on milk, of course you can get drunk by mixing gin and whisky and rum. But it will be your silly belief in a thoroughly exploded superstition that causes your drunkenness and not the fact that you mixed your drinks.

So much for *your* side of the equation. On the liquor side, of course, the all-important question is the quantity of proof alcohol consumed. If you take a 3-ounce drink of bonded bourbon, which is 100 proof, you have consumed 1½ ounces of pure alcohol. The same quantity of 87-proof gin means 1⅓ ounces of alcohol. The use of citrus juices, aromatic wines, etc., in the cocktail, of course, reduces proportionately the amount of alcoholic content. But, given a certain quantity of alcohol, it does not make the slightest bit of difference whether that alcohol is taken in the form of whisky, gin, rum, brandy, or any other *dry*, spirituous liquor, either separately or in any combination you may choose.

There is just one exception to this well-established principle. For some reason that medical science has not yet been able to fathom, there are some individuals whose systems simply will not tolerate certain liquors, just as there are some individuals who are allergic to certain foods. Nine times out of ten this is pure imagination. A man has Manhattan cocktails and a lobster dinner and later suffers an attack of acute indigestion. He invariably looks for a whipping boy. He may blame it on the lobster; he may blame it on the whisky; or he may blame it on the Italian vermouth. Probably he took his meal when he was tired or nervously upset and simply unable properly to digest and assimilate any food whatsoever. The *particular* food—or drink—had nothing whatsoever to do with his upset. Nevertheless, there still remain a substantial number of cases where the repugnance to certain liquors is genuine. I personally have trouble with certain red wines—including some of my favorites, such as Chambertin. I also have to be extremely cautious about drinking brandy—including cognac, of which I am extremely fond. These liquors do not make me drunk, nor do they cause any nausea, but they do cause severe stomach-burn. All these cases are purely individual idiosyncrasies and, of course, they have nothing whatsoever to do with *mixing* different types of liquor.

Finally, there is one caution to be observed respecting the kind of liquors consumed (and, of course, in all I am saying, I assume that the liquors are pure, wholesome, and well made). I have already called attention to the danger of consuming large quantities of sugar in combination with alcohol. A man drinks, let us say, one 50-50 Manhattan, one standard-recipe Alexander, and one standard-recipe Stinger, after which he suffers violent indigestion and nausea. Perhaps he becomes downright drunk. Of course he blames "mixing 'em." Well, no wonder he gets sick! His Manhattan was half sweet wine; his Alexander was one-third syrupy, sickish-sweet crème de cacao; and his Stinger was half crème de menthe—also a sweet, heavy cordial. But it wasn't mixing his drinks that did it. If he had had three Stingers he would probably have been twice as sick, and if he had had the same quantity of straight crème de menthe he might well have been three times as sick. Would you think of sitting down and drinking three cocktail glasses of honey or of maple syrup? Wouldn't you expect to be sick if you did? And a sugar-alcohol combination is even worse.

Cordials are utterly delightful after-dinner drinks. These are served in a liqueur glass which holds about ¾ ounce —about half the amount you will get in one Stinger. Seldom does one take more than one of these small glasses of any liqueur, and if the slogan "No more than two to a customer" was ever appropriate for any drink, it is here. Liqueurs are also excellent in place of sugar in a cocktail, but when so used the quantity should seldom, if ever, exceed one or two teaspoonfuls to a drink. If you want to have a good, thorough, disgusting, reeling, puking drunk, and get that way as fast as possible, my advice is to get a bottle of any heavy, sweet liqueur, such as crème de menthe or Parfait Amour or liqueur verte, and take it *straight!* Don't mix!

That, *mes amis*, is one reason why the cocktails I recommend are *always* dry. The other reason, of course, is their superior flavor. Note my standard 1-2-8 Sour recipe. *Never* anything like 1-1-1. God forbid! Frequently, at one of my cocktail parties, some friend will say to me (especially the ladies—bless their dear little innocent, misguided hearts): "Good lord, Dave, but you make your cocktails strong!" They say that *while* they are drinking them, not two hours later. For never, since I learned years ago what makes a cocktail tick, *never* has anyone become sick on cocktails made and served by me—not even after four or five or even more of them!

JUDGING LIQUOR

Professional liquor tasting—both of wines and of spirits—is a highly skilled art requiring an exceptionally discriminating sense both of smell and of taste. You may have heard the story of two experts, both of whom agreed that a certain hogshead of whisky was off flavor. However, one insisted that it tasted of leather and the other claimed that the taste was that of iron. Finally the cask was drained and, in the bottom, there was found one small leather-covered upholstery tack!

Few can hope to attain any such sensitivity to component flavors, nor is that at all necessary for a full appreciation and enjoyment of the best in liquors. On the other hand, the man to whom liquor is just liquor—the man who doesn't care whether his whisky is a bonded straight whisky or a 20-per-cent blend, or whether his cognac is two years old or twenty, so long as it has plenty of alcoholic strength—is missing the real joy of drinking and is wasting his money when he buys any alcoholic beverage other than pure raw alcohol. Furthermore, he is in grave danger of becoming an alcoholic. If he is truly wise, he will stop drinking entirely.

The average man can, however, acquire sufficient discrimination to distinguish readily between liquors that are good, those that are indifferent, and those that are definitely bad. By learning to do so he will increase his enjoyment of real quality products many-fold. He can also, if he will, save money as well, for, while he may pay more per bottle for what he buys, he will get more real gustatorial delight out of one bottle of high-quality liquor than he now gets out of five or ten bottles of the cheaper product. And now for the method by which you can test your liquors for yourself.

Use a small glass, preferably with a wide bottom and a small mouth. A small brandy snifter—from two to four ounces—is excellent. Pour into the glass a small quantity of the liquor—not more than a tablespoonful, preferably less. Hold the glass in the cupped hands to warm both glass and liquor. It is an excellent idea to preheat the glass with hot water, then dry it, and to have the liquor at room temperature. Twirl the glass to spread the liquor over as much of the inside surface as possible, thereby bringing a large area of it in contact with the air and helping to vaporize the volatile ingredients. Then, holding the glass in the cupped hand, sniff for the odor. Sniff at first gently, then swish the liquor around the glass again and sniff vigorously. Do this several times, for the odor may vary as the liquor in the glass gradually becomes warmer. The odor should be full-bodied—not thin—but it should produce no acrid "sting" in the nasal passages.

Then take a *very* small sip—just a few drops—of the liquor. Do not swallow this but roll it about the tongue. Breathe in gently through the mouth, close the lips, and exhale through the nose. Finally swallow. By now, if it is really good liquor, you will probably have to swallow because your mouth will be watering for more! Do not take more, however, but note carefully how long the taste lingers after you first took your sip. Note also whether the taste merely fades out gradually with, perhaps, an even more delightful flavor as it fades or whether the aftertaste is acrid or musty or, in the case of liqueurs, sickish-sweet and flavorless.

The flavor, like the odor, should be full-bodied, not thin. It should be mellow and smooth and not harsh or sharp. There should be no "tinny" flavor (particularly noticeable in the case of poorly made gins). And the taste should persist for a substantial length of time. In the case of full-bodied, well-matured liquors, the taste may last as long as four or five minutes! This exquisitely delightful, long-lingering aftertaste is one of the best tests of high quality. A raw, green liquor, or one that consists merely of a small quantity of real liquor blended with raw alcohol (neutral spirits) and water, will first assault the palate with the force of a charge of nitroglycerin, then quickly vanish, leaving either no aftertaste whatsoever or one that is brackish and disagreeable.

Finally, after the taste of the liquor has completely disappeared, empty and drain the glass, warm it in the hands again, and again note the odor. If it smells at all woody, or tinny, or musty, or moldy, it is inferior liquor. The residue of a well-made, well-aged liquor should have the same mellow, appetizing appeal as existed before the glass was drained.

Remember, in the case of liqueurs, that in cocktails—as distinguished from taking a pony straight as an after-dinner cordial—only a comparatively small amount is used in each drink for incidental flavoring and coloring. They are merely used as a substitute for sugar or a fruit syrup. Therefore, so long as they are well made and adequately flavored, there is no necessity of their meeting the same critical test that you should apply to a base liquor. Judge your liquor in the light of the manner in which you are going to use it.

The best method of judging liquor is by comparison. Before you can say with any assurance that a liquor is exceptionally fine or only moderately good or rather poor, you must have some standard by which to judge it. Therefore, particularly at the start, you should test two brands or samples together, rinsing the mouth thoroughly with warm water after testing one sample and before trying the other.

Since whiskies and brandies are easier to test than gins or rums, I suggest that you start with them. I also suggest that you start with two brands that differ widely. You will be better able to pass comparative judgment on two brands of closely similar excellence later, but don't start off with such a test or you may well become confused and give up entirely. I therefore suggest that, with Scotches, you compare Fulstrength or John Begg Liqueur or Johnnie Walker Black Label or Haig & Haig Pinch Bottle with Cutty Sark or Johnnie Walker Red Label. With ryes, compare Mount Vernon (if you are fortunate enough to have any of their old-time bonded) or Old Overholt or Large's Monongahela with Old Drum or Three Feathers. With bourbons, compare James E. Pepper or Old Forester or Old Taylor with Old Mr. Boston or any bourbon blend. With cognacs, compare Rémy Martin V.S.O.P. or Monnet V.V.S.O.P. or Courvoisier V.S. with Hennessy Three Star or with any California brandy.

After making a few tests with whiskies and brandies you can try gins and rums. Compare Booth's House of Lords or an *imported* Gordon with Three Feathers or Old Mr. Boston gins. Compare Cuban Bacardi or Havana Club Cuban rums with Government House. I am sorry that I cannot suggest any apple brandies for you to compare because I know of none on the market that I consider sufficiently mature to constitute a satisfactory standard of excellence.

Make these tests whenever you acquire a bottle of a new brand of liquor. Compare it with a brand that you have found you like. After you have fully acquired the knack of making comparative tests, compare a good, mature, full-bodied bourbon with a Scotch. If you now think you like Canadian whiskies, compare the bourbon with one of them. And keep some sort of record, even if only a mental one, of the results of your tests from time to time. Continual testing will greatly improve your judgment and you may well be surprised to see how your tastes change at the same time.

BUREAUCRATIC AND OTHER IDIOSYNCRASIES

Webster spells it idiosyncrasy. My own preferred spelling is idiot-sin-crazy! What used to be cause for a wry smile—the damnfoolishness of the professional do-gooders and the nitwit legislators and bureaucrats trying to keep the do-gooders happy—has now become cause for serious alarm. Let us look at a few of these items, some merely funny and some definitely frightening.

INTERNAL REVENUE TAXES

A few years before prohibition repeal, I sat on the Country Club porch just outside Charleston, West Virginia, and watched the spirals of smoke curling up from a half dozen stills in the nearby mountains. I was told that I could have a keg of White Mule shipped to me, express prepaid, packed in a barrel of carefully selected apples, at a cost—as I recall—of some four or five dollars per gallon for the liquor, with the apples thrown in for free! When repeal finally became effective, the Internal Revenue tax was fixed at $1.10 per proof gallon and I fondly imagined that moonshining would become pretty much a thing of the past. However, within a year, the tax was increased to $2.00 per gallon and then, through a series of five successive increases, to its present rate of $10.50 per gallon. To make matters worse, the government now insists that the tax must be paid at the end of eight years in bond even though the liquor is not withdrawn for sale until many years later! Small wonder that the twelve-, sixteen-, and twenty-year-old whiskies that I used to prize so highly (see page 55) are now, for the most part, a matter of memory only.

But will the distillers take this regulation without putting up a fight? Well, this question bids fair to split the industry wide open. On the one hand, as has already been pointed out, there is much more profit in the manufacture and sale of green whiskies and whisky blends than in top-quality, well-matured products. On the other hand, there is grave danger that if only immature ryes and bourbons are available, discriminating drinkers may turn to well-aged Scotch and Irish and even—God save the mark!—to Canadian. As to what the outcome will be, your guess is, perhaps, as good as mine.

And, in the meantime, as might well be expected, the illegal manufacture and sale of liquor that pays no tax whatsoever is increasing by leaps and bounds. Nearly 23,000 bootleg stills were seized in 1956; but, for every one seized, at least one remains and one or two new ones soon spring up. It is estimated that 70-odd million gallons of bootleg liquor were sold in 1956 or approximately 25 per cent of our total consumption. That represents a tax loss, at present rates, of nearly a billion dollars. Not only the liquor industry but many state enforcement agencies believe that a cut of 40 to 50 per cent in the Internal Revenue tax would so lower the cost to the consumer as to cripple the bootleg business with no substantial loss of revenue to the government. But will our federal bureaucrats and our Congressmen from the deep South, many of whom like their "Cawn Likker," see the point?

Frederick Othman, who is one of my favorite newspaper columnists, has recently called attention to a few other silly features of our federal laws. The first is the differentiation between still and sparkling wines. He points out that the tax on still wines amounts to $80 on each ton of grapes used in their manufacture; but, use the same ton of grapes to make champagne, and the tax is multiplied almost sevenfold. The only difference is carbon dioxide —CO_2—which you get tax-free at the soda fountain and in such bottled drinks as ginger ale and White Rock. Why?

The second is the tax on beer which used to be known as the poor man's drink. Othman doesn't argue for the return of the days when you could get a scuttle of suds for a nickel with a bountiful repast, known as the free lunch, thrown in. He does, however, feel that when a 12-ounce bottle of beer which, a few years ago, cost 10¢ sells for 25¢ or even more, primarily because of tax increases, things have gone a bit too far. He points out that, since 1950, approximately one third of the breweries in the United States have been forced out of business and, of course, there has been a corresponding resumption of the manufacture of home brew.

JIFFY QUICK JUNK

Today, Milady brings home from the market her precooked dinner of filet mignon, French-fried potatoes, and asparagus Hollandaise, all on an aluminum plate which she pops under the broiler for fifteen minutes and her dinner is ready. With it she drinks her decaffeinized instant coffee, sweetened with calory-free saccharin. While waiting for her dinner to heat, she decides to have a Daiquiri. No time to squeeze limes, so she takes a can of frozen lime juice (or, perhaps, lemon juice), shakes it up with her rum, and maybe a bit of sugar, and there is her synthetic Daiquiri. Ugh!! Ye shades of Constante Ribalagua! Perhaps it is as well that he died in time to escape this final insult to a noble drink. And, believe it or not, there are at least two rum manufacturers who, in the interest of promoting the sale of their products among those who are too lazy to make a real drink, recommend this short cut in their advertising.

At this point I suggest that you reread what I have said on pages 97–98 about using only fresh fruit, freshly squeezed. And along the same lines, perhaps I should warn against trying to keep cocktails in the icebox. One writer once said that you can no more keep a Martini in the refrigerator than you can keep a kiss in the refrigerator. He might well have expanded this to include all cocktails—at least all that are made with aromatic wines, such as vermouth, or with fruit juices. And Old-Fashioned can, perhaps, be kept in the refrigerator for a reasonable length of time but not a Manhattan or a Daiquiri, or a White Lady or a Jack Rose. To my admonition (page 98) regarding fruits to buy 'em fresh, squeeze 'em fresh, and use 'em fresh, I might well have added, as to the resultant cocktails, "Drink 'em fresh."

VODKA DRINKS

From time to time, my friends have said to me, "Dave, I have been given a bottle of vodka. What the [mustn't say the naughty word] do I do with it?"

Well, first of all, let us realize that vodka is an absolutely characterless neutral grain spirit (grain alcohol), watered down to 110 proof or less with no flavor characteristics of its own whatsoever. It will, therefore, blend with *anything*, just as water will blend with anything. But, when it is used in a mixed drink, reliance must be placed entirely on the other components for the flavor of the drink.

There are people who like Vodka Martinis but, unless you use much more vermouth than I recommend, you will have nothing but raw alcohol with a faint herb flavor from the vermouth. The all-persuasive juniper flavor of the gin is entirely absent. There are those who like a Vodka Old-Fashioned, but here we have only sweetened alcohol and water with a dash of bitters—absolutely no flavor except what comes from the bitters. I suppose there may be those who like Vodka on Rocks, but they should realize that they are drinking diluted pure grain alcohol and they are getting merely "kick" with no flavor whatsoever.

Nevertheless, there are many drinks—and excellent drinks—that can be made with vodka. It is necessary only to remember that the flavor characteristics must come from the other ingredients. You can substitute vodka for gin in the *WHITE LADY; ORANGE BLOSSOM; PINK LADY; GREENBACK; RED LION;* or *BEAUX ARTS*.

You can substitute it for the rum in the MORNING ROSE; MIAMI; CUBAINE; KNICKERBOCKER; and so on. You can use it in HIGHBALLS; BUCKS; RICKEYS; COLLINSES; FIZZES; DAISIES and FIXES; COBBLERS; COOLERS; SLINGS and TODDIES; LEMONADES, LIMEADES, and ORANGEADES (page 333); individual PUNCHES; SQUIRTS; Party PUNCHES and CUPS; and SWIZZLES. You can even use it in an ALEXANDER, though why anyone should want to, God only knows.

There are, however, a number of drinks the recipes for which specifically call for vodka and, for whatever they may be worth, here are some two dozen of the more common ones. And when it comes to "rolling your own," here is a liquor with which you can experiment endlessly. Just remember that it has absolutely no flavor of its own. Use it solely for alcoholic content, relying entirely on your quinquinas, fruit juices, cordials, and other spirits for your flavor, and there is practically no limit to the concoctions that you can devise—some good, some so-so, and some (as in the case of other concoctions) absolutely putrid!

BLOODY MARY A classic example of combining in one potion both the poison and the antidote. It was *not* invented by Rodgers and Hammerstein. As usual, proportions vary all over the map according to the whim of the individual author or bartender. Essentially, however, it consists of 1 part vodka and 2 to 6 parts tomato juice. Frequent additions are a few drops of Tabasco, Worcestershire, or A 1 Sauce. Sometimes a little lemon juice is mixed with the drink or a paper-thin slice of lemon is floated on top.

CANCAN Pour 1 to 1½ ounces of vodka into a champagne glass and fill with chilled champagne. Decorate with a twist of lemon or orange peel. See the BURRA PEG, and the RUSSIAN.

COSSACK

    1 part Sugar Syrup
    2 parts Lime Juice
    4 parts Vodka
    4 parts Cognac

Shake with crushed ice.

CZARINA

    1 part French Vermouth
    1 part Italian Vermouth
    6 parts Vodka
    3 or 4 parts Apricot Brandy to each drink

Stir. Note that this is a *VODKA MEDIUM MARTINI* or *VODKA PERFECT* with the addition of a little apricot flavor. A different version of the Czarina calls for equal parts of pineapple juice and vodka with a dash of bitters.

GOLDEN SCREW

    1 part Vodka
    1 to 3 parts Orange Juice

Shake or stir.
    Also sometimes called the *GOLDEN SPIKE*. Compare the *ORANGE BLOSSOM*, and the *SCREWDRIVER*.

GRAND DUCHESS

    1 part Grenadine
    2 parts Lime Juice
    2 parts Gold Label or other heavy Rum
    4 parts Vodka

Shake with cracked or crushed ice.

GYPSY or GYPSY QUEEN

    1 part Benedictine
    2 to 6 parts Vodka

1 dash Orange Bitters to each drink

Shake.

The original recipe calls for a proportion of 1 to 2. This, however, is rather sweet. About 5 to 6 parts vodka to 1 of Benedictine makes a much better drink.

HURRICANE
- 1 part Vodka
- 2 parts Cognac
- 1 teaspoonful Absinthe to each drink

Shake with cracked ice.

KANGAROO
- 3 to 4 parts Vodka
- 1 part French Vermouth

Stir. Twist of lemon on top.

KATINKA
- 1 part Apricot Liqueur
- 2 parts Lime Juice
- 8 parts Vodka

Shake well with crushed ice.

KRETCHMA
- 1 part Lemon Juice
- 2 parts Crème de Cacao
- 3 to 5 parts Vodka
- 1 or 2 dashes Grenadine to each drink

Shake with cracked ice. If the grenadine is omitted, this drink is also called the *NINITCHKA*.

MOSCOW MULE Place 1 or 2 cubes of ice in a large glass or mug. You can get special Moscow Mule mugs of copper, holding about 12 ounces, if you want to spend the money for them. Add the juice of a medium-sized lime, 2 to 3 ounces of vodka (depending on how hard you want the Mule to kick), and fill up with ginger beer (*not* ginger ale). This drink was invented by Heublein, whose Smirnoff vodka I recommend. However, while they specify their own Cock 'n' Bull ginger beer, I still prefer Schweppes' from England.

RUSSIAN This cocktail is, in effect, a *BURRA PEG* without the sugar. Take 1 jigger cognac and 1 dash Angostura for each drink. Shake with cracked ice and strain into pre-chilled saucer champagne glass. Fill glass with chilled champagne and decorate with a twist of lemon.

Another cocktail of the same name—and the ingredients of which more truly justify the name—consists of 1 part crème de cacao to 3 or 4 parts vodka. Shake with cracked ice.

RUSSIAN BEAR The Russian, with the addition of 2 or 3 teaspoonfuls of sweet cream to each drink.

SCREWDRIVER Simply an *ORANGE BLOSSOM*, using vodka in place of gin.

SOVIET
- 1 part French Vermouth
- 1 part Dry Sherry
- 6 parts Vodka

Stir with large ice cubes.

TOVARICH
- 1 part Kümmel
- 2 parts Lime Juice
- 8 parts Vodka

Shake with cracked ice.

TWISTER This is a *VODKA HIGHBALL*, but using Seven-Up instead of ginger ale or soda and with the addition of ⅓ lime to each drink. Drop the squeezed lime into the drink.

VODKA Straight vodka with 1 or 2 dashes of your favorite bitters.

VODKA ICEBERG Vodka on Rocks, with the addition of a dash of absinthe.

VODKA SPECIAL
- 1 part Crème de Cacao
- 2 parts Lemon Juice
- 8 parts Vodka

Shake thoroughly with cracked or crushed ice.

Another Vodka Special uses cherry liqueur in place of crème de cacao and lime juice in place of lemon.

VODKA TALL DRINKS Because of the current craze for vodka drinks, the manufacturers of White Rock have come out with a special citrus-flavored mixer for vodka tall drinks. They recommend the *VODKA PLUNGE* and the *VODKA SPLASH*. The former is merely a Vodka Highball, using their special mixer, decorated with a slice of lime or lemon. The latter is made in the same way but, in place of plain vodka, uses 3 parts vodka to 1 part of a cranberry-juice concentrate known as Cran.

VOLGA
- 1 part Lime Juice
- 1 part Orange Juice
- 4 parts Vodka
- 2 dashes Grenadine to each drink
- 1 dash Orange Bitters to each drink

Shake thoroughly with cracked or crushed ice.

VOLGA BOATMAN
- 1 part Orange Juice
- 1 part Kirsch
- 3 to 5 parts Vodka

Shake with cracked ice. Compare the Volga, above.

SHORT DRINKS, INCLUDING MORE COCKTAILS

There is only one reason for setting forth any further cocktail recipes for the person who has learned to "roll his own." For the past fifteen years I doubt that I have looked at a recipe book more than once for every hundred times I have made cocktails. However, from time to time you will hear some good friend sing loud praises over the cocktail he had at some party called the Alamagoopus Bazunk or the Silly Streptococcus and you may want to find out whether it is a standard drink that you never chanced to hear about and, if so, how it is made. I shall therefore try to give you a list of the more commonly known cocktails (and a few not so common) even though many of them are, in my opinion, decidedly inferior drinks. Where the usual recipes are bad merely because they are too sweet or too creamy or too something else that I think can be ironed out to some extent by a slight change in the formula, I have made that change. Many of them are intrinsically hopeless and, in such cases, I have given the usual recipe for whatever it may be worth.

In addition to more cocktails, this chapter also covers miscellaneous short drinks of various kinds from after-dinner cordials—about ¾ ounce to 1 ounce—up to Sours and similar drinks served in Sour or Delmonico glasses of 4 to 5 ounces. As a general proposition, however, I am leaving for a later chapter on long drinks all drinks containing any appreciable quantity of carbonated beverages. True, some bars may serve you a Rickey or a Highball in a

Delmonico glass. Nevertheless, the fact remains that the drink is, inherently, a tall drink even though it is possible to serve a reduced portion in a small glass.

ABACAXI RICAÇO (ah-bah'-kah-shee' rich-kah'-so) Abacaxí is the Brazilian (Portuguese) word for pineapple. "Rico" means delicious and "ricaço" means extra-delicious. This drink, therefore, is the Brazilian "Extra Delicious Pineapple." Cut off the top of a small pineapple and carefully scoop out the center leaving a shell about ½" thick. A sharp grapefruit knife is the best tool for this. Chill the shell in the refrigerator freezing compartment while mixing the drink. Remove the hard core from the pineapple center and beat up the pulp in your Waring Blendor. Add the juice of 1 large lime, about 2 teaspoonfuls sugar syrup, and 3 to 4 ounces of Cuban gold label or Barbados rum. A mixture of about 1 part Jamaica and 3 parts Cuban white label rum also works very well. Beat until well blended (about 2 minutes), add a small tumblerful of crushed ice, beat about 1 minute more, and pour the entire mixture, without straining, into the chilled pineapple shell. Serve with long straws. Some recipes call for blending the non-alcoholic ingredients only and pouring the rums over the mixture. I believe that the flavors "marry" better when they are beaten together.

"ABSINTHE DRINKS"

ABSINTHE COCKTAIL
3 parts Absinthe
2 parts Water
1 teaspoonful Sugar Syrup to each drink

Shake with crushed ice. A twist of lemon over each cocktail. Some recipes call for a dash of anisette.

If grenadine is substituted for the sugar syrup the drink becomes the TOMATE (toh-maht'), so called because of its tomato color. This is a popular French variety of the Absinthe Cocktail.

ABSINTHE DRIP The proper preparation of this drink requires an absinthe glass with a French drip top. Mix 1 teaspoonful sugar syrup and 1 jigger absinthe and place in the glass. Fill the top with finely shaved ice and water and, holding it high above the glass, let the water drip into the glass until the absinthe turns first milky, then cloudy and opalescent.

ABSINTHE A LA WOOLWORTH The Absinthe Drip requires a special drip glass which, if not entirely missing from the American market, is at least hard to find. A reasonably satisfactory substitute can be had in the top section of a toy Silex which can be bought at Woolworth's. If you find the stem inconveniently long, you can have it cut back to a more suitable length.

ABSINTHE FRAPPE
- 1 part Anisette
- 3 to 4 parts Absinthe
- 1 teaspoonful Sugar Syrup to each drink

Shake thoroughly with finely crushed or shaved ice. There are several methods of serving this drink. One method is to strain into an Old-Fashioned glass, adding ice water, if necessary, to fill the glass. My favorite method is to pour, ice and all, into a saucer champagne glass and serve with short straws.

ABSINTHE, ITALIAN STYLE
- 1 part Anisette
- 3 to 4 parts Absinthe
- ½ teaspoonful Maraschino to each drink

Place ingredients in a bar glass with cracked ice. Pour ice water slowly into glass until drink turns cloudy. Stir and strain into cocktail glass.

ACACIA

- 1 part Benedictine
- 3 to 4 parts Gin
- 1 teaspoonful Kirsch to each drink

This cocktail could not have been named for my fraternity, but it is worthy of it. The original recipe, with a larger proportion of Benedictine, won the first prize at the championship cocktail contest at Biarritz in 1928. It can be still further improved by adding 2 parts of lemon juice and another 3 to 4 parts of gin.

ADAM AND EVE

- 1 part Forbidden Fruit
- 1 part Cognac
- 1 part Gin

Shake. This cocktail is improved by adding a small amount of lemon or lime juice.

ADMIRAL

- 1 part Cherry Heering
- 2 parts Lime Juice
- 8 parts Gin

Shake with cracked ice.

AFTER-DINNER CORDIALS

For a complete list of cordials or liqueurs, see pages 199–208. As an after-dinner drink, these are served in a small liqueur glass and at room temperature.

The ladies usually like the sweet liqueurs, such as crème de cacao, Apry, Parfait Amour, etc. Most men prefer the highly aromatic liqueurs, such as Benedictine, Chartreuse, Drambuie, etc. Men also like the very dry fruit brandies, such as Himbeergeist (Zwack's raspberry brandy), kirschwasser, etc. Thus, normally, the ladies would prefer an apricot liqueur whereas the men would prefer an apricot brandy.

The fruit brandies may be served in a liqueur glass, the same as cordials.

Cordials are also sometimes served as *FRAPPES*.

Certain of the cordials are sometimes blended half and half with another spirituous liquor such as B & B (*Benedictine & Brandy*) and D & S (*Drambuie & Scotch*). For the latter, use a liqueur Scotch, such as Fulstrength.

AKVAVIT 'N' BITTERS It has already been pointed out that *AKVAVIT* should be chilled in the bottle, served in pre-chilled glasses, and not diluted by shaking with ice.

Nevertheless, many Americans like a dash of bitters with the akvavit. The best method is to put a dash of bitters in each glass, twirl the glass to coat the sides with the bitters, shake out the excess, then pour in the pre-chilled akvavit.

ALAMAGOOZLUM
- 1 part Bitters
- 1 part Curaçao
- 3 parts Sugar Syrup
- 3 parts Yellow Chartreuse
- 3 parts Jamaica Rum
- 4 parts Holland Gin
- 4 parts Water
- 1 Egg White to each 4 or 5 drinks

Shake with cracked or crushed ice.

This cocktail is supposed to have been a specialty of the elder Morgan of the House of Morgan, which goes to prove that as a bartender he was an excellent banker.

ALASKA
- 1 part Yellow Chartreuse
- 5 to 7 parts Gin

Stir. A twist of lemon over each drink. Note that this is merely a Dry Martini with Chartreuse in place of vermouth. Because of the sweetness of the Chartreuse, a larger proportion of gin may be used than with the Dry Martini.

This is also sometimes called the ORIENTAL. It can be greatly improved by using less Chartreuse and adding 1 or 2 parts dry sherry. This is the NOME.

ALEXANDER

- 1 part Sweet Cream
- 1 part Crème de Cacao
- 4 parts Gin

Shake with cracked ice.

The above is a modified Alexander that can be consumed with reasonable safety before a meal, although why anyone should take it if dry cocktails are available, I wouldn't know.

Reference has been made several times to the original Alexander consisting of equal parts of the three ingredients—a nice midafternoon snack in place of a half pound of bonbons, but deadly as a pre-prandial drink. If brandy is substituted for the gin, this drink becomes the BRANDY ALEXANDER or PANAMA. If made with gin and cognac, half and half, it is known in Paris as the BLOND NEGRESS (LA NEGRESSE BLONDE).

ALPINE GLOW

- 1 part Cointreau
- 2 parts Lemon Juice
- 4 parts Cognac
- 4 parts Gold Label Rum
- 1 or 2 dashes Grenadine to each drink

Shake with cracked or crushed ice.

AMBROSIA Soak a small lump of sugar in Angostura. Place in a saucer champagne glass, add 1 pony of cognac, and fill with champagne.

See my comments on the *CHAMPAGNE COCKTAIL*. Ambrosia, phooey!

AMERICAN BEAUTY
- 1 part French Vermouth
- 1 part Grenadine
- 1 part White Crème de Menthe
- 1 part Orange Juice
- 4 parts Cognac

Shake well with crushed ice. Float 1 teaspoonful claret on top of each drink.

This drink is sometimes served in a tall glass filled with crushed ice and is then called *AMERICAN BEAUTY PUNCH*.

AMERICAN FLAG A *POUSSE-CAFE* consisting of grenadine, maraschino, and Parfait Amour or Crème Yvette.

AMER PICON See *PICON COCKTAILS*.

ANGEL'S DREAM A *POUSSE-CAFE* consisting of Apry and sweet cream.

ANGEL'S KISS A *POUSSE-CAFE* consisting of crème de cacao, Crème Yvette, prunelle, and sweet cream. Sometimes the Crème Yvette and prunelle are omitted.

ANGEL'S TIT A *POUSSE-CAFE* consisting of crème de cacao, maraschino, and sweet cream.

ANGLER'S GIN 'N' BITTERS with a dash of grenadine. Sometimes served in a Sour glass filled with crushed ice.

APPETIZER
- 1 part Orange Juice

2 parts Dubonnet
4 parts Gin
1 dash Bitters to each drink

Stir.

APRICOT

1 part Apricot Brandy
3 parts Gin
1 dash Orange Bitters to each drink

Shake with cracked ice. Decorate with a cherry.

The APRICOT BRANDY SOUR is also sometimes called an Apricot Cocktail and sometimes an APRICOT DELIGHT.

AQUITANIA

1 part Apricot Liqueur
2 parts Lime Juice
8 parts Gin

Shake with cracked or crushed ice. Decorate with a cherry.

ARMY & NAVY

1 part Lemon Juice
1 part Orgeat
2 parts Gin

I have given the original recipe which, to my mind, is horrible. If made to my 1:2:8 formula, it is merely the GIN SOUR with orgeat used in place of sugar syrup.

AROUND THE WORLD

1 part Green Crème de Menthe
2 parts Pineapple Juice
8 parts Gin

Shake with cracked or crushed ice. Decorate with a green cherry.

AUNT EMILY
- 1 part Apricot Liqueur
- 2 parts Gin
- 1 part Orange Juice
- 2 parts Applejack
- 1 dash Grenadine to each drink

Shake with cracked ice.

BACARDI FLYER
A *BACARDI COCKTAIL* strained into a saucer champagne glass and the glass filled with iced champagne.

BALTIMORE BRACER
- 1 part Anisette
- 1 part Cognac
- 1 Egg White to each drink

Shake with cracked or crushed ice.

BERLIN BINGE
Invented by Jean Gaste at Le Tangage in Paris and dedicated to the harmonious association of the four great world powers. It consists of American bourbon, English gin, French cognac, and Russian vodka, garnished with an olive (preferably a green olive), symbolizing the olive branch of peace. Equal parts of the four liquors, symbolizing equality of the four powers.

Not as bad as it sounds, but *definitely* not recommended. It is also sometimes called the *LEAGUE OF NATIONS*.

BETSY FLANAGAN
This is merely a *JAMAICA RUM MANHATTAN* with a dash of Angostura and ½ teaspoonful sugar syrup to each drink.

BIARRITZ
A *BRANDY SOUR* with curaçao in place of sugar syrup.

BIG APPLE
Another exotic "what-is-it." The distin-

guishing characteristic is the manner in which it is served. Cut a conical plug about as large around as a silver dollar from the top of a large, preferably red apple and trim the point of the cone off to leave a plug about ½" thick. Scoop out the pulp and core of the apple (see Abacaxí Ricaço, above), leaving a shell about ¾" thick. Chill the shell as in the Abacaxí Ricaço. In the Waring Blendor beat 1 part lemon juice, 2 parts orange juice, and 3 parts apple brandy with a small amount of honey and the pulp from the apple. Strain into the chilled apple and serve with straws. The ingredients of the *JACK ROSE* or the *APPLEJACK SOUR* can be substituted for those given above.

This drink is sometimes called the *COUNTRY COCKTAIL* but the original Country Cocktail consists of equal parts of lemon juice, applejack, and port with about 1 teaspoonful of sugar syrup and ¼ to ½ an egg to each drink.

BITTERSWEET A RYE SOUR with 4 parts orange juice in place of 2 parts lemon juice.

BLACKBERRY BEAUTY
    1 part Lime Juice
    2 parts Blackberry Liqueur
    5 parts Gin

Shake vigorously with cracked ice.

BLACKBERRY JULEP This is a 26 proof domestic blackberry wine made by the Berriwyne Co. of New Jersey. It may be served hot (but don't let it boil), at room temperature, or chilled. It may be served "On the Rocks" or as a "Mist," either plain or with a dash of bitters, and it blends satisfactorily with gin, rum, vodka, or with dry white brandies such as kirsch.

BLACKBERRY PUNCH
    1 teaspoonful Sugar Syrup

THE FINE ART OF MIXING DRINKS 249

>   Juice of 1 large Lemon
>   1 ounce Rum (preferably a dark Rum)
>   2 ounces Blackberry Liqueur

Shake, strain into a goblet of shaved ice, garnish, and serve with straws.

BLACKOUT A BLACKBERRY BRANDY SOUR. Also sometimes made with part blackberry brandy and part gin as a base.

BLACK STRIPE
>   1 part Water
>   1 part New Orleans Molasses
>   3 parts Jamaica Rum

Shake vigorously with cracked ice.

This one is submitted as a curiosity rather than as a drink. It is definitely *not* an apéritif cocktail.

This is also sometimes served as a hot drink. See HOT GROG.

BLINKER
>   1 part Grenadine
>   3 parts fresh Grapefruit Juice
>   6 to 8 parts Rye or Bourbon

One of the few cocktails using grapefruit juice. Not particularly good but not too bad.

BLOSSOM
>   1 part Pineapple Juice
>   2 parts Lime Juice
>   8 parts White Label Rum

Shake with cracked or crushed ice.

BLUE MONDAY
>   1 part *Blue Curaçao* or Blue Cointreau

3 to 5 parts Vodka

Stir with large ice cubes.

BLUE SKIES
- 1 part Sugar Syrup
- 2 parts Lemon Juice
- 4 parts Gin
- 4 parts Applejack
- 1 or 2 dashes Grenadine to each drink

Shake with cracked or crushed ice.

BOLO
- 1 part Sugar Syrup
- 2 parts Lime Juice
- 1 part Orange Juice
- 8 parts White Label Rum

Shake with cracked or crushed ice.

BOOMERANG
- 1 part Passion-Fruit Nectar
- 1 part Gin
- 1 part White Label Rum
- 1 dash each of Lemon Juice and Angostura to each drink

The ingredients in this drink are all excellent but the drink itself violates practically every principle of cocktail mixing. It is given here as a horrible example of what *not* to do.

BOYD
- 2 parts French Vermouth
- 2 parts Lime Juice
- 6 parts White Label Rum
- 1 teaspoonful Raspberry Syrup to each drink

Shake with cracked ice. Grenadine can be substituted for the raspberry syrup.

BRAINSTORM
    1 part French Vermouth
    4 parts Rye
    2 or 3 dashes Benedictine to each drink

Stir. Decorate with a twist of orange peel.
Another version of this drink calls for Irish whisky instead of rye.

BUGHOUSE
    1 part Italian Vermouth
    3 parts Cognac
    1 teaspoonful Absinthe to each drink

Stir.

BULLFROG An Apricot Brandy Sour but with no sugar. This drink is also sometimes called the *HOP TOAD*. Some recipes call for equal parts of apricot brandy and Jamaica rum.

CAFE KIRSCH Equal parts of kirsch and strong, cold coffee, sugar to taste, and 1 egg white to each drink. Shake with cracked ice and strain into cocktail glass.

CANADIAN This cocktail is straight Canadian whisky with 2 or 3 dashes each of curaçao and Angostura and 1 teaspoonful of sugar syrup to each drink. Maple syrup is sometimes used in place of the sugar.

CANASTA
    1 part Lemon Juice
    2 parts Southern Comfort

Shake well with cracked ice.
Not too bad but, if you don't mind, you can have your Canasta; I'll take bridge!

CAPTAIN'S BLOOD
- 1 part Lime Juice
- 2 to 3 parts Jamaica Rum
- 2 or 3 dashes Bitters to each drink

Shake with finely cracked ice.

CARIOCA
This is merely the name given by the manufacturers of Carioca-brand rum to a Daiquiri made with Carioca gold label. Compare *BACARDI*.

CARMEN
This is merely the *MORNING ROSE* with lime juice in place of lemon juice, which is an improvement.

CHAMPAGNE COCKTAIL
This drink should be served in a pre-chilled saucer champagne glass. Place a medium-sized loaf of sugar in the glass and saturate it with Angostura bitters—about 2 dashes. Fill with thoroughly chilled champagne. Add a twist of lemon or orange peel, or both.

The addition of cognac in the ratio of 1 part of cognac to about 4 or 5 of champagne converts this cocktail into the *MAHARAJAH'S BURRA PEG*. The Burra Peg is also served as a long drink in a Highball or Collins glass, decorated with a spiral of lemon or lime peel, like a Horse's Neck. See also the *RUSSIAN*.

Why some people rave about the Champagne Cocktail is a complete mystery to me. The only known reason for regarding it as "ultra-ultra" is the fact that champagne is expensive. From every point of view, other than cost, this cocktail is a decidedly inferior drink, and no true champagne lover would ever commit the sacrilege of polluting a real vintage champagne by dunking even plain sugar—much less bitters—in it. So, if you must, on occasion, serve this incongruous mess just for the sake of "putting on the dog," then, in the name of all that a true lover of the grape holds sacred, use a cheap domestic champagne or even an artificially carbonated white wine.

The cocktail will be just as good, the burden on your pocketbook will be less, and you will have refrained from desecrating the memory of Dom Perignon, the Benedictine monk who, by accident, first discovered champagne.

CHAMPERELLE or SHAMPARELLE The Champerelle is nothing but a large *POUSSE-CAFÉ* served in a sherry glass instead of a Pousse-Café glass. For some unknown reason it is usually called a *BRANDY CHAMPERELLE*, although kirsch, Goldwasser or some other very dry liquor is frequently used instead of cognac with the cordials. As with all Pousse-Cafés, care must be taken to prevent the different liquors from running together.

Any combination of liqueurs and spirits that will remain separate can be used. One of the oldest recipes I have calls for the following—to be poured in the order named: orange Curaçao, Yellow Chartreuse, anisette, and either kirschwasser or cognac.

Compare the *GOLDEN SLIPPER*, the *LUNE DE MIEL*, the *KNICKEBEIN*, and the *POUSSE L'AMOUR*, in which an egg yolk is also used. See also the *SCAFFA*.

CHAPPARA
    1 part Italian Vermouth
    1 part Gold Label Rum
    Peel of an entire Lime, thoroughly squeezed

This drink is nothing to brag about at best. The Havana bar that makes a specialty of it does not ice and shake it but mixes it in advance and leaves it several days in the refrigerator to "ripen." Ugh! Every principle of cocktail mixing is violated, with the result that one would expect.

CHARLIE CHAPLIN
    2 parts Lime Juice

3 parts Sloe Gin
3 parts Apricot Brandy

Shake with crushed or cracked ice. The original recipe for this drink calls for three times as much sloe gin as brandy, which is far too sweet a drink for a cocktail.

CHARLOTTE RUSSE One half teaspoon sugar syrup, 1 dash each Angostura and orange bitters to each drink of gin. Shake with cracked or crushed ice. Rinse pre-chilled cocktail glass with a few drops of absinthe and strain the gin mixture into it.

Not a bad drink despite the gooey-sounding name.

CHAUNCEY OLCOTT
1 part Italian Vermouth
1 part Dry Sherry
6 parts Irish Whisky

Stir.

CHERRY BLOSSOM
1 part Curaçao and Grenadine, half and half
2 parts Lemon Juice
3 parts Cognac
5 parts Kirsch

Shake with cracked ice. Decorate with a cherry.

CHINESE Two or 3 dashes each of curaçao, grenadine, maraschino, and Angostura to each drink of gold label or other medium- or heavy-type rum.

Shake with cracked ice. A twist of lemon over each glass. Decorate with a cherry.

CHOCOLATE SOLDIER
1 part Lime Juice
2 parts Dubonnet
4 parts Gin

Shake with cracked ice.

CLASSIC

- 1 part Curaçao
- 1 part Maraschino
- 4 parts Lemon Juice
- 8 parts Cognac

Shake with cracked ice. A twist of lemon over each drink.

CLUB Perhaps it would not be too much of an exaggeration to say that there are as many CLUB COCKTAILS as there are clubs. Here are a few examples:

NO. 1 Equal parts of dry sherry and tawny port with a dash of orange bitters to each drink. Stir.

NO. 2 Straight gin with 2 dashes each of orange bitters, Chartreuse, and Jamaica rum to each drink. Stir. Decorate with stuffed olive.

NO. 3 Straight whisky with 1 or 2 dashes each of Angostura and grenadine to each drink. Stir. Decorate with a cherry. (Note the similarity of this cocktail to the Old-Fashioned.)

NO. 4 Straight cognac with 2 dashes each of maraschino, crème d'ananas, and orange bitters to each drink. Stir. A twist of lemon over each glass.

COMMANDO

- 1 part Cointreau
- 2 parts Lime Juice
- 8 parts Whisky
- 2 or 3 dashes Absinthe to each drink

Shake with cracked ice.

COMMODORE

- 1 part Sugar Syrup
- 2 parts Lemon Juice
- 8 parts Gold Label Rum

2 dashes Grenadine or Raspberry Syrup to each drink and 1 Egg White to each two drinks

Shake. Decorate with a cherry.

Another version of the Commodore calls for whisky instead of rum, omits the egg white, and uses orange bitters in place of the grenadine. Obviously, the two Commodores command two different fleets.

CONTINENTAL

 1 part Sweet Cream
 2 parts Lemon Juice
 8 parts Rye
 3 dashes Jamaica Rum to each drink

Shake with crushed ice.

Another version of the Continental calls for 1 part each of Benedictine, lime juice, and French vermouth, and 4 parts gin.

CORNELL Straight gin with 1 egg white and a few dashes of maraschino to each drink. Shake well with cracked ice and strain into cocktail glass.

CORONATION Just as the Club Cocktail depends on whose club it is, so does the Coronation depend on who is being crowned. Here are four versions:

NO. 1 Two parts French vermouth and 3 parts sherry with 2 or 3 dashes each of maraschino and orange bitters to each drink. Stir.

NO. 2 Equal parts of French vermouth, Dubonnet, and gin. Stir.

NO. 3 Equal parts of French vermouth, Italian vermouth, and applejack with 1 or 2 dashes apricot liqueur to each drink.

NO. 4 Straight cognac with 1 or 2 dashes each of curaçao and orange bitters to each drink. Shake with a bruised sprig of mint. A twist of lemon over each drink, and decorate with a small mint leaf.

COUNTRY CLUB Equal parts of French vermouth and white label rum with a few dashes of orange curaçao to each drink. Stir.

As previously noted, I believe that gold label rum blends better than white label in aromatic-type drinks. Try this drink both ways and see which you like the better.

See also the whisky cocktail by the same name.

CRESCENT CITY
> 1 part Lime Juice
> 2 parts Italian Vermouth
> 4 parts Gold Label Rum
> 1 or 2 dashes Angostura to each drink

Shake or stir.

This cocktail, while not particularly good, is interesting in that it is a compromise between the aromatic type and the Sour type.

CRUSTAS The distinguishing feature of the Crusta is that the entire inside of the glass is lined with lemon or orange peel. The drink may be served in either a wineglass or an Old-Fashioned glass, although it is much harder to make the peel fit in the Old-Fashioned glass.

Take a large lemon or a small orange of a size approximating that of the glass to be used. Cut off both ends and peel the remainder in spiral fashion so as to keep the peel all in one piece. Line the inside of the glass with this peel, wet the edge of the glass, and dip in powdered sugar to frost the edge of both peel and glass. In a bar glass mix 1 part sugar syrup, 2 parts lemon juice, and 8 parts brandy with 1 or 2 dashes each of maraschino and bitters to each drink. Shake with finely crushed ice and strain into the prepared glass.

While the BRANDY CRUSTA is the most common form of this drink, it is, after all, merely a Sour-type drink served in fancy style. Substitution of a different liquor as a base will give you a GIN CRUSTA, a RUM CRUSTA, an APPLEJACK CRUSTA, a WHISKY CRUSTA, and so on.

CUBAN

    1 part Curaçao
    2 parts Lime Juice
    2 parts Pineapple Juice
    8 parts White Label Rum

Shake with crushed ice. A twist of lemon over each drink.

Another version of the Cuban omits the pineapple juice and substitutes equal parts of grenadine and maraschino for the curaçao.

Still another version omits the pineapple and substitutes apricot liqueur for the curaçao and cognac for the rum. This is high treason! How could any drink be truly Cuban unless made with rum?

CUBAN DREAM Straight gold label rum with a few dashes each of Benedictine and French vermouth to each drink. Shake or stir.

This cocktail is also sometimes called simply the DREAM.

DAWN

    1 part Apricot Liqueur
    2 parts Orange Juice
    8 parts White Label Rum
    1 dash Grenadine to each drink

Shake well with crushed ice.

There is a very similar drink in flavor called the GOLDEN DAWN and there are several versions of that drink. Here are three. The drink should be thoroughly chilled and may be decorated with a cherry.

GOLDEN DAWN, NO. 1   One part apricot liqueur, 1 part lime juice, 2 parts orange juice, 6 parts gin, 1 dash grenadine to each drink. Compare the Paradise, page 280.

GOLDEN DAWN, NO. 2   One part apricot brandy, 1 part lemon juice, 2 parts orange juice, 4 parts applejack, 1 dash grenadine to each drink.

GOLDEN DAWN, NO. 3   Same as No. 1 but with rum instead of gin.

DEMI-VIRGIN

    1 part Grenadine
    2 parts Lime Juice
    8 parts Gin
    1 dash Orange Bitters to each drink

Shake well with cracked or crushed ice.

This is simply a Gin Sour with grenadine substituted for sugar syrup.

DERBY

    1 part Peach Brandy
    4 parts Gin

Crush 1 small sprig of mint to each drink in bar glass or shaker; add the liquor and shake well with crushed ice. This drink is improved by the addition of a small quantity of sugar syrup—not over 1 teaspoonful to each drink.

There is also another cocktail called the Derby consisting of straight cognac with 1 or 2 dashes each of curaçao, pineapple syrup, and bitters. The cocktail glass is filled about ½ to ⅔ full with this mixture and the glass then filled up with champagne.

DIKI-DIKI

    1 part Grapefruit Juice

1 part Gin
4 parts Applejack

Shake with crushed ice.

This is a very dry cocktail. Another version of the Diki-Diki, not so dry, calls for Swedish Punch in place of the gin. If this is used, the quantity should be reduced to about ½ part. Otherwise, the cocktail will be too sweet.

DIVAN (pronounced dee-vahn′) Equal parts lemon juice, orange juice, and rye with 1 teaspoonful grenadine to each drink. This drink can be improved by increasing the proportion of whisky to 2 or 3 parts.

DOCTOR There are numerous recipes for this drink. Here are several. Shake well with cracked ice.

NO. 1 Equal parts of lime juice and Swedish Punch.

NO. 2 Equal parts of lemon juice, Swedish Punch, and gin. This is also known as the GRETA GARBO.

NO. 3 One part lemon juice, 1 part orange juice, 2 parts Swedish Punch.

NO. 4 One part lime juice, 2 parts Jamaica rum, 3 parts Swedish Punch.

DOLORES
1 part Dubonnet
1 part Dry Sherry
2 parts Jamaica Rum

Stir. A twist of lemon over each glass.

Jamaica rum blends perfectly with Dubonnet. A mixture of 1 part rum to 3 or 4 parts Dubonnet is most palatable and, while rum drinks generally should be stinging cold, the high proportion of Dubonnet in this drink makes it pleasing even without chilling.

There is another quite different drink also called the Dolores consisting of equal parts of crème de cacao, kirsch, and Spanish brandy with the white of an egg to each 2 drinks.

DOROTHY or DOROTHY GISH
    1 part Orange Juice
    1 part Pineapple Juice
    6 parts White Label Rum
    2 or 3 dashes Apricot Brandy to each drink

Shake well with cracked ice.

DOUBLE RAINBOW
    1 part Lemon Juice
    3 parts Orange Juice
    6 parts Southern Comfort
    3 dashes Grenadine to each drink

Shake well with cracked or crushed ice. This makes a very satisfactory frozen cocktail also.

DOUGLAS FAIRBANKS
    1 part Apricot Brandy
    2 parts Lemon Juice
    4 parts Gin
    1 Egg White to each 2 drinks

Shake with cracked or crushed ice.

Note that this drink is, in effect, a Golden Dawn (see page 259) with egg white substituted for the orange juice.

EAGLE
    1 part Parfait Amour
    2 parts Lemon Juice
    8 parts Gin
    1 Egg White to each 2 drinks

Shake with cracked ice.

EMERALD STAR

- 1 part Green Curaçao
- 2 parts Lemon Juice
- 2 parts Apricot Brandy
- 4 parts Gin
- 4 parts White Label Rum

Shake with cracked ice.

EPICUREAN

- 1 part Kümmel
- 2 parts French Vermouth
- 4 parts Cognac
- 1 dash Bitters to each drink

Stir.

ERIN

- 1 part Green Crème de Menthe
- 3 parts Gin

Shake. Decorate with a green cherry. Some recipes call for the addition of a few dashes of lemon and orange juice, the white of an egg to each 2 drinks, and a dash of nutmeg in each glass.

ETHIOPIA A Sweet Martini with several dashes of Fernet-Branca to each drink and a twist of lemon.

FEDORA

- 1 part Curaçao
- 2 parts Lemon Juice
- 3 parts Gold Label Rum
- 3 parts Whisky
- 2 parts Cognac

Shake.

Some recipes call for sugar syrup in addition to the curaçao. Also, some recipes make one or another of the rum, whisky, and cognac the dominant base with only a few dashes of the other two.

FERNET   Equal parts of cognac and Fernet-Branca with a few dashes of sugar syrup and Angostura. Stir. A twist of orange over each glass.

If crème de menthe is substituted for the cognac, this becomes a FERNET MENTHE.

FIBBER McGEE   A Sweet Martini with a dash of Angostura and about 2 teaspoonfuls of grapefruit juice to each drink.

FLAMINGO
   1 part Apricot Brandy
   1 part Lime Juice
   3 parts Gin
   1 or 2 dashes Grenadine to each drink

Shake with cracked ice.

FLIPS   A Flip is any wine or liquor shaken up with sugar and a whole egg. The usual proportions are 1 teaspoonful sugar or sugar syrup, 1 whole egg, and 2 ounces liquor to each drink. Shake with cracked or finely crushed ice and strain into a small Sour or Delmonico glass (about 3 to 4 ounces). Decorate with a dash of grated nutmeg.

The most common spirituous-liquor Flips are the *BRANDY FLIP* and *GIN FLIP*. The most common wine Flips are the *SHERRY FLIP* and *PORT FLIP*. There are also *APPLEJACK FLIPS*, *RUM FLIPS* (using gold label Cuban, Jamaica, or any of the intermediate rums), *WHISKY FLIPS*, *CLARET FLIPS*, *MADEIRA FLIPS*, and so on. All are made exactly the same except for the wine or liquor used as a base.

The *CHOCOLATE FLIP* is made with equal parts of cognac and sloe gin. The *COFFEE FLIP* is made with equal parts of cognac and port.

See also *SHERRY AND EGG*.

FLORIDA
- 1 part Sugar Syrup
- 2 parts Lime Juice
- 2 parts Pineapple Juice
- 8 parts White Label Rum
- 1 dash Green Crème de Menthe to each drink

Shake. Decorate with a sprig of mint. The Orange Blossom is also sometimes called the *FLORIDA*.

FORBIDDEN FRUIT Equal parts French vermouth, gin, and Forbidden Fruit. Shake.

FOUR W Equal parts Jamaica or Cuban gold label rum and unsweetened grapefruit juice with a dash each of Angostura and maple syrup to each drink. Invented by Herb Smith, formerly of Larchmont, N. Y., and put out as a specialty years ago by his friend, Oscar of the Waldorf, in honor of the Duke of Windsor and his then bride. The four W's stand for *WALLY WARFIELD WINDSOR WALLOP*.

FRAPPES To frappé is to chill with shaved or very finely crushed ice. Some recipes call for shaking the drink with the snow ice and then straining into a glass. The more usual method, however, is to pour the drink with the ice into a cocktail or saucer champagne glass and serve with a short straw. In the case of liqueurs, the glass is usually filled with the ice first and the liqueur merely poured into the glass of ice without shaking.

Practically any liqueur or, for that matter, any other drink can be served as a Frappé. Absinthe and crème de menthe (both white and green), however, are the two drinks most commonly served as a Frappé.

The *FRAPPEED CAFE ROYAL* consists of 1 part cognac and 3 parts strong black coffee shaken and served as a Frappé.

FRESCO Crush a small piece of pineapple for each drink with a muddler or, if you have a Waring Blendor, whip in the Blendor. To the muddled pineapple add

   1 part Sugar Syrup
   2 parts Lime Juice
   8 parts White Label Rum

Shake with crushed ice and strain into pre-chilled and frosted glasses.

FRIAR Equal parts French vermouth, pineapple juice, and gin. Shake vigorously with crushed ice and strain into glasses while still frothy.

FROZEN COCKTAILS Frozen cocktails require the use of a Waring Blendor or similar electric mixer of the type used at soda fountains. The egg-beater type of electric mixer cannot be used.

The cocktail ingredients are poured into the mixer with approximately the same quantity of crushed ice and mixed at high speed for about 2 minutes until the entire mass is the consistency of fine snow. The drink is then served in a large cocktail or saucer champagne glass with short straws. The mixture should be heaped up in the glass in the shape of an inverted cone. This may be accomplished by pouring part of the drink into a medium-meshed strainer, holding the strainer above the glass, and tapping its side.

Practically any Sour-type cocktail is adaptable to being served "frozen" style. The most common of all is the *FROZEN DAIQUIRI.*

Others suggested are the *FROZEN SOUTHERN COMFORT SOUR, FROZEN ORANGE BLOSSOM, FROZEN RHETT BUTLER, FROZEN RED LION, FROZEN SCARLETT O'HARA, FROZEN SNOW WHITE, FROZEN MIAMI, FROZEN STINGER,* and *FROZEN HONEYMOON.*

Do not serve egg or cream cocktails frozen style. The

FU MANCHU
   1 part Sugar Syrup
   2 parts Lime Juice
   4 parts Jamaica Rum
   2 dashes each Curaçao & White Crème de Menthe to each drink

Shake with crushed ice.

FUTURITY
Equal parts Italian vermouth and sloe gin with a few dashes each of Angostura and grenadine to each drink. Stir.

GABY DES LYS (gah'-bee day lee')
   1 part Orgeat
   4 parts Gin
   3 or 4 dashes Absinthe to each drink

Shake vigorously with crushed ice.

GLOOM LIFTER
   1 part Sugar Syrup
   2 parts Lemon Juice
   6 parts Irish Whisky
   1 Egg White to each 2 drinks

Shake with cracked ice.
Compare the GLOOM CHASER and GLOOM RAISER.

GOLDEN SLIPPER
Fill a sherry glass about ⅓ full with Yellow Chartreuse; carefully float an egg yolk on the Chartreuse; then fill the glass to within ⅜" of the top with Danziger Goldwasser.

Compare the CHAMPERELLE, the KNICKEBEIN, and the LUNE DE MIEL.

GRAND PASSION
   1 part Passion-Fruit Nectar
   2 parts Gin
   1 dash Angostura to each drink

This drink can be greatly improved by adding 1 to 2 parts lemon or lime juice and increasing the gin to at least 5 or 6 parts.

GRAND SLAM   Manhattan with the addition of 1 or 2 teaspoonfuls lime juice and 2 or 3 dashes curaçao to each drink. Stir.
   Another drink also known as the Grand Slam consists of 1 part grenadine and curaçao (half and half), 2 parts lemon juice, and 8 parts white label rum.

GRAPEFRUIT BLOSSOM   Same as the Orange Blossom but with grapefruit juice in place of orange juice. A few dashes of maraschino to each drink to counteract the sharpness of the grapefruit. This drink is also sometimes made with white Cuban rum in place of the gin.

GRASSHOPPER   Originally this drink was a two-color Pousse-Café consisting of crème de cacao and crème de menthe, with or without a cream float. Recently, however, it has developed into a so-called cocktail consisting of equal parts of white crème de cacao, green crème de menthe, and sweet cream, shaken with cracked ice. One bar in New York City cuts down on the cream and adds blackberry brandy. This results in a rather muddy-looking locust; but, with or without the blackberry, as a cocktail it is strictly vile.

GREENWICH   Equal parts of crème de cacao, applejack, and gin. Shake with cracked ice.

HELEN TWELVETREES   Equal parts of gin and pineapple juice with a dash or two of Parfait Amour to give the whole a blue tint. Shake with crushed ice. Some recipes (e.g., Sloppy Joe's of Havana, Cuba) call for 1 part gin to 2 parts pineapple juice.

HIGH HAT
   1 part Cherry Heering
   2 parts Lemon Juice
   4 parts Whisky

Shake with cracked or crushed ice.

HOLLANDS or HOLLAND GIN Holland gin is a pungent, highly aromatic drink. While most Americans do not like it and regard its flavor as rather brackish, nevertheless, if taken straight and *very* cold (like vodka and akvavit), it is a splendid drink. The gin should be thoroughly chilled in the bottle rather than stirred or shaken with ice. It should be served in a small whisky glass, not in a cocktail glass. Finally, like vodka and akvavit, it should be downed at one swallow and not sipped.

Holland gin does not blend well with other flavors and, while dozens of recipes have been written for Holland-gin cocktails, they are generally regarded (and properly so) as pretty much worthless. There are two or three possible exceptions. Here they are:

1. HOLLAND GIN 'N' BITTERS One or 2 dashes Angostura or other aromatic bitters to each drink of Holland gin.

2. HOLLAND GIN COCKTAIL One dash Absinthe and 2 dashes each of sugar syrup and orange bitters to each drink of the gin. Stir quickly with crushed ice.

3. HOLLAND'S PRIDE One part Italian vermouth and 2 parts Holland gin. Add Absinthe, sugar syrup, and orange bitters, as in the Holland Gin Cocktail. Stir quickly with cracked ice.

THE FINE ART OF MIXING DRINKS

IDEAL

- 1 part Sugar Syrup
- 2 parts Grapefruit Juice
- 2 parts French Vermouth
- 6 parts Gin

Shake with cracked ice.

With the vermouth omitted and the grapefruit juice increased to 4 parts, this becomes the *LILLY*.

IRISH COFFEE & RUSSIAN TEA

Here are two delicious hot drinks for the end of your dinner and, believe it or not, the Russian Tea does *not* use vodka. The Irish Coffee has attained great popularity in a number of New York restaurants. Different restaurants have their own special formulas and hocus-pocus for serving it but, essentially, a jigger of Irish whisky is blended in the cup or mug with sugar to taste, hot coffee is added to within about a half inch from the top, and then extra-heavy (even clotted) cream is floated gently on top.

The Russian Tea consists of very strong, black tea flamed with cognac in exactly the same manner as the *CAFE ROYAL*.

ISLE OF PINES

- 1 part Sugar Syrup
- 2 parts Grapefruit Juice
- 6 parts White Label Rum

Shake with cracked ice.

JACKAROO

- 3 parts Passion-Fruit Nectar
- 4 parts Rye
- 1 dash Angostura to each drink

To my taste, the fruit syrups and liqueurs do not blend well with whisky. This drink can be improved by adding lemon juice and increasing the quantity of rye. See the *GRAND PASSION*.

JITTERS Equal parts of French vermouth, gin, and ojen. Stir.

JOCKEY CLUB Sweet Manhattan with 2 dashes maraschino to each drink. Stir.

KAHLUALEXANDER An *ALEXANDER* or, better still, a *PANAMA* with kahlua or crème de café substituted for the crème de cacao.

KENTUCKY COLONEL No less an authority than the late G. Selmer Fougner, author of the famous *Wine Trail* series, vouches for the proportions of this drink as 1 part bourbon to 2 parts pineapple juice. The Kentucky colonels of my acquaintance would be more likely to reverse that proportion.

Another and, to my mind, better version of this drink is 1 part Benedictine to 3 parts bourbon, stirred and decorated with a twist of lemon peel.

KINA LILLET DRINKS In commenting on *Lillet vermouth*, I warned not to confuse this brand of vermouth with the apéritif wine, originally known as Kina Lillet but now called simply Lillet. If, by accident, you get a bottle of the wine instead of the vermouth, what do you do with it? Well, here are a few of the old-time recipes using Kina Lillet. I definitely do *not* recommend any of them, but some of them can be made reasonably palatable by varying the proportions in accordance with the principles heretofore set forth.

1. *COLONEL LINDBERGH* Equal parts of Lillet and Plymouth gin with a few dashes of orange juice and of apricot liqueur to each drink. I'll bet he never could have flown the Atlantic on this!

2. *KINA* Equal parts of Kina Lillet and Italian vermouth with 4 parts gin. The so-called *PERFECT*, using Lillet in place of French vermouth.

3. *LILLET* Equal parts of Kina Lillet, gin and crème de noyaux. See the *LILLY*.

4. *MAIDEN'S WISH*
    - 2 parts Kina Lillet
    - 1 part Apple Brandy
    - 1 part Apricot Brandy
    - 2 parts Gin

See the *FOOLISH VIRGIN*. The same remarks apply to both drinks.

5. *ODDS McINTYRE* Equal parts of lemon juice, Kina Lillet, cognac, and Cointreau. Shake with cracked ice. Also known by several other names and I hope that Odds, whose writings I admire, is not responsible for it.

6. *RICHMOND* (Reesh-mawn)
    - 1 part Kina Lillet
    - 2 parts Gin
    - A twist of Lemon

This is an ordinary bar Martini (horrible!) with Lillet in place of vermouth. If a dash of Angostura and a twist of orange peel are substituted for the twist of lemon, it becomes the *GREAT SECRET*. Or, again, if a few dashes of curaçao are added, it becomes the *H. & H.* Or substitute a few dashes of Dubonnet and it becomes the *JIMMY BLANC*.

7. *SELF-STARTER*
    - 1 part Apricot Brandy
    - 2 parts Kina Lillet
    - 3 parts Gin

8. *SILVER BULLET*
    - 1 part Kina Lillet
    - 1 part Lemon Juice
    - 2 parts Gin

KINGSTON
- 1 part Sugar Syrup
- 2 parts Lime or Lemon Juice
- 3 parts Gin
- 5 parts Jamaica Rum

Shake well with cracked or crushed ice. A few dashes of grenadine or a small quantity of orange juice may be added if desired.

KNICKEBEIN
This drink consists of several liqueurs or fruit syrups, with or without cognac or a fruit brandy, with an unbroken egg yolk and a dash of bitters. Beyond this, authorities differ as to how it is made.

The oldest recipe book in my possession treats it as being made like the Golden Slipper and the Pousse l'Amour—i.e., as a Pousse-Cafè containing an egg yolk. For this variety of Knickebein a sherry glass is used. The glass is filled ⅓ full with vanilla syrup or crème de vanille. An egg yolk is then carefully floated on the vanilla, a dash of bitters squirted on the egg, and enough Benedictine added to cover the yolk. Finally the remainder of the glass (about ⅓) is filled with cognac or kirsch. As with a Pousse-Café, great pains must be taken to prevent the liquors from running into one another.

With another version of this drink, several liqueurs such as Benedictine, curaçao, and maraschino are blended together. The glass is filled ⅔ full of the mixed liqueurs and the egg yolk floated on the liqueurs. The egg white is beaten to a stiff froth and piled over the yolk to form an inverted cone, and the bitters are squirted over the beaten whites.

In consuming the drink, where beaten egg white is used, this is first sucked from the top. The liquors are then sipped, and, at the end, the egg yolk is taken with the last swallow of the liquid.

LADY ALEXANDER
As if the Alexander and the Scotch

Alexander were not bad enough, someone had to think up this drink which is even less of a cocktail and more of a dessert drink than the original Alexander. It consists of equal parts of crème de cacao and sloe gin with the white of an egg and a dash of Angostura. Shake well.

LEVIATHAN
 1 part Sugar Syrup
 2 parts Lemon Juice
 2 parts Orange Juice
 4 parts Scotch

Shake.

LIBERTY
 1 part Sugar Syrup
 2 parts Lime Juice
 3 parts White Label Rum
 5 parts Applejack

Shake with cracked or crushed ice.

Another version of the Liberty omits the sugar syrup and substitutes sloe gin for the rum and apricot brandy for the applejack.

LITTLE COLONEL
 1 part Lime Juice
 2 parts Bourbon
 4 parts Southern Comfort

Shake with cracked or crushed ice.

An excellent drink except that it is a bit sweet. It can be made drier, and therefore improved, by reversing the proportions of bourbon and Southern Comfort.

LOVER'S DELIGHT
 1 part Cointreau
 1 part Forbidden Fruit
 2 parts Cognac

Shake.

The original recipe for this drink calls for equal parts of the three liquors. Even the above modification is still much too sweet. It can be greatly improved by adding about 2 parts lemon juice and increasing the proportion of cognac to 8 parts.

LUNE DE MIEL This is essentially the same as the *GOLDEN SLIPPER*, *KNICKEBEIN*, and *POUSSE L'AMOUR*, except for the liqueurs used. Cointreau is placed in the bottom of the sherry glass, the egg yolk is floated in the Cointreau and Parfait Amour added to the top of the egg, and finally, kümmel is floated on top.

MADAGASCAR

    1 part Lemon Juice
    3 parts Orange Juice
    8 parts White Cuban Rum

Shake with cracked ice. Sprinkle a small pinch of grated nutmeg on each drink.

This is, in effect, an Orange Blossom, using rum in place of gin.

MAIDEN'S PRAYER

    1 part Cointreau
    2 parts Lemon Juice
    8 parts Gin
    1 dash Orange Bitters to each drink

Shake well with cracked ice.

Here is another drink that illustrates the ease of "rolling your own." It is nothing but a Gin Sour with Cointreau substituted for sugar. Or, put another way, it is a Side Car with Gin used in place of Cognac.

Compare the *MIAMI*, *OLYMPIC*, *SANTIAGO*, and *SUNRISE*.

MANGAREVA

    1 part Cointreau

THE FINE ART OF MIXING DRINKS

> 2 parts Lime Juice
> 1 part Honey
> 7 parts Applejack

The exotic aspect of this cocktail lies in the manner in which it is served; viz., in coconut shells filled with crushed ice. Decorate with small sticks of fresh pineapple and serve with straws. The bottled apple and honey combination may be substituted for the honey and applejack above listed.

MEMPHIS or MEMPHIS BELLE   Place half of a fresh peach or apricot in a saucer champagne glass and fill the glass with crushed or shaved ice; add 1 to 1½ jiggers Southern Comfort and decorate with a cherry. A spoonful of sherry or port may be floated on top if desired. Serve with straws for sipping the liquor and a demitasse spoon with which to eat the fruit.

MIAMI BEACH   Equal parts of French vermouth, grapefruit juice, and Scotch.

Another horror that can be classed as a vestigial remainder of prohibition days. I have yet to find any truly good cocktail made with Scotch. This, however, is probably about as good—and as bad—as any.

Compare the *MIAMI*.

MIKADO   Straight cognac with a dash of Angostura and 2 or 3 dashes each of curaçao, crème de noyaux, and orgeat to each drink. Shake with cracked ice. A twist of lemon over each drink. Decorate with a cherry.

MILLION   This is simply a Jamaica Rum Sour with a dash of Angostura to each drink. Shake with crushed ice and decorate with a cherry.

This cocktail is also sometimes called *OLD PLANTATION*.

See also *MILLIONAIRE* and *MILLIONAIRE ROYAL*.

MILLION DOLLAR

    1 part Italian Vermouth
    1 part Pineapple Juice
    6 parts Gin
    2 or 3 dashes Grenadine & ½ Egg to each drink

Stir with cracked ice. A spoonful of orange-flower water (*Eau de Fleurs d'Oranger*) may be floated on each drink, if desired.

MISSOURI MULE

This is the Southland's answer to the Moscow Mule. Fill a large goblet or mug about half full of cracked ice. Add the juice of ¼ large lemon and 2 ounces of Southern Comfort and fill the mug with ginger beer (*not* ginger ale). Stir briskly and serve. Lime juice may be used in place of the lemon but is not as satisfactory.

MONKEY GLAND

    1 part Grenadine
    2 parts Orange Juice
    6 parts Gin
    1 or 2 dashes Absinthe to each drink

Shake with crushed ice.

MONTE CARLO

    1 part Benedictine
    2 parts Rye
    1 or 2 dashes Angostura to each drink

Shake with cracked ice.

This drink is a bit on the sweet side. It can be improved by adding 2 parts lemon juice and increasing the rye from 2 parts to about 4 or 5. Compare the KENTUCKY COLONEL.

MORNING [1]

    1 part French Vermouth

[1] See also MORNING ROSE.

3 parts Cognac
2 dashes each of Absinthe, Curaçao, & Angostura to each drink

Stir with ice cubes. A twist of lemon over each drink. Decorate with a cherry.

There are a number of variations of this drink. Some recipes omit the vermouth, some use both cognac and whisky, some add a few dashes of maraschino, and some use orange bitters in place of Angostura.

MORNING GLORY [1]

1 part Lemon Juice
3 parts Gin
1 dash White Crème de Menthe & ½ Egg White to each drink

Shake with cracked ice. Some recipes use 1 part whisky and 2 parts gin, and some use grenadine in place of the crème de menthe.

MORNING STAR [1]

1 part Sugar Syrup
3 parts Dry Sherry
6 parts White Cuban Rum
1 Egg Yolk to each 2 drinks

Shake with cracked ice. A pinch of powdered nutmeg sprinkled over each drink.

MOSS ROSE

1 part Sloe Gin
2 parts Grapefruit Juice
4 parts Oloroso Sherry

Shake with cracked ice.

This drink is not recommended because it is too much on the sweet side. It is included here because it is one of the few cocktails calling for grapefruit juice.

[1] See also MORNING ROSE.

MY OWN PASSION
- 1 part Passion-Fruit Nectar
- 2 parts Lime Juice
- 8 parts White Label Cuban Rum

This can be shaken with crushed ice but is best mixed in a Waring Blendor. The cocktail is dry, yet is liked by those who, as a rule, do not like alcoholic drinks. The proportions, of course, can be varied if you wish. You might also add a dash of orange bitters. My many friends have almost unanimously joined me in voting this the ultra-ultra cocktail de luxe.

NECTARINE JULEP
Mash a dozen very ripe nectarines, press through a strainer, blend with 2 ounces of bourbon, and strain into a Julep mug packed with finely cracked ice. Muddle to frost the mug, pack with more ice to top of mug, adding more bourbon if needed. Garnish with a slice of lemon and dust with powdered sugar. Then, in the words of my friend Colonel Elliott Springs, who gave me the recipe, "forget the art of raising nectarines."

NEVADA
- 1 part Sugar Syrup
- 2 parts Grapefruit Juice
- 2 parts Lime Juice
- 8 parts White Label Rum

Shake with cracked ice. This is merely a Daiquiri with grapefruit juice added.

NEW ORLEANS
There are two cocktails of entirely different types that have been given this name. The first is simply a LOTUS CLUB or WEYLIN with the addition of 1 or 2 dashes each of anisette and orange bitters. The other consists of 1 part grapefruit juice to 2 parts Southern Comfort. Shake.

OJEN Straight ojen with 2 or 3 dashes of bitters to each drink.

OLYMPIA or *OLYMPIC* This is a Daiquiri or Rum Sour with Cherry Heering substituted for the sugar syrup.
  Compare the *MAIDEN'S PRAYER, SANTIAGO,* and *SUNRISE.*

OMAR KHAYYAM This drink is a specialty of Saber Khouri's restaurant, the Omar Khayyám, in San Francisco, famous for its Balkan cuisine. Essentially, it is the *RHETT BUTLER* or the *FROZEN RHETT BUTLER.* It can be still further improved by adding a few drops of rose-petal flavoring, which is also a dessert specialty of the Omar Khayyám.

OPAL
  1 part Chartreuse
  6 parts Absinthe

Shake vigorously and long with crushed ice.

OPALESCENT
  1 part Grenadine
  2 parts Lemon Juice
  8 parts Gin
  1 Egg White to each 2 drinks

Shake with cracked ice. Some recipes call for the addition of a sprig of mint and some call for a teaspoonful of cream to each drink in place of the egg white.
  Compare the *PINK LADY.*

OPERA Equal parts of Dubonnet and white label rum with a dash of lime juice and a twist of orange peel over each drink.
  Another recipe uses gin in place of rum and maraschino liqueur in place of lime juice.

ORGEAT   There are three types of cocktails by this name. The first is a Whisky Sour with a dash of Angostura and a teaspoonful of orgeat to each drink. The second is a variation of the first, but with cognac in place of whisky. The third is a Gin Sour with orgeat substituted for the sugar syrup. Some recipes also substitute orange juice for the lime juice.

PALISADES   Equal parts of gin and cider (preferably hard cider) with a dash of Angostura. Shake.
Not recommended.

PALMETTO
>   1 part Italian Vermouth
>   2 parts Jamaica Rum
>   1 dash Bitters to each drink

Stir. A twist of orange peel over each drink. Some recipes call for French vermouth instead of Italian, but this makes a much inferior drink.

PARADISE
>   1 part Apricot Brandy
>   2 parts Orange Juice
>   8 parts Gin

Shake with cracked ice and add a twist of orange peel to each drink. Some recipes call for white label rum in place of gin. Compare the *DAWN* and *GOLDEN DAWN*.

PARK AVENUE
>   1 part Italian Vermouth
>   2 parts Pineapple Juice
>   4 parts Gin
>   2 dashes Curaçao to each drink

Shake with cracked ice.
Compare the *PINEAPPLE BLOSSOM* and *PINK PINEAPPLE*, below.

PENNSYLVANIA
    1 part Grenadine
    2 parts Pineapple Juice
    8 parts White Label Rum

Shake with cracked ice.

PINEAPPLE BLOSSOM Same as an *ORANGE BLOSSOM* but using pineapple juice instead of orange juice. Add a dash of orange bitters. Shake.

Compare the *PARK AVENUE*, above. See also the *PINEAPPLE BLOSSOM* made with whisky.

PINK PINEAPPLE
    1 part Grenadine
    2 parts Pineapple Juice
    6 parts Gin

Shake with cracked ice.

PLUIE D'OR
    1 part Kümmel
    1 part Orange Juice
    2 parts Vieille Cure
    4 parts Gin

Shake with cracked ice.

PONCE DE LEON ½ ounce each of grapefruit juice, Cointreau, gold label rum, and cognac, shaken with cracked ice and strained into a saucer champagne glass. Fill the glass with champagne. Another variation of the Champagne Cocktail. Not too bad, but don't waste a good vintage French champagne on it. It is no fountain of youth, despite its name.

POUSSE-CAFES (poohs kah-fay'[2]) Pousse-Cafés consist of a series of different-colored liqueurs floated one

[2] And *please* don't say "pussy käffy" or "pussy" anything else.

on top of another in a tall liqueur glass specially made for this purpose. Great care must be exercised to prevent the liqueurs from running together and spoiling the rainbow effect. Some bartenders pour the liqueurs slowly down the inside rim of the Pousse-Café glass from a spoon or from a sherry glass; others pour them carefully over the back of a spoon held inside the Pousse-Café glass. Even after the liqueurs have been poured a sudden jar or movement of the glass may cause the liqueurs to run together.

The liqueur of the greatest density is poured into the glass first, then the next heaviest, and so on to the top, the drink frequently being topped off with a spoonful of sweet cream. Unfortunately, it is impossible to furnish any table of densities of different liqueurs because the same flavor (such as an apricot or crème de cacao) made by one distiller may have a different density from that made by another. This depends, of course, upon the sugar content. As a general rule, the higher the proof (i.e., the greater the alcoholic content), the less the sugar content and therefore the lighter the liqueur. Non-alcoholic syrups, therefore, such as grenadine and raspberry syrups, are usually the heaviest and should be poured first. This rule is not infallible because it is possible to have a thin, watery non-alcoholic syrup on the one hand and a heavy, sugary, but high-proof liqueur on the other. Nevertheless, it will furnish a rough guide to density in most cases.

Pousse-Cafés are usually made in 3, 5, 6, or 7 colors. Following is a typical 7-ring or 7-color Pousse-Café in the order in which the liqueurs are poured:

1. *Grenadine or Raspberry Syrup (red)*
2. *Crème de Cacao (brown)*
3. *Maraschino (white)*
4. *Orange Curaçao (orange)*
5. *Crème de Menthe (green)*
6. *Parfait Amour (violet)*
7. *Cognac (amber)*

The various "ANGEL'S" drinks are all of the Pousse-Café type. Following are some of the various combinations that have been specially named:

FAIVRE'S POUSSE-CAFE   Benedictine, orange curaçao, kirschwasser, 2 or 3 drops of bitters on top.

PARISIAN POUSSE-CAFE   Green Chartreuse, orange curaçao, kirschwasser, cognac.

RAINBOW POUSSE-CAFE   Crème de violette, crème de cassis, maraschino, crème de menthe, yellow Chartreuse, curaçao, cognac.

SANTINAS POUSSE-CAFE   Maraschino, orange curaçao, cognac.

WALDORF POUSSE-CAFE   Raspberry syrup, anisette, Parfait Amour, yellow Chartreuse, Crème Yvette, green Chartreuse, cognac.

POUSSE L'AMOUR (poohs lah-moor')   This is another of the Pousse-Café—egg-yolk drinks like the *GOLDEN SLIPPER, KNICKEBEIN,* and *LUNE DE MIEL.* Maraschino is first placed in the sherry glass, the egg yolk is dropped in and surrounded with crème de vanille, and the glass is topped off with cognac.

PRINCETON
   1 part Port
   3 parts Gin
   2 dashes Orange Bitters to each drink

Authorities differ as to the proper mixing of this drink. Under one version, all the ingredients are stirred together; under another version the gin and bitters are shaken with crushed ice, poured into a chilled cocktail glass, and the port is then poured into the glass and allowed to settle through the gin and bitters. A twist of lemon over the top.

PUSSYFOOT

- 1 part Lemon Juice
- 3 parts Orange Juice
- 1 teaspoonful Grenadine to each drink
- 1 Egg Yolk to each 2 or 3 drinks

Shake thoroughly with cracked ice.

You will find one or two teetotalers at practically every cocktail party—thoroughly good scouts who, for one reason or another, just don't drink cocktails. Rather than serve them plain orange juice or tomato juice or, worse still, have them stand around empty-handed, try giving them this non-alcoholic "cocktail." It really does not deserve the name it bears because the drink is both good and honest.

Other very palatable *PROHIBITION COCKTAILS* (i.e., non-alcoholic) can be made by combining 1 part lime juice with about 4 to 5 parts grape juice or the sweet juice from almost any canned fruit, such as cherries, peaches, apricots, raspberries, etc. See also *SOUTHERN BEAUTY*.

RHETT BUTLER

- 1 part Curaçao
- 1 part Lime Juice
- 1 part Lemon Juice
- 8 parts Southern Comfort

Shake with crushed ice. Like all Sour-type Southern Comfort drinks, this makes an excellent frozen cocktail also.

ROCKS AND MISTS Apparently as a symptom of the general revulsion against overly sweet drinks and wishy-washy drinks, there has been a steadily increasing popularity during the last few years of the Scotch Mist, Bourbon on Rocks, etc. To make any drink "on Rocks," merely place one or more cubes of ice in an Old-Fashioned glass and pour the straight liquor over it.

No "garbage," please, for this is a he-man's drink and not a fruit salad. If you use crushed ice, instead of cubes, the drink becomes a "Mist." This, of course, is merely a Frappé. These, you will note, are not true cocktails but they are not bad (if the liquor is good), and they are infinitely superior, as apéritifs, to some of the syrupy liquid hash concoctions frequently served as cocktails.

ROSE Here is a cocktail that was highly popular in Paris during the twenties and early thirties. My good friend, Frank Meier, for thirty-odd years the manager of the Ritz Bar in Paris, states that it was invented by Johnny Milta of the Chatham Bar in Paris. In a compilation called *Cocktails de Paris*, published by La Maison du Cocktail of Paris in 1929, a slightly different formula is credited to Albert of the Chatham. There are also several other formulas, both French and American. The distinguishing feature of all the recipes, of course, is the rose color of the drink. (Compare the MORNING ROSE.) Here are several of the various formulas:

NO. 1 (original by Johnny Milta of the Chatham Bar)
    1 part Kirsch
    2 parts Noilly Prat Vermouth
    1 teaspoonful Raspberry Syrup to each drink

Stir. Decorate with a cherry. This drink can be greatly improved by using 1 part vermouth to 3 or 4 parts kirsch.

NO. 2 (by Albert of the Chatham Bar)
Same as No. 1, but with the addition of a teaspoonful of cherry liqueur to each drink. The comments with respect to improving No. 1 apply equally to No. 2.

NO. 3 (also Parisian recipe)
    1 part Noilly Prat Vermouth
    4 parts Gin
    1 teaspoonful Cherry Liqueur to each drink

Stir. Decorate with a cherry.

NO. 4 (American recipe)
- 1 part Noilly Prat Vermouth
- 1 part Dubonnet
- 8 parts Gin
- 1 teaspoonful Grenadine to each drink

Stir. Decorate with a cherry. A twist of lemon over each drink.

RUMBA
- 1 part Gin
- 2 parts Jamaica Rum
- 1 or 2 dashes Grenadine to each drink

Shake thoroughly with crushed ice.

Whoever thought up this snootful of liquid dynamite certainly liked his liquor hard! While the above is the original recipe, it can be greatly improved by adding 1 part lime or lemon juice and either an extra few dashes of grenadine or an equivalent amount of sugar syrup.

SANTIAGO
- 1 part Curaçao
- 2 parts Lime Juice
- 8 parts White Label Rum
- 2 or 3 dashes Jamaica Rum to each drink

Shake with cracked or crushed ice. A *DAIQUIRI GRENADINE* is sometimes called a Santiago.

SAVANNAH
- 1 part Orange Juice
- 3 parts Gin
- 1 teaspoonful Crème de Cacao to each drink
- 1 Egg White to each 2 drinks

Shake.

If you have any friends who are Alexander addicts, try this drink on them. I do not especially recommend it except as a means of weaning an Alexander baby.

SCAFFAS The Scaffa is the same as the *CHAMPE-RELLE*. It is usually called a *BRANDY SCAFFA*. The usual liquors, served in a sherry glass and poured carefully to keep them separate—like a Pousse-Café—are as follows: raspberry syrup, maraschino, green Chartreuse, cognac. A dash of Angostura is sometimes used to top the drink.

SCARLETT O'HARA

- 1 part Cranberry Juice
- 2 parts Lime Juice
- 8 parts Southern Comfort

Shake with crushed ice. You can use canned cranberry juice for this drink or you can substitute grenadine.

The original recipe calls for 1 part cranberry juice to 2 of Southern Comfort, with merely a dash of lime juice. However, although I am a devoted Cape Codder, I just don't like cranberries in any form, and I therefore recommend keeping the proportion of this brackish, puckery liquid at a minimum. This also makes an excellent frozen cocktail—even with the cranberry juice.

SEESAW Straight cognac with 3 or 4 dashes each of Benedictine and French vermouth and 1 dash of bitters to each drink. Shake.

SEVENTH HEAVEN

- 1 part Maraschino
- 2 parts Grapefruit Juice
- 8 parts Gin

Shake with cracked ice.

O.K. if you like it, but I'll take the fourth or fifth heaven with lime or lemon juice instead of grapefruit.

SHAKES A Shake contains the same ingredients as a Sour but in somewhat different proportions. The usual proportion is 2 teaspoonfuls sugar syrup and 3 teaspoonfuls lemon juice with 2 or 3 ounces of spirituous liquor.

Observing these proportions with the proper base liquor, you can produce the BRANDY SHAKE, GIN SHAKE, RUM SHAKE, APPLEJACK SHAKE, WHISKY SHAKE, VODKA SHAKE, and so on.

SHANGHAI

 1 part Cointreau
 2 parts Lime Juice
 2 parts Italian Vermouth
 8 parts Rye

Shake with cracked ice.

SHERRY AND BITTERS Like vermouth and the other aromatic wines, a good dry sherry—preferably an amontillado—may be combined with Angostura or other aromatic bitters to make an excellent tonic and appetizer. Use 2 to 3 dashes of bitters to each jigger of sherry and stir thoroughly. If ice is used at all (and it is preferable not to use it), use only large cubes and do not allow the wine to remain in contact with the ice any longer than necessary.

SHERRY AND EGG This drink is akin to the various Pousse-Café and egg drinks, such as the POUSSE L'AMOUR, etc., except that it uses only one liquor instead of a galaxy of them. Like the others, however, and like the Flips, it is both food and drink.

Put about a tablespoonful of sherry in a sherry glass and twirl to wet the entire inside of the glass. Break into the glass a whole egg. Then fill the glass with sherry. Some recipes call for the yolk only, but the whole egg is preferable. This is an excellent tonic.

Any other fortified wine or a spirituous liquor can be used in place of the sherry. Thus you may have PORT AND EGG, MADEIRA AND EGG, BRANDY AND EGG, BOURBON AND EGG, etc.

SHIRLEY JANE Straight rye with a teaspoonful of sugar and 2 or 3 dashes grenadine to each drink. Prepare and serve like an Old-Fashioned.

SIGMA CHI One of my good interfraternity friends, a member of Alpha Chi Rho, has accused me of partiality for including a cocktail bearing the name of my own fraternity (the ACACIA) and deliberately omitting the Sigma Chi. Of course I am partial. Moreover, for reasons heretofore fully explained, this drink is not a true cocktail. However, in the interests of interfraternity comity, here it is:
- 1 part Benedictine
- 2 parts Sloe Gin
- 1 dash Bitters to each drink

SLEEPY HOLLOW
- 1 part Sugar Syrup
- 1 part Apricot Liqueur
- 4 parts Lemon Juice
- 10 parts Gin
- 1 sprig Mint to each drink

Muddle the mint with the lemon juice and sugar. Add the liquors and shake thoroughly with crushed ice.

SLOEBERRY Sloe gin with 2 dashes each of Angostura and orange bitters to each drink.

This and the sloe gin cocktails below are included as a matter of information only and are not recommended. Sloe gin is too sweet for use as a cocktail base.

SLOE GIN There are two version of this cocktail, one made with Italian vermouth and lemon juice, the other with French vermouth. Here they are:

SWEET: One part lemon juice, 2 parts Italian vermouth, and 4 parts sloe gin. A dash of Angostura to each drink. Stir.

DRY: Equal parts of French vermouth and sloe gin. One dash each of Angostura and orange bitters to each drink. Stir.

SLOPPY JOE'S

1 part Port
1 part Cognac
2 parts Pineapple Juice
1 dash each of Grenadine & Curaçao to each drink

Shake with cracked ice. Not a true cocktail because of the large proportion of pineapple juice. This defect can be remedied by increasing the cognac from 1 to 3 or 4 parts and reducing the pineapple juice from 2 parts to 1.

SMASHES The Smash is a short Julep. In other words, it consists of fresh mint, sugar, and any spirituous liquor.

For each drink, gently crush a sprig of mint with a teaspoonful of sugar syrup and, if desired, a dash of bitters in a bar glass. Add crushed ice and 2 to 4 ounces (according to the size of the glass in which the drink is to be served) of the desired liquor. Shake thoroughly and strain into the glasses.

Originally the smash was served in a Sour or Delmonico glass or in a fancy wineglass and was decorated with pineapple, berries, slices of orange and lemon, and a sprig of mint. It may, however, be served in a Sour glass or even in a cocktail glass with no decorations other than perhaps a cherry and a small sprig of mint.

According to the liquor used, you can have a *BRANDY SMASH*, a *GIN SMASH*, a *BOURBON SMASH*, a *RYE SMASH*, a *SCOTCH SMASH*, a *RUM SMASH*, an *APPLEJACK SMASH*, a *VODKA SMASH*, etc.

SNAPPER Except for the base liquor used, the original recipe for this drink is like the original recipe for the Stinger—equal parts of white crème de menthe and gin.

Like the Stinger, it can be converted into a more acceptable drink by using 1 part lime juice, 2 parts crème de menthe, and 6 to 8 parts of the base liquor—in this case gin.

Compare the STINGER, EMERALD, DEVIL and SHAMROCK.

SOUL KISS Equal parts of French vermouth, Italian vermouth, and Dubonnet, with 1 or 2 teaspoonfuls of orange juice to each drink.

What a placid, unemotional soul the guy that named this drink must have had!

Two other drinks also bear this same misleading name. The first is a Pousse-Café of maraschino and Crème Yvette, decorated with a maraschino cherry. The second is a bit more vigorous and consists of equal parts of French vermouth, Byrrh, and whisky with a dash of sugar syrup and 1 or 2 spoonfuls of orange juice to each drink.

SOUTHAMPTON
   1 part Cherry Heering
   4 parts Cognac
   1 dash Bitters to each drink

Shake with cracked ice. A twist of lemon over each glass. The original recipe also calls for sugar syrup, but the liqueur makes the drink more than sweet enough without the sugar.

SOUTHERN BEAUTY Juice of half a large lime, 1 egg white, and 2 dashes of Angostura to each drink. Shake vigorously and long with crushed ice.

This is another drink for the teetotalers. Compare the PUSSYFOOT.

SOUTHERN COMFORT
   1 part Lime Juice

4 parts Southern Comfort
1 dash French Vermouth to each drink

Shake with cracked ice. Note that the Southern Comfort is, in itself, sweet enough so that no sugar is necessary and none should be used.

STOLEN KISS

1 part Sugar Syrup
2 parts Absinthe
6 parts Gin
1 Egg White to each 2 drinks

Shake with cracked or crushed ice.

STONE

1 part Dry Sherry
1 part Italian Vermouth
4 parts White Label Rum

Stir with large ice cubes.

SUISSESSE Straight absinthe with 1 teaspoonful sugar syrup and 1 egg white to each 2 drinks. A few dashes of anisette may be added if desired. Also, some recipes call for 1 part French vermouth to 2 parts absinthe instead of straight absinthe.

This drink should be shaken long and vigorously with crushed ice. It is usually served in a Delmonico or Sour glass. An interesting variation is to serve in hollow-stemmed champagne glasses. Fill the stem with green crème de menthe, drop a maraschino cherry over the hollow stem opening, and then pour in the drink. This, supposedly, is a picker-upper for the cold, gray dawn of the morning after.

SUNRISE

1 part Cointreau
2 parts Lemon Juice

8 parts White Label Rum
1 or 2 dashes Benedictine to each drink

Shake with cracked ice.
Compare the MAIDEN'S PRAYER, OLYMPIC and SANTIAGO.

SUNSHINE

1 part French Vermouth
2 parts Pineapple Juice
6 parts White Label Rum
1 or 2 dashes Grenadine to each drink

Stir with cracked ice.
See also the SUNDOWNER.

SWEET AND LOVELY

1 part Maraschino & Grenadine, half & half
2 parts Lime Juice
3 parts Gin
5 parts Applejack

Shake with cracked ice.

SWEET DREAM

1 part Apricot Liqueur
2 parts Pineapple Juice
4 parts White Label Rum
4 parts Gin

Shake with cracked ice. Decorate with a cherry or a twist of orange peel.

SWISS SPECIAL

1 part Gin
1 part Swiss Kirsch
2 parts Rye

Shake with cracked ice. Decorate with a cherry and float ½ teaspoonful Grand Marnier on each drink. Swiss kirsch is prescribed because it is somewhat sweeter than other varieties. If a dry kirsch, such as Schwarzwälder, is used, add 1 or 2 dashes sugar syrup for each drink.

TAMMANY This is a Medium Martini with a dash of absinthe.

TEQUILA This is simply a Tequila Sour, made like any other Sour, but with tequila as the base liquor.

THISTLE A sweet Manhattan using Scotch whisky.

TIGER'S TOOTH Straight Irish whisky with one dash each of lemon juice, Italian vermouth, bitters, and kirsch.

TIPPERARY
- 1 part French Vermouth
- 3 parts Gin
- 1 teaspoonful each Orange Juice & Grenadine to each drink
- 1 sprig Mint to each drink

Muddle the mint with the orange juice and grenadine. Add the vermouth and gin and stir with cracked ice. Some recipes call for Italian vermouth instead of French. Others call for sloe gin instead of dry gin and omit the mint.

TROPICAL
- 1 part Lime Juice
- 4 parts Jamaica Rum
- Crushed, sweetened Pineapple
- 1 dash Grenadine to each drink

Sprinkle a fair-sized slice of fresh pineapple with sugar and crush in a bar glass with a muddler or, better still, in a Waring Blendor. Place the crushed pineapple with the other ingredients in a shaker with crushed ice and shake long and vigorously. The drink may be strained into a cocktail glass or may be poured, ice, pineapple shreds, and all, into a large wineglass and served with straws.

There are two other and quite dissimilar drinks that are also called Tropicals. The first consists of 1 part crème de vanille to 2 parts cognac. The second consists of 1 part crème de cacao, 1 part maraschino, and 2 parts dry vermouth, with a dash of orange bitters to each drink. Neither of these latter two Tropicals can properly be called a cocktail.

TURF   A Dry Martini with 1 or 2 dashes each of maraschino, Angostura, and orange bitters to each drink. The same drink with a dash of absinthe is called the TUXEDO.

UNION CLUB

    1 part Orange Curaçao
    2 parts Lime Juice
    8 parts Rye
    2 dashes each Orgeat & Grenadine to each drink
    1 Egg White to each 2 drinks

Shake with cracked ice.

UPTOWN

    1 part Lime Juice
    1 part Orange Juice
    1 part Pineapple Juice
    6 parts Jamaica Rum
    1 dash each Cointreau, Grenadine, & Orange Bitters to each drink

Shake with cracked or crushed ice.

VALENCIA   There are two entirely different cocktails that bear this name. The first consists of equal parts of dry sherry and applejack with 2 or 3 dashes of orange juice. The second consists of 1 part orange juice to 2 parts apricot brandy with 2 or 3 dashes of orange bitters.

In each case the drink should be thoroughly shaken with cracked or crushed ice.

VIRGIN Equal parts Forbidden Fruit, white crème de menthe, and gin. Shake.

Should be called the *FOOLISH VIRGIN*, for only someone very young, very unsophisticated, and very foolish would want this conglomeration as a cocktail.

The Sweet Martini, when made with orange bitters instead of Angostura, is also sometimes called the Virgin.

WAGON WHEEL
- 1 part Grenadine
- 2 parts Lemon Juice
- 3 parts Cognac
- 5 parts Southern Comfort

Shake with cracked ice. Also makes a good frozen cocktail.

WALTZING MATILDA
- 1 part Passion-Fruit Nectar
- 1 part White Gin (I recommend Beefeater)
- 2 parts Dry White Wine
- A few dashes Orange Curaçao to each drink

Shake well with cracked ice and strain into Collins glasses, filling each glass about ⅓ full. Add ice cubes and fill glass up with club soda or ginger ale.

The above, which is the original recipe, is a tall drink. It can be served as a cocktail, omitting the soda or ginger ale.

WHITE
- 1 part Anisette
- 5 parts Gin
- 1 dash Orange Bitters to each drink

Shake with cracked ice. A twist of lemon peel over each glass.

WHITE BABY

   1 part Cointreau
   2 parts Lime Juice
   8 parts Gin

Shake with cracked ice.

This, of course, is simply a WHITE LADY without the egg white and with lime juice in place of lemon.

WHITE LION

   1 part Grenadine
   2 parts Lime Juice (put in shell of ½ lime)
   1 part Curaçao
   7 parts White Label Rum

Shake.

WHITE ROSE
Equal parts of gin and kirsch with 1 teaspoonful sugar syrup to each drink and 1 egg white to each 2 drinks.

There is also another cocktail called the White Rose which is the White, above, with the addition of 1 egg white to each 2 drinks.

WHITE VELVET
This is the same as the White Baby, above, but with pineapple juice substituted for the lime juice.

WIDOW'S DREAM
This is a Benedictine Flip (see FLIPS), topped off in the glass with sweet cream.

And may heaven help the poor widows if that is what their dreams are like!

YACHT CLUB

   1 part Italian Vermouth
   3 parts Gold Label Rum
   1 dash Apricot Liqueur to each drink

Stir.

YOU AND I A Whisky Sour with orange curaçao in place of sugar syrup.

ZA-ZA The most common version of this drink is equal parts of gin and Dubonnet, decorated with a twist of lemon peel.

A second version substitutes sloe gin for the dry gin.

A third version substitutes dry sherry for the gin.

Still another version consists of a Sweet Martini with a dash of crème de menthe.

ZOMBIE This is undoubtedly the most overadvertised, overemphasized, overexalted, and foolishly feared drink whose claims to glory ever assaulted the eyes and ears of the gullible American public.

Actually, as a drink, it is not bad at all; but the claims made for it and the advertising by which it has been touted, as well as one feature of the formula, offend my sensibilities in three respects.

First of all, I am allergic to secret formulas for mixing drinks at a bar or in the home. The Zombie formula is supposed to be the jealously guarded secret of Don the Beachcomber, of Hollywood. One of the rum distilleries, however, states that they devised the original formula. Charles Baker, Jr., states that he invented a quite different formula some two years ahead of Don the Beachcomber. All this mystery, of course, is calculated to inspire curiosity and thus advertise the drink.

Second, I am also allergic to any fear-inspiring slogan such as "Only two to a customer." Everyone except Caspar Milquetoast, of course, comes back for a third just to pit his personal prowess against the allegedly devastating power of the drink. This not only is the cheapest type of advertising; it is also a steal and a perversion of the old claim of Southern Comfort of a "self-imposed limit of two to a person."

Third, the multiplicity of various rums and other ingredients is an offense against the first principles of drink mixing and adds nothing to the flavor or other value of the drink. Two rums—white Cuban for the base and a dash of Jamaica for flavor—would do as well as four or five. The 151-proof Demerara adds nothing to the flavor of the drink, and the quantity used is too microscopic to add appreciably to the alcoholic strength. The mere mention of 151-proof liquor, however, is sufficient to add to the mental hazard of the unsophisticated consumer of the drink.

Twenty different bars serving this drink will probably put out eighteen to twenty different versions of it. In the main, however, each drink will be concocted approximately as follows:

> 1 teaspoonful Sugar Syrup [3]
> ½ to ¾ ounce Lime Juice
> ¾ ounce fresh Pineapple Juice [4]
> 1 ounce White Label Rum
> 2 ounces Gold Label Rum [5]
> 1 ounce Jamaica Rum
> 2 teaspoonfuls Apricot Liqueur [6]
> ½ to ¾ ounce mysterious ingredient [7]

The above ingredients are shaken with crushed ice and poured, with the ice, into a Zombie glass (a 14- to 16-ounce Collins glass will do just as well). From ½ to 1 teaspoonful of 151-proof Demerara rum is then floated on top and the drink is decorated with slices of orange and lemon, pink and green cherries, a pineapple stick,

---

[3] Falernum or orgeat may be used in place of the sugar syrup.

[4] The less conscientious bars, of course, may use canned, unsweetened pineapple juice.

[5] Just for the sake of making it more complicated this may be changed to 1 ounce gold label rum and 1 ounce Barbados or Haitian rum.

[6] For the same reason this may be changed to 1 teaspoonful apricot and 1 teaspoonful cherry. Sometimes the liqueurs are used and sometimes brandies.

[7] This is usually papaya juice. Sometimes it is coconut juice. Sometimes—and preferably—this ingredient is omitted altogether.

and several sprigs of mint. Finally, powdered sugar is sprinkled over all. And there, brother, is your Zombie, grandfather of all pixies, and great-uncle to the gremlins.

This, of course, is not a cocktail at all but a tall drink. However, since it is commonly, although erroneously, referred to as a ZOMBIE COCKTAIL, I am putting the formula here near the end of the cocktail recipes and, if you please, as an introduction to the chapter on tall drinks.

ZOOM

1 part Honey
2 parts Sweet Cream
8 parts Cognac

Shake vigorously with cracked or crushed ice. The honey may be dissolved in a small amount of boiling water if desired.

While the Zoom is basically a cognac drink, other liquors may be substituted, thereby providing a *GIN ZOOM, KIRSCH ZOOM, RUM ZOOM, WHISKY ZOOM*, etc., as desired.

TALL DRINKS

As noted at the beginning of the last chapter, I regard as a short drink anything that *should* be served in a glass holding up to 4 or 5 ounces and as a long or tall drink anything that *should* be served in a glass containing 6 ounces or more. Many bars have three sizes of so-called Highball glasses: the standard Highball glass holding 6 ounces, the tall Highball glass holding 8 ounces, and the short Highball glass holding only 4 ounces. To me, nothing smaller than a 6-ounce glass can properly be called a Highball glass, and even that is rather skimpy. Moreover, as previously pointed out, I regard any drink containing any appreciable amount of carbonated beverage as inherently a tall drink. One can, of course, if his taste is sufficiently perverted, serve a Tom Collins in a liqueur glass or a Martini in a 16-ounce Collins glass. The Collins would still remain, in character, a tall drink despite the Lilliputian size of the glass, and the Martini would still remain a cocktail—or perhaps four or five cocktails served in a single glass. It is for this reason that I regard the Old-Fashioneds served at most bars, not as Old-Fashioned cocktails, but as short Rye or Bourbon Highballs because they are topped off with an ounce or more of water, either charged or plain.

When we come to classifying our tall drinks we at once find ourselves in serious difficulty. What is a Highball? How does it differ from a Buck? What is the difference between a Collins and a Fizz? Between a Collins and a Rickey? The real trouble is that one bar devised a certain combination of ingredients and called it by a certain name—say, a Highball, and another bar put out a wholly analogous drink with a different base liquor and called it by a different name—say, a Buck. The drinks were invented and named by different people in different places with no effort to stick to any generic designations. There is little, if any, difference between Fixes and Daisies or between Punches and Cups. A Cup should be made in large quantity and served in individual cups. But a Punch also—when made for a large party—is made in a Punch bowl and is served in cups. And, if so desired, either may be made and served in individual portions.

Where there are recognizable distinctions between one type of drink and another I have tried to point them out. Let us remember, however, that there are different schools of thought on many matters of nomenclature and it is, at the best, difficult to say who is right and who is wrong.

HIGHBALLS

What is a Highball? The best dictionary definition that I have been able to find says that it is a drink of whisky diluted with a carbonated beverage and iced. But what kind of whisky—Scotch, rye, bourbon, Irish, or Canadian? How about vodka, which is also a whisky? And what kind of carbonated beverage? And, if Scotch and soda is a Highball, why not brandy and soda? Or applejack and soda? One writer on mixology who has compiled what is probably one of the largest collections of recipes ever published under the covers of a single book treats a Highball as almost any combination of alcoholic (or even non-alcoholic) liquor with a so-called "filler" served in a 4-, 6-, or 8-ounce Highball glass. Who is right?

Actually it matters but little. No one ever orders merely "a Highball," nor "a Whisky Highball," nor even "a Scotch Highball" or "a Bourbon Highball." The wise drinker does not even order "a Scotch and soda" or "a bourbon and ginger ale"; he names not only the type but also the *brand* of whisky along with the type and, perhaps, the brand of carbonated beverage.

In an effort to start a movement for the purpose of bringing some semblance of order out of chaos, however, let us define a Highball as any tall iced drink (6 ounces or more) consisting of a base liquid (alcoholic or non-alcoholic) in combination with a carbonated beverage and with or without auxiliary coloring and flavoring agents, but definitely *without* lemon or lime juice. If citrus juices are used the drink becomes a Buck or a Collins or a Rickey and is no longer a Highball.

Let us also agree that, while *any* carbonated beverage can be used in a Highball, such as ginger ale, Coca-Cola, etc., it will always be assumed that, unless otherwise specified, a charged water, either plain or alkaline (and preferably plain), is to be used, such as seltzer, White Rock, Canada Dry Water, etc.

The usual proportions for a Highball are 1½ ounces of the base liquid with 1 large cube of ice in a 6-ounce Highball glass, with enough carbonated beverage added to fill the glass to approximately ⅜" from the top. Stir quickly and lightly with a stirring rod or small bar spoon. For an 8-ounce glass, use 2 ounces of base liquid and 2 cubes of ice. For a very tall Highball or any other long drink that is to be sipped over a fairly long period of time (such as at the bridge table) be sure to use plenty of ice. Four to five cubes is none too much for a 14- to 16-ounce Collins glass. There is nothing more insipid than a lukewarm drink. But remember, too, that as the ice melts the drink will be diluted. Use plenty of liquor as well as plenty of ice. A safe rule is 1 part of liquor to 4 parts of ice and carbonated beverage combined for a small Highball (6 to 8 ounces) and 1 to 3 for a very long one. It is, of course, much better to make two small or medium-sized drinks than one very large one, but there are times when the host needs to participate in other activities of the evening and cannot conveniently be running to the kitchen every few minutes to replenish glasses.

Following the above rules, you can turn out at will any of the following: *APPLEJACK HIGHBALL, BOURBON HIGHBALL, BRANDY HIGHBALL, BYRRH HIGHBALL, DUBONNET HIGHBALL, GIN HIGHBALL, IRISH HIGHBALL, RUM HIGHBALL, RYE HIGHBALL, SCOTCH HIGHBALL, VERMOUTH HIGHBALL,* or *VODKA HIGHBALL*. You can also make delicious *PROHIBITION HIGHBALLS* for your teetotaler friends by combining grape juice or other fruit syrups with ginger ale. In this case, however, you should use a larger proportion of the fruit juice—about 1 to 2. If your stomach is a bit upset or squeamish and you don't feel up to hard liquor, even in a dilute form, try using, as the Highball base, 1 part of grenadine to 2 or 3 parts of bitters and make an *ANGOSTURA HIGHBALL*, a *FERNET HIGHBALL*, or a *PICON HIGHBALL*.

You are by no means limited to the Highballs above listed. Here, again, learn to "roll your own." Cognac and applejack are not the only brandies that can be used in Highballs. Cherry brandy with about half as much grenadine as brandy makes an excellent *KIRSCH HIGHBALL*. Try the other brandies, such as apricot, peach, pear, and raspberry, but, with these brandies, use a few teaspoonfuls of a liqueur or syrup to give body and character to the drink. You can use either a liqueur of the same flavor as the brandy or of a neutral flavor, such as maraschino, or a citrus flavor, such as Triple Sec.

As a matter of fact, you can also create many interesting variations of your other Highballs by adding a few dashes of either a liqueur or bitters. Try Angostura or Peychaud bitters with your bourbon and ginger ale; Drambuie with your Scotch and soda; orgeat with your Rum Highballs, and so on. Gin and ginger ale, with a dash of Angostura, is sometimes called a *GIN SPIDER*. Roll 'em yourself! Half the fun of drink mixing consists of mentally "tasting" some new and untried combination and then putting it together and finding out whether or not it tastes the way you thought it would.

Here are a few more tall drinks that fall within the category of Highballs as we have now defined Highballs.

POMPIER—EXPORT-CASSIS—VERMOUTH-CASSIS
This triple-named drink is a very mild, refreshing, and altogether excellent drink, particularly for a hot summer afternoon or evening.

> 1 pony Crème de Cassis
> 1 jigger French Vermouth
> 1 large cube Ice

Stir quickly in a 6- to 8-ounce glass, add charged water to fill, stir once more, and serve.

The BYRRH-CASSIS uses Byrrh in place of the vermouth; the DUBONNET-CASSIS uses Dubonnet, and so on. The CASSISCO, a popular French drink, uses cognac in place of the vermouth.

CASSIS-KIRSCH or POLINCHELLE
Made like a Vermouth-Cassis, but with kirschwasser in place of the vermouth.

VERMOUTH-CURAÇAO
Made like a Vermouth-Cassis, but with curaçao in place of the crème de cassis.

BYRRH-CITRON
> 1 pony Citron Syrup [1]
> 1 jigger Byrrh

Prepare like the Vermouth-Cassis.

DUBONNET-CITRON
Made like a Byrrh-Citron, but with Dubonnet in place of Byrrh.

PICON-CITRON
Made like a Byrrh-Citron, but with Amer Picon in place of Byrrh.

---

[1] *Citron* (seé-trohń) is French for lemon. Citron syrup is lemon syrup. In Europe it can be obtained ready-made and bottled. It is better, however, when freshly prepared by mixing lemon juice and sugar syrup, about 2 to 1.

PICON-CURAÇAO Made like a Picon-Citron, but with curaçao in place of the citron syrup.

SUISSESSE HIGHBALL First frappé a *SUISSESSE*, using a whole egg white and anisette. Pour, ice and all, into a Highball glass, add more ice if needed, and fill with charged water.

Like the Suissesse, this is supposed to be a picker-upper.

CANADIAN GRENADIER Gin and ginger ale, but with a small scoop of orange or lemon ice in place of ice cubes to chill the drink.

HORSE'S NECK This is the great *what-is-it* of the Highball tribe. Originally it was a whisky drink and Scotch, Irish, rye, or bourbon was used, as requested. Then it degenerated into a prohibition drink by leaving out the whisky. Then it degenerated still further by putting in gin.

While listed in some recipe books as a Collins (because served in a Collins glass), it definitely is not a Collins: first, because it contains no lemon; second, because it contains no sugar; and third, because it is made with ginger ale, not club soda.

Peel a medium or large lemon in one continuous spiral. Hang the peel in a Collins glass with just enough over the edge of the glass and hanging outside to keep the peel in place. Place 3 or 4 large cubes of ice in the glass and—

(a) for our teetotaler friend, fill with ginger ale. This is known as a *PLAIN HORSE'S NECK*.

(b) for others, add 2 to 3 ounces of gin, Scotch, Irish, rye, rum, applejack, or bourbon, as desired, and then fill up with ginger ale. This is known as a *HORSE'S NECK WITH A KICK*.

TAIL FEATHERS Place 1 ounce of orange juice in a Collins glass filled with ice. Fill the glass with ginger beer, (*not* ginger ale) and decorate with mint and a thin slice of lime. An excellent Prohibition Highball.

SPRITZER A Rhine-wine Highball consisting of Rhine wine and charged water, approximately half and half.

CONCERNING CARBONATED BEVERAGES

Note that we have defined a Highball as a combination of some base liquid with a carbonated beverage. Now, water, H_2O, just plain water, is one of the most necessary and useful substances to be found on this earth of ours. On occasion it is a most satisfying and refreshing beverage. In fact, there are times when no other beverage whatsoever can quite take the place of water. It is useful in making infusions, such as tea and coffee. It is necessary to sustain vegetable as well as animal life. It can be used to warm our houses and to cool our automobile engines. We need it to wash our bodies, our dishes, and our clothes. So indispensable is it that it was classed by the ancients as one of the four essential elements, along with earth, air, and fire. It is, indeed, one of the greatest of God's gifts to man.

But, like the other three elements of the ancients, there are places where it does belong and places where it does not belong. You don't want earth in your soup, air in your intestinal tract, or fire in your icebox. And one of the places where plain water distinctly does not belong is in any alcoholic beverage. There may be a few well-marked exceptions, such as the Absinthe Drip, where the water serves a specific and well-defined purpose, but these exceptions are very, very few indeed.

A carbonated beverage in a Highball or Collins or Rickey, of course, dilutes the liquor as much as would the same quantity of plain water, but, to compensate for this dilution, it adds to the drink a tang, a zip, a zest, a sparkle. A good carbonated beverage actually points up and enhances the flavor of the liquor. It stimulates the taste buds and renders them more truly appreciative of the bouquet of the accompanying liquor.

Plain water, on the other hand, merely dilutes. It takes away and gives nothing in return. You wouldn't think of pouring water in your milk or your ginger ale or your Coca-Cola, would you? Then, in heaven's name, why think of pouring it in your bourbon or your Scotch? A watered drink is always necessarily a flat drink, a lifeless drink, an insipid drink. If you don't like carbonated beverages (though it is hard to imagine anyone not liking them), don't drink them; but don't pour water in your whisky and call it a Highball. Drink the whisky straight and use the water as a chaser. Or take a claret or some other still wine, or a lemonade, or a glass of milk, or a cup of coffee—or even a glass of plain water. And, if you simply *must* use still water in your whisky or other liquor, use hot water, add a dash of soap flakes, and throw it down the drain, where dishwater belongs. Then dry the glass and pray for forgiveness for the sin of wasting good liquor.

BUCKS

The Bucks, the Rickeys, the Collinses, and the Fizzes all differ from the Highball in that they contain citrus juice, whereas the Highball does not. It is easier, however, to distinguish them from the Highball than it is to distinguish them from one another. The original Buck was the Gin Buck—a favorite of the prohibition era—and it was made with ginger ale. From the Gin Buck there developed various other Bucks, and many bartenders and recipe writers started switching the carbonated beverage along with the base liquor, while still calling the finished product a Buck. Actually, in many cases, what they turned out under the name of a Buck was a Rickey or a Collins.

Another distinguishing feature of the original Gin Buck was that a quarter of a lemon was squeezed into the glass with a hand squeezer and the lemon itself dropped into the glass with the juice.

Still another feature of the Buck is that no sugar is used,

the ginger ale—even a very dry, pale ginger ale—furnishing sufficient sweetening.

In making our Bucks, therefore, let us retain all three of these features. The amounts given below are for a 10- to 12-ounce Highball glass.

GIN BUCK Cut a large lemon into quarters and squeeze one quarter into a Highball glass, dropping the lemon in with the juice. Add 2 or 3 ice cubes and 3 ounces gin, fill glass with ginger ale, and stir. Some recipes call for ½ lime in place of the ¼ lemon.

The *APPLEJACK BUCK, BRANDY BUCK, RUM BUCK,* and *WHISKY BUCK* are all made exactly the same except for using the appropriate liquor to replace the gin.

When made with Scotch whisky, this drink is called a *MAMIE TAYLOR*.[2] This drink antedates even the Gin Buck, but, as originally concocted, the juice of the lemon only was used and not the flesh and rind.

An interesting variation of the Rum Bucks may be had by adding a few dashes of Cointreau or orgeat when using Cuban rum and a few dashes of falernum when using Jamaica rum.

RICKEYS

Here is another drink as to which confusion reigns among both authors and dispensers. Even as painstaking a dictionary as Macmillan's defines a Rickey as a "drink containing spirituous liquor, lime *or lemon* juice, and carbonated water." One bartender's manual distinguishes Rickeys from Collinses and Fizzes as being a shorter drink and drier in that more lime *or lemon* juice is used and less sugar.

---

[2] Some of the other Bucks are sometimes dubbed "Taylors" also. Thus the Gin Buck is called *MAMIE'S SISTER*, the Bourbon Buck is *MAMIE'S SOUTHERN SISTER*, and the Rum Buck is *SUSIE TAYLOR*.

Actually, all true Rickeys are made with limes—*never* with lemons. Your bartender may *substitute* lemon juice if he lacks limes or if he has prepared lemon juice on hand and is in a hurry, but, if he does, the drink is no longer a Rickey. The size of the glass is purely incidental. The Collins is usually served in a 10- to 14-ounce glass, but the Fizz, like the Rickey, is usually served in an 8-ounce or even smaller glass.

The two most common and best-known Rickeys are the Gin Rickey and the Sloe Gin Rickey. However, any spirituous liquor may be used, and liqueurs, perhaps, make the most palatable Rickeys of all. I have introduced dozens of people, ranging all the way from strict teetotaler to confirmed rum hound, to the *APRICOT RICKEY* and each and every one has pronounced it one of the most delicious beverages he has ever tasted. The tartness of the lime cuts the cloying sweetness of the apricot liqueur, and the two flavors blend into one indescribably delectable whole. Of course, in offering this drink to my prohibitionist friends, I have first made sure that they were familiar with the *GRAPE JUICE RICKEY* (a splendid non-alcoholic drink) and have told them I was substituting apricot juice for the grape juice!

The original Gin Rickey was a very dry drink, using little or no sugar. In the case of Liqueur Rickeys no sugar is needed, for the liqueur itself is plenty sweet. With spirituous liquors, such as gin, applejack, rum, and whisky, however, the drink is greatly improved for most tastes by the addition of a teaspoonful of sugar or liqueur. With gin, try maraschino or grenadine; with rum, try orgeat or falernum; and with whisky or brandy, try curaçao.

Here is the basic formula and, according to the liquor used, you can use it to make any of the following: *APPLE-JACK RICKEY, APRICOT RICKEY, BOURBON RICKEY, CHERRY RICKEY, GIN RICKEY, SLOE GIN RICKEY, GRENADINE RICKEY, IRISH RICKEY, MANDARINE RICKEY* (especially delicious),

PEACH RICKEY, RUM RICKEY (any type of rum), *SOUTHERN COMFORT RICKEY* (also splendid), *SCOTCH RICKEY* (see the *MAMIE TAYLOR*), *VODKA RICKEY*, etc.

> Juice of 1 small or ½ large Lime
> 2 ounces of the selected liquor
> With dry spirituous liquors use 1 tsp. Sugar Syrup

Stir together in an 8-ounce glass, add 2 large ice cubes, fill the glass with charged water, stir again, and serve with stirring rod or small bar spoon.

For your teetotaler friends, do not overlook the *PROHIBITION RICKEYS*, made with grape juice, grenadine, or any other fruit syrup. Also the *LIME RICKEY*, made with a teaspoonful of sugar and the juice of a whole lime—really a Limeade. If you like a drink a bit on the bitter side (but not too much so), try Amer Picon. *VERMOUTH RICKEYS, DUBONNET RICKEYS*, etc., are also refreshing, palatable, and very mild. The *ROYAL RICKEY* is a Gin Rickey with the addition of a pony of vermouth and either a half dozen crushed, fresh raspberries or a teaspoonful of raspberry syrup.

Before the development of the large seedless Florida limes, the small Persian limes were squeezed with a hand squeezer and the lime shell was dropped in the glass just as is done with the lemon in making a Buck. Today it is optional to use the shell or only the juice.

An interesting and delicious variation of the Rickeys may be had by using kumquats in place of limes. We usually think of kumquats as belonging to the orange family. The Chinese, however, call them golden limes. Use 2 to 3 kumquats in place of 1 lime. Squeeze with a small lime squeezer and add the shell of half a squeezed kumquat to the juice. A dash of orange-flower water may also be added if desired. The French Eau de Fleurs d'Oranger is the best.

COLLINSES

The Collins is the tallest of tall drinks and is so served at practically all bars. A special glass has even been created for it—the Collins glass—which holds 12, 14, or even 16 ounces as against the ordinary bar Highball glass of 6 ounces.

Basically, the Collins is simply a Sour served in a tall glass with ice and charged water. Or, stated in another way, it is a lemonade made with charged water and spiked with gin or some other liquor.

Originally there were two brothers only in the Collins family—Tom and John. During recent years, however, numerous cousins have appeared on the scene—Pedro, Pierre, Sandy, Mike, Jack, the Colonel, and several others whose first names have not yet been officially recorded in the baptismal registry.

The original Collinses were always made with gin but, strangely enough, never with London dry gin—the very liquor that is practically always used in making a Collins today. The Tom Collins was made with Old Tom gin and the John Collins with Holland gin. Holland gin has a strong, aromatic flavor all its own and, as has previously been noted, it does not blend satisfactorily with any other liquor, with citrus juices, or, in fact, with anything except, perhaps, bitters. Consequently, the John Collins was never popular in this country and today it is practically unknown.

The adoption of London dry gin as a Collins base gave rise to two schools of nomenclature. With one school it was simply substituted for Old Tom gin in the Tom Collins. The other school, however, preferred to retain the Tom Collins name for the original drink made with Old Tom gin and, since Holland gin was practically never used any more in a Collins, they transferred the John Collins name to the Collins made with London dry gin. This accounts for the confusion that exists in present-day books of recipes. In some the Tom recipe calls for Old Tom gin and the John recipe for dry gin; in others the Tom recipe calls for dry gin and the John recipe for Holland gin. Actually, of course, Old Tom gin is merely a sweetened London gin. Consequently, we can make our Tom Collins with either Old Tom or London dry gin, but, if Old Tom gin is used, the quantity of sugar should be reduced by about a half.

Another modern innovation in the making of Collinses is the use of a special citric-flavored, carbonated beverage called "Tom Collins Mix." All that is necessary is to add the gin or other liquor to the "Tom Collins Mix" and sweeten to taste. This produces a reasonably palatable drink and, of course, much time and effort are saved. The beverage does not, however, compare with a real Collins made with fresh lemon juice.

In making a Collins, have the charged water thoroughly pre-chilled. Use 3 to 4 large cubes of ice and a 14- to 16-ounce Collins glass. Stir quickly and briefly. This is a long drink, to be consumed slowly and with reverence and meditation. It should not be allowed to go flat, and either the use of a warm charged water or prolonged stirring will release the carbon dioxide in the water and render the drink stale and insipid.

Here is the Tom Collins formula together with the list of the various other relatives and the liquor used in each:

TOM COLLINS

    1 tablespoonful Sugar Syrup
    Juice of 1 medium-sized Lemon
    3 to 4 ounces (2 jiggers) Gin

Stir together in Collins glass, add 4 large ice cubes, fill glass with charged water, stir again quickly, and serve. If Old Tom gin is used, reduce sugar by half.

JOHN COLLINS   Use Holland gin in place of Old Tom or London dry.

COLONEL COLLINS or BOURBON COLLINS   Use bourbon in place of gin.

MIKE COLLINS or *IRISH COLLINS*   Use Irish whisky.

JACK COLLINS or *APPLE COLLINS*   Use Applejack.

PEDRO COLLINS or *RUM COLLINS*   Use Cuban rum, either white or gold label.

The Rum Collins, decorated with sprigs of mint, is sometimes called a *MOJITO* (moe-hee'-toe).

PIERRE COLLINS or *BRANDY COLLINS*   Use cognac.

SANDY COLLINS or *SCOTCH COLLINS*   Use Scotch whisky.

RYE COLLINS   Use rye whisky.

VODKA COLLINS   Use vodka.

CANADIAN COLLINS   Use Canadian whisky and, in place of sugar syrup, use maple syrup.

TEQUILA COLLINS   Use tequila.

GIN 'N' TONIC   This varies somewhat from the regular Collins formula, as will be noted. Add 1 or 2 thin slices of lemon to 3 ounces of gin in a Collins glass. Put 3 or 4 large cubes of ice in the glass and fill it up with quinine water.

Remember that this is not merely a thirst quencher but also a tonic. It *does* contain real quinine, and too much quinine, while not intoxicating in the ordinary sense, nevertheless can produce a head that feels like a fully inflated balloon. Take due notice and govern yourself accordingly.

FIZZES

What is the difference, if any, between a Tom Collins and a Gin Fizz? No less an authority than the late G. Selmer Fougner insisted that there was no difference and that the two "are identically the same drink, made in the same manner with the same ingredients, the sole difference being that for the 'Tom Collins' a larger glass is used." As his authority (as if the colonel needed any higher authority!) he quoted from *The Professional Bartenders Guide*.

It is, of course, true that the ingredients of both drinks are the same. Unfortunately, it is also true that today, at many bars, a Gin Fizz is made and served like a short Tom Collins. This, however, is because the old-time siphon bottle has largely disappeared from our bars and has been replaced by the individual metal-capped bottle of club soda or sparkling water.

Now, for long drinks, such as the Collins and the Highball, that are to be consumed slowly over a substantial length of time, the modern bottled carbonated waters have a tremendous advantage over the old-time siphon. The carbonic acid gas is given off slowly in minute bubbles and the life of the drink is many times as long as it is in a drink in which the charged water is added under high pressure with much fizzing and foaming. (See *Soda and Ginger Ale*.) Nevertheless, I insist that a Fizz should actually fizz—just as a soda fizzes when the soda jerker reverses the handle at the fountain and delivers a fine stream of the carbonated water under high pressure into the glass. The good colonel, unfortunately, overlooked certain differences in the method of preparing and serving the two drinks, and it is those differences that distinguish the Collins from the Fizz.

The Collins is made in a tall glass (14 to 16 ounces) with several ice cubes or an equivalent amount of cracked ice in the glass and with the charged water poured in slowly and the whole drink stirred very briefly in order that it may retain its carbonation as long as possible. The drink should be clear, like a Highball, and should never be permitted to "fizz." The Fizz, on the other hand, should be thoroughly frappéed with fine ice (three or even five minutes of shaking are none too long), after which it is strained into a 6- to 8-ounce glass and "fizzed" by adding charged water in a fine stream under pressure. It should be served foaming exactly as the drinks served you at a soda fountain foam. Harry Johnson, in his *Bartender's Manual* published in the early eighties, says, "Bear in mind that all drinks called Fizz's must be drank as soon as handed out, or the natural taste of the same is lost to the customer." Harry's grammar might be improved upon, but he knew what a Fizz was. And if you can't get siphon bottles to use in making your Fizzes, I suggest that you acquire one of those clever little gadgets that can be attached to the ordinary sparkling-water bottle and enable you, by shaking the bottle and then depressing the valve, to deliver a stream under pressure similar to the siphon. Or, as an emergency measure, shake the bottle while holding the thumb over the top and then, holding the bottle at an angle of about 45°, tilt the thumb slightly and thus squirt the water into the glass.

The Fizz is a drink with which you can really go to town in "rolling your own." Just remember that basically it is simply a Sour (but with somewhat different proportions from those of the Sour-type cocktail) thoroughly frappéed and then fizzed up with charged water. But remember, too, that the charged water will cut down the sweetness of the sugar and the sourness of the lemon or lime juice as well as the strength of the liquor. For the Sour-type cocktail I have recommended the 1-2-8 formula, not to make the cocktail "strong," but to prevent it from being either sickish-sweet from the sugar or puckerish-sour from the citrus juice. For the Fizz, you will find it hard to improve on the old formula of 1—or a little less—sweet (sugar, fruit syrup, or liqueur), 2 sour (lime or lemon juice), 3—or a little more—strong (spirituous liquor), and 4 weak (charged water and ice). If you will keep these simple principles firmly in mind, you can ad lib *ad infinitum*—or at least as long as your supply of liquid ingredients holds out. However, just to get you started, here are some of the better-known formulas, both plain and fancy:

GIN FIZZ
    1 tablespoonful Sugar Syrup

Juice of 1 medium-sized Lemon
1½ jiggers Gin

Shake vigorously with crushed ice for several minutes and strain into pre-chilled 8-ounce glass. Fizz up with siphon of charged water, stirring continuously as water is added. In this and practically all other Fizzes, lime juice or a combination of lime and lemon juice may be used in place of the lemon.

SILVER FIZZ   Frappé 1 egg white with the other ingredients constituting the Sour base. Otherwise the same as the Gin Fizz.

GOLDEN FIZZ   Same as Silver Fizz, except that 1 egg yolk is used instead of the egg white.

ROYAL FIZZ   Gin Fizz using 1 whole egg.

DIAMOND FIZZ   Gin Fizz using champagne instead of charged water. Stir vigorously while adding the champagne.

HOFFMAN HOUSE FIZZ   Gin Fizz with maraschino used in place of sugar syrup and with a tablespoonful sweet cream and a teaspoonful orange juice added.
This is also sometimes called the GRAND ROYAL.

ALBEMARLE FIZZ   Add 1 teaspoonful raspberry syrup to the finished Gin Fizz in the glass.

CRIMSON FIZZ   Crush a half dozen strawberries with the other ingredients. Otherwise same as Gin Fizz.

GREEN FIZZ   Same as Silver Fizz with the addition of 1 teaspoonful green crème de menthe.

VIOLET FIZZ   Same as Gin Fizz but with crème de violette substituted for the sugar syrup.

MERRY WIDOW FIZZ   Same as Gin Fizz but with juice of ½ lemon and ½ orange.

PURPLE FIZZ Equal parts sloe gin and grapefruit juice in place of gin and lemon juice. Otherwise same as Silver Fizz.

ALABAMA FIZZ Plain Gin Fizz decorated with 2 or 3 sprigs of mint. This is also sometimes called the *SOUTHSIDE FIZZ*.

NEW ORLEANS GIN FIZZ
    1 tablespoonful Sugar Syrup
    Juice of ½ medium-sized Lemon
    Juice of ½ large Lime
    1 Egg White
    ½ ounce Heavy Cream
    3 ounces Gin

The secret of this Fizz is the long shaking with cracked or crushed ice. Use long strokes and shake for at least five minutes. Strain into 8-ounce glass and add about 1½ ounces charged water from the siphon. The drink should be thick even after the charged water is added.

RAMOS GIN FIZZ Same as New Orleans Fizz, but with the addition of ½ to 1 teaspoonful Eau de Fleurs d'Oranger. This genuine orange-flower water is manufactured by Warrick Frères of Grasse, France, and is imported and distributed in the United States by J. Manheimer of New York City.

ORANGE AND LIME FIZZ A Gin Fizz using the juices of ½ lime, ½ orange, and ¼ lemon, and no sugar.

ORANGE FIZZ A Gin Fizz using juice of ½ orange and 2 or 3 dashes orange bitters in place of the lemon juice. No sugar.

PINK LADY FIZZ A Silver Fizz with grenadine substituted for the sugar syrup.

TEXAS FIZZ A plain Gin Fizz with 1 teaspoonful grenadine and 2 teaspoonfuls orange juice in place of the sugar syrup.

MORNING GLORY FIZZ
    2 teaspoonfuls Sugar Syrup
    Juice of ½ Lime
    Juice of ½ Lemon
    1 Egg White
    1 pony Absinthe
    1 jigger Scotch

Prepare and serve same as Silver Fizz.

Supposed to be a grand picker-upper for the morning after. Johnson says it "will give a good appetite and quiet the nerves."

The following are all made the same as the Gin Fizz except for the substitution of ingredients as noted:

APPLEJACK FIZZ   Applejack in place of gin.

APPLE BLOW FIZZ or *APPLE BLOSSOM FIZZ*   A Silver Fizz made with applejack.

BRANDY FIZZ   Brandy in place of gin.

DERBY FIZZ   A Royal Fizz made with bourbon and a few dashes of curaçao.

MAY BLOSSOM FIZZ   Swedish Punch in place of gin and grenadine in place of sugar syrup.

PINEAPPLE FIZZ   A White Label Rum Fizz with pineapple juice substituted for the lemon juice.

RUBY FIZZ   A Sloe Gin Fizz with the addition of 1 egg white and a few dashes of raspberry syrup.

RUM FIZZ   Cuban rum, either white or gold label, in place of gin.

SEA FIZZ   A Silver Fizz with absinthe in place of the gin.

SLOE GIN FIZZ   Sloe gin in place of dry gin.

SNOW BALL   A Silver Fizz with whisky in place of the gin and ginger ale in place of the charged water.

WHISKY FIZZ   Rye or bourbon, as you prefer, in place of gin.

And in making our Fizzes let us not forget our teetotaler friends. We can have PROHIBITION FIZZES, just as well as other prohibition drinks. Grape juice, grenadine, orgeat, or any fruit syrup, frappéed with lime or lemon juice and fizzed up with charged water, will make a tasty and refreshing drink. It won't have the snap and tang that a good alcoholic Fizz will have, but remember that it is just that snap and tang that your "tomato-juicer" friend does not like or want. With a little understanding and conscientious care you can make him drinks that will delight and satisfy him, and the chances are that that is more than he can—or will—do for you. But be comforted by the thought that it is more blessed to give than to receive.

AUSTRALIAN SNOW   This is another Prohibition Tall Drink—a passion-fruit soda. Blend together in a 14-ounce Collins glass 2 ounces of passion-fruit nectar with an equal quantity of vanilla ice cream (or, better still if available, lime ice cream). Fizz up with the siphon bottle or equivalent (see *FIZZES*), stirring constantly. When glass is nearly full, add 1 scoop of ice cream. Serve with straws.

DAISIES AND FIXES

As previously noted, there is little, if any, difference between these two classes of drinks. Most of the old Fix recipes call for pineapple syrup, whereas the Daisies usually use raspberry syrup or grenadine. This, however, is relatively unimportant. Both drinks are of the Sour type, employing citrus juices, fruit syrups or liqueurs, and a spirituous liquor.

The Fix is regularly served with straws in a glass or a goblet filled with shaved or crushed ice. The Daisy is sometimes strained into a Delmonico or a small Highball glass, but it is also proper—and, in my opinion, preferable—to serve it with straws in a goblet, a stein, or—best of all—a silver mug full of fine ice, exactly the same as a Fix. The drink should be muddled with a long spoon until the outside of the glass or mug becomes frosted.

Both drinks are also customarily decorated with whatever fruit may be available and desired—orange, lemon, cherries, pineapple, strawberries, raspberries, small grapes, sprigs of mint, etc. For please bear in mind the fact that these are drinks of the Mid-Victorian Era. Put on your hoop skirt and bustle or wax your mustache, and sip them to the dreamy rhythm of a Viennese waltz. All of the following are to be stirred or shaken with cracked ice, poured into a goblet or mug, and decorated as above indicated:

GIN DAISY

    1 part Grenadine
    2 parts Lemon or Lime Juice
    8 parts Gin

Mix and pour into prepared goblet as above indicated. Float 1 or 2 teaspoonfuls yellow Chartreuse on top.

APPLEJACK DAISY [3] or BRANDY DAISY or RUM DAISY or WHISKY DAISY
Except for the base liquor used, these are all made and served exactly like the Gin Daisy.

GIN FIX

    1 part Pineapple Syrup
    2 parts Lime or Lemon Juice
    8 parts Gin

Prepare and serve the same as a Gin Daisy. If pineapple syrup is not available substitute maraschino or Cointreau.

[3] The Applejack Daisy is also known as the STAR DAISY.

Or you can use 1 part sugar syrup and add 1 to 2 parts fresh pineapple juice. A spoonful of green Chartreuse may be floated over the top of each drink if desired.

APPLEJACK FIX or **BRANDY FIX** or **RUM FIX** or **WHISKY FIX** Except for the base liquor used, these are made and served exactly like the Gin Fix.

There you are, my children. Now you tell me the difference between a Daisy and a Fix. Maybe it is that one is pink and the other white.

And, once again, don't forget *PROHIBITION DAISIES* and *FIXES* for your teetotaler friends. Use plain raspberry syrup, pineapple syrup, or whatever fruit syrup you may have. Add orange juice along with the lime and lemon. This is sometimes called a *DUMMY DAISY*. You can use grape juice instead of raspberry or pineapple. And, now that the color is purple, is it a Fix or a Daisy? Perhaps we might call this the *DAISY PROHIBITION FIX*. The color would seem appropriate.

JULEPS

In the whole category of tall drinks there is probably none that is more delicious and certainly none that has caused more violent disagreement and acrimonious debate than the *MINT JULEP*. Should the mint be bruised or not bruised? Should it be left in the glass or removed? Should it be blended with the whisky or should it be used merely as a decoration on the top of the glass? Should the drink be served with straws or not? Should it be decorated with fruit or not? If you are interested in these and other similar details about the Julep, I suggest that you write to the National Distillers Product Corporation, New York City, for their excellent little booklet on Mint Juleps. If it is not out of print (it was copyrighted in 1939), I am sure they will be glad to send you a copy.

I have, in all, probably some thirty or forty different recipes for Juleps, some good, some bad, some indifferent.

THE FINE ART OF MIXING DRINKS 323

I shall give you just three—my own and two others that I consider excellent. It takes two hours or more advance notice to prepare one of the latter. The other is for those who like only a very mild mint flavor. First of all, however, there are certain cardinal principles to be observed, no matter what recipe you follow, if you want to turn out a Julep that is really good and that is attractively frosted.

1. *Use very tall 14- or 16-ounce containers, whether of glass or of silver. Silver mugs are best because they frost better than glass, and mugs with handles—especially insulated handles—are best of all because they keep the warm hand from coming in contact with the outer surface of the container, thus melting the frost. If glasses are used, the thinner the glass, the better. It is well to serve paper napkins with which to handle the glasses, thereby insulating them to some extent from the warm hand. Also serve saucers or large coasters in which to set the glasses or mugs, for some of the frost will always melt and drip.*

2. *Unless the drink itself is to be chilled in the refrigerator, thoroughly pre-chill the glasses by leaving them in the refrigerator as close as possible to the freezing compartment for at least a half-hour. When filling the glasses, wear woolen gloves or wrap the glass in a clean dry towel to keep the warm hand from coming in contact with the glass.*

3. *Use only fresh mint and (except as a garnish) only the small, tender leaves at the end of each sprig. Discard all stems and all the old and large leaves.*

4. *Use only the best-quality bonded bourbon—the older, the better. If you want to make a RYE JULEP, or a RUM JULEP, or a GIN JULEP, or a BRANDY JULEP, or an APPLEJACK JULEP, well and good, but you will be on your own. I am not a Kentucky colonel—in fact, I have been in Kentucky only once—but I am*

firmly convinced that all other Juleps are only inferior imitations of those made with good Kentucky bourbon.

5. Use sugar syrup, not dry sugar. It not only saves time but it blends with the liquor as dry sugar and water never can.

6. For the garnish use nothing but tender, young sprigs of mint. Rinse them well in cold water, dry with a clean towel, and, while still slightly moist, dip in powdered sugar. Clip off the end of each stem just before immersing in the drink, thus allowing the juice to bleed into the liquor.

7. Use shaved or finely crushed ice—not merely cracked ice. If you have a mechanical crusher—such as the Dazey—set it for the finest crush. If you use a canvas bag and mallet, pound until the ice is like snow. Discard all lumps.

With these warnings and advance preparations, proceed with the actual preparation of your Juleps as below indicated. No. 1 is my own favorite; No. 2 is the time consumer; No. 3 is the one with just a faint mint flavor.

JULEP NO. 1   In a bar glass place, for each drink, 1 tablespoonful sugar syrup, about a dozen tender young mint leaves, and 2 or 3 good dashes of Angostura. If you don't like bitters, leave them out, but, in my opinion, they add enormously to the character of the drink. Bruise the mint gently with a muddler and blend the three ingredients by stirring and pressing gently for several minutes. Do not crush the leaves, for this releases the bitter, inner juices. Pour about 2 ounces of bourbon for each drink into the bar glass and stir all thoroughly together.

Remove the Julep glasses from the refrigerator, pack them with the crushed ice (don't let the bare hands touch the glasses) and strain the contents of the bar glass into them. With a long bar spoon churn the contents of the glasses up and down for a few minutes. Add more ice and fill each glass to within about ⅜" to ¼" of the top with bourbon and repeat the churning process until the glasses start to frost.

Insert long straws in the glasses, decorate with the sugared mint sprigs, and serve.

The glasses may be returned to the refrigerator after the drinks are mixed if so desired, but this is not necessary. If they are returned, insert the straws but do not add the garnish until the moment of serving. The dry cold of the refrigerator will wilt the mint sprigs if they have been added. Also it may freeze the ice into a solid mass, making it difficult or impossible to insert the straws later.

JULEP NO. 2 Prepare the mint, sugar, Angostura mixture as in No. 1, but do not add the bourbon. Pour half of this mixture into the bottom of the Julep glass. Half fill the glass with crushed ice, firmly packed down. Add the balance of the mint mixture and fill the glass to the top with the ice. Insert straws and place the glass in the refrigerator as close as possible to the freezing compartment. Leave it there for at least an hour.

Remove glass from refrigerator (insulated hands again) and gently pour into it all the bourbon it will hold up to about ¼" from the top. Return to the refrigerator for at least another hour, then remove, add garnish, and serve.

JULEP NO. 3 Pre-chill the glasses. In the bottom of each glass place a tablespoonful of sugar syrup and, if desired, stir into it a few dashes of Angostura.

Distribute three or four small sprigs (not just the leaves) of mint over the bottom of the glass but do not bruise or crush. Pack the glass full with crushed ice and fill with bourbon to within about an inch of the top. Churn with a long spoon to settle the ice and start the frosting process. Refill with ice, add enough bourbon to bring to desired height, and insert straws.

Place drinks in refrigerator for at least 5 or 10 minutes (a half-hour is better), add garnish, and serve.

One of the greatly disputed points about Juleps is whether or not to float a spoonful of rum on top of each drink. To your true Kentucky colonel, this is rank heresy. It does, however, add an exotic touch which many like. I like Juleps either with or without the rum, but, if you do use rum, use only a good Jamaica rum at least 8 years old and use not more than 1 teaspoonful.

I will also make one single concession to my rule of "nothing but bonded bourbon" for a Julep. Southern Comfort, which, of course, has a bourbon base, makes an excellent Julep. The ladies, in particular, will like it better than one made with straight bourbon.

If any of your teetotaler friends attend your Julep party I fear you will have to serve them plain ice water. I know of no prohibition variety of the Julep.

COBBLERS

Like the Fixes and the Daisies, the Cobblers are served with straws in a goblet filled with finely crushed or shaved ice and are decorated with fruit and a sprig or two of mint. They differ from Fixes and Daisies (which are basically Sours) primarily in that the Cobblers contain either no citrus juice at all or, at the most, only one or two dashes. They consist of either a wine or a spirituous liquor combined with either sugar syrup or some sweet liqueur. While seldom served today, Harry Johnson, circa 1880, said of the Sherry Cobbler: "This drink is without doubt the most popular beverage in this country, with ladies as well as with gentlemen. It is a very refreshing drink for old and young."

In making any of the Cobblers, the goblet is first filled with fine ice. If goblets are not available an 8- to 10-ounce Highball glass can be substituted. The ingredients of the drink are not separately shaken but are poured over the ice in the glass, the sugar or liqueur first and the wine or spirituous liquor last. The contents of the glass are then churned with a bar spoon until frost appears on the outside of the glass. Straws are then inserted and the drink is decorated with fruit and mint and served.

APPLEJACK COBBLER or BRANDY COBBLER or GIN COBBLER or RUM COBBLER or WHISKY COBBLER Prepare glass with ice as above directed. Add 2 teaspoonfuls sugar syrup. Fill glass to within ½" of top with the desired liquor and stir. When glass begins to frost, decorate and serve. A teaspoonful of pineapple syrup or a few dashes of curaçao are frequently used with the sugar syrup. Also a fruit liqueur, such as maraschino, Cointreau, apricot, or peach, may be substituted for the sugar syrup. With rum, orgeat or falernum will make a pleasing substitute for the sugar.

CLARET COBBLER or MADEIRA COBBLER or PORT COBBLER or RHINE WINE COBBLER or SAUTERNE COBBLER or SHERRY COBBLER or TOKAY COBBLER Same as the Cobblers made with spirituous liquors, but with the port, sauterne, or other sweet wines, omit the sugar syrup and use a few dashes of curaçao. With the Rhine wine, add a few dashes of lemon juice. With the sherry, add a twist of lemon peel.

CHAMPAGNE COBBLER Made like the other Cobblers but with champagne. Use sugar syrup and a twist each of lemon and orange peel.

COFFEE COBBLER Made like the other Cobblers but with 1 part port wine to 2 parts cognac. Add a twist of lemon peel.

ENGLISH COBBLER Made with 2 parts heavy rum (preferably London Dock) to 1 part strong black tea and 1 teaspoonful lemon juice.

VANILLA COBBLER Made with 1 part crème de vanille to 2 parts cognac, plus 1 tablespoonful heavy cream. Instead of fruit decorations, sprinkle grated nutmeg over the top.

COOLERS

A Cooler is essentially a *HORSE'S NECK WITH A KICK*, although there are also Prohibition Coolers made with non-alcoholic ingredients. So far as I have been able to ascertain, the original Cooler was the Remsen Cooler and, while most modern recipe books indicate gin for the Remsen Cooler, this is incorrect. This Cooler derived its name from the fact that it was made with Remsen Scotch whisky, a brand no longer seen, at least in this country.

The Cooler is served in a Collins glass decorated with the skin of a whole lemon or orange cut in a continuous spiral and hung over the edge of the glass exactly as in the Horse's Neck. Sometimes both a lemon peel and an orange peel are used for decoration.

Whereas the Horse's Neck is made with ginger ale, the original Remsen Cooler was made with club soda. Today some Coolers are made with charged water and some with ginger ale. There are also Coolers made with other carbonated beverages, at least one or two made with cider, and some modern recipes even stoop to prescribing plain water. The Cooler should be very dry, but sugar can be used if desired and perhaps the best advice here is "sweeten according to taste." If you want the drink to be thirst-quenching, refreshing, and satisfying, however, you must keep it definitely on the dry side. The base of the Cooler may be a spirituous liquor, a wine, a liqueur, or even a fruit syrup. With sweet wines or liqueurs it is usually advisable to use a few dashes of lime or lemon juice, but this is optional. It is also optional whether or not to use bitters and how much.

With the above principles well in mind you should be able to "roll your own" Coolers with whatever ingredients may be at hand and of any type and strength to suit any taste from that of an Andy Volstead to that of the Old Soak. However, the following are offered as specimens:

REMSEN COOLER (The original Cooler) Decorate a Tom Collins glass with a lemon peel as above directed and place 3 or 4 large ice cubes in the glass. Add 2 to 3 ounces Scotch whisky and fill the glass with charged water. Stir quickly with bar spoon and serve.

APPLEJACK COOLER or *BRANDY COOLER* or *GIN COOLER* or *RUM COOLER* or *WHISKY COOLER* Except for the liquor used, these are made exactly like the Remsen Cooler. Ginger ale may be substituted for the charged water if desired.

The Rum Cooler, when made with Jamaica rum, is sometimes called a *BLACKSTONE COOLER.*

STONE FENCE or *STONEWALL JACKSON* An Applejack Cooler with hard cider in place of the carbonated beverage.

BOSTON COOLER A Rum Cooler with the addition of 1 teaspoonful sugar syrup and the juice of half a lemon.

MOONLIGHT COOLER or *HARVARD COOLER* Made like a Boston Cooler but with applejack instead of rum.

LONG TOM COOLER Made like a Boston Cooler but with Old Tom gin instead of rum.

WINE COOLERS Use any wine desired and make the same as other Coolers except that with the light, unfortified wines a larger quantity should be used than in the case of spirituous liquors. With very sweet wines, such as sauterne and port, add 1 teaspoonful lemon juice. With very dry wines, such as Rhine wines, a teaspoonful of sugar syrup or of a liqueur such as maraschino or curaçao may be added.

A Claret Cooler plus a few dashes of rum is sometimes called a MANHATTAN COOLER.

COUNTRY CLUB COOLER or VERMOUTH COOLER Use 1 ounce grenadine, 3 ounces French vermouth, and charged water. Italian vermouth may also be used, in which case omit the grenadine and add 1 teaspoonful lemon juice.

DUBONNET COOLER or BYRRH COOLER Made like the Italian Vermouth Cooler except for the base wine.

And now here are a few *PROHIBITION COOLERS* for your teetotaler friends:

MINT COOLER Crush one or two sprigs of mint with 1 or 2 teaspoonfuls sugar in the bottom of the glass, add the ice, decorate with the lemon peel, and fill glass with ginger ale.

RAIL SPLITTER One ounce sugar syrup, juice of 1 medium-sized lemon. Fill up with ginger ale.

SARATOGA COOLER Ginger ale and sarsaparilla, half and half.

The Rail Splitter plus a few dashes of Angostura is also sometimes called a Saratoga.

LONE TREE COOLER Juice of 1 lemon and ½ orange with 1 ounce grenadine. Fill up with charged water.

SANGAREES

A Sangaree is a chilled and sweetened beer, wine, or liquor, served in a Highball glass, and dusted over the top with grated nutmeg. Many present-day recipe books overlook the Sangarees made of beer, ale, and porter and, on the other hand, in recent years the category has been broadened to take in drinks made with spirituous liquors diluted with water. These, of course, are substantially the same as cold Toddies and Slings.

ALE SANGAREE or *BEER SANGAREE* or *PORTER SANGAREE* Place 2 teaspoonfuls of sugar syrup in an 8-ounce Highball glass; fill glass with the ale, beer, or porter; stir gently with a bar spoon; dust top with grated nutmeg and serve.

BURGUNDY SANGAREE or *CLARET SANGAREE* or *SAUTERNE SANGAREE* Made the same as the Beer Sangarees except that one or two lumps of ice are placed in the glass to chill the wine. It is discretionary whether to leave the ice in the glass or to remove it before serving the drink.

MADEIRA SANGAREE or *PORT SANGAREE* or *SHERRY SANGAREE* Made the same as the other wine Sangarees except that only about 3 ounces of the fortified wine is used and the glass is then filled up with ice water.

APPLEJACK SANGAREE or *BRANDY SANGAREE* or *GIN SANGAREE* or *RUM SANGAREE* or *WHISKY SANGAREE* Made exactly the same as those with a base of sherry or other fortified wine.

HOT SANGAREES

The Sangarees are also sometimes served hot. In the case of the Ale, Beer, and Porter Sangarees, this is accomplished by heating a poker or other iron rod to white heat and then immersing it in the drink. The nutmeg is not added until the drink has been heated. The Sangarees made of spirituous liquors and fortified wines are heated by using hot instead of cold water. The Sangarees made of light wines are not served hot, although they could be so served by heating the wine itself either separately or by the hot-poker method.

SLINGS AND TODDIES

The dictionaries define both Slings and Toddies as "mixtures of sweetened spirits and water." While Slings have always been served both hot and cold, the Toddy was originally a hot drink only. Today, however, Toddies, as well as Slings, are served both hot and cold. Slings are usually made with lemon and either sugar or some sweet liqueur. Toddies usually contain a thin slice of lemon or a piece of lemon peel but no lemon juice. Also, they usually contain one or more spices, such as cinnamon, cloves, or nutmeg. These differences, however, are merely incidental and, when served hot, it is difficult, if not impossible, to distinguish between a Sling and a Toddy. One distinction between the cold drinks is that Toddies are usually made with plain water, Slings with charged water or ginger ale.

APPLEJACK SLING or *BRANDY SLING* or *GIN SLING* or *IRISH SLING* or *RUM SLING* or *SCOTCH SLING* or *WHISKY SLING*
  1 teaspoonful Sugar Syrup
  2 teaspoonfuls Lemon Juice
  3 ounces of the selected Liquor

Combine the above in a goblet or large Highball glass. Fill the glass with chilled, charged water for a cold Sling or with boiling water for a hot Sling. Some recipes omit the lemon juice. Others omit both the lemon juice and sugar and use a few dashes of Angostura. Some recipes also call for dusting the top with nutmeg. Query, is it then a Sling or a Sangaree?

PAPAYA SLING A Gin Sling using 1 tablespoonful papaya syrup in place of sugar syrup.

SINGAPORE GIN SLING Of all the recipes published for this drink, I have never seen any two that were alike. Essentially it is simply a Gin Sling with the addition of cherry brandy. The following is typical of the various recipes:

- 1 teaspoonful Sugar Syrup
- Juice of ¼ large Lemon or ½ large Lime
- 1 pony Cherry Brandy (Kirsch)
- 1½ jiggers Gin
- 1 dash Angostura

Shake and strain into 8-ounce Highball glass or use 10-ounce glass and leave 1 large ice cube in the glass. Fill glass with charged water. Some recipes call for the addition of a pony of Benedictine. Also, some call for ginger ale in place of the charged water. A slice of lemon peel should be twisted over and dropped into the drink.

APPLEJACK TODDY or BRANDY TODDY or GIN TODDY or IRISH TODDY or RUM TODDY or SCOTCH TODDY or WHISKY TODDY

- 1 ounce Sugar Syrup
- 3 ounces of the selected Liquor
- 2 or 3 Cloves
- 1 dash ground Cinnamon or small piece Cinnamon Bark
- 1 dash ground Nutmeg
- 1 thin slice Lemon

Combine all ingredients except the nutmeg in a goblet or tall Highball glass. Fill the glass with either hot or cold water and dust the nutmeg over the top.

LEMONADES, LIMEADES, AND ORANGEADES

Lemonades, either plain or spiked, are delicious, refreshing summer drinks. When spiked with a spirituous liquor, of course, the Lemonade becomes a Collins. Delightful variations in flavor, however, may be obtained by adding 1 or 2 ounces of practically any liqueur to the Lemonade or by adding a wine, either mixed with the other ingredients or floated on top of the drink. Limeades and Orangeades are equally tasty, and any two or all three of these citrus fruits may be used in combination.

LEMONADE (*Plain*)
    1 tablespoonful Sugar Syrup
    Juice of 1 large Lemon

Combine and pour into Collins glass full of cracked ice. Fill glass with either plain or charged water, stir thoroughly, decorate with fruits, and serve. A sprig of mint may be added if desired.

LIMEADE   Use 2 large limes in place of lemon.

ORANGEADE   Use 1 large or 1½ to 2 small oranges in place of lemon. A combination of either lemon or lime with the orange greatly improves this drink.

LIME-LEMONADE or *LIME-ORANGEADE* or *LEMON-ORANGEADE*   Made like a plain Lemonade but with mixed fruit juices as follows:
    ½ large Lemon, 1 large Lime
    1 large Orange, 1 Lime
    1 large Orange, ½ Lemon

WINE LEMONADES   With light-colored wines—sauterne, Rhine wine, sherry, etc.—the wine should be stirred in with the other ingredients in the proportion of about 1 part of wine to 2 or 3 of the water or perhaps a bit less in the case of a fortified wine such as sherry.

With deep-colored wines—claret, red burgundy, port, etc.—the same proportions should be observed and the wine may be either stirred into the drink or floated on top.

LIQUEUR LEMONADES   Omit the sugar syrup and add 1 pony of practically any liqueur. The citrus- and fruit-flavored liqueurs—Cointreau, curaçao, maraschino, apricot, cherry, etc.—are better for this purpose than a strongly aromatic liqueur such as Chartreuse.

PINK LEMONADE Use raspberry syrup or grenadine in place of sugar.

GREEN LEMONADE Use green crème de menthe in place of sugar.

ORGEAT LEMONADE Use orgeat in place of sugar.

EGG LEMONADE Plain Lemonade with the addition of 1 whole egg. Shake the lemon, sugar, and egg thoroughly in a cocktail shaker; pour into glass without straining; add the water, stir, and serve.

PICON LEMONADE Plain Lemonade with the addition of 1 jigger Amer Picon.

The various combinations above suggested can be employed with limes or oranges as well as with lemons. If kumquats are available, try using the juice of 3 or 4 kumquats with that of 1 lime. This is a *KUMQUAT LIMEADE*.

For party use I suggest serving plain Lemonades and having on a serving table bottles of claret, grenadine, orgeat, port, and a few liqueurs. Let each guest spike his drink to suit is individual fancy.

INDIVIDUAL PUNCHES

There are two types of Punches according to the manner in which they are to be served: individual Punches which, like Highballs, Juleps, etc., are made in the glasses in which they are to be served, and party Punches which are made in a Punch bowl and ladled from the bowl into the cups in which they are served. The party Punches will be considered in a later chapter.

Of the individual Punches there are two types: the Sour-type, which, like the Collins, the Julep, the Daisy, etc., is a thirst-quenching drink especially suited to a hot summer afternoon, and the Milk Punch, which is really a combination of food and drink. Let us consider the Milk Punch first, and this time we will start with our teetotaler friend and, after serving him, we will spike the remaining drinks to suit the several individual tastes. Since there is no liquor in the prohibition drink, we shall try to compensate in part for its absence by the use of an egg.

MILK SHAKE or *MILK PUNCH*, Plain
> 1 whole Egg
> ½ pint (1 cup) Sweet Milk
> Sugar to taste (1 to 3 teaspoonfuls Syrup)

Shake with cracked ice until thoroughly blended and chilled, then strain into Collins glass. Dust with ground nutmeg if desired.

APPLEJACK MILK PUNCH, BRANDY MILK PUNCH,[4] *GIN MILK PUNCH,*[5] *IRISH MILK PUNCH, RUM MILK PUNCH,*[4] *SCOTCH MILK PUNCH, WHISKY MILK PUNCH* [5]
> 2 to 3 ounces of the selected Liquor
> ½ pint (1 cup) Sweet Milk
> Sugar to taste

Prepare same as plain Milk Punch. Decorate with a dash of grated nutmeg or a sliver of lemon or orange peel.

HOT MILK PUNCHES Any of the above Punches can also be served hot. Combine the sugar and liquor in a Highball glass or goblet and fill glass with boiling hot milk.

TIGER'S MILK
> 1 teaspoonful Sugar Syrup
> 2 ounces Brandy or Applejack
> 1 Egg White to each 2 drinks

---

[4] A Milk Punch made with 2 parts rum and 3 parts brandy is known as *BULL'S MILK*.
[5] The Whisky Milk Punch is also known as *WHITE PLUSH*. So also is the Gin Milk Punch. With the White Plush made of gin, maraschino is usually used in place of the sugar syrup.

1 drop each of Vanilla, Orange, Clove & Cinnamon Extracts to each 4 drinks

Beat the egg white with the sugar and extracts, then shake with ice and brandy. Strain into Collins glass and fill up glass with sweet cider and milk, half and half. Dust with nutmeg.

PUFFS The Puff is a combination Milk and Soda Punch. Mix equal parts of the desired liquor and milk in the shaker, strain into a Sour glass until the glass is from ½ to ⅔ full, and top off with charged water—preferably from a siphon. Stir quickly and serve.

According to the liquor used, the drink is called a *BRANDY PUFF, GIN PUFF, RUM PUFF, WHISKY PUFF*, etc.

PLANTERS' PUNCH Of all the Sour-type Punches, the Planters' Punch, made with Jamaica rum, is probably the most popular. It is an excellent drink and its popularity is well deserved. The Myers Company, makers of Planters' Punch Rum, gives 2 formulas for this drink. The first they designate as the Old Plantation formula, which is 1 sour (lemon or lime), 2 sweet (sugar), 3 strong (rum), and 4 weak (ice and water combined). The second, which they call the American formula, is 1 sweet, 2 sour, 3 weak, 4 strong. I personally recommend 1 sweet, 2 sour, 3 strong, 4 weak.

- 1 part Sugar Syrup
- 2 parts Lemon Juice
- 3 parts Jamaica Rum
- 2 or 3 dashes Angostura to each drink

Shake vigorously with crushed ice and pour, without straining, into Collins glasses. Pack glasses to top with crushed ice, fill to within ½" to ⅜" of top with charged water and churn with a bar spoon until glasses start to frost. Decorate with fruit as desired and serve with straws.

BRANDY PUNCH or ROMAN PUNCH

- 1 part Raspberry Syrup
- 2 parts Lemon Juice
- 3 parts Cognac
- 1 part Jamaica Rum
- 2 or 3 dashes Curaçao to each drink

Prepare and serve like Planters' Punch. Benedictine may be used in place of the raspberry syrup, in which case omit the curaçao.

MISSISSIPPI PUNCH

- 1 part Sugar Syrup
- 2 parts Lemon Juice
- 3 parts Bourbon
- 1 part Cognac

Prepare and serve like Planters' Punch. Float 1 tablespoonful Jamaica rum on top of each drink.

If pineapple juice is substituted for the cognac and the rum float is omitted, this drink becomes a FLORIDA PUNCH.

AMERICAN BEAUTY PUNCH

- 1 part White Crème de Menthe
- 3 parts Orange Juice
- 2 parts Cognac
- 2 parts French Vermouth

Prepare and serve like Planters' Punch. Float 1 teaspoonful claret on top of each drink.

WHISKY PUNCH

- 1 part Curaçao
- 2 parts Lemon Juice
- 3 parts Whisky

Prepare and serve like Planters' Punch.

GIN MINT PUNCH

   1 part Sugar Syrup
   2 parts Lemon Juice
   3 parts Gin
   1 or 2 sprigs Mint to each drink

Muddle the mint with the sugar and lemon juice and prepare like Planters' Punch. Ginger ale may be used in place of charged water.

PICON PUNCH

   1 part Grenadine
   2 parts Lemon Juice
   3 parts Amer Picon

Prepare and serve like Planters' Punch.

YACHT CLUB PUNCH

   1 part Grenadine
   2 parts Lemon Juice
   3 parts Rum
   2 or 3 dashes Absinthe to each drink

Prepare and serve like Planters' Punch.

NEW ORLEANS PUNCH

   1 part Raspberry Syrup
   2 parts Lemon Juice
   1 part Jamaica Rum
   2 parts Bourbon

Prepare like Planters' Punch except that strong, cold, black tea is used in place of charged water.

CREOLE PUNCH

   1 part Sugar Syrup
   2 parts Lemon Juice
   1 part Brandy
   2 parts Port

Prepare like Planters' Punch except that orange juice and water in the ratio of 3 to 1 are used in place of charged water.

PIMM'S CUPS These are bottled Cups from England. My Canadian friends are extremely fond of them, especially Pimm's No. 2. There are three of them, No. 1 made with gin, No. 2 with Scotch, and No. 3 with cognac.

To serve, place a thin piece of lemon and a small piece of cucumber rind in a tall glass filled with ice. Add 2 ounces of Pimm's of the desired type and fill up with lemon soda or Tom Collins Mix.

With these illustrative Punches as examples for your general guidance you should be able to "roll your own" Punches as readily as any other drink. The all-important item to remember is that the drink must be thoroughly frosted. It is a frappéed drink to be served with straws and not merely a cold drink to be served, like a Highball or a Collins, with a few cubes of ice in the glass. Compare, for example, the *PLANTERS' PUNCH*, and the *SOUTHSIDE SPECIAL*.

MISCELLANEOUS

There are a number of tall drinks that are interesting—some rather good and some not so good—that do not properly fall within any of the foregoing categories. They will be discussed under this heading of "Miscellaneous." Note, however, that this book does not consider either malt beverages or wines, except in so far as they are used as ingredients in mixed drinks.

'ARF AND 'ARF or HALF AND HALF Originally half ale and half porter. Also half old or still ale and half new or sparkling ale. Also half beer and half ale. Serve in a beer or Highball glass or mug.

SHANDY GAFF Half ale and half ginger ale. Serve

same as 'Arf and 'Arf. Pour the ale first, then the ginger ale, or pour both together. Stir quickly with bar spoon and serve.

BLACK VELVET [6] Half Guinness's stout and half champagne. Pour the stout first, then the champagne, or both simultaneously.

If porter is used in place of stout, the drink is known simply as *VELVET*. If beer is used, it is known as the *HALSTEAD STREET VELVET*.

I was first introduced to Black Velvet at the home of a very dear friend of mine in Montreal and I received one of the greatest of all the drinking surprises of my whole life. The combination of champagne and stout sounds terrifying—something like molasses and horse-radish. Actually, it is excellent. The champagne cuts the heavy, syrupy consistency of the stout, and the stout takes the sharp, tart edge off the champagne. Each is the perfect complement of the other. Be sure, however, that you use (a) a good bottling of the stout, (b) an extra-dry champagne—preferably a *brut* or *nature*.

TURKISH BLOOD Champagne and red burgundy, half and half.

In this mixture each ingredient fights the other with disastrous results. I definitely do not recommend it. If you must have a sparkling burgundy (an American drink that is anathema to any true Burgundian), buy a sparkling burgundy. Don't combine a still burgundy with a sparkling champagne and thus ruin both.

MIMOSA Orange juice and champagne, half and half.

Just another freak champagne mixture. It is not half bad and the ladies usually like it. Use a good quality domestic champagne, medium-dry.

DOG'S NOSE One part gin to 2 parts porter. Serve in

---

[6] Also sometimes called the *BISMARK*.

Highball glasses. This drink is sometimes chilled in the glass with cracked ice.

A slight modification of the 'Arf and 'Arf theme. It is included as a curiosity and is not recommended.

WARD EIGHT The Ward Eight is probably more frequently served as a tall drink than as a cocktail. See WARD EIGHT cocktail.

NORTHSIDE SPECIAL
  2 teaspoonfuls Sugar Syrup
  Juice of 1 Orange
  2 ounces Jamaica Rum

Shake with crushed ice, pour into Collins glass, ice and all, fill glass with charged water, and serve with straws.

SOUTHSIDE SPECIAL Same as Northside Special except that the Southside is made with the juice of 1 lemon instead of an orange.

This is really a Jamaica Rum Collins. It is *not* a PLANTERS' PUNCH.

SQUIRTS

A Squirt is a very sweet drink made of a spirituous liquor or wine in combination with fresh fruit or fruit syrups and charged water. A fruit liqueur, such as maraschino, apricot, etc., may be used in place of a plain fruit syrup. The Whisky Squirt is a typical example.

WHISKY SQUIRT Crush ½ small peach in a bar glass. Add 1 tablespoonful sugar syrup, 1 teaspoonful curaçao, and 1 jigger bourbon. Shake with crushed ice, pour into tall Highball glass, and fill glass with charged water.

Orgeat and crushed pineapple are recommended for use with the *RUM SQUIRT*. Raspberry syrup or grenadine and strawberries are recommended for use with the *GIN SQUIRT*.

In making *WINE SQUIRTS*, use 2 jiggers wine and any appropriate fruit and fruit syrup or liqueur.

LALLA ROOKH One ounce each of cognac, gold label rum, and crème de vanille with ½ teaspoonful sugar syrup and 1 tablespoonful whipped cream to each drink. Shake with crushed ice, strain into 8-ounce Highball glass, and fizz up with siphon.

This relic of the Gay Nineties is a syrupy-sweet and wholly deceptive concoction. It was one of my favorites during college days before I had learned the wisdom of sticking to dry drinks. I am including it here because of nostalgic memories.

CUBA LIBRE or *RUM AND COCA-COLA* Juice of 1 small Lime (drop ½ lime shell in, too), 2 ounces White Label Rum.

Put ingredients in Collins glass, add 3 or 4 large ice cubes, fill up with Coca-Cola, stir quickly, and serve.

FRENCH 75
  Juice of 1 Lime or ½ Lemon
  2 teaspoonfuls Sugar Syrup
  2 ounces Cognac

Shake with crushed ice, pour into Collins glass, ice and all, and fill up with champagne.

Gin is sometimes used in place of cognac in this drink, but then, of course, it no longer should be called French.

PARTY DRINKS

Of all the various party drinks, Punches and Cups (which, as already pointed out, are pretty much synonymous) occupy first place. There are certain very special drinks such as the Wassail Bowl (little known in this country) and the Egg Nog which occupy a prominent position during the holiday season, but the Punch bowl is the rallying point for teas, receptions, "at homes," and all manner of occasions, formal and informal, at all seasons of the year.

Cups are frequently mixed in a glass pitcher with ice cubes or cracked ice and are poured from the pitcher, whereas Punches are mixed in a Punch bowl. This, however, is purely incidental. Cups can equally well be mixed in and served from a Punch bowl.

And here is your opportunity to "roll your own" with a vengeance. With a few basic principles kept firmly in mind, there is practically no limit to the variety of utterly delicious flavor effects you can produce with the wide range of fruits, fruit juices, wines, spirits, cordials, spices, and so on, that can be used. Those basic rules, however, are as important in the case of Punches as they are in the case of cocktails. A good Punch is something more than a mélange of mixed fruits floating around in sugared water. Here are the more important rules, together with a number of incidental suggestions that should prove helpful.

1. *First of all, there are several rules that we noted in connection with our cocktails that are equally important in making Punches. They are:*

(a) Use only the best-quality liquors, particularly spirits. You are looking primarily for flavor; "kick" is purely secondary. From this point of view one bottle of bonded rye or bourbon is better than two or three of the average blend.

(b) For unsweetened fruit juices, use only fresh fruits, freshly squeezed. Canned or bottled sweet fruit syrups may be used but *never* canned lemon juice, canned orange juice, etc. And, above all, never use any chemical substitutes for the citrus juices.

(c) Use only pure, clean, clear ice uncontaminated by any foreign flavors.

2. *Use not only good-quality liquor but a good quantity as well. If you want to make a prohibition Punch (and there are many very good ones), do so. But if you want to make an alcoholic Punch, it should be neither so strong as to resemble knockout drops, nor so weak that the guests will have any doubt as to whether or not it contains liquor. A watery Punch is no better than a watery cocktail.*

3. *Do not use too many different kinds of liquor and be sure that those you do use are not inconsistent in type. Be sure that they will "marry" into one harmonious whole. You can blend almost any liqueurs, especially the fruit-flavored liqueurs, with gin or Cuban rum. Be careful, however, what you try to blend with whisky. Don't try to mix several strong, pungent liqueurs, such as Chartreuse, kümmel, and Grand Marnier, in one drink. That is like trying to combine mince pie, strawberry shortcake, and chocolate ice cream in one dessert.*

4. *By the same token, go easy on your cut-up fruits. The Punches of the Gay Nineties were thick with sliced oranges, lemons, bananas, cherries, chunks of pineapple, peaches, apricots, and whatever berries might be in season. Today people seek a refreshing drink rather than a fruit cocktail when they come to the Punch bowl.*

There are some Punches that are started by macerating the fruits with sugar and spirits. Even where this is done, I believe it is best to strain off the resultant liquid and discard the pulps. Most Punches, however, are made with fruit juices and syrups, and to use also a lot of cut-up fruits adds nothing to the flavor and is a source of nuisance to the drinker.

5. *Use a solid block of ice in the Punch bowl—as large a block as the bowl will accommodate—and not ice cubes. If you cannot obtain a large cake of ice, remove the separators from your ice trays and freeze blocks the full size of the trays instead of separate cubes. The larger the ice block used, the less the dilution of the drink.*

6. *Blend your fruit flavors, spices, and liquors or wines well in advance of using and leave them at room temperature for an hour or two to ripen and blend. Then place the mixture in the refrigerator to chill for at least an hour before emptying into the Punch bowl. Warm liquids poured over the ice melt it and quickly dilute the drink.*

7. *When ready to serve the drink, pour the chilled mixture over the block of ice in the bowl, add the carbonated or other sparkling beverages—champagne, club soda, etc.—and stir briefly with the ladle before serving. When serving, stir occasionally from the bottom of the bowl in order to maintain a constant blend of uniform consistency.*

8. *Cucumber peel imparts a peculiarly elusive and delicate flavor to wine Punches. Peel very thin and leave in the Punch for a few minutes only, then remove and discard. Bitters can be used to reduce both oversweetness and oversharpness of the drink. A fairly liberal seasoning with bitters will frequently point up and give character to an otherwise insipid drink. Various herbs—sprigs of mint or wintergreen tied together in a small bunch, caraway seeds, anise seeds, juniper berries tied up in small cheese-*

cloth bags, etc.—can be used to produce interesting and exotic flavors. Be sure, however, that these flavors are consistent with the flavors of your liquors and fruit juices.

9. Tea is used in many Punches and Cups. See that it is well made. Use fresh water—not water that has been boiled before and then reheated—and have it actively boiling. Remember that the tea will be diluted by the other liquids and the ice and that it must, therefore, be strong. Use 2 to 3 teaspoonfuls to each cup of water. Pour the boiling water over the tea in an earthenware or glass vessel, allow it to stand for 5 to 7 minutes, stirring once or twice during that time, and then strain off. And don't use tea balls. Tea balls do not and cannot make good tea; they make lazy man's cambric tea.

Another method sometimes employed, where the tea flavor is desired without the dilution resulting from using water, is to put the tea in a cheesecloth bag and leave it in the Punch for 15 or 20 minutes before adding the ice.

10. How much Punch should you make? Well, of course, that depends on the nature of the party and the capacity of your guests. Is it a "how-d'ye-do, glad-to-see-you, good-by" party or a "sit-around-all-afternoon-and-talk" party? For the usual run of formal and semiformal affairs you can figure about two 4-ounce cups to a person. For a longer and wholly informal affair, at least three cups to a person. Some will drink more and some less, but that will be about the average. Two 4-ounce cups are 8 ounces or ½ pint per person. That means, then, that each quart of Punch will serve four persons. The recipes that follow are all for serving twenty persons. That is to say, they average about 5 quarts or, in some cases, a little more.

So much for the general instructions; now for a few recipes. Any of the Sour-type *INDIVIDUAL PUNCHES* can, of course, be used for party Punches by merely increasing the amounts proportionately.

FISH HOUSE PUNCH This is probably the most famous of all Punches. It is also one of the most potent and one of the best. The formula is supposed to have originated in 1732 with that famous old Philadelphia Club called the "State in Schuylkill." I have at least a dozen recipes for this drink, all different and all purporting to be the original and official recipe. If the one below given is not the original recipe, it at least comes very close to it. It is a still Punch—that is to say, it employs plain water (which, in theory, should be fresh spring water) in place of any carbonated beverage.

¾ pound Loaf Sugar
1½ pints Lemon Juice
2 bottles [1] Rum
1 bottle [1] Cognac
3½ pints Water
4 ounces Peach Brandy

Dissolve the sugar in part of the water in the Punch bowl. Add the lemon juice and the balance of the water and stir thoroughly. Then add the liquors and allow the mixture to stand for at least 2 to 3 hours to ripen and blend, stirring a bit from time to time. Place a large block of ice in the bowl, stir to cool, and serve.

The original recipe, I believe, calls for Jamaica rum. In my opinion, the drink is improved by using 1 bottle Jamaica and 1 bottle gold label Cuban. I also prefer to use an equivalent amount (about ½ pint) of sugar syrup in place of the loaf sugar. Some recipes call for peach liqueur in place of peach brandy. If this is used the quantity of sugar should be reduced somewhat. One recipe recently published as "State in Schuylkill's Own Recipe" omits the peach entirely.

---

[1] The word "bottle" is used in these Punch recipes to indicate the customary "fifth" or approximately 25 ounces.

XALAPA PUNCH This is another simple but potent Punch (although not as powerful as Fish House) and is one employing tea.

>2½ quarts strong Black Tea
>1 pint Sugar Syrup
>Grated peel of 2 medium Lemons
>1 bottle Applejack
>1 bottle Gold Label Rum
>1 bottle Claret
>1 large Lemon, sliced very thin

Pour the hot tea over the lemon peel and allow to stand 10 to 15 minutes. Add the sugar syrup and stir thoroughly. Cool, add the liquors and claret, and let stand an hour or more to ripen. Pour over ice in Punch bowl and add lemon slices just before serving.

ARTILLERY PUNCH This is, indeed, well named. The effect of three or four salvos is devastating.

>1 quart Rye
>1 quart Claret
>1 quart strong Black Tea
>1 pint Jamaica or Gold Label Rum
>½ pint Gin
>½ pint Cognac
>1 jigger Benedictine
>1 pint Orange Juice
>½ pint Lemon Juice

Blend, allow to ripen, and pour over ice in Punch bowl.

Note that this is a *very* dry mixture. For most palates it can be improved by adding at least ½ pint sugar syrup.

Another, also powerful, formula for the Artillery Punch uses sugar, lemon juice, bitters, claret, sherry, Scotch, brandy, and club soda. The one above given is, in my opinion, the better of the two.

APPLEJACK PUNCH

    8 ounces Grenadine
    1 pint Lemon Juice
    1 pint Orange Juice
    2 bottles Applejack
    2 quarts Ginger Ale

Blend all the ingredients other than the ginger ale and allow to ripen. Add ginger ale in Punch bowl at time of serving.

DRAGOON PUNCH This is the cavalry's answer to the Artillery Punch.

    ½ pint Sugar Syrup
    ½ pint Sherry
    ½ pint Brandy
    3 pints Porter
    3 pints Ale
    3 pints Champagne
    3 Lemons, sliced very thin

Blend all ingredients except champagne in the Punch bowl. Add champagne at last minute.

WHISKY CUP Place 1 quart strawberries in bowl with 1 teacupful or more of crushed, fresh pineapple, sprinkle with ¾ pound powdered sugar, pour 1 pint Jamaica rum over them, and allow to stand, covered, overnight to ripen. Add 1 pint lemon juice, 1½ pints orange juice, 2 quarts bourbon, and ½ pint grenadine. Blend and pour over ice in the Punch bowl. At time of serving add 2 quarts club soda or ginger ale.

CARDINAL PUNCH The various recipes for Cardinal Punch have one thing, and one thing only, in common: they all employ a certain amount of red wine to produce the red or cardinal color. Most of them are combinations of red and white wines and fruit juices, but some also use rum or brandy and one even uses a vermouth. The following recipe is chosen at random from many:

½ pint Sugar Syrup
1 pint Lemon Juice
Grated rind of 4 Lemons
1 quart Rhine Wine
2 quarts Red Burgundy
2 quarts Club Soda

Blend and ripen all ingredients except the soda. Add club soda at time of serving.

BRANDY PUNCH

½ pint Sugar Syrup
½ pint Curaçao
1 pint Lemon Juice
1 pint Orange Juice
2 ounces Grenadine
2 bottles Cognac
2 quarts Club Soda

Blend and ripen all ingredients except the soda. Add soda at time of serving.

ROCKY MOUNTAIN PUNCH

4 ounces Sugar Syrup
4 ounces Maraschino
1 pint Lemon Juice
1 bottle Jamaica Rum
4 quarts Champagne

Blend and ripen other ingredients and add champagne at time of serving.

FRUIT BOWLS or *PEACH BOWL* or *PINEAPPLE BOWL* or *APRICOT BOWL* or *STRAWBERRY BOWL* The Bowls all consist of fresh fruit, sugar, and a dry white wine. Peel and slice 6 ripe peaches, or 6 to 8 apricots, or 1 pineapple, or wash and slightly crush 1 full quart strawberries. Place the fruit in a glass bowl or glazed crock, sprinkle with about ¾ pound sugar. Pour ½ bottle Rhine wine over the fruit, cover, and allow to stand overnight. Stir mixture, pour over ice in Punch bowl, and add Rhine wine or a similar dry white wine to bring total quantity up to 5 quarts. Serve 1 or 2 berries or slices of other fruit in each drink.

A heavy wine—Madeira or dry sherry—may be used in macerating the fruit, but a very dry white wine should be the principal ingredient of the Punch.

LAFAYETTE PUNCH This is the simplest to prepare of all Champagne Punches. Slice a half dozen oranges and arrange in bottom of Punch bowl. Sprinkle heavily with sugar, pour 1 bottle moselle wine over the fruit, and allow to stand 1 hour or more to ripen. Place large block of ice in bowl and add 4 quarts champagne or 1 quart moselle and 3 quarts champagne at time of serving.

CHAMPAGNE PUNCH There are many varieties of Champagne Punches employing all manner of other wines and liquors in addition to the champagne. Some of them use both champagne and charged water. Personally, I like either of these liquids in a Punch, but I do not like to see them used in combination. The following is, I think, as good as any Champagne Punch I know.

Peel, slice, and crush three or four thoroughly ripe pineapples. Place in a glass bowl, cover with a pound or more of powdered sugar, and allow to stand an hour or more for fruit to soak up the sugar. Add 1 pint lemon juice, 4 ounces maraschino, 4 ounces curaçao, 1 pint cognac, and 1 pint Jamaica rum. Stir, cover, and allow to stand overnight to ripen. Put in Punch bowl with large block of ice and, at time of serving, add 4 quarts champagne.

RHINE WINE PUNCH
    ½ pint Sugar Syrup
    1 pint Lemon Juice

1 pint Dry Sherry
½ pint Cognac
½ pint strong Black Tea
3 quarts Rhine Wine
1 quart Club Soda
Cucumber Peel

Blend ingredients other than soda in Punch bowl. Leave thin slices green cucumber peel in for about 10 minutes, then remove. Add charged water at time of serving and stir.

MAY WINE This is a famous old German drink which depends for its flavor upon the herb *Waldmeister* or woodruff, which can be gathered green in the spring of the year.

Sprinkle a half dozen bunches of *Waldmeister* with ½ to ¾ pound powdered sugar. Place in glass bowl or glazed crock and add ½ pint cognac and 1 quart Moselle or other white wine. Cover and let stand overnight. Stir and strain. Pour over ice into Punch bowl and add 3 quarts Moselle and 2 quarts of champagne. Charged water may be substituted for the champagne if desired.

BALAKLAVA NECTAR
½ pint Sugar Syrup
½ pint Lemon Juice
Grated peel of 3 or 4 Lemons
2 quarts Claret
3 quarts Champagne

Mix ingredients other than champagne and allow to ripen. Add champagne at time of serving. Some recipes substitute charged water for 1 or 2 bottles of the champagne.

POOR MAN'S PUNCH
½ pint Sugar Syrup

½ pint Raspberry Syrup
1 pint Lemon Juice
2 quarts Claret
2 quarts Club Soda

Mix and ripen all except the soda. Add soda at time of serving.

CLARET CUP

½ pint Sugar Syrup
½ pint Lemon Juice
1 pint Orange Juice
4 ounces Curaçao
4 ounces Pineapple Juice
2 ounces Maraschino
2 quarts Claret
2 quarts Club Soda

Add charged water only at time of serving.

BURGUNDY CUP Same as Claret Cup, but use red burgundy in place of the claret and use Benedictine in place of maraschino.

SAUTERNE CUP Same as Burgundy Cup, but use Sauterne in place of burgundy and use 4 ounces cognac in place of the pineapple juice.

STIRRUP CUP

1 part Brown Sugar, dissolved in water
2 parts Lime Juice
4 parts Pineapple Juice
12 parts Rum

This drink is frequently served as an individual Punch in a tall glass full of cracked ice and decorated with a lemon-peel spiral like a Horse's Neck. There is no reason, however, why it should not be served, like other Punches, as a party drink.

MISSOURI PUNCH
  ½ pint Sugar Syrup
  ½ pint Lemon Juice
  1 bottle Brandy
  1 bottle Bourbon
  1 bottle Jamaica Rum
  2 quarts Club Soda

Add soda at time of serving.

This Punch, too, is commonly served as an individual Punch. It is then made according to the usual Sour proportions and is served in a tall glass of crushed ice with only a small quantity of charged water.

PROHIBITION PUNCHES

The possibilities in making non-alcoholic Punches are almost as unlimited as with spirituous and vinous Punches. Starting with lemon or lime juice for the Sour, practically any kind of fruit syrup can be used for the sweet, or sugar can be used with orange, pineapple, or some similar fresh fruit juice, and the combination can then be made sparkling with ginger ale or soda. Here are two or three that are offered merely by way of suggestion.

LEMON ICE PUNCH or ORANGE ICE PUNCH
Put lemon or orange ice in the Punch bowl and add ginger ale in the proportion of 1 quart of ginger ale to each pint of the ice. Raspberry, pineapple, or any other water ice or sherbet can be substituted.

This Punch can, of course, be spiked if so desired. Either plain or spiked, it has just one thing to recommend it—it requires only a quick dash to the corner drugstore to secure the water ice, after which it can be prepared instantaneously.

WHITE ANGEL PUNCH
  ½ pint Sugar Syrup
  1 pint Lemon Juice

>   1 quart strong Green Tea
>   2 quarts White Grape Juice
>   2 quarts Club Soda

Prepare like any other Punch, adding the soda at time of serving.

BLUE ANGEL PUNCH   Same as White Angel, but use black tea and ordinary purple grape juice.

GOLDEN DAWN PUNCH
>   1 pint Apricot Syrup
>   1 pint Lime Juice
>   3 pints Orange Juice
>   3 quarts Club Soda

Prepare and serve same as the Angel Punches. The juice from canned apricots can be used in place of the apricot syrup. In this case use a quart in place of the pint of the heavier syrup.

SWIZZLES

A Swizzle is simply a Sour-type drink churned with a swizzle stick until it attains a foamy appearance and the container becomes frosted. A swizzle stick is any long rod —wood, metal, plastic, or what have you—with several short blades or fingers attached to the bottom at right angles to the shaft, like an old-fashioned paddle wheel and axle stood on end. The bladed end is immersed in the drink, the shaft is held between the palms of the hand, and the whole stick is rapidly rotated by sliding the hands back and forth against one another.

The Swizzle is commonly served at bars as an individual drink in Highball glasses partly filled with fine ice. A miniature swizzle stick is frequently furnished the customer who does his own swizzling. This gives the customer an extra kick and saves the bartender both time and effort. Strictly speaking, however, the Swizzle is a party drink. It should be made in a large glass or silver pitcher. Fill the pitcher about two-thirds full of finely crushed or shaved ice, pour in the drink, churn with the swizzle stick until the pitcher is well frosted, and then pour into pre-chilled glasses. The individual drinks may be decorated with fruit or a sprig of mint if desired.

Since the Swizzle comes from the West Indies, the original Swizzle is, of course, made with Rum—Jamaica rum. Like any other drink of the Sour type, however, it can be made of any other liquor if desired. Liqueurs can, of course, be substituted for the sugar syrup. There are also some who like to swizzle aromatic-type drinks, such as whisky and vermouth. This is, in effect, a swizzled Manhattan. A few dashes of bitters will lend character to any Swizzle, either Sour or aromatic.

RUM SWIZZLE or APPLEJACK SWIZZLE or BRANDY SWIZZLE or GIN SWIZZLE or WHISKY SWIZZLE

1 part Sugar Syrup or a Liqueur
2 parts Lime or Lemon Juice
8 parts Rum or other Liquor
1 or 2 dashes Angostura to each drink

With rum or gin, use lime juice. With the other liquors, use lemon juice.

With rum, try orgeat or falernum in place of the sugar. With whisky, try Chartreuse.

I do not recommend swizzling the aromatic-type drinks. However, try them if you wish. Remember, though, that swizzling, like shaking, will give the vermouth a cloudy, muddy appearance.

SHRUBS

A Shrub is a ripened mixture of fruit juice, sugar, and spirits. The aging can be done in a wooden cask, a stone crock, or glass bottles. If the Shrub is to be kept any appreciable length of time before using, it is best to bottle it and cork it tight when it is made. In using, the Shrub is diluted with water (either plain or carbonated) and thoroughly chilled. Shrubs are usually fortified with either brandy or Jamaica rum, but this is optional. Applejack can be used as well and, with fruits such as raspberries, strawberries, and cherries, a white Cuban rum or even gin can be used. The original Shrub was made with lemons, but, as above noted, any fruit juice can be used.

LEMON-RUM SHRUB

  1 pint Lemon Juice
  Grated Rind of 3 Lemons
  2 pounds Sugar
  2 quarts Jamaica Rum
  1 quart Water

Pour the rum over the lemon rind and let stand 2 or 3 days. Add the other ingredients, mix thoroughly until sugar is dissolved, strain, and bottle. Should remain in bottles 5 to 6 weeks before using. It is well to heat the water and sugar until sugar is thoroughly dissolved before adding to other ingredients.

ORANGE-RUM SHRUB

  2 quarts Orange Juice
  Grated Rind of 2 Oranges
  1 pound Sugar
  2 quarts Rum (any type)

Proceed same as with Lemon-Rum Shrub. If sugar is to be separately dissolved, use as little water as possible for this purpose.

FRESH FRUIT SHRUBS Use fruits that are somewhat tart, such as cherries, currants, strawberries, raspberries, etc. Cook the fruit to extract the juice and strain it. Add sugar and boil with the juice, keeping it well skimmed. The quantity of sugar depends on the acidity of the fruit. With currants or strawberries use about ¾ pound to each pint of juice; with sweet cherries or raspberries, about ½ pound. Cool, add 2 to 4 ounces of cognac for each quart of syrup, and bottle.

WASSAIL BOWL

While the Wassail is a hot drink, it is included here because it is traditionally a party drink for feast days and, particularly, for Christmas Eve. The Wassail Bowl never gained the popularity in this country that it enjoyed in England. The drink may be made of wine, cider, beer, or almost any combination of those three liquids. White wine, if used, is used alone. The heavy wines, such as sherry and Madeira, are used either alone or in combination with beer. Some wassailers, seeking greater potency in the beverage, add a spot of brandy to the sherry or Madeira. Here is a typical recipe:

OLD ENGLISH WASSAIL Boil together in ½ pint of water, 1 tablespoonful powdered nutmeg, 2 teaspoonfuls ginger, 6 cloves, ½ teaspoonful mace, a half dozen allspice berries, and a 2-inch stick of cinnamon. Add 2 pounds sugar and 4 bottles sherry or Madeira. Cook over a slow fire.

Core and bake a dozen apples.

Beat separately the yolks and whites of 12 eggs and fold together. Put the beaten eggs in a large bowl and add the heated wine and spice mixture, pouring in, at first, very small quantities and stirring briskly with each addition.

After the hot wine and eggs have been thoroughly beaten together, add the baked apples to the foaming mixture. If cognac is to be added, do this toward the end of the beating and just before adding the apples. If both beer and wine are to be used, cook the spices and sugar in about a pint of the beer, then add the rest of the beer and sherry, using 1 part sherry to 3 or 4 of beer.

BROWN BETTY Boil ½ pound brown sugar, juice of

1 lemon, and 1 teaspoonful assorted spices in 1 pint water. Add ½ pint cognac and 1 quart ale, bring all to the boiling point, and pour into a bowl over slices of toasted raisin bread that has been dusted with cinnamon and ginger.

This is not a true Wassail Bowl, but it is included here because of its close similarity. This drink is also sometimes iced and served cold.

NOGS

What the Wassail Bowl failed to achieve in popularity in this country the Egg Nog has made up for. It is the traditional drink of the holiday season from Christmas Eve to New Year's night, and it is also served on many other festive occasions.

There are almost as many battles over Egg Nogs as over Juleps. Should the Nog be made liquid, to drink, or solid, to eat? Should the whole egg be used or only the yolk? If the white is used, should it be beaten stiff and folded in? Should cream be used, or milk, or both? If cream is used, should it be whipped? Should the Nog be consumed at once after making or allowed to stand several days to ripen? What liquor or liquors give the best flavor?

Different schools of thought on these various questions have given rise to scores of recipes. A few typical ones will be given here, including both the simple Egg Nog as an individual drink, shaken up and consumed at once, and several party Nogs to be served from the Punch bowl, in cups and, preferably, with small spoons. In making party Nogs, there are a few rules that should be carefully followed.

1. *The yolks should be beaten until they are light and frothy. Usually the sugar is then beaten into the yolks and the liquor is then stirred gradually into the mixture, and this is allowed to stand for an hour or more to cook the eggs. Some, however, prefer to add the liquor to the eggs first and the sugar later.*

2. When using stiffly beaten egg whites, these must be folded, not beaten, into the mixture. This is done by beating the whites separately and pouring them on top of the rest of the mixture. With a large spoon, cut through the whole mixture to the bottom of the bowl, dip up a spoonful of the mixture, bring it up along the side of the bowl, and pour it over the top. Continue cutting, dipping, and pouring in this manner until the whites are fully blended into the mixture. Even a small amount of beating will ruin the entire Nog.

3. When beating the egg whites, it is helpful to add about ¼ teaspoonful salt for each 4 whites.

4. The Nog should be kept in a cool place until used. It may be poured into a pre-chilled Punch bowl, but no ice is ever put in the Nog. Dust the top of each cup with grated nutmeg when serving.

INDIVIDUAL EGG NOG
- 1 Egg
- 1 teaspoonful Sugar
- 2 ounces Liquor
- 8 ounces Milk

Shake vigorously with cracked ice, strain into a tall glass, and serve with a dash of nutmeg over the top.

This may be made with sherry, port, Madeira, applejack, gin, cognac, rum, or whisky, as desired. Sometimes two liquors such as cognac and rum or sherry and cognac are used.

BALTIMORE EGG NOG
- 12 Eggs
- 1 pound Sugar
- 1 pint Cognac
- ½ pint Jamaica Rum
- ½ pint Peach Brandy
- 3 pints Milk
- 1 pint Cream

Beat yolks to a foam, add the liquor slowly, then the sugar, stirring constantly. Then add the milk and cream and, finally, fold in the stiffly beaten whites.

KENTUCKY EGG NOG

- 12 Eggs
- 2 pounds Sugar
- 1 quart Bourbon
- 1 pint Jamaica Rum
- 1 pint Cognac
- 1 pint Milk
- 3 pints Heavy Cream

Beat yolks, beat in the sugar, then slowly stir in the bourbon and rum. Stir in the milk and cream and then the cognac. Finally, fold in the stiffly beaten whites.

FRANKLIN FARMS EGG NOG

- 12 Eggs
- 1 pound Sugar
- 1 quart Jamaica Rum
- 1 pint Peach Brandy
- 3 pints Heavy Cream

Beat yolks to a froth and slowly stir in the cream. Stir in sugar and then add the liquors very slowly, stirring constantly. Fold in half of the beaten egg whites. Beat the other half very stiff and pour over top of the mixture in the Punch bowl.

This recipe differs from all others in that the liquor is not added until the cream has been mixed with the yolks. It produces a Nog of a different consistency because the liquor does not cook the yolks as it does when added directly to them. It is easier to make because there is less danger of curdling the eggs.

PENDENNIS CLUB EGG NOG

- 12 Egg Yolks
- 1 pound Sugar

1 quart Bourbon
2 quarts Heavy Cream

Mix the bourbon and sugar and allow them to stand for 3 hours or more.

Beat the yolks to a froth and combine gradually with the sweetened whisky, stirring constantly. Allow the egg-and-whisky mixture to stand for 2½ to 3 hours to cook the yolks.

Whip the cream stiff and fold into the egg-whisky mixture. Place in bowl, pack bowl in ice, and allow to stand for an hour. Note that this recipe does not use the egg whites.

WESTERN EGG NOG

12 Eggs
½ pound Sugar
1 bottle (fifth) Bourbon
1 jigger Jamaica Rum
3 pints Heavy Cream

Beat the yolks to a froth and beat in the sugar. Slowly stir in the liquor. Whip the cream and stir it into the mixture. Beat the whites until light, but not stiff, and stir them into the mixture.

Note that this Nog has a different consistency and texture from most, owing to the fact that the whites are not beaten stiff and folded in but are beaten only until light and foamy and are then stirred in.

There are hot as well as cold Egg Nogs. In general, the *INDIVIDUAL EGG NOG* can be made as a hot drink by using either hot water or, preferably, hot milk in place of cold milk and omitting the chilling process. There is, however, one drink of a distinctly party-Nog type that, in the pre-prohibition days, was to be found at practically every bar during the entire Christmas season. It was served, piping hot and frothing, in Tom and Jerry mugs which very much resembled the old-time shaving mugs. Here it is:

TOM AND JERRY

- 1 dozen Eggs
- ½ pound Sugar
- 4 ounces Jamaica Rum
- 1 tablespoonful each ground Allspice, Cinnamon & Cloves

Beat yolks and whites separately. Beat in the sugar and spices with yolks, then pour in the rum gradually, stirring constantly. Finally, fold in the whites. Store this in a large bowl.

Put a ladleful of the mixture in a large mug, add 2 ounces bourbon, fill mug with boiling water or hot milk, and stir vigorously until the whole drink foams. Dust with ground nutmeg and, if desired, float 1 teaspoonful of cognac on top.

HOT DRINKS

Mention has already been made of the *WASSAIL BOWL* as a hot party drink and of a number of other drinks that are served sometimes cold and sometimes hot, such as the *SANGAREES*, the *TODDIES* and *SLINGS*, the *PUNCHES*, and the *NOGS*, particularly the *TOM AND JERRY*.

There are also a number of other hot drinks of which at least a brief mention should be made, although they are seldom seen today, at least in this country. Some are individual drinks and some are party drinks.

POSSETS

A Posset consists of sweetened and spiced milk curdled with hot ale or wine. Eggs are frequently added to the mixture and sometimes, when eggs are used, the milk is omitted and the mixture is called an Egg Posset.

ALE POSSET
  1 quart Heavy Cream
  1 pint Ale
  10 Eggs
  1 tablespoonful Sugar
  Spices as desired

Beat the yolks of the 10 eggs and the whites of 5 with the sugar and cream and, when thoroughly blended, stir in the ale. Sprinkle liberally with nutmeg and, if desired, ground cinnamon, cloves, or other spices. Cook over a slow fire until mixture thickens and serve in mugs or Punch cups.

WINE POSSET

    1 quart Milk
    ½ pint Dry White Wine
    1 tablespoonful Sugar
    1 teaspoonful grated Lemon Peel
    Spices as desired.

Boil the milk and wine together until the milk curdles. Strain off the whey and dissolve the sugar and grated lemon in it. Press the curdled milk through a sieve, sprinkle with nutmeg and any other desired spices, beat into the sweetened whey, and serve piping hot.

EGG POSSET

    Yolks of 12 Eggs
    2 quarts Dry White Wine
    ½ teacupful Sugar
    1 teaspoonful ground Spices (Nutmeg, Cinnamon, Cloves, etc., as desired)

Beat yolks to a froth and beat in the sugar and spices. Heat the wine to boiling point and pour slowly into the egg mixture, stirring constantly. Serve at once.

If desired, ½ pint Jamaica rum may be substituted for 1 pint of the wine. This makes a more potent drink which is sometimes called *RUM BOOZE*.

MULLS

A Mull or Mulled Wine is simply a spiced and sweetened wine served piping hot. Traditionally, the wine was placed in a pitcher and heated by thrusting a white-hot poker into it. This, of course, is the spectacular way of doing it, and it may have answered very well in the days of large fireplaces and correspondingly large and heavy pokers. Perhaps a bit of soot and ash on the poker may even have tended to reduce the acidity of the wine. In the present super-sanitary air-conditioned age, however, white-hot pokers are not usually lying around handy, and it is more practicable and, in my opinion, much more satisfactory to heat the mixture over the kitchen range or even on an electric grill.

GLUHWEIN or MULLED WINE

    1 quart Wine
    Peel of 1 Lemon & 1 Orange
    Spices to taste
    1 tablespoonful Sugar

If ground spices are used, cook 1 to 2 teaspoonfuls of them with the lemon and orange peels and sugar in 1 cup water until flavor is well dissolved and then add the wine. It is even better to use 1 crushed, but not grated, nutmeg, 2 to 3 inches stick cinnamon, and a half dozen whole cloves; boil them with the sugar and lemon and orange peels in the wine and strain out.

With the heavy wines—Madeira, port, or sherry—heat to the desired temperature and serve immediately. Do not allow the wine to boil, as this detracts from the flavor. With light wines, such as claret and burgundy, the mixture may be allowed to simmer over a low flame for 5 to 10 minutes.

NEGUS

The Negus is a sweetened, spiced wine (usually port) served with hot water. It is quite similar to the Mulls but differs from them traditionally in that, with the one, the wine is heated by the hot-poker (or saucepan) method, whereas, with the other, the wine is heated by the addition of hot water. The drink is said to have been invented during the reign of Queen Anne by one Colonel Francis Negus.

NEGUS

    1 quart Port
    1 tablespoonful Sugar
    Grated Peel of 1 Lemon
    Juice of 2 Lemons
    Spices as desired
    1 quart boiling Water

Warm the wine but do not let it boil. Pour into a heated jug with the sugar, lemon, and spices and let stand where all will keep warm for 10 to 15 minutes. Add the boiling water, stir well, and serve piping hot. If preferred, the sugar and spices may be boiled in the water and then added to the warm wine.

Other wines, either heavy or light, may be used. The light wines, such as claret or burgundy, may be boiled, but port, sherry, or Madeira should never be allowed to boil.

For choice and quantity of spices, see under Mulls, above.

BISHOPS

The Bishop is quite similar to the *WASSAIL BOWL* (page 359) except that ale is never used and baked or roasted oranges are used instead of apples.

ENGLISH BISHOP Stick from 1 to 2 dozen whole cloves in an orange and bake or roast it. Cut hot orange in quarters, place in glass double boiler, and pour over it 1 quart port together with 1 tablespoonful sugar or honey. Allow to simmer over boiling water in double boiler (or in saucepan over *very* low flame) for 20 to 30 minutes and serve hot. Remember that boiling the port will damage its flavor.

Other wines may be substituted for the port. When claret is used the drink becomes a *CARDINAL;* and a very fancy variety, using bitter oranges, letting the roasted oranges stand in the claret for a day, then pressing out the juice and reheating, is called BISHOP A LA PRUSSE. When champagne is used in place of port the drink is called a POPE. There is also a CIDER BISHOP and, in making this one, the cider is usually spiked with applejack or cognac.

GROGS

My Modern Dictionary defines Grog as a mixture of spirits and cold water, unsweetened. This, undoubtedly, is the good nautical meaning of the term, dating back to the time when the men of England first commenced to go down to the sea in ships. Nevertheless, in American parlance the term is more usually used to refer to a hot drink and one that not only is sweetened but also contains lemon juice or, at the very least, is served with a slice of lemon.

HOT GROG
    1 jigger Jamaica Rum
    1 teaspoonful Sugar Syrup
    1 tablespoonful Lemon Juice

Stir the above ingredients together in a Highball glass or mug, fill up with hot water, and add a twist of lemon peel. Any other spirituous liquor can, of course, be substituted, but the traditional Grog is made with a heavy-bodied rum such as Jamaica, New England, or Demerara. Hot tea is sometimes used instead of water and makes a better drink.

If molasses is used in place of sugar, this drink becomes a *BLACK STRIPE*.

HOT SPICED RUM or HOT BUTTERED RUM
While not strictly a Grog because it is both sweetened and spiced, this may be as good a place as any to mention Hot Spiced Rum. Any place that it might be mentioned, to me, would be out of place. Hot liquors have a number of definite medicinal uses. They are excellent to warm up on *after* exposure to cold. Taken

upon retiring, they are excellent diaphoretics and hypnotics—that is, they promote both perspiration and sleep. With one or two exceptions, such as the Tom and Jerry, however, their use should, in my opinion, be strictly limited to medicinal purposes. How anyone can possibly consume them for pleasure is utterly beyond me. And, of all the hot liquors, I regard Buttered Rum as the worst. The Hot Spiced Rum without the butter is bad enough, but the lump of butter is the final insult. It blends with the hot rum just about as satisfactorily as warm olive oil blends with champagne! I believe that the drinking of Hot Buttered Rum should be permitted only in the Northwest Passage and, even there, only by highly imaginative and overenthusiastic novelists. However, just as a curiosity, here is the recipe:

1 jigger Jamaica or New England Rum
1 teaspoonful Sugar Syrup
Spices to taste
1 small lump Butter
Hot Water

Stir rum and sugar in mug or Highball glass. Fill with hot water, add spices, float butter on top, and stir gently until butter is dissolved. Some recipes call only for a few whole cloves, others call for ½ teaspoonful mixed ground spices—cloves, allspice, mace, etc. Frequently a little ground cinnamon or nutmeg is dusted over the top when the drink is served.

The above is the usual recipe. Trader Vic, in his excellent *Book of Food and Drink,* a copy of which should be in the hands of every true gourmet, recommends that the sugar (brown) and butter be first thoroughly creamed together with the spices and that the hot water and rum be added to this batter and stirred well. He has even prepared a ready-mixed batter for the market and it is excellent. This unquestionably makes a much better drink than the usual formula given above. As medicine, it is not too bad, but, to me, it is still definitely and solely a medicinal drink.

COFFEE DRINKS

Café noir with cognac or a liqueur constitutes the perfect finale to a dinner. The two may be sipped separately and alternately or they may be combined, either with or without igniting the liqueur. Here are a few flaming coffee specials.

CAFE ROYAL Float 1 or 2 teaspoonfuls cognac on a cup of hot coffee. Place a cube of sugar in a teaspoon, fill the spoon with cognac, and warm it over the coffee or by holding near a lighted candle (but not over the flame lest the spoon be coated with soot). Light the liquor in the spoon and, as it burns, lower it gently into the coffee, holding it barely below the surface of the liquid, thereby igniting the whole top surface of the liquid. Swish spoon gently back and forth in cup until flame dies out.

ALHAMBRA ROYAL Same as Café Royal, but made with hot chocolate instead of coffee. You probably will not be able to get the cognac to burn in the chocolate, but you can try.

CAFE KIRSCH Same as Café Royal, but use kirsch instead of cognac.

Any other fruit brandy or any citrus liqueur may be used in the same manner. I recommend curaçao and Grand Marnier. With the sweet liqueurs, omit the sugar cube.

CAFE DIABLE To each full cup (8 ounces) of coffee, use 1 cup cognac, 1 slice each orange and lemon peel, 2 large cubes sugar, and 2 whole cloves. Warm the above ingredients (other than the coffee) in a silver bowl. Dip out a ladleful of the cognac and light. Lower it into bowl and dip up a ladleful at a time and pour back, at the same time gradually pouring the hot coffee into the mixture. Continue until the flame dies out, then serve in cups.

Another method of serving this—spectacular but not altogether practical—is to cut through the outer skin of an orange all around the center and gently pry back each half of the skin and turn inside out as you would the finger of a glove. Leave each half attached at the end. One half serves as the base of this citrus chalice, the skinned orange rests above this base, and the other half of the skin reposes on top of all and serves as the cup. Fill this orange cup ⅔ full of hot coffee, add the cognac, cloves, sugar, and lemon peel. Ignite and, when flame has burned out, serve. Each orange cup should be set on a saucer. The skinned orange center is used as the handle or stem. Very sensational, but also very tricky and likely to be rather messy. I recommend using a silver bowl and ladling the mixture into demitasses.

CAFE BRULOT Made in a silver bowl the same as Café Diable but, in addition to the cloves and lemon and orange peels, use stick cinnamon and vanilla bean. If desired, the sugar cubes may first be rubbed with citrus fruits—grapefruit, tangerines, kumquats, limes, etc.—for additional flavor.

BLUE BLAZER

I have not seen a Blue Blazer mixed at any bar for more than thirty years. However, it must be that someone, somewhere, still mixes them, for even today practically every recipe book gives the formula and calls attention to the fact that "if properly done, this will have the appearance of a continual stream of fire." My good old manual of the eighties also adds, "This is a very elegant drink in cold weather and has a wonderful effect of healing an old cold, especially when the party goes to bed soon after drinking it." Here it is.

BLUE BLAZER In one silver or pewter mug dissolve 1 tablespoonful honey in enough hot water to fill the mug half full. Put an equal amount of Scotch in the other mug. Ignite the liquor and, while it is burning, pour back and forth from one mug to the other four or five times until the flame dies out. Pour into a heavy, heatproof glass, add a twist of lemon peel, dust nutmeg over the top, and serve.

SCANDINAVIAN HOT DRINKS

These might have been included with the other hot drinks, such as the Wassail Bowl, under "Party Drinks." Glögg is to a Swedish Christmas what the Wassail Bowl was to Old England and what the Egg Nog is in this country. Both the Swedish Glögg and the Danish Øgge go with winter sports.

GLOGG

- 1 quart Cognac
- 1 pint Sherry
- ½ cup Sugar
- 1 dozen Cloves
- 2- or 3-inch stick of Cinnamon
- ½ cup Raisins
- ½ cup blanched but unsalted Almonds

Put all the ingredients except the sherry in a silver bowl, warm, ignite, and stir until sugar is dissolved and flame dies down. Stir in the sherry and serve while still hot. Port, Madeira, burgundy, or claret may be substituted for the sherry.

Any leftover Glögg may be bottled, corked tight, and kept. Reheat to temperature just below boiling point before serving.

ØGGE

- 1 quart Beer
- 2 ounces Sugar Syrup
- 4 Egg Yolks

Beat the sugar into the yolks, heat the beer to the boiling point, and stir gradually into the yolks. Dust with nutmeg and serve.

PICKER-UPPERS

Picker-uppers are drinks that are supposed to restore the tired brain and body to a semblance of normalcy on the morning after the night before. Actually, little, if any, beneficial effect will be obtained from any of them. Excessive doses of alcohol act as acute irritants on the mucous membranes of the intestinal tract, producing intestinal catarrh, hyperacidity, and extreme fatigue. Because of its great affinity for nerve tissue, alcohol induces a partial paralysis, mental or muscular, or both. As previously pointed out, there is a dilatation of the peripheral blood vessels (giving a false sense of warmth) and a certain amount of cardiac stimulation, resulting in a strong, full, and active pulse. Respiration is increased, the lungs working hard to oxidize and eliminate the alcohol.

So long as any of the alcohol remains in the stomach, relief may be obtained by emptying and washing out the stomach. Filling the stomach to capacity with hot water, inducing regurgitation (tickling the throat with the finger tip being the most common means), refilling the stomach with hot water, again emptying it, and finally drinking one or two glasses of warm water with a bit of aromatic ammonia or sodium bicarbonate will usually give decided relief.

The morning after, however, is far too late for any such treatment. Bromo-Seltzer, Alka-Seltzer, sodium bicarbonate, or some similar alkaline agent may help reduce the acidity and reduce the catarrhal condition. Caffeine, strychnine, or some other stimulant may allay some of the fatigue. Warm milk or a small quantity of olive oil may help soothe the irritated membranes of the stomach. Complete relief will be obtained, however, only after the alcohol has been entirely eliminated—through the lungs, through the skin, through the kidneys, and through the intestines. Such elimination can be accelerated to some degree by inducing perspiration (as in a Turkish bath), by increasing respiration (a brisk walk in the fresh air), and by accelerating the emptying of the bowels (a saline laxative such as Epsom salts). By the morning after, however, most of the alcohol has already found its way into the blood stream and time, and time only, will oxidize and eliminate it. And during that time the great restorer is rest, and more rest, and still more rest.

All of which is by way of pointing out that any supposedly beneficial effects from the consumption of still more alcohol are psychological rather than physiological. You don't treat arsenic poisoning by taking more arsenic or ptomaine poisoning by eating more contaminated food. Why be so naïve as to imagine that you can cure alcohol poisoning by drinking more alcohol?

Nevertheless, superstitions, however absurd, are hard to kill off and, in order that you may know at least a few of the theoretical "eye-openers," "restorers," "bracers," and what not, here are some of the more common of them.

The Suissesse (page 292) and Suissesse Highball (page 306) as well as the Morning Glory Fizz (page 319) have already been mentioned. Next in importance, perhaps, is champagne—and lots of it. There are many advocates of Sours and, just to tie the "mixing-drinks-will-make-you-drunk" superstition in with the equally silly one of using a "hair of the dog that bit you," the Sour devotees insist that the drink must be made of whatever the liquor may have been that knocked you out the night before.

Hot coffee, milk—either warm or cold—and tomato juice have all been recommended. These all do have a certain merit and none of them commits the error of pouring more alcohol into an alcohol-raw stomach. Egg Nogs also can be defended to a degree, particularly if the amount of cognac or other liquor content is kept at a minimum.

And now, as a final type of picker-upper, here are two that must be based on the theory of using a counterirritant.

PRAIRIE OYSTER Mix together in an Old-Fashioned or Sour glass the following:
- 1 ounce Cognac
- 1 tablespoonful Vinegar
- 1 tablespoonful Worcestershire
- 1 teaspoonful Catsup
- 1 teaspoonful Angostura

Drop the yolk of an egg into the mixture, add a small dash of cayenne. Swallow, without breaking the yolk of the egg.

OLD PEPPER
- 1 jigger Whisky
- Juice of ½ Lemon
- 1 teaspoonful Worcestershire
- 1 teaspoonful Chili Sauce or 1 tablespoonful Tomato Juice
- 2 or 3 dashes Angostura
- 1 dash Tabasco

Mix thoroughly and serve in Sour glass.

FOOD AND DRINK

We in America are just beginning to wake up to the value of wines and, to a somewhat lesser degree, of spirituous liquors in cooking. The well-recognized and peculiar excellence of French cooking has been due in no small part to the lavish use of wines: first, in marinating and tenderizing meats before cooking; second, during the cooking process; and, third, in the making of all manner of sauces.

Alcohol, of course, vaporizes at a very low temperature, and even the most rabid prohibitionist need have no fear of any alcoholic residue in a dish, such as a pot roast, a casserole, etc., that has cooked for an hour or more, even if the liquid used consisted solely of wine. Furthermore, in most cases, the taste of the finished product bears no resemblance to the taste of the wine or liquor used in the cooking. The flavor of the food and that of the wine "marry" and produce an entirely new taste effect that is delicious and quite indescribable. Until you have tasted venison marinated in red wine, ham baked with Madeira, roast beef basted with stout, or steak and lobster broiled over charcoal and basted with Spanish brandy, you have not tasted any of those meats at its best.

It is not my purpose, however, to take up the subject of cooking with wines and liquors. There are a number of books on the market on this type of cookery, several of which are of outstanding excellence. There are, however, a number of wine and liquor mixtures that may well be classed as both food and drink. Practically all the egg or milk and liquor combinations fall into this category, including the *FLIPS*, the *SHERRY AND EGG* and similar drinks using a whole egg or an egg yolk, the *NOGS*, the *POSSETS*, and the *MILK PUNCHES*.

There are two more to which I wish to call your attention, the Sabayon and the Syllabub, the first of which is, in effect, a hot Nog or Custard and the second a Milk Punch.

SABAYON or *ZABAGLIONE* The first spelling given is the French, the second the Italian. It is also sometimes spelled *ZABAIONE* and sometimes *ZAMBAGLIONE*.

    6 Egg Yolks
    6 tablespoonfuls Sugar
    8 ounces Marsala

Beat the eggs and sugar thoroughly together, stir in the marsala, and cook in a double boiler, stirring constantly until the mixture thickens. Serve hot in small goblets or saucer champagne glasses and eat with a spoon. Sherry (an oloroso or other sweet type) or a madeira is frequently used in place of the marsala.

The French recipes frequently call for pouring the cooked mixture into the beaten egg whites before serving.

The Sabayon is also frequently used as a sauce poured over a dessert pudding.

SYLLABUB

    1 part Sherry (sweet)
    1 part Milk
    1 part Heavy Cream
    Sugar to taste

Beat all together and serve in saucer champagne glasses. Port or Madeira may be used in place of the sherry. Some recipes call for the addition of cognac or Jamaica rum. Other recipes omit the milk and use from ¼ to ½ as much lemon juice in place of the milk.

A small piece of cake soaked in the wine used for the drink is sometimes placed in the glass and the Syllabub is poured over it as a dessert dish.

CONCLUSION

Is there anything else you would like to know about mixed drinks? I have described at some length all manner of mixed drinks—short drinks and tall drinks, hot drinks and cold drinks, temperance drinks and old-soak drinks, party drinks and individual drinks, special-occasion drinks and everyday drinks, sour drinks and sweet drinks, morning drinks and evening drinks, pre-prandial drinks and post-prandial drinks, good drinks, bad drinks, and indifferent drinks.

While I have given the recipes for some seven or eight hundred different drinks, this book is not intended as a recipe book. If you use it as a recipe book it will have wholly failed of its purpose. There are hundreds—perhaps thousands—of drink recipes that are not included and new drinks are being invented by someone, somewhere, everyday. It would be a hopeless task to try to catch up with them all and include them in any one book or series of books. Furthermore, it would be a foolish and useless task.

The recipes herein contained are intended solely as specimens of what others have done, in order that you may examine them, analyze them, criticize them, and improve upon them. Whether it be a cocktail, a Highball, a Rickey, a Daisy, a Punch, or what not, pick out a recipe that strikes you as being well thought out. Try it. If you find it too sweet, cut down on the sugar or liqueur. If you find it too sour, cut down on the lime or lemon juice. If you find it too sharply alcoholic, add a dash of bitters. Play around with it until you find the proportion that just suits your taste. Learn to "roll your own" and then throw away all your recipe books—including this one!

One of the many things that I have always admired about Chinese cookery—the most perfect cooking in the world—is that a good Chinese cook will take just one meat —such as pork—and half a dozen vegetables and then, with his various sauces—Soyu, Ho Yeou, Ham Har, etc.—he will feed you for a week and never give you the same dish twice. You should be able to do the same thing with drinks. Your base liquor—such as gin or rum—takes the place of the meat; your syrups and liqueurs take the place of the vegetables; and your citrus juices, vermouths, and bitters take the place of the sauces. With these few ingredients —including only one base liquor—you should be able to roll out drinks by the hundred, all different—cocktails, Highballs, Collinses, Fizzes, Rickeys, Daisies, Fixes, Cobblers, Coolers, Slings, Toddies, and so on, and on, and on.

You will find that not only the cocktail but many others, such as the Rickey and the Daisy, are delicious drinks. However, I believe you will also find that the most useful, the most flexible, and the best all-around drink of them all is that great American institution, the COCKTAIL.

As a final word, therefore, may I paraphrase the Artillery song,

"Let the cocktails keep rolling along."

"KEEP THEM ROLLING"

INDEX

Aalborg Taffel Akvavit, 74
ABACAXI RICACO, 240
ABBEY, 177
Abbot's bitters, 96
Abricotine, 200
Absinthe, 79–80
ABSINTHE À LA WOOLWORTH, 241
ABSINTHE, ITALIAN STYLE, 241
ABSINTHE COCKTAIL, 240–41
ABSINTHE DRIP, 80, 241
ABSINTHE FRAPPÉ, 80, 241
Absorption method of avoiding drunkenness, 216–17
ACACIA, 242
ADAM & EVE, 242
ADIRONDACK, 146
ADMIRAL, 242
ADONIS, 196
Advocaat, 200
AFFINITY, 188
Aguardiente, 81
AIRMAIL, 144–45, 150
Akvavit. *See* Aquavit
AKVAVIT 'N' BITTERS, 243
ALABAMA FIZZ, 318
ALAMAGOOZLUM, 243
ALASKA, 243–44
ALBEMARLE FIZZ, 317
Alcohol, as a stimulant, 219
ALE POSSET, 365–66
ALE SANGAREE, 331
ALEXANDER, 20, 114, 244
ALHAMBRA ROYAL, 371
Allasch Doppelt Kümmel, 94, 200, 205
Allergies to liquor, 40, 214–15, 222–23
ALLIES, **175**
ALPINE GLOW, 244

Ambassador Scotch, 50
AMBER DREAM, 176
AMBROSIA, 245
AMERICAN BEAUTY, 245
AMERICAN BEAUTY PUNCH, 245, 338
American brandies, 70, 228
AMERICAN FLAG, 245
Amer Picon, 96, 245
Amontillado sherry, 88–89
Amoroso sherry, 89
AMOUR, 196
Ancient Bottle gin. *See* Seagram's yellow gin
Añejo rum, 61
ANGEL'S DREAM, 245
ANGEL'S KISS, 245
ANGEL'S TIT, 245
ANGLER'S, 245
Angostura bitters, 95
ANGOSTURA HIGHBALL, 304
Anis, 200
Anisette, 200
ANNIVERSARY, 191
Apéritif wines, 82–87
APPENDICITIS, 143–44
APPENDICITIS DE LUXE, 144
APPETIZER, 245–46
APPLE BLOSSOM, 195
APPLE BLOSSOM FIZZ, 319
APPLE BLOW FIZZ, 319
Apple brandy, 64, 71–72. *See also* Calvados, Applejack
APPLE CAR, 132–33, 141
APPLE CART, 132–33
APPLE COLLINS, 314
Applejack, 71
Applejack, as a cocktail base, 71
APPLEJACK BUCK, 309

INDEX

APPLEJACK COBBLER, 327
APPLEJACK COCKTAIL, 194
Applejack cocktails, aromatic type, 194–95
APPLEJACK COOLER, 329
APPLEJACK CRUSTA, 258
APPLEJACK DAISY, 321
APPLEJACK DYNAMITE, 166
APPLEJACK FIX, 322
APPLEJACK FIZZ, 319
APPLEJACK FLIP, 263
APPLEJACK HIGHBALL, 304
APPLEJACK JULEP, 323
APPLEJACK MANHATTAN, 124, 195
APPLEJACK MILK PUNCH, 336
APPLEJACK OLD-FASHIONED, 127, 194
APPLEJACK PUNCH, 350
APPLEJACK RABBIT, 166
APPLEJACK RICKEY, 310–11
APPLEJACK SANGAREE, 331
APPLEJACK SHAKE, 288
APPLEJACK SLING, 332
APPLEJACK SMASH, 290
APPLEJACK SOUR, 133 n., 141
Applejack Sour, cocktails based on, 133–34, 166–70
APPLEJACK SWIZZLE, 357
APPLEJACK TODDY, 333
APRICOT BOWL, 351–52
Apricot brandy, 64, 73
APRICOT BRANDY COCKTAIL, 246
APRICOT BRANDY SOUR, 142
APRICOT COCKTAIL, 246
APRICOT DELIGHT, 246
Apricot liqueur, 26, 200
APRICOT RICKEY, 310, 311
Apry, 200
Aquavit, 74–75
Aqua vitae, 64
AQUAVIT SOUR, 142
AQUITANIA, 246
Arak rum, 59
'ARF & 'ARF, 340
Armagnac, 68–69

ARMY, 123 n.
ARMY & NAVY, 246
Aromatic cocktails, 170–71
Aromatic wine cocktails, 195–98
Aromatic wines as modifying agents, 23–25, 82, 170
AROUND THE WORLD, 246
Arrack, 80–81
Arrack Punsch, 59, 200, 207
Artemisia, 79
Arteriosclerosis and drinking, 217
ARTILLERY PUNCH, 349
AUNT EMILY, 247
Austin, Nichols & Co. rum, 63
AUSTRALIAN SNOW, 320
AVIATION, 145

B. & B., 243
BACARDI COCKTAIL, 127
Bacardi Elixir, 200
BACARDI FLYER, 247
Bacardi rum, 61, 228
BAHIA, 197
BALAKLAVA NECTAR, 353
BALD HEAD, 174
BALTIMORE BRACER, 247
BALTIMORE EGG NOG, 361–62
BAMBOO COCKTAIL, 23, 196–97
BANANA BACARDI, 131
Bandana from Havana, 131, 200
Barack Pálinka, 73
Barbados rum, 59, 61, 62, 63
BARBADOS RUM COCKTAIL, 62
BARBARY COAST, 181
Bardinet liqueurs, 94
Bardinet rum, 63
Bar glasses, 35–36
Barley malt, use in making whisky, 47–48, 50, 56
BARRY, 176
Basel kirsch, 73
Basic principles, 19–26, 136–38 26, 136–38

INDEX 383

Batavia Arak. *See* Arak rum
Bathtub gin, 20, 40
BEACHCOMBER, 145, 150
BEADLESTON, 188
BEAUX ARTS, 174
Beefeater gin, 43
BEER SANGAREE, 331
BEE'S KNEES, 20, 144
Bellows' liqueur rum, 61
Bellows' rums, 62
Bell's Royal Reserve Scotch, 50
Benedictine, 26, 43, 92, 94, 200
Benedictine & Brandy, 243
Benedictine Society liqueurs, 94, 200
BERLIN BINGE, 247
BERMUDA, 191
BERMUDA ROSE, 191
Berreteaga rum, 63
Berry Brothers' gin, 43
BETSY FLANAGAN, 247
BETSY ROSS, 163
BETWEEN THE SHEETS, 165
Bianco vermouth, 84
BIARRITZ, 247
BIG APPLE, 247–48
BIJOU, 176
Bishop, definition of, 368
BISHOP À LA PRUSSE, 369
BISHOP COCKTAIL, 181
BISHOPS, 368–69
BISMARK, 341 n.
Bisquit Dubouché cognac, 68
Bitters, 24, 94–97, 196 n.
BITTERSWEET, 248
BLACKBERRY BEAUTY, 248
Blackberry brandy, 73
BLACKBERRY BRANDY SOUR. *See* BLACKOUT
Blackberry Julep, 248
Blackberry liqueur, 200
BLACKBERRY PUNCH, 248–49
BLACKOUT, 249
BLACKSTONE COOLER, 329
BLACK STRIPE, 249, 369

BLACK VELVET, 341
Blandy Madeira, 90
Blended cognacs, 67–68
Blended whiskies, 47–53
BLINKER, 249
BLOND NEGRESS, 244
BLOODY MARY, 234
BLOSSOM, 249
BLUE ANGEL PUNCH, 356
BLUE BELL, 188
BLUE BIRD, 147
BLUE BLAZER, 372–73
BLUE CURAÇAO, 147
BLUE DEVIL, 146
BLUE MONDAY, 249–50
BLUE MOON, 146
BLUE SKIES, 250
BOBBIE BURNS, 187–88
Boissière vermouth, 85
BOLERO, 153
BOLO, 250
Bols Geneva gin, 41–42
Bolskümmel. *See* Kümmel
Bols liqueurs, 93, 94, 96
BOMBAY, 191
BOOMERANG, 176, 250
Boonekamp bitters, 96
Booth's London gin, 43–44, 228. *See also* House of Lords gin
Bootlegging and taxes, 229–30
Borovicka, 81–82
BOSTON COOLER, 329
BOULEVARD, 183–84
Bourbon, 50–51. *See also* Whisky
BOURBON & EGG, 288
BOURBON BUCK, 309 n.
BOURBON COCKTAIL, 157–58, 180 n.
BOURBON COLLINS, 313
BOURBON HIGHBALL, 304
BOURBON RICKEY, 310–11
BOURBON SMASH, 290
BOWLS, FRUIT, 351–52
BOYD, 250–51

384 — INDEX

BRACERS. *See* Picker-uppers
BRADFORD, 117 n.
BRAINSTORM, 251
Brandy, 32, 63–64, 92. *See also* Armagnac; Apple brandy; Cherry brandy; Cognac, etc.
BRANDY ALEXANDER, 193–94, 244
BRANDY & EGG, 32, 288
BRANDY BUCK, 309
BRANDY CHAMPERELLE, 253
BRANDY COBBLER, 327
BRANDY COCKTAIL (aromatic type), 190
BRANDY COCKTAIL (sour type), 163
BRANDY COLLINS, 314
BRANDY COOLER, 329
BRANDY CRUSTA, 258
BRANDY DAISY, 321
BRANDY FIX, 322
BRANDY FIZZ, 319
BRANDY FLIP, 263
BRANDY HIGHBALL, 304
Brandy inhaler, 31, 32
BRANDY JULEP, 323
BRANDY MANHATTAN, 124
BRANDY MILK PUNCH, 336
BRANDY OLD-FASHIONED, 127, 190
BRANDY PUFF, 337
BRANDY PUNCH, 338, 351
BRANDY SANGAREE, 331
BRANDY SCAFFA, 287
BRANDY SHAKE, 288
BRANDY SLING, 332
BRANDY SMASH, 290
Brandy snifter, 32
BRANDY SOUR, 141
Brandy Sour, cocktails based on, 162–66
BRANDY SWIZZLE, 357
BRANDY TODDY, 333
BRANDY ZOOM, 300
BRAZIL, 197
BRONX, PINEAPPLE, 177

BRONX, SILVER, 177
BRONX COCKTAIL, 25–26, 177
BROOKLYN, 177, 183
BROWN BETTY, 359–60
Brunnen kirsch, 73
BUCKS, 308–9
BUGHOUSE, 251
BULLFROG, 251
BULL'S MILK, 336 n.
Burdon's sherry, 89
Bureaucratic Idiosyncracies, 229–32
BURGUNDY CUP, 354
BURGUNDY SANGAREE, 331
Burnett's London gin, 43
BURRA PEG, 252
Burrough's Beefeater gin, 43
BUSTER BROWN, 159–60
BUTTERED RUM, 369–70
B.V.D., 195
Byass. *See* Gonzales Byass
Byrrh, 86–87
BYRRH-CASSIS, 305
BYRRH-CITRON, 305
BYRRH COCKTAIL (gin), 198
BYRRH COCKTAIL (rye), 198
BYRRH COOLER, 330
BYRRH HIGHBALL, 304

CAFÉ BRÛLOT, 372
CAFÉ DIABLE, 371–72
CAFÉ KIRSCH, 251, 371
CAFÉ ROYAL, 371
CAFÉ ROYAL, FRAPPÉED, 264
California brandy, 69–70, 228
Caloric Punsch, 200
Calvados, 71
Campari bitters, 96
Canada Dry carbonated beverages, 104
Canadian Club whisky, 50
CANADIAN COCKTAIL, 251
CANADIAN COLLINS, 314
CANADIAN GRENADIER, 306
Canadian whisky, 49–50
CANASTA, 251

INDEX

385

CANCAN, 234
CAPITOL, 184
CAPTAIN'S BLOOD, 252
Carbonated beverages, brands of, 104, 302–3, 307–8
CARDINAL, 368
CARDINAL PUNCH, 350–51
CARIOCA, 252
Carioca rum, 61
Carlshamm's Punsch, 94, 200
CARMEN, 252
Carta blanca rum, 61
Carta oro rum, 61
CASINO, 145
CASSISCO, 305
CASSIS-KIRSCH, 305
Caussade. *See* Marquis de Caussade
Certosa, 200–1
CHAMPAGNE COBBLER, 327
CHAMPAGNE COCKTAIL, 252–53
Champagne glasses, 29, 31, 32
CHAMPAGNE PUNCH, 352
Champagne wine, 65
CHAMPERELLE, 253
CHAPPARA, 253
Charente River, 64
Charleston rum, 63
Charley's Royal Reserve rum, 62
CHARLIE CHAPLIN, 253–54
CHARLOTTE RUSSE, 254
Chartreuse, 43, 93–94, 201
CHAUNCEY OLCOTT, 254
CHERBOURG, 184
CHERRY BLOSSOM, 254
Cherry brandy, 64, 72–73
Cherry Heering, 63, 201
Cherry liqueur, 201
CHERRY RICKEY, 310–11
CHICAGO, 193
CHINESE COCKTAIL, 254
Chives Regal Scotch, 50
CHOCOLATE FLIP, 263
CHOCOLATE SOLDIER, 254
CHURCHILL, 189

CIDER BISHOP, 369
Cinzano vermouth, 83–84, 85–86
Cirrhosis, not caused by liquor, 211
Citrus juices, rules for using, 24, 97, 137–39
CLARET COBBLER, 327
CLARET CUP, 354
CLARET FLIP, 263
CLARET SANGAREE, 331
CLASSIC, 255
C.L.O.C., 201
CLOVER CLUB, 42, 147–48
CLOVER LEAF, 148
CLUB COCKTAIL, 255
Club soda, brands of, 103–4
Coates London gin, 43
COBBLERS, 326–28
Cockade rum, 63
Cocktail, definition of, 21–22
Cocktail base, 22–23, 136–37
Cocktail glasses, 28–29, 31, 32
"Cocktail King" and his Daiquiris, 129–31
Cocktails, rules for making, 21–26, 136–38, 149
six basic, 115–34
Cocktails based on the Applejack Sour. *See* Applejack Sour
Cocktails based on the Brandy Sour. *See* Brandy Sour
Cocktails based on the Gin Sour. *See* Gin Sour
Cocktails based on the Rum Sour. *See* Rum Sour
Cocktails based on the Whisky Sour. *See* Whisky Sour
COFFEE COBBLER, 327
COFFEE COCKTAIL, 163–64
Coffee drinks, 371–72
COFFEE FLIP, 263
Coffee Southern, 201
Cognac and other grape brandies, 63–71

COGNAC ZOOM, 300
Cointreau, 26, 93, 94, 201
Cointreau S.A.R.L. liqueurs, 94
Collins, Tom, John, & others, 313–14
COLONEL COLLINS, 313
COLONEL LINDBERGH, 270
COMMANDO, 255
COMMODORE, 255–56
CONNECTICUT, 194
CONTINENTAL, 256
COOLERS, 328–30
COOPERSTOWN, 175
Cordial glasses, 29, 30
Cordial Médoc, 94, 201–2
Cordials. *See* Liqueurs
CORNELL, 256
CORONATION, 256–57
COSSACK, 235
COUNTRY CLUB, 181, 257
COUNTRY CLUB COOLER, 330
COUNTRY COCKTAIL, 248
COUNTRY GENTLEMAN, 168–69
COURTNEY RILEY COOPER, 191
Courvoisier cognac, 68, 228
Cream, rule for using, 25, 101
Cream sherry, 88
Crème d'Ananas, 202, 207
  use in daiquiris, 128
Crème de Bananes, 202
Crème de Cacao, 202
Crème de Café, 202
Crème de Cassis, 202
Crème de Fraises, 202
Crème de Framboise, 202
Crème de Menthe, 26, 101, 202, 204
Crème de Moka, 202
Crème de Noyaux, 202, 206
Crème de Rose, 202
Crème de Thé, 202
Crème de Vanille, 202
Crème de Violette, 203
Crème Yvette, 203
CREOLE PUNCH, 339–40
CRESCENT CITY, 257

CRIMSON FIZZ, 317
CRUSTAS, 257–58
Crusted port, 91
Császár, 203
CUBAINE, 153
CUBA LIBRE, 343
CUBAN, 258
CUBAN APRICOT, 154
CUBAN DREAM, 258
CUBAN PEACH, 154
Cuban rum, 58–61
Cuervo tequila, 79
CUPS & PUNCHES, 344–56
Curaçao, 26, 94, 203
  blue, 147
CURAÇAO COCKTAIL, 160
Cusenier cognac, 68
Cusenier liqueurs, 94
Cutty Sark Scotch, 228
CZARINA, 235

D. & S., 243
Daiquiri, discussion of, 62, 87, 101, 127–31, 232
DAIQUIRI, original recipe, 127
DAIQUIRI DE LUXE, 129
DAIQUIRI GRENADINE, 127, 129, 131
DAIQUIRIS, La Florida recipes, 130–31
DAISIES, 320–21
DAISY PROHIBITION FIX, 322
Damiana, 203
Danish Akvavit, 74–75
Danziger Goldwasser, 203, 204, 205
Dash, definition of, 38
DAWN, 258
DEAUVILLE, 168
DEEP SEA, 175
De Kuyper's bitters, 96
De Kuyper's liqueurs, 94
DELMONICO COCKTAIL, 190
Delmonico glasses, 30, 33
DELMONICO SPECIAL, 190
Demerara rum, 59, 62

DEMI-VIRGIN, 259
Deo Optimo Maximo, 200
Deptford gin, 43
DEPTH BOMB, 169–70
DERBY, 259
DERBY FIZZ, 319
DEVIL, 164
DIAMOND FIZZ, 317
DIKI-DIKI, 259–60
DIPLOMAT, 196
Ditta Giuseppe Alberti liqueurs, 94
DIVAN, 260
DIXIE, 160
DOCTOR, 260
DOG'S NOSE, 341–42
DOLORES, 260–61
D.O.M., meaning of, 200
Domecq. *See* Pedro Domecq
DOROTHY, 261
DOROTHY GISH, 261
DOUBLE RAINBOW, 261
DOUGLAS FAIRBANKS, 261
Douro River valley, 90
DRAGOON PUNCH, 350
Drambuie, 92, 94, 203
Drambuie & Scotch, 243
Drambuie Liqueur Co., 50, 94
DREAM, 258
Drinking, relief from effects of, 374–76
Drinks, effect of mixing, 220–24
Drop, definition of, 38
Drunkenness, 215–17
DRY MARTINI, 116
Dry Sack, 89
DRY STINGER, 164
Dubonnet, 86–87
DUBONNET-CASSIS, 305
DUBONNET-CITRON, 305
DUBONNET COCKTAIL, 198
DUBONNET COOLER, 330
DUBONNET HIGHBALL, 304
DUBONNET RICKEY, 311
Duff Gordon sherry, 89

DUMMY DAISY, 322
DUPLEX, 196
Dutch gin. *See* Holland gin
Dykaree. *See* Daiquiri

EAGLE, 261
EAST INDIA, 192
Eau de Fleurs d'Oranger. *See* Orange Flower Water
Eau de vie, 64
Eau de Vie de Danzig, 203
Eau de vie de marc, 69
Eau d'Or, 203
EGG LEMONADE, 335
EGG NOGS. *See* NOGS
EGG POSSET, 366
Eggs, 24–25, 101–2, 113–14, 360–61
EL PRESIDENTE, 127, 178
EMERALD, 164
EMERALD STAR, 262
ENGLISH BISHOP, 368–69
ENGLISH COBBLER, 327
English gin. *See* London gin
EPICUREAN, 262
Equipment for the bar, 27–38
ERIN, 262
Erin's Antique Irish, 50
ETHIOPIA, 262
Ets. Marnier Lapostolle liqueurs, 94
EXPORT-CASSIS, 305
EXPRESS, 187
Extrait d'Absinthe, 79–80
EYE-OPENERS. *See* Picker-uppers

FAIVRE'S POUSSE-CAFÉ, 283
Falernum, 26, 203–4
FARMER'S DAUGHTER, 169
FARMER'S WIFE, 195
FEDORA, 262–63
Feeble-mindedness and alcohol, 217–18
Fernet bitters, 96
FERNET COCKTAIL, 263
FERNET HIGHBALL, 304

FERNET MENTHE, 263
FIBBER MCGEE, 263
Field, Son & Co.'s bitters, 96
Fine champagne, 64, 67, 68, 93
Fino sherry, 88
Fior d'Alpe, 204
Fiori Alpini, 204
FISH HOUSE PUNCH, 348
FIXES, 321–22
FIZZES, 314–20
FLAMINGO, 263
Flavoring agents, 25–26
FLIPS, 263
Flora della Alpi, 204
FLORIDA, 146, 264
FLORIDA PUNCH, 338
Floridita bar in Havana, 129–30
FLYING DUTCHMAN, 119
Fockink's Geneva gin, 41
Fockink's liqueurs, 93, 94
Fockink Tavern, 41n.
FOOLISH VIRGIN, 296
FORBIDDEN FRUIT COCKTAIL, 264
Forbidden Fruit liqueur, 43, 204
Fortified wines, 87–91
FORTY-SEVEN, 156
FOUR W, 264
Framboise, 64, 204
Framboisette, 26, 204
FRANKLIN FARMS EGG NOG, 362
FRAPPÉED CAFÉ ROYAL, 264
Frappéed cordials, 243, 264
FRAPPÉS, 264
Freezomint. See Crème de Menthe
French kirsch, 73
FRENCH 75, 343
FRESCO, 265
FRIAR, 265
FRISCO, 161
FROZEN COCKTAILS, 265–66
FROZEN DAIQUIRI, 265
FROZEN HONEYMOON, 265
FROZEN MIAMI, 265
FROZEN ORANGE BLOSSOM, 265
FROZEN RED LION, 265
FROZEN RHETT BUTLER, 265
FROZEN SCARLETT O'HARA, 265
FROZEN SNOW WHITE, 265
FROZEN SOUTHERN COMFORT SOUR, 265
FROZEN STINGER, 265
FRUIT BOWLS, 351–52
FRUIT BRANDY HIGHBALLS, 304
Fruit juices, 24, 97–99
FRUIT SHRUBS, 358–59
Fruit syrups, 99–101
Fulstrength Scotch, 49–50, 228
FU MANCHU, 266
Funchal, Madeira from, 89–90
Fundador brandy, 71
FUTURITY, 266

GABY DES LYS, 266
Garnier liqueurs, 93, 94
Gautier cognac, 68
Geneva gin. See Holland gin
Get cognac, 68
Get liqueurs, 94
GIBSON COCKTAIL, 117
GIBSON DE LUXE, 117–18
Gilbey London gin, 43
Gilka kümmel. See Kümmel
GIMLET, 42, 146
Gin, 40–46
GIN BUCK, 309, 309n.
GIN COBBLER, 327
GIN COCKTAIL, 171–72
Gin cocktails, aromatic type, 171–77
GIN COOLER, 329
GIN CRUSTA, 258
GIN DAISY, 321
GIN FIX, 321–22
GIN FIZZ, 314–15, 316–17
GIN FLIP, 263
Ginger ale, brands of, 104
Ginger beer, 237
Ginger liqueur, 204

INDEX

GIN HIGHBALL, 304
GIN JULEP, 323
GIN MILK PUNCH, 336
GIN MINT PUNCH, 339
GIN 'N' BITTERS, 171–72
GIN 'N' IT, 173
GIN 'N' ROCKS, 173
GIN 'N' SIN, 172
GIN 'N' TONIC, 314
GIN OLD-FASHIONED, 127
GIN PAHIT, 172
GIN PUFF, 337
GIN RICKEY, 146, 310–11
GIN SANGAREE, 331
GIN SHAKE, 288
GIN SLING, 332
GIN SMASH, 290
GIN SOUR, 140
Gin Sour, cocktails based on, 142–49
GIN SPIDER, 304
GIN SQUIRT, 342–43
GIN SWIZZLE, 357
GIN TODDY, 333
GIN ZOOM, 300
Glassware, Gimmicks, and Gadgets, 27–38; illustrations, 30–31
GLÖGG, 373
GLOOM CHASER, 175
GLOOM LIFTER, 266
GLOOM RAISER, 175
Gloria Mundi Madeira, 90
GLUHWEIN, 367
Goddard rum, 63
GOLDEN DAWN, 258–59
GOLDEN DAWN PUNCH, 356
GOLDEN FIZZ, 317
GOLDEN GLOVE, 131
GOLDEN GLOW, 176
GOLDEN MARTINI, 117 n.
GOLDEN SCREW, 235
GOLDEN SLIPPER, 266
GOLDEN SPIKE, 127 n., 235
Gold label rum. See Carta oro
Goldwasser. See Danziger

Goldwasser
Gomme syrup. See Sugar syrup
Gonzales Byass brandy, 71
Gonzales Byass sherry, 89
GORDON, 118
Gordon London gin, 43, 228
Government House rum, 63, 228
GRAND DUCHESS, 235
Grande Champagne, 64
Grand Marnier, 43, 44, 92–93, 94, 204
GRAND PASSION, 267
GRAND ROYAL, 317
GRAND SLAM, 267
Grant's Scotch, 50
GRAPEFRUIT BLOSSOM, 267
Grape brandies, 63–71
GRAPE JUICE RICKEY, 310
Grappa, 69–70
GRASSHOPPER, 267
GREAT SECRET, 271
Greek brandies, 70–71
GREENBACK, 147
GREEN BRIAR, 188
GREENBRIER, 176
GREEN FIZZ, 317
GREEN LEMONADE, 335
GREENWICH, 267
Grenadine, 26, 100, 101, 204–5
GRENADINE RICKEY, 310–11
GRETA GARBO, 260
GROGS, 369–70
Gum syrup. See Sugar syrup
GYPSY, 235–36
GYPSY QUEEN, 235–36

H. & H., 271
HABITANT, 184–85
Haig & Haig Pinch Bottle, 50, 228
"Hair of the dog," 375
Haitian rum, 59, 61, 62, 63
HAITIAN RUM COCKTAIL, 62
HALF & HALF, 340

HALSTEAD STREET VELVET, 341
Hankey Bannister Scotch, 50
HARMONY, 166
HARVARD, 190
HARVARD COOLER, 329
Harvey's Bristol Cream, 89
HAVANA, 179
HAVANA BEACH, 131
HAVANA CLUB COCKTAIL, 178
Havana Club rum, 61, 228
HAWTHORNE, 184
Heering, Peter, liqueurs, 94
HELEN TWELVETREES, 267–68
Hennessy cognac, 228
Herbs, use in punches, 346–47
Herbsaint, 80
Highball glasses, 30, 32–33
HIGHBALLS, 109, 302–7
HIGH HAT, 268
HIGHLAND, 187
HIGHLAND FLING, 187
Himbeergeist, 64, 73
HOFFMAN HOUSE FIZZ, 317
HOLE IN ONE, 189
Holland gin, 40–42, 268
HOLLAND GIN 'N' BITTERS, 268
HOLLAND GIN COCKTAIL, 268
HOLLAND'S PRIDE, 268
Holloway London gin, 43
Holloway's bitters, 96
HONEY BEE, 144–45, 150
HONEYMOON, 169
HONEYSUCKLE, 144–45, 150
HONG KONG, 175
HOP TOAD, 251
HORSE'S NECK, 306
Horse's Neck, 328
HORSE'S NECK, PLAIN, 306
HORSE'S NECK WITH A KICK, 306
Hostetters bitters, 95
HOT BUTTERED RUM, 369–70
HOT DRINKS, 365–73
HOT EGG NOGS, 363–64
HOT GROG, 369
HOT MILK PUNCHES, 336
HOT SANGAREES, 331

HOT SPICED RUM, 369–70
House of Lords gin, 43, 44, 228
Hulstkamp Geneva gin, 41
HURRICANE, 236

Ice, 102–3, 109–11
IDEAL, 269
Insulation method of guarding against drunkenness, 215–17
Internal Revenue taxes, 44, 53, 60, 95, 229–31
INTERNATIONAL, 119
IRISH COFFEE, 269
IRISH COLLINS, 314
IRISH HIGHBALL, 304
IRISH MILK PUNCH, 336
IRISH MIST, 205
IRISH RICKEY, 310–11
IRISH SLING, 332
IRISH TODDY, 333
Irish whisky, 47, 48, 50
ISLE OF PINES, 269

J. & B. Liqueur Scotch, 50
JACK COLLINS, 314
JACK IN THE BOX, 167–68
JACK ROSE, discussion of, 133, 141, 232
JACK ROSE DE LUXE, 133–34
JACKAROO, 269
Jacquin liqueurs, 94
Jamaica rum, 59, 60, 61–62
James E. Pepper bourbon, 228
JAPANESE, 190
Jarzebiak, 76
Jerez, sherry from, 89
JERSEY CITY, 168
Jersey Lightning, 72
JERSEY SOUR, 133 n.
Jiffy Quick Junk, 231–32
JIMMY BLANC, 271
Jitters, 270
JOCKEY CLUB, 270
John Begg Liqueur Scotch, 228
JOHN COLLINS, 313
John Jameson Irish, 50

INDEX

JOHN MCCLAIN, 187
Johnnie Walker Black Label Scotch, 50, 228
Johnnie Walker Red Label Scotch, 228
Jourde liqueurs, 94
Judging liquor, 225–28
JULEP NO. 1 (author's favorite), 324–25
JULEP NO. 2 (time consumer), 325
JULEP NO. 3 (faint flavor), 325–26
JULEPS, 322–26
Julep mugs, 30
Jules Robin cognac, 68

Kahlua, 205
KAHLUALEXANDER, 270
KANGAROO, 236
KATINKA, 236
KENTUCKY COLONEL, 270
KENTUCKY EGG NOG, 362
KIDDIE CAR, 132–33, 141
KINA, 270
Kina Lillet, 85
Kina Lillet Drinks, 270
King's Ginger Liqueur, 204, 205
KINGSTON, 272
Kirsch, 63, 64, 72–73
KIRSCH HIGHBALL, 304
KIRSCH SOUR, 142
Kirschwasser. See Kirsch
KIRSCH ZOOM, 300
Kirsebaer, 73
KLONDIKE, 195
KNICKEBEIN, 272
KNICKERBOCKER, 154
KNIGHT, 165
Korkmaster, 36
KRETCHMA, 236
Kümmel, 94, 200, 205
KUMQUAT LIMEADE, 335
Kumquats, use in place of limes, 311

L'Abbaye de Cenon liqueurs, 94
LADY ALEXANDER, 272–73
LAFAYETTE, 182
LAFAYETTE PUNCH, 352
LALLA ROOKH, 343
Lambert rum, 63
LAMBS' CLUB, 176
LARCHMONT, 155
Large's rye. See Monongahela
Leacock & Co. Madeira, 90
LEAGUE OF NATIONS, 247
LEMONADE, 334
Lemonades, party service, 335
Lemon Hart Liqueur rum, 61
Lemon Hart rums, 61, 62
LEMON ICE PUNCH, 355
LEMON-ORANGEADE, 334
LEMON-RUM SHRUB, 358
Leroux liqueurs, 94
Levert & Co. Genever gin, 41
LEVIATHAN 477, 273
LIBERTY, 273
Licor de Café. See Kahlua, 205
Lightbourn's rum, 63
LILLET, 85, 271
Lillet apéritif wine, 85
Lillet vermouth, 85
LILLY, 269
LIMEADE, 311, 334
LIME-LEMONADE, 334
LIME-ORANGEADE, 334
LIME RICKEY, 311
Liqueur d'Anis, 80, 205
Liqueur d'Or. See Danziger Goldwasser
Liqueur glasses, 29, 30
Liqueur Jaune, 205
LIQUEUR LEMONADES, 334
LIQUEUR RICKEYS, 309–11
Liqueurs, 25, 26, 92–94, 199–208
Liqueur Strega, 94, 205, 207
Liqueur Veritas, 80
Liqueur Verte, 205

Liquor, 209–28
LITTLE COLONEL, 273
LITTLE ONE, 155
LOCH LOMOND, 187
Løitens aquavit, 75
London Dock rum, 61
London dry gin, 42–43. See also London gin
London gin, 40–43
  white & yellow, 42–43
London sweet gin. See Old Tom gin
LONE TREE, 176
LONE TREE COOLER, 330
LONG TOM COOLER, 329
LOTUS CLUB SPECIAL, 186
LOVER'S DELIGHT, 273–74
LUNE DE MIEL, 274

MADAGASCAR, 274
Madeira, classes of, 89–90
MADEIRA & EGG, 288
MADEIRA COBBLER, 327
MADEIRA FLIP, 263
MADEIRA SANGAREE, 331
MADISON AVENUE, 153
MAHARAJAH'S BURRA PEG, 252
MAIDEN'S PRAYER, 274
MAIDEN'S WISH, 271
MAISON CHARLES, 152–53
Malt. See Barley malt
MAMIE'S SISTER, 309 n.
MAMIE'S SOUTHERN SISTER, 309 n.
MAMIE TAYLOR, 309
MAMMY BOY, 179
MAÑANA, 151
Mandarine, 205
MANDARINE RICKEY, 310–11
Mandarinette, 205
MANGAREVA, 274–75
MANHATTAN, 35, 86–87, 95, 107–8, 121–24, 183–85, 232
MANHATTAN DRY, 123–24
MANHATTAN MEDIUM, 123
MANHATTAN SWEET, 123

MANHATTAN COOLER, 330
MANHATTAN DE LUXE, 124
Manzanilla sherry, 88–89
Maraschino, 26, 205–6
Marasquin, 205–6
Marc. See Eau de vie de marc
MARIANNE, 184
Marie Brizard cognac, 68
Marie Brizard Fine Champagne, 67
Marie Brizard kirsch, 73
Marie Brizard liqueurs, 93, 94
Marie Brizard rum, 63
Marquis de Caussade armagnac, 69
Marsala, uses of, 91
Marseille, vermouth from, 84–85
Martin's Scotch, 50
MARTINEZ, the original Martini, 121
MARTINI, 35, 107, 108, 114, 115–21, 174–76, 232
MARTINI, DRY, 116, 117
MARTINI, GOLDEN, 117 n.
MARTINI MEDIUM, 116–17, 119
MARTINI, SWEET, 117
MARTINI, The Ideal, 120–21
Martini & Rossi grappa, 69
MARTINI DE LUXE, 117–18
Martinique rum, 59, 63
MARY PICKFORD, 179
MAXIM, 176
MAY BLOSSOM FIZZ, 319
MAY WINE, 353
Mazarine, 206
Mead, 81
Mead Makers, Ltd., 81
Measurements, table of, 38
Measuring, 105–8
MECCA, 177
Médoc. See Cordial Médoc
MEMPHIS, 275
MEMPHIS BELLE, 275
MERRY WIDOW, 197
MERRY WIDOW FIZZ, 317

INDEX

Metaxa brandy, 71
Metheglin, 81
METROPOLITAN, 191–92
MEXICAN ITCH, 78
Mexican rum, 59, 63
MIAMI, 152
MIAMI BEACH, 275
MIKADO, 275
MIKE COLLINS, 314
MILK PUNCHES, hot and cold, 336–37
MILK SHAKE, 336
MILLION, 275
MILLIONAIRE, 159
MILLIONAIRE ROYAL, 159
MILLION DOLLAR, 276
MIMOSA, 341
MINT COOLER, 330
MINT JULEP. See JULEPS
Mirabelle, 64, 72
MISSISSIPPI PUNCH, 338
MISSOURI MULE, 276
MISSOURI PUNCH, 355
MISTS & ROCKS, 284–85
MIXED VERMOUTH, 196
Mixing drinks, effect of. See Drinks
Modifiers. See Modifying agents
Modifying agents, 23–25
MOJITO, 314
Mona rum, 61
Monastique, 206
MONKEY GLAND, 276
Monnet cognac, 68, 228
Monnet 1858 cognac, 67
Monongahela rye, 228
MONTANA, 191
MONTE CARLO, 276
MONTREAL GIN SOUR, 142–43
MOONLIGHT COOLER, 329
MORNING, 276–77
MORNING GLORY, 277
MORNING GLORY FIZZ, 319, 375
MORNING ROSE, 150–51
MORNING STAR, 277

MOSCOW MULE, 236–37
MOSS ROSE, 277
Mount Vernon rye, 55, 228
MULLED WINE, 367
MULLS, 366–67
MY OWN PASSION, 278
Myer's rums, 61–62

NACIONAL, 131
Napoleon 1811 cognac, 67
NATURAL, 165
NAVY, 123 n.
Nectar of Tokay, 206
NECTARINE JULEP, 278
NEGRESSE BLONDE, LA, 244
Negrita rum, 63
Negus, Col. Francis, 367
NEGUS, recipe for, 367–68
NEVADA, 278
NEW ALGONQUIN, 183
NEW DEAL, 182
New England rum, 59, 63
NEW ORLEANS, 278
NEW ORLEANS GIN FIZZ, 318
NEW ORLEANS PUNCH, 339
NEW YORKER, 158–59
Nicholson London gin, 43
NINITCHKA, 236
NOGS, 360–64
Noilly Cassis, 206
Noilly Prat vermouth, 84–85
NOME, 119, 244
Nomenclature of drinks, 301–2
Non-alcoholic drinks. See Prohibition Cocktails; Prohibition Highballs; Prohibition Rickeys, etc.
NORTHSIDE SPECIAL, 342
Norwegian Aquavit, 74–75
Noyaux. See Crème de Noyaux
Nuyens liqueurs, 94

ODDS MCINTYRE, 271
ØGGE, 373
OISEAU BLEU, 147
Ojen, 80

OJEN COCKTAIL, 279
Okolehao, 80
Old Bushmill's Irish, 50
Old Drum rye, 228
OLD ENGLISH WASSAIL, 359
Old-Fashioned, 100, 103, 124–27, 232
OLD-FASHIONED DE LUXE, 125
Old-Fashioned glasses, 29, 31
Old Forester bourbon, 228
Old Gentry gin, 43
Old Granddad bourbon, 55
Old Medford rum, 63
Old Mr. Boston bourbon, 228
Old Mr. Boston gin, 228
Old Overholt rye, 228
OLD PEPPER, 376
OLD PLANTATION, 275
Old St. Croix rum, 63
Old Taylor bourbon, 228
Old Tom gin, 42
OLD VERMONT, 166–67
Oloroso sherry, 88, 89
OLYMPIA, 279
OLYMPIC, 279
OMAR KHAYYAM, 279
Oorlam Genever gin, 41
OPAL, 279
OPALESCENT, 279
OPERA, 279
Oporto, port from, 90
ORANGEADE, 334
ORANGE & LIME FIZZ, 318
Orange bitters, 95
ORANGE BLOSSOM, 20, 25, 146
Orange brandy, 64
ORANGE FIZZ, 318
Orange Flower Water, 311, 318
ORANGE ICE PUNCH, 355
Orange liqueur, 206
Orange peel, use of, 112
ORANGE-RUM SHRUB, 358
Orgeat, 26, 101, 206
ORGEAT COCKTAIL, 280
ORGEAT LEMONADE, 335

ORIENTAL, 244
Otard Dupuy cognac, 68
Ouzo, 206

Paddy's Old Irish, 50
PALISADES, 280
PALMER, 141
PALMETTO, 280
PANAMA, 193–94, 244
Papaya juice, 99
PAPAYA SLING, 332
PARADISE, 280
Parfait Amour, 43, 101, 206
PARISIAN, 175
PARISIAN POUSSE-CAFÉ, 283
PARK AVENUE, 280
Party drinks, 344–56, 373
Passion Fruit Nectar, 206–7
PEACH BOWL, 351–52
Peach brandy, 64
Peach liqueur, 207
PEACH RICKEY, 310–11
Pear brandy, 73
Pêche, 207
PEDRO COLLINS, 314
Pedro Domecq brandy, 71
Pedro Domecq sherry, 89
PENDENNIS CLUB EGG NOG, 362–63
PENNSYLVANIA, 281
Peppermint, 207
Pères Chartreux liqueurs, 94
PERFECT, 116
Pernod, 79–80
Peruvian brandy, 70
Peychaud bitters, 96, 187 n.
PICCADILLY, 184
PICKER-UPPERS, 374–76
PICON-CITRON, 305
PICON COCKTAIL, DRY, 197
PICON COCKTAIL, SWEET, 197
PICON CRÉMAILLÈRE, 197–98
PICON-CURAÇAO, 306
Picon, G., bitters, 96
PICON HIGHBALL, 304
PICON LEMONADE, 335

PICON PUNCH, 339
PIERRE COLLINS, 314
PIMM'S CUPS, 340
PINEAPPLE BACARDI, 131
PINEAPPLE BLOSSOM (gin), 281
PINEAPPLE BLOSSOM (whisky), 161
PINEAPPLE BOWL, 351-52
PINEAPPLE BRONX, 177
Pineapple Cordial, 207
PINEAPPLE FIZZ, 319
PINK DAIQUIRI. See Daiquiri Grenadine
PINK GIN, 172 n.
PINK LADY, 148
PINK LADY FIZZ, 318
PINK LEMONADE, 335
PINK PINEAPPLE, 281
Pippermint, 207
Pisco brandy, 70
PLANTERS' PUNCH, 337
Planters' Punch rum, 62
PLAZA, 176
PLUIE D'OR, 281
Plum brandy, 64, 72
Plymouth gin. See Coates London gin
Pokers, use in making hot drinks, 366-67
POLINCHELLE, 305
POMPIER, 305
PONCE DE LEON, 281
POOR MAN'S PUNCH, 353-54
POPE, 369
Port, 90-91
PORT & EGG, 288
Portal, Dingwall & Norris rum, 62
PORT COBBLER, 327
PORT FLIP, 263
PORT SANGAREE, 331
PORTER SANGAREE, 331
POSSETS, 365-66
Pot stills, 47, 65
Pousse-Café, glasses, 29, 30
POUSSE-CAFÉS, 99, 281-83

POUSSE L'AMOUR, 32, 283
Power's Three Swallows, 50
PRAIRIE OYSTER, 376
PRESIDENT, AMERICAN; PRESIDENT, CUBAN. See El Presidente
Prima (1ma) Aquavit, 75
PRINCETON, 283
PROHIBITION COCKTAILS, 284
PROHIBITION COOLERS, 330
PROHIBITION DAISIES, 322
PROHIBITION FIXES, 322
PROHIBITION FIZZES, 320
PROHIBITION HIGHBALLS, 304
PROHIBITION PUNCHES, 336, 355-56
PROHIBITION RICKEYS, 311
Proof, as a factor in quality of liquor, 44-46
Prune brandy, 64
Prunella, 207
Prunelle, 207
Puerto Rican rum, 59, 60-61
PUFFS, 337
Pulque, 78
PUNCHES & CUPS, 335-40, 344-56
PURPLE FIZZ, 318
PUSSYFOOT, 284

QUEEN, 117
QUEEN OF SHEBA, 148-49
Quetsch, 64, 72
Quinquina, 82-83

RAIL SPLITTER, 330
RAINBOW POUSSE-CAFÉ, 283
Rain Water Madeira, 90
RAMONCITA LOPEZ SPECIAL, 131
RAMOS GIN FIZZ, 318
Raspail, 207
Raspberry brandy, 64, 73
Raspberry syrup, 99
Reaction time of drinks, 39-40, 113-14, 126
RED LION, 147

REMSEN COOLER, 329
Rémy Martin cognac, 68, 228
RHETT BUTLER, 284
RHINE WINE COBBLER, 327
RHINE WINE COOLER, 329
RHINE WINE PUNCH, 352–53
Ribalagua, Constante, The Cocktail King, 129–30
RICHMOND, 271
RICKEYS, 309–11
Rigi kirsch, 73
ROB ROY, 187
R.O.C. curaçao, 203
Rocher Frères liqueurs, 94
Rock & Rye, 207
ROCKS & MISTS, 284–85
ROCKY MOUNTAIN PUNCH, 351
ROMAN PUNCH, 338
Ron Añejo, 61
Ronrico rum, 61
ROSE, 285–86
Rouyer cognac, 68
ROYAL FIZZ, 317
Royal Reserve rum, 62
ROYAL RICKEY, 311
ROYAL SMILE, 167
RUBY FIZZ, 319
Ruby port, 91
RUM & COCA-COLA, 343
Rum, 58–63
RUMBA, 286
RUM BOOZE, 366
RUM BRONX, 179
RUM BUCK, 309, 309 n.
RUM COBBLER, 327
RUM COCKTAIL, 179
Rum cocktails, aromatic type, 177-80
RUM COLLINS, 314
RUM COOLER, 329
RUM CRUSTA, 258
RUM DAISY, 321
RUM FIX, 322
RUM FIZZ, 319
RUM FLIP, 263
RUM HIGHBALL, 304

RUM JULEP, 323
RUM MANHATTAN, 124, 178
RUM MARTINI, 119
RUM MILK PUNCH, 336
RUM OLD-FASHIONED, 127, 179
RUM PUFF, 337
RUM RICKEY, 310–11
RUM SANGAREE, 331
RUM SHAKE, 288
RUM SIDE CAR, 152
RUM SLING, 332
RUM SMASH, 290
RUM SOUR, 140
Rum Sour, cocktails based on, 149–56
RUM SQUIRT, 342
RUM SWIZZLE, 357
RUM TODDY, 333
RUM ZOOM, 300
RUSSIAN, 237
RUSSIAN BEAR, 237
RUSSIAN TEA, 269
Rye. See Whisky
RYE COLLINS, 314
RYE HIGHBALL, 304
RYE JULEP, 323
RYE SMASH, 290
Rye whisky, brands of, 50–51

Sabayon, 378
St. Croix rum, 63
St. James Club, Montreal, 142
St. James rum, 63
ST. MORITZ, 183
St. Raphael, 86
Sandeman Madeira, 90
Sandeman sherry, 89
SANDY COLLINS, 314
Sangarees, definition of, 330–31
SANGAREES, 330–31
SANTIAGO, 129, 286
SANTINAS POUSSE-CAFÉ, 283
Santo Domingan rum, 59
SARATOGA COCKTAIL, 190
SARATOGA COOLER, 330

INDEX

Sarthe rum, 63
SAUTERNE COBBLER, 327
SAUTERNE CUP, 354
SAUTERNE SANGAREE, 331
SAVANNAH, 286
SAZERAC, 96, 185–86
SCAFFAS, 287
SCARLETT O'HARA, 287
Schiedam gin. See Holland gin
Schnapps, 41 n.
Schwarzwälder kirsch, 72–73
SCOTCH & SODA, 56, 302
Scotch as a cocktail base, 56, 186–87
SCOTCH COCKTAIL, 187
Scotch cocktails, aromatic type, 186–89
SCOTCH COLLINS, 314
SCOTCH HIGHBALL, 304
SCOTCH MANHATTAN, 124, 187–89
SCOTCH MILK PUNCH, 336
SCOTCH MIST, 284
SCOTCH OLD-FASHIONED, 127, 187
SCOTCH RICKEY, 310–11
SCOTCH SAZERAC, 188
SCOTCH SLING, 332
SCOTCH SMASH, 290
SCOTCH TODDY, 333
Scotch whisky, 46–58
SCREWDRIVER, 237
SEA FIZZ, 319
Seagram's Ancient Bottle gin, 43
Seagram's Golden gin, 43, 44
Seagram's Pedigree whisky, 50
Seagram's V.O. whisky, 50
Seagram's yellow gin, 43–44
SEESAW, 287
SELF STARTER, 271
SEPTEMBER MORN, 150
SEVENTH HEAVEN, 287
Severy liqueurs, 94
SHAKES, 287–88

Shaking and stirring, 108–9
SHAMPARELLE. See Champerelle
SHAMROCK, 184
SHANDY GAFF, 340–41
SHANGHAI, 288
SHEEPSHEAD BAY, 184
SHEIK, 148
Sherry, 87–89
SHERRY & BITTERS, 288
SHERRY & EGG, 32, 288
SHERRY COBBLER, 327
SHERRY FLIP, 263
Sherry glasses, 29, 31, 32
SHERRY SANGAREE, 331
SHIRLEY JANE, 289
Short drinks, 239–300
SHRUBS, 357–59
Side Car, a Brandy Sour, 141; discussion of, 67, 93, 132–33
SIDE CAR DE LUXE, 132
SIDNEY, 183
SIGMA CHI, 289
SILVER BRONX, 177
SILVER BULLET, 271
SILVER FIZZ, 317
Silver mugs, 30, 33, 34
SINGAPORE GIN SLING, 332–33
Skaal, 75
SLEEPY HOLLOW, 289
SLINGS & TODDIES, 332–33
Slivovitz, 64, 72, 79
SLOEBERRY, 289
Sloe Gin, 40, 207
SLOE GIN COCKTAIL, DRY, 290
SLOE GIN COCKTAIL, SWEET, 289
SLOE GIN FIZZ, 320
SLOE GIN RICKEY, 310–11
SLOPPY JOE'S, 290
SMASHES, 192, 290
Smirnoff vodka, 75
SNAPPER, 290–91
SNOW BALL, 320
SNOW WHITE, 151–52
Soda and ginger ale, 103–4
Solera, definition of, 87–88

SOMERSET, 116
SOUL KISS, 291
Sour glasses, 30, 33
Sour mash whisky, 51
SOURS, 138–42
SOUTHAMPTON, 291
SOUTHERN BEAUTY, 291
Southern Comfort, 73–74, 207
SOUTHERN COMFORT COCKTAIL, 291–92
SOUTHERN COMFORT JULEP, 326
SOUTHERN COMFORT OLD-FASHIONED, 126–27
SOUTHERN COMFORT RICKEY, 310–11
SOUTHSIDE FIZZ, 318
SOUTHSIDE SPECIAL, 342
SOVIET, 237
Spanish brandies, 70–71
SPICED RUM. *See* Hot Spiced Rum
Sp. Vini Gall., 64
Sp. Vini Vitis, 64
SPRITZER, 307
SQUIRTS, 342–43
STAR, 195
STAR DAISY, 321 n.
STINGER, 164
Stirring and shaking, 108–9
STIRRUP CUP, 354
STOLEN KISS, 292
STONE, 292
STONE FENCE, 329
STONEWALL JACKSON, 329
STRAWBERRY BOWL, 351–52
Strega. *See* Liqueur Strega
STUBBY COLLINS, 127 n.
Sugar syrup, how made, 100
SUISSESSE, 292, 375
SUISSESSE HIGHBALL, 306, 375
SUNDOWNER, 164
SUNRISE, 292–93
SUNSHINE, 293
SUPREME, 167
SUSIE TAYLOR, 309 n.

Swedish aquavit, 74–75
Swedish Punch. *See* Arrack Punsch
SWEET & LOVELY, 293
SWEET DREAM, 293
Sweet mash whisky, 51
SWISS, 198
Swiss kirsch, 73
SWISS SPECIAL, 293–94
Swizzled Manhattan, 357
SWIZZLES, 356–57
SYLLABUB, 378

TAIL FEATHERS, 306–7
Tall drinks, definition of, 301–2
TAMMANY, 294
Tangerine, Dolfi, 207–8
Tanqueray's gin, 43
Tawny port, 91
Taxes and Bootlegging, 229–31
TENNESSEE, 161
Tequila, 78–79, 294
TEQUILA COCKTAIL, 294
TEQUILA COLLINS, 314
TEQUILA MARTINI, 119
TEQUILA SOUR, 142
Testing liquor. *See* Judging liquor
TEXAS FIZZ, 318–19
THIRD RAIL, 179–80
THISTLE, 294
Three Dagger rum, 62
Three Feathers bourbon, 228
Three Feathers gin, 228
Three Swallows Irish, 50
TIGER'S MILK, 336–37
TIGER'S TOOTH, 294
TIPPERARY, 294
T.N.T. SPECIAL, 195
TODDIES, hot and cold, 332–33
TOKAY COBBLER, 327
TOM & JERRY, 364
Tom & Jerry mugs, 31, 33–34
TOMATE, 240–41
TOM COLLINS, 42, 313, 314–15

INDEX

Tom Collins Mix, 313
Torino, vermouth from, 83–84, 86
TORONTO, 181
TOVARICH, 237
TRINITY, 188
Triple Sec, 93, 208
TROPICAL, 294–95
TURF, 295
TURKISH BLOOD, 341
TUXEDO, 295
TWISTER, 237

Ulcers, alcohol as a cause of, 217
Unicum bitters, 96, 97
UNION CLUB, 295
Union of South Africa liqueurs, 94
UPTOWN, 295
UPTOWN MANHATTAN, 184

VALENCIA, 295–96
Van der Hum, 94, 208
VANILLA COBBLER, 328
VELVET, 341
VERMONT. See OLD VERMONT
Vermouth, 83–86
VERMOUTH-CASSIS, 305
VERMOUTH COCKTAIL, 23, 196
VERMOUTH COOLER, 330
VERMOUTH-CURAÇAO, 305
VERMOUTH HIGHBALL, 304
VERMOUTH RICKEY, 311
VERMOUTH RINSE, 115–16
VERMOUTH SPRAY, 115–16
Vieille Cure, 43, 94, 208
Vin & Spritcentralen aquavit, 75
Vin & Spritcentralen liqueurs, 94
Vinmonopolet aquavit, 75
Vino de Pasto sherry, 88–89
Vintage port, 91
VIOLET FIZZ, 317
VIRGIN, 123 n., 296

Virgin Islands rum, 59, 63
Vodka, 75–78
VODKA COCKTAIL, 238
VODKA COLLINS, 314
Vodka drinks, 233–38
VODKA HIGHBALL, 304
VODKA ICEBERG, 238
VODKA MARTINI, 119
VODKA MEDIUM MARTINI, 235
VODKA PERFECT, 235
VODKA PLUNGE, 238
VODKA RICKEY, 310–11
VODKA SHAKE, 288
VODKA SMASH, 290
VODKA SPLASH, 238
VODKA SOUR, 142
VODKA SPECIAL, 238
Vodka tall drinks, 238
VOLGA, 238
VOLGA BOATMAN, 238

WAGON WHEEL, 296
Waldmeister, use in May wine, 353
WALDORF POUSSE-CAFÉ, 283
WALLY WARFIELD WINDSOR WALLOP, 264
WALTZING MATILDA, 296
WARD EIGHT, 158, 342
WASSAIL BOWL, 359–60
Welsh Bros. Madeira, 90
WESTCHESTER SPECIAL, 182
WESTERN EGG NOG, 363
WEYLIN, 186
Whisky, 46–58, 122–23, 156–57
WHISKY BUCK, 309
WHISKY COBBLER, 327
WHISKY COCKTAIL, 180
Whisky cocktails, aromatic type, 180–86
WHISKY COOLER, 329
WHISKY CRUSTA, 258
WHISKY CUP, 350
WHISKY DAISY, 321
WHISKY FIX, 322

WHISKY FIZZ, 320
WHISKY FLIP, 263
Whisky glasses, 29, 31
WHISKY MILK PUNCH, 336
WHISKY PUFF, 337
WHISKY PUNCH, 338
WHISKY SANGAREE, 331
WHISKY SHAKE, 288
WHISKY SLING, 332
WHISKY SOUR, 140–41
Whisky Sour, cocktails based on, 156–62
WHISKY SQUIRT, 342
WHISKY SWIZZLE, 357
WHISKY TODDY, 333
WHISKY ZOOM, 300
WHITE, 296
WHITE ANGEL PUNCH, 355–56
WHITE BABY, 297
White Italian vermouth, 83–84
White label rum. *See Carta blanca*
WHITE LADY, 143, 232
WHITE LION, 297
White Mule, 54, 77, 81
WHITE PLUSH, 336 n.
White port, 90
WHITE ROSE, 297
WHITE VELVET, 297
WIDOW'S DREAM, 297
Williams & Humbert sherry, 89
WINE COOLERS, 329–30
WINE LEMONADES, 334
WINE POSSET, 366
WINE SANGAREES, 330–31
WINE SQUIRTS, 343
Woodruff. *See Waldmeister*
Wormwood, 79
Wray & Nephews rums, 61

XALAPA PUNCH, 349

YACHT CLUB, 297
YACHT CLUB PUNCH, 339
YALE, 175
YALE FENCE, 175
YELLOW GIN, 172 n.
YOU & I, 298
Young's gin, 43

ZABAGLIONE. *See* SABAYON
ZABAIONE. *See* SABAYON
ZAMBAGLIONE. *See* SABAYON
ZA-ZA, 298
ZOMBIE, 33, 62, 298–99
Zombie glasses, 33
ZOOM, 300
Zubrowka, 76
Zug kirsches, 73
Zwack's bitters, 96, 97
Zwack's kirsch, 72–73
Zwack's liqueurs and brandies, 64, 73, 93, 94